COGNITIVE NEUROPSYCHOLOGY AND NEUROLINGUISTICS:

Advances in Models of Cognitive Function and Impairment

COGNITIVE NEUROPSYCHOLOGY AND NEUROLINGUISTICS:

Advances in Models of Cognitive Function and Impairment

Edited by
Alfonso Caramazza
Johns Hopkins University

LAWRENCE ERLBAUM ASSOCIATES, PUBLISHERS
1990 Hillsdale, New Jersey Hove and London

Lawrence Erlbaum Associates, Inc., Publishers
365 Broadway
Hillsdale, New Jersey 07642

Library of Congress Cataloging-in-Publication Data

Cognitive neuropsychology and neurolinguistics : advances in models of cognitive function and impairment / edited by Alfonso Caramazza.
p. cm.
Contents: Cognitive representations and processes in number production : evidence from cases of acquired dyscalculia / Michael McCloskey . . . [et al.] — phonological deficits in aphasia / Sheila E. Blumstein — Neuropsychology of sentence parsing / Marcia C. Linebarger — Lexical processing and sentence comprehension in aphasia / Edgar Zurif, David Swinney, and Merrill Garrett — Short-term memory impairment and language processing / Eleanor M. Saffran — Image generation in the two cerebral hemispheres / Jeffrey D. Holtzman and Stephen M. Kosslyn — Hierarchical distributed networks in the neuropsychology of selective attention / Michael I. Posner — the effects of attentional deficits on reading and spelling / Argye E. Hillis and Alfonso Caramazza.
ISBN 0-89859-892-3
1. Cognition disorders. 2. Neuropsychology. 3. Neurolinguistics.
I. Caramazza, Alfonso.
RC553.C64C64 1990
616.85′5—dc 20 89-37789
CIP

Printed in the United States of America
10 9 8 7 6 5 4 3 2 1

Contents

List of Contributors

Sheila E. Blumstein, Department of Cognitive and Linguistic Sciences, Brown University, Providence, Rhode Island 02912

Alfonso Caramazza, Cognitive Science Center, The Johns Hopkins University, Baltimore, Maryland 21218

Merrill Garrett, Department of Psychology, University of Arizona, Tucson, Arizona 85721

Roberta A. Goodman–Schulman, Department of Speech Pathology, Loyola College, 4501 N. Charles Street, Baltimore, Maryland 21210-2699

Argye E. Hillis, HealthSouth Rehabilitation Center, 9512 Harford Road, Baltimore, Maryland 21234

Jeffrey D. Holtzman*, Formerly at Department of Neurology, Cornell Medical Center, New York, New York 10021

Stephen M. Kosslyn, Department of Psychology, Harvard University, Cambridge, Massachusetts 02138

Marcia C. Linebarger, Research and Development Division, System Development Corporation/A Burroughs Company, Box 517, Paoli, Pennsylvania 19301

---

*Deceased.

Michael McCloskey, Cognitive Science Center, The Johns Hopkins University, Baltimore, Maryland 21218

Michael I. Posner, Department of Psychology, University of Oregon, Eugene, Oregon 97403

Eleanor M. Saffran, Department of Neurology, Temple University School of Medicine, Philadelphia, Pennsylvania 19140

Scott M. Sokol, Massachusetts General Hospital, Neurolinguistics Laboratory, 15 River Street, Boston, Massachusetts 02108-3402

David Swinney, Department of Psychology, CUNY, 33 W. 42nd Street, New York, New York 10036

Edgar Zurif, Program in Linguistics and Cognitive Science, Brandeis University, Waltham, Massachusetts 02254

Preface

Since the mid 1950s, the cognitive paradigm has enjoyed a prominent position in the psychological sciences as the grip of behaviorism slowly lost its hold over increasingly larger domains of psychology. In part, this development was the result of the failure of the behavioristic paradigm to provide significant insights into the nature of intelligent behavior. Equally important for the emerging prominence of the cognitive paradigm were developments in computer science and linguistics, which provided important conceptual tools for the development of a framework within which to articulate hypotheses about the structure of cognitive mechanisms. The cognitive paradigm quickly spread from its early domains of application (language and reasoning) to other areas of human performance.

In the mid to late 1960s, the cognitive paradigm began to influence neuropsychological research, shifting the focus of explanation of impaired performance in brain-damaged patients from appeals to the neuroanatomical site of damage to hypotheses about transformations of a cognitive system as a result of pathology (Goodglass, 1968; Jakobson, 1964; Warrington & Shallice, 1969). This shift in focus has continued over the past 20 years. However, it was not until the early 1980s that the shift from neuroanatomically based to cognitively based explanations of cognitive disorders became sufficiently marked to be identified by a distinct name—Cognitive Neuropsychology (Caramazza, 1984; Coltheart, 1984). This shift in focus does not imply a rejection of the goal to develop a theory of the neural basis for cognitive mechanisms. It represents instead the realization that, even when the goal is to develop a theory of the neural basis for cognition, the use of neuropsychological data for this purpose necessarily involves claims about the structure of the normal cognitive system. In other words, any claim about brain/cognition relationships is necessarily a claim about normal cognitive mechanisms. Obviously, then, if the performance of brain-damaged subjects could be used to inform theories of brain/cognition relationships, it must equally be able to inform theories of normal cognitive functioning.

Aside from the potentially important contribution for clinical practice, research on the nature of cognitive dysfunction is justified by the belief that it may serve to constrain theories of normal cognitive functioning. This belief is motivated, in turn, by the assumption that deviation from normality consequent to brain damage is not indefinite or random but obeys precise constraints determined by the intrinsic structure of the premorbid system. On this assumption, one may reason backwards, as it were, from impaired performance to infer what the structure of the normal cognitive system must be like so that it may be transformed in such a way as to lead to the observed performance—the not uncommon process of *retrodiction* (Caramazza, 1986). This reasoning has been applied with increasing sophistication to various domains of cognition (see Ellis & Young, 1988; Shallice, 1988).

The chapters in this volume represent several examples of current cognitive neuropsychological research carried out in the United States, and they share the important characteristic of placing considerable emphasis on the development of detailed models of normal cognitive functioning through the analysis of cognitive impairment. They differ, however, in terms of the cognitive domain investigated and in the dominant methodology of the reported research. The domains of investigation include imagery, attention, memory, and language; however, it must be recognized that a disproportionate number of the chapters deal with one aspect or another of language processing. This reflects both the interests of the editor and the fact that research on language disorders has been a major focus of interest in cognitive neuropsychological research. The chapters also differ in terms of the emphasis that is placed on single-patient versus patient-group research methodology. Thus, some of the authors only report research based on single-patient analyses, whereas others primarily report studies based on patient-group research.

As anyone who has tried to edit a book knows, this task is fraught with all kinds of dangers. One of the most unpleasant aspects concerns the inevitable delays that are introduced when a collection of individuals work at their own, sometimes quite different, pace. I am grateful to the contributors of this volume for their patience.

REFERENCES

Caramazza, A. (1984). The logic of neuropsychological research and the problem of patient classification in aphasia. *Brain and Language, 21*, 9–20.

Caramazza, A. (1986). On drawing inferences about the structure of normal cognitive systems from the analysis of patterns of performance: The case for single-patient studies. *Brain and Cognition, 5*, 41–66.

Coltheart, M. (Ed.). (1984). Editorial. *Cognitive Neuropsychology, 1*(1), 1–8.

Ellis, A., & Young, A. (Eds.). (1988). *Human Cognitive Neuropsychology.* Hillsdale, NJ: Lawrence Erlbaum Associates.

Goodglass, H. (1968). Studies on the grammar of aphasics. In S. Rosenberg & K. Joplin (Eds.), *Developments in applied psycholinguistics research*. New York: Macmillan.

Jakobson, R. (1964). Toward a linguistic typology of aphasic impairments. In A. V. S. de Reuck & M. O'Connor (Eds.), *Disorders of language*. London: Churchill.

Shallice, T. (Ed.). (1988). *From Neuropsychology to Mental Structure*. Cambridge: Cambridge University Press.

Warrington, E., & Shallice, T. (1969). The selective impairment of auditory verbal short-term memory. *Brain, 92*, 885–896.

1 Cognitive Representations and Processes in Number Production: Evidence from Cases of Acquired Dyscalculia

Michael McCloskey
Scott M. Sokol
Johns Hopkins University

Alfonso Caramazza
Johns Hopkins University

Roberta Ann Goodman-Schulman
Loyola College of Maryland

Traditionally, research involving subjects with acquired cognitive deficits has focused on defining clinical syndromes and exploring relationships between deficits and lesion loci. However, recent years have seen a growing realization that the impaired performance of brain-damaged subjects also represents a rich source of information about normal cognition. In essence, inferences about normal cognitive processes may be drawn from a pattern of impaired performance by asking, What must the normal cognitive system be like such that damage to the system could produce this specific performance pattern (e.g., Caramazza 1984, 1986; Shallice, 1979)? This approach, which involves the detailed analysis of single cases, can offer insights into the general architecture of a cognitive system and also into the internal structure and functioning of the system's components.

In this chapter, we present data from several brain-damaged subjects in support of claims about the cognitive processing of numbers. Numbers, like sentences, are sequences of symbols generated and interpreted in accord with syntactic and semantic rules. Thus, many of the questions arising in the study of sentence processing have counterparts in the realm of number comprehension and production. For example, how in number comprehension is a sequence of digits (e.g., 902) or number words (e.g., nine hundred two) transformed into an internal representation? And how in number production is an internal representation of a number converted into the appropriate sequence of digits or words?

The cognitive mechanisms for number comprehension and production are of interest first because numbers are implicated in a variety of everyday activities (e.g., using money, telephones, clocks, and addresses). Further, an understanding of number processing is important in research on several number-related topics, including research on calculation (e.g., Ashcraft &

Battaglia, 1978; Miller, Perlmutter, & Keating, 1984), clinical neuropsychological research on the classification, diagnosis, and treatment of dyscalculia (for reviews, see Boller & Grafman, 1983; Levin & Spiers, 1985), and developmental research on the acquisition of number concepts (e.g., Gelman & Gallistel, 1978; Siegler & Robinson, 1982). Finally, studies of numbers may have relevance for research on language in general. The number systems are naturally occurring yet relatively simple symbolic systems, with circumscribed sets of basic symbols and largely straightforward syntax. Analyses of the processing mechanisms for these simple systems may suggest hypotheses about the processing of language in general (e.g., with regard to issues of lexical representation and retrieval).

In this chapter, we focus specifically on the production of numbers in the form of words (e.g., six thousand seventy-four). We describe single-case studies of five brain-damaged subjects, arguing that the subjects' error patterns converge on a set of conclusions about the levels of representation involved in number production, and about the processes operating on the representations at each level. We begin by sketching the general model of number processing that guides our research.

COGNITIVE MECHANISMS IN NUMBER PROCESSING

McCloskey, Caramazza, and Basili (1985) suggested that the cognitive mechanisms for number processing comprise several functional components. At the most general level, their model distinguishes components for number comprehension from those for number production. Within the comprehension and production components, a further distinction is drawn between components for processing Arabic numbers (i.e., numbers in digit form, such as 4,027) and components for processing verbal numbers (i.e., numbers in the form of words, such as four thousand twenty-seven).

The Arabic and verbal number comprehension components are assumed to convert numerical inputs into semantic representations specifying the basic quantities in a number, and the power of 10 associated with each. For example, given the number 8,040, the Arabic number comprehension process might generate as output a representation taking the form {8}10EXP3, {4}10EXP1. The digits in brackets stand for semantic representations of the basic quantities in the number, and 10EXPn indicates the power of 10 associated with each quantity. EXP abbreviates *exponent*, so that 10EXP3, for example, stands for 10 to the third power, or thousand. We adopt this particular notation merely to avoid confusion between semantic representations of numbers and numbers in the form of digits or words. The important assumption is that the semantic representation specifies the basic quantities in a number and their associated powers of 10.

The semantic representations generated by the Arabic or verbal number comprehension processes provide the basis for internal processing of the numerical inputs (e.g., in comparing two basketball scores to determine which team won, in deciding whether a price is reasonable, in calculating a tip at a restaurant).

Finally, the Arabic and verbal number production components translate semantic representations of numbers into Arabic or verbal form for output. For example, the verbal number production process, given the semantic representation {8}10EXP3, {4}10EXP1, would generate the word sequence *eight thousand forty* in phonological form (for spoken production) or graphemic form (for written production).

These assumptions about the general architecture of the cognitive number-processing mechanisms are supported by patterns of dissociations observed in brain-damaged subjects. For example, brain damage may impair production of Arabic numbers while leaving comprehension of Arabic numbers intact, and so forth (e.g., McCloskey et al., 1985; McCloskey & Caramazza, 1987).

In this chapter, we focus on the verbal number production component, with the aim of characterizing its internal structure and functioning.

LINGUISTIC STRUCTURE OF VERBAL NUMBERS

In attempting to delineate the processes by which semantic representations of numbers are transformed into sequences of number word representations, it is worthwhile to consider the linguistic structure of verbal numbers. An appreciation of this structure helps to make clear the nature of the input-output mappings a verbal number production process must compute. Further, the rich lexical and syntactic structure of verbal numbers may well be reflected in the cognitive mechanisms for verbal number production.

In the verbal number system, the words *one* through *nine*, which we will call the ones words, represent the basic quantities {1} through {9}. In contrast, the tens words (e.g., twenty, thirty) represent basic quantities times 10. Numbers including both tens and ones are represented by combining the appropriate tens word with the appropriate ones word (e.g., thirty-six). The single exception to this rule concerns numbers involving one ten and some ones. The verbal number system does not include a word for one ten that combines with ones words to represent one ten and some ones—there is no word like *onety* that combines with ones words to produce numbers like onety-six.

Instead, numbers made up of one ten and some ones are represented by a special set of words, the teens words. For instance, the number consisting of one ten and two ones is represented by the word *twelve*, and the number made up of one ten and six ones is represented by the word *sixteen*.

To represent numbers larger than 99, the verbal number system associates ones, teens, and tens words with multiplier words such as *hundred, thousand*, and *million*. The basic unit in a verbal number is the sequence [ONES hundred TENS ONES] (e.g., six hundred thirty-seven). In this unit, the word *hundred* serves as a multiplier for the preceding ones word. Of course, in any given unit, some elements may not be present, as in *six hundred seven* (in which there is no tens word). Further, the sequence TENS ONES may be replaced by TEENS, as in *six hundred seventeen*.

Whereas hundred acts as a multiplier for a single word, the multipliers thousand, million, billion, and so forth, multiply entire units. For example, in the number six hundred thirty-seven thousand, thousand multiplies the entire unit *six hundred thirty-seven*.

A complete number is represented simply by assembling the basic units, with their associated multipliers, in order of decreasing magnitude. Thus, the number 634,546,321 is represented by arranging the following units in the order shown:

((six) hundred thirty-four) million
((five)hundred forty-six) thousand
((three) hundred twenty-one)

The parentheses show the scope of the multipliers: Each multiplier applies to the expression enclosed by the set of parentheses to its immediate left. Thus, in the millions unit, hundred multiplies six, and million multiplies the entire unit.[1]

Having considered briefly the general architecture of the cognitive number-processing mechanisms and the linguistic structure of verbal numbers, we turn now to the performance of several brain-damaged subjects with verbal number-production impairments.

SUBJECT HY: LEXICAL REPRESENTATION AND RETRIEVAL IN VERBAL NUMBER PRODUCTION

HY is a right-handed man with a ninth-grade education who owned and ran a construction company until he suffered a left-hemisphere cerebrovascular accident (CVA) in 1981, at the age of 66. He reports that many aspects of his work involved dealing with numbers, and that he had no difficulty with numbers prior to the CVA. HY's speech is fluent, although he has word-finding problems that are apparent both in conversation and in formal testing.

HY was tested with several tasks involving number comprehension and production. Here we focus on a task chosen to probe spoken production of

[1]For further discussion of the linguistic structure of verbal numbers, see Hurford, 1975; Menninger, 1969; or Power & Longuet-Higgins, 1978.

TABLE 1.1
Examples of HY's Errors in Reading Aloud Arabic Numbers

Stimulus	*Response*
1	*two*
681	six hundred *fifty*-one
916	*five* hundred sixteen
4,014	four thousand *nineteen*
16,906	*eighteen* thousand nine hundred six

verbal numbers. In this task, Arabic numbers were presented one at a time, and HY was asked to read each number aloud (e.g., given 4,056, say "four thousand fifty-six"). Over a period of several months, HY read aloud nearly 5,000 Arabic numbers ranging in size from one to seven digits, with an error rate of about 14%.

Table 1.1 presents examples of HY's errors. Nearly all of the incorrect responses were lexical substitution errors in which an incorrect word was substituted for the corresponding correct word. For example, in the response of "four thousand nineteen" to the stimulus 4,014, the incorrect word *nineteen* was substituted for the correct word *fourteen*.

Our working model of the cognitive number-processing system suggests that reading an Arabic number aloud implicates the Arabic number comprehension process, which generates a semantic representation of the number, and the verbal number production process, which converts the semantic representation into a sequence of phonological number word representations. Hence, HY's number-reading errors could stem from an Arabic number comprehension deficit, a verbal number production deficit, or both.

Considering first the possibility of a comprehension deficit, HY may be impaired in encoding the individual digits in the stimulus numbers. Thus, for example, when presented with 681, HY may have encoded the 8 as a 5, leading to generation of the incorrect semantic representation {6} 10EXP2, {5} 10EXP1, {1}10EXP0. An intact verbal number production process may then have produced the sequence of phonological representations /six/ /hundred/ /fifty/ /one/, which contains the incorrect representation /fifty/ in place of the correct representation /eighty/. (We indicate phonological representations by words enclosed in slashes.)

In contrast, HY's Arabic number comprehension may be intact, and his errors may have resulted from a verbal number production deficit in which the production process generated, from a correct semantic representation, a sequence of phonological number word representations in which one or more of the words was incorrect. For example, for the stimulus 681, the Arabic number comprehension process may have generated the correct semantic representation {6}10EXP2,{8}10EXP1,{1}10EXP0. However, a disrupted verbal number production process may have selected the representation /fifty/ to represent the eight tens in the number, instead of the correct representation /eighty/.

Results from several number-processing tasks clearly point to a verbal number production deficit as the source of HY's number-reading errors. On several tasks requiring comprehension of Arabic digits, HY showed excellent performance. For example, he was 100% correct in judging which of two Arabic numbers was larger (e.g., 34,567 vs. 34,489). However, on tasks requiring spoken production of verbal numbers, HY made lexical substitution errors. For example, in several different testing sessions we asked HY the question, How many days are there in a year? On five occasions when he was asked to write the answer in Arabic form, HY consistently produced the correct response 365, indicating that he understood the question and knew the answer. When, however, he was asked on six occasions to say the answer aloud, he made lexical substitution errors four of the six times (i.e., "three hundred forty-two," "three hundred sixty-three," "three hundred sixty-seven," and "three hundred fifty-four"). Another relevant observation is that on tasks requiring written responses, HY often gave an incorrect spoken response while writing the correct response. For example, when asked to write the number of eggs in a dozen, HY said "sixteen" while writing 12.

These results suggest that HY's errors in reading Arabic numbers aloud stem from disruption of the verbal number production process. Given this conclusion, we can ask what the errors can tell us about the production process.

In attempting to answer this question, we conducted an analysis comparing HY's responses in the number-reading task word-by-word with the correct responses. Consider, for example, the stimulus 374:

Correct response:	three	hundred	seventy-four
HY's response:	five	hundred	seventy-four

A word-by-word comparison for this response shows that in place of the correct word *three*, HY said "five." The remaining words (i.e., *hundred, seventy, four*) were produced correctly. We focus here on the results for the ones, teens, and tens words; for a discussion of HY's errors in production of multiplier words (i.e., *hundred, thousand*, and *million*), see McCloskey, Sokol, and Goodman (1986).

Figure 1.1 presents a confusion matrix constructed from the word-by-word comparisons. The rows of the matrix represent the correct response words, and the columns represent the words produced by HY. For example, the row for the word *two* indicates that when the correct response word was *two*, HY never said "zero," but said "one" 10 times, "two" 649 times, "three" once, and so forth. Note that the unit of analysis is now the individual word, and not the response as a whole.

	zero	one	two	three	four	five	six	seven	eight	nine	ten	eleven	twelve	thirteen	fourteen	fifteen	sixteen	seventeen	eighteen	nineteen	twenty	thirty	forty	fifty	sixty	seventy	eighty	ninety
zero	64																											
one		615	15		1	5		2	3	2	1																	
two		10	649	1	7	1	14	1	2	1	1																	
three			14	618	2	27	8	10	3	1		1										2						
four		1	1	2	653	3	7	7	8	3																		
five		1	2	4	9	646	3	17	6	5	1					2												
six			8	3	7	4	649	1	17	1															1			
seven		7	1	1	12	10	2	624		13																5		
eight		1	3	2	8	9	17	7	607	2																		
nine			1		2	2	4	12	1	615	2																	
ten		1	1					1			181				2		1			1	1							
eleven										1	1	158		1	1	1		2										
twelve							1				1		154	1	4	1	30		1		1							
thirteen												2		172		1	3	7										
fourteen													1		164		2	3	1	1								
fifteen											4	2		1	1	129	3	8										
sixteen													1				151	1	2									
seventeen												1		1	4	1		135	2	2								
eighteen													1				11	1	137	2								
nineteen											1	1			1		4	5	2	150								1
twenty			1				2				1		1								263	4	4	3	9		3	
thirty						1		1	1					2							2	277		8	3	3	3	
forty					3										3						7	2	277	1		5	2	2
fifty						1					4					1					3	6	4	266	5	7		
sixty																	1				7	1	1	2	277		3	
seventy								4										1					7	4	2	263	2	1
eighty																			1		3	1	6	1	10	4	247	3
ninety										1											1		1	5	2	10	3	269

FIG. 1.1 Word confusion matrix for subject HY. Rows represent the correct words, and columns represent the words produced by HY. (Reproduced from McCloskey et al., 1986)

It is evident from the confusion matrix that HY's errors are not evenly distributed across the possible incorrect response words. Rather, the errors fall into three distinct clusters. When the correct word was a ones word (i.e., between one and nine), nearly all of the incorrect words produced by HY were also ones words. For example, when the correct word was *six*, Hy sometimes said "two" or "eight," but not "twelve" or "fifty." When the correct word was a teens word (i.e., between ten and nineteen), nearly all of HY's errors were also teens words. Finally, when the correct word was a tens word (i.e., twenty, thirty, forty, . . ., ninety), HY's errors were almost always tens words. Over 90% of HY's errors fell into one of these three clusters.

What must the normal verbal number production process be like so that disruption of the process could result in this pattern of performance? In the following section, we present a model of spoken verbal number production and argue that HY's error pattern motivates the principal assumptions of the model.

A MODEL OF SPOKEN VERBAL NUMBER PRODUCTION

The major assumptions of the model concern the representation of number words in the phonological production lexicon (i.e., the store of phonological word representations underlying the production of spoken language), and the processes that determine from an input semantic representation the sequence of words to be retrieved from the lexicon.

The Phonological Production Lexicon. We assume that within the phonological production lexicon, the representations of the basic number words (i.e., *one, two, . . ., eighty, ninety*) are partitioned into three functionally distinct classes, as shown in Table 1.2. The ONES class contains phonological representations of the words *one* through *nine*; the TEENS class contains phonological representations of the words *ten* through *nineteen*; and the TENS class contains phonological representations of the words *twenty, thirty*, and so forth, up to *ninety*. Retrieval of a phonological representation thus involves specifying the appropriate lexical class (e.g., TENS), and the appropriate position within the class (e.g., the position for the quantity {5}). For example, the phonological representation /fifty/ would be addressed by the class/position-within-class specification TENS:{5}, and TEENS:{2} would specify /twelve/.

We assume further that the production lexicon includes a MULTIPLIER class containing phonological representations of the multiplier words *hundred, thousand, million*, and so forth.[2]

The Number Production Process. We assume that when the verbal number production system receives a semantic representation of a number, the largest power of 10 in the number is identified, and on this basis a syntactic frame is generated. Consider, for example, the semantic representation {4}10EXP3, {6}10EXP2, {3}10EXP0, corresponding to the Arabic stimulus number 4,603. From this input, the following frame would be generated:

---

[2]Deloche and Seron (1982a, 1982b; 1984) and Seron and Deloche (1983, 1984) also invoked the concept of number-lexical classes (*stacks*, in their terminology) in classifying the errors made by groups of aphasic subjects on various number-processing tasks. However, Deloche and Seron's assertions about the stack structure of number words may not have been intended as claims about cognitive number-processing mechanisms, but rather as descriptions of the verbal number system considered as a formal symbolic system. (See Seron & Deloche, 1984: "Thus, there is evidence that stack notions are relevant to neuropsycholinguistics, but this does not mean that the mental lexicon is organized according to such structures. . . ." p. 233).

TABLE 1.2
Number-Lexical Classes in the Phonological Production Lexicon

Ones	*Teens*	*Tens*
—	ten	—
one	eleven	—
two	twelve	twenty
three	thirteen	thirty
four	fourteen	forty
five	fifteen	fifty
six	sixteen	sixty
seven	seventeen	seventy
eight	eighteen	eighty
nine	nineteen	ninety

[ONES:____] MULT:T [[ONES:____] MULT:H TENS:____ ONES:____]
"10EXP3" "10EXP2" "10EXP1" "10EXP0"

This frame specifies, among other things, that for numbers in which 10EXP3 is the largest power of 10, the generalized verbal form is a ONES word, followed by the MULTIPLIER thousand, followed by a ONES word, and so forth.

After the syntactic frame is generated, each basic quantity in the input semantic representation is assigned to the appropriate slot in the frame. This filling of the frame is guided by the syntactic category labels beneath each slot. For example, the label under the leftmost slot specifies that this slot should be filled with the quantity associated with 10EXP3 (i.e., {4}). Thus, for 4,603 the filled frame takes the following form:

[ONES:{4}] MULT:T [[ONES:{6}] MULT:H TENS:____ ONES:{3}]
"10EXP3" "10EXP2" "10EXP1" "10EXP0"

The filled syntactic frame represents a plan for production of the sequence of words comprising the verbal form of the number. (See, e.g., Garrett, 1980, for a discussion of planning structures in sentence production.) The elements in the frame (e.g., ONES:{4}) are, in essence, abstract lexical-semantic representations of the to-be-produced words. These abstract representations, we assume, are used to address phonological representations in the production lexicon. For each filled slot, the class label (e.g., ONES) indicates the number-lexical class, and the quantity representation (e.g, {4}) identifies the position within class. Thus, for example, the leftmost specifies retrieval of the phonological representation /four/. An empty slot (such as the "10EXP1" slot in the foregoing frame) indicates that no phonological representation should be retrieved.

Multiplier words are specified in terms of the MULTIPLIER class (abbreviated MULT in our depictions of syntactic frames) and the particular item within that class. In the foregoing frame, the MULT:T and MULT:H represent instructions for retrieval of the phonological representations /thousand/ and /hundred/, respectively.

The final step in the production process is thus the retrieval of the phonological representations specified by the filled syntactic frame. In the present example, the retrieval process would yield the sequence /four/ /thousand/ /six/ /hundred/ /three/.

The lexical retrieval process unfolds as described, unless a {1} is encountered in a TENS-class slot. In this event, a special teens procedure is invoked. This procedure does not retrieve a phonological representation from the TENS class, but instead proceeds to the next slot and pairs the quantity value in that slot with the class label TEENS, in order to address a phonological representation in the TEENS class. For example, for the following filled frame, the teens procedure would generate TEENS:{3}, so that the lexical retrieved stage would yield the sequence /six/ /hundred/ /thirteen/.

[[ONES:{6}] MULT:H TENS:{1} ONES:{3}]
"10EXP2" "10EXP1" "10EXP0"

If the slot that specifies the position within the TEENS class is empty (as it would be for 610), then the teens procedure generates the specification TEENS:{0}, leading to the retrieval of /ten/.

Finally, one additional assumption about multipliers and empty slots is needed. The brackets in the syntactic frame indicate the slots to which the multipliers apply. If all slots within the scope of a multiplier are empty, then the multiplier word is omitted. Consider, for example, the filled frame for the number 4023:

[ONES:{4}] MULT:T [[ONES:___] MULT:H TENS:{2} ONES:{3}]
"10EXP3" "10EXP2" "10EXP1" "10EXP0"

The multiplier *hundred* applies only to the ONES slot to its immediate left. Because this slot is empty, the phonological form /hundred/ is not retrieved. Thus, the retrieval process yields the sequence /four/ /thousand/ /twenty/ /three/. Similarly, multipliers that apply to entire units (e.g., thousand, million) are omitted when all slots in the unit are empty. For example, in the case of the number 3,000,789, all of the slots within the scope of the multiplier *thousand* would be empty, and consequently /thousand/ would not be retrieved.

Application of the Model to HY's Performance. This model allows us to provide a straightforward account of HY's error pattern in terms of a deficit affecting the retrieval of phonological number word representations from the production lexicon. Specifically, we assume that given a specification of a to-be-retrieved number word, HY is largely intact in accessing the correct number-lexical class, but is impaired in accessing the appropriate position within class. For example, given the specification TENS:{7}, the lexical retrieval process would almost always access the TENS class, and so would not retrieve a ones word or a teens word. However, the retrieval process might access the wrong position within the TENS class, resulting in the substitution of an incorrect tens word (e.g., forty, sixty) for the correct word *seventy*.

A deficit of this sort should lead to lexical substitution errors in which the incorrect word is from the same number-lexical class as the correct word. This is, of course, just what the confusion matrix in Fig. 1.1 shows—HY substituted ones words for ones words, teens words for teens words, and tens words for tens words.

The critical feature of this interpretation is the assumption that verbal number production involves a level of representation at which to-be-retrieved number words are represented in terms of number-lexical class and position within class (e.g., TENS:{3}). This assumption allows us to specify a deficit that would result in the observed pattern of errors (i.e., an impairment in using the position-within-class part of the class/position representations to address phonological representations in the production lexicon).

If we do not assume a class/position-within-class level of representation, and a corresponding organization of the number word representations in the production lexicon, we cannot readily explain the clustering of HY's errors. Thus, the error pattern provides strong support for these assumptions about normal number production.

The errors falling outside of the three major clusters offer further support. Over half of these errors were class errors, in which the class was incorrect but the position within class was correct. For example, HY said "twelve" in response to the stimulus 20, and "ten thousand *ninety*" in response to 10,019.

The class errors may be interpreted by assuming that the lexical retrieval process occasionally accessed the wrong number-lexical class but the right position within the class. For example, the substitution of "twelve" for "twenty" may have occurred when the retrieval process accessed the position corresponding to the quantity {2} in the TEENS class instead of the TENS class.

The second subject we discuss, JG, presents with an error pattern complementary to that of HY.

Subject JG

JG is a 25-year-old right-handed woman who sustained left-hemisphere damage as a result of a closed-head injury in September, 1983. She is a high school graduate, and reports that she had no difficulties with numbers prior to her accident. JG's spoken language comprehension and production are essentially normal, although she evidences impairments in spelling, and in reading aloud words and nonwords.

Over a testing period of several months, JG read aloud approximately 2,800 Arabic numbers ranging in size from one to nine digits, with an error rate of 6%. Like HY, JG made lexical substitution errors involving the ones, teens, and tens words. However, it is evident from the confusion matrix in Fig. 1.2 that JG's pattern of performance was somewhat different from that of HY.

JG's error pattern is notable first for the predominance of class errors (e.g., stimulus 916, response "*nineteen* hundred sixteen"; see Table 1.3 for other examples). Whereas only 4% of HY's lexical substitutions were class errors, 60% of JG's errors fell into the class error category. Further, all of JG's lexical substitutions for the ones, teens, and tens words were either class errors or within-class errors (e.g., stimulus 908, response "nine hundred *seven*"); she made no responses in which both the class and the position within class were incorrect.

JG's performance provides further support for the assumption that verbal number production involves a level of representation at which to-be-retrieved number words are specified in terms of class and position within class (e.g., TEENS:{6}). As in the case of HY's errors, JG's within-class errors may be interpreted by assuming that the lexical retrieval process, given a correct specification of a to-be-retrieved number word (e.g., ONES:{6}), occasionally accessed the correct class but the wrong position within class, leading to errors such as "two" produced in place of "six." Similarly, her class errors (e.g., "sixty" substituted for "six") may be explained by positing that the retrieval process occasionally accessed the wrong number-lexical class (e.g., the TENS class given ONES:{6}), but the correct position within the class (e.g., the position for the quantity {6}).

A potential alternative explanation is that JG's lexical substitutions resulted from errors in comprehending the Arabic stimulus numbers. In the case of her within-class errors, this alternative account cannot be excluded entirely. JG's within-class error rate was only .5%—she made within-class lexical substitutions for only 39 of the 7,692 ones, teens, and tens words she produced in the Arabic number-reading task. Thus, even a very low rate of digit encoding errors could account for the within-class errors. Although JG's performance on several tests of Arabic number comprehension was excellent, the comprehension results cannot rule out the possibility that encoding errors occurred at such a rate.

The class errors, however, are not attributable to errors in comprehending the Arabic stimulus numbers—the form taken by these errors is inconsistent with comprehension error interpretations. McCloskey et al. (1986) discussed this point in some detail; here we simply sketch the argument.

The class errors clearly cannot be interpreted as resulting from simple digit encoding errors. First, for 9 of the 59 class errors (e.g., stimulus

	zero	one	two	three	four	five	six	seven	eight	nine	ten	eleven	twelve	thirteen	fourteen	fifteen	sixteen	seventeen	eighteen	nineteen	twenty	thirty	forty	fifty	sixty	seventy	eighty	ninety
zero	15	1																										
one		619		1						2																		
two		1	488	2																	2							
three			1	488			2																					
four					512										1								1					
five			1			474		2																1				
six			2				509																		2			
seven								496		1																2		
eight								2	491	2																	1	
nine							1			505										5								3
ten											143			1														
eleven		1										151	1															
twelve													149			1					2							
thirteen				1										149														
fourteen					3							1	2		142								1					
fifteen																147	1	1						1				
sixteen							1										149	1										
seventeen								1						1		1		156										
eighteen																			150	1							1	
nineteen										1		1	1					1		145								
twenty			5																		202							
thirty														1								217						
forty					7										1								184					
fifty						2										2								194		2		
sixty																	2								173	1		
seventy								4										1								173		
eighty									1										1								195	
ninety										1												1						193

FIG. 1.2 Word confusion matrix for subject JG. Rows represent the correct words, and columns represent the words produced by JG. (Reproduced from McCloskey et al., 1986)

TABLE 1.3
Examples of Class Errors Made by JG in the Arabic Number-reading Task

Stimulus	*Response*
312	three hundred *twenty*
14,890	*four* thousand eight hundred ninety
916	*nineteen* hundred sixteen
50,300	*five* thousand three hundred
60,980	*sixteen* thousand nine hundred eighty
20,417	twenty thousand *fourteen* hundred seventeen
607,500	six hundred *seventy* thousand five hundred

20,417, response "twenty thousand *fourteen* hundred seventeen"), no account in terms of digit encoding errors can be given. Further, 41 of the remaining 50 errors would require the assumption of encoding errors for two adjacent digits. For example, a digit encoding error interpretation of the response "forty" to the stimulus 14 must assume that the 1 was encoded as a 4, and the 4 was encoded as a 0. This multiple encoding error interpretation proves untenable. Multiple encoding errors will, of course, not always lead to responses taking the form of class errors. For example, for the stimulus 618, multiple encoding errors could lead to the responses "four hundred twenty-eight," "six hundred fifty-four," "two hundred thirteen," and many others that, like these examples, are not class errors. In fact, multiple encoding errors must take very specific forms to yield class errors, so that we would expect the vast majority of multiple encoding errors not to result in responses falling into the class error category. However, aside from the class errors, JG made only three responses interpretable as multiple encoding errors. Clearly, it is difficult to maintain the position that JG made 41 multiple encoding errors that happened to result in class errors, and only 3 multiple encoding errors that did not yield class errors.

Attempts to interpret the class errors as digit transpositions (e.g., transposition of 2 and 0 to yield the response "one hundred twenty" to the stimulus 102) encounter similar difficulties. Thus, whereas the model we have proposed offers a straightforward interpretation of JG's class errors, potential alternative accounts prove inadequate. Hence, JG's performance pattern converges with that of HY in supporting the assumptions of a class/position-within-class level of representation and a corresponding partitioning of the number-word representations in the phonological production lexicon.

SUBJECT AT: MORPHOLOGY AND THE PRODUCTION LEXICON

In interpreting the performance of subjects HY and JG, we have assumed that phonological number-word representations are retrieved from the production lexicon in whole-word units (e.g., /sixteen/, /forty/). Another possibility is that the lexical retrieval process is morphologically productive, such that retrieval of a number word involves assembling a base (e.g., /six/) and the appropriate suffix (e.g., /ty/), with some special provision being made for irregular words such as *twelve*. The morphological productivity hypothesis would interpret within-class errors as the result of accessing the wrong base (e.g., /four/ instead of /six/). Similarly, class errors (at least those involving regular words) could be interpreted as the result of accessing the wrong suffix.

Some form of knowledge about lexical morphology is certainly available in the cognitive system. For example, most speakers of English can presumably generate a plausible plural for a nonsense noun (e.g., bokes for the nonsense noun *boke*), or a plausible past participle for a nonsense verb (e.g., blinched for the nonsense verb *blinch*). Further, data from several

TABLE 1.4
Examples of Errors in Writing Verbal Numbers in Response to Arabic Stimuli

Stimulus	*Response*
13	threeteen
15	fiveteen
20	twoty
30	threety

brain-damaged subjects suggest specifically that information about morphological structure is available in the case of number words. Table 1.4 presents examples of errors observed in a task where Arabic numbers (e.g., 17) were presented, and the subjects were asked to write the corresponding verbal numbers (e.g., seventeen). These regularization errors, which we have observed in several brain-damaged subjects, apparently resulted from the inappropriate combination of a base (e.g., two) and a suffix (e.g.,–ty). It is also worth mentioning in this context that children learning to count occasionally produce words such as twelveteen, fivety, and eleventy (Fuson, Richards, & Briars, 1982).

The availability of information about morphological structure does not, however, necessarily mean that retrieval from the production lexicon normally involves accessing and assembling root and affix representations. Production of plural nouns, for example, may normally involve the retrieval of whole-word representations, with assembly of a root form with a plural suffix taking place only in the case of novel words for which no whole-word representation is available in the lexicon. Similarly, verbal number production may, as we have assumed, normally involve retrieval of whole-word representations (e.g., /sixteen/).

The results for subject HY and JG do not speak directly to the issue of whole-word retrieval versus morphological assembly of number word representations. However, the performance of another brain-damaged subject, AT, can be brought to bear on this issue.

AT is a right-handed woman with an 11th grade education who suffered a left-hemisphere CVA (secondary to toxemia of pregnancy) in 1964, at the age of 20. AT was tested in our laboratory for a period of several months in 1984 and 1985. During the testing period, she read aloud 6,700 Arabic numbers ranging in magnitude from one to six digits, with an error rate of 13%. Like HY and JG, AT made lexical substitution errors in the number-reading task. Examples of her errors are presented in Table 1.5. AT's performance pattern was similar to that of HY—virtually all of her lexical substitutions (i.e., 850 of 861, or 99%) were within-class errors.

On tests of Arabic digit comprehension (e.g., judging which of two single- or multidigit Arabic numbers was larger), AT showed excellent performance. Further, her error pattern in the number-reading task (see following) does not fit the pattern expected for a digit comprehension deficit. Hence, we assume that AT's number-reading errors reflect a lexical retrieval deficit in the production of the spoken verbal responses, and not an impairment in comprehension of the Arabic stimulus numbers.

A striking feature of AT's performance is that some number words were much less likely than others to be produced correctly. Table 1.6 presents the percentage of correct responses for each of the ones, teens, and tens words.

TABLE 1.5
Examples of AT's Errors in Reading Aloud Arabic Numbers

Stimulus	*Response*
3,090	*two* thousand ninety
7,016	seven thousand *fourteen*
398	three hundred ninety-*six*
9,618	nine thousand six hundred *eighteen*
752	seven hundred *forty*-two

TABLE 1.6
AT's Percentage of Correct Responses in Spoken Production of Number Words

Word	*Percent Correct*
one	98
two	91
three	93
four	93
five	96
six	94
seven	97
eight	90
nine	95
ten	99
eleven	97
twelve	99
thirteen	90
fourteen	93
fifteen	89
sixteen	59
seventeen	81
eighteen	68
nineteen	95
twenty	100
thirty	99
forty	99
fifty	98
sixty	98
seventy	93
eighty	85
ninety	96

It is evident from the table that for most of the number words, AT's performance was in the 90%–100% correct range. However, two of the words—*sixteen* and *eighteen*—showed substantially poorer performance.

This pattern of performance creates serious problems for the morphological productivity hypothesis. Consider first the data for the word *sixteen*. AT was only 59% correct in producing "sixteen." All of her errors were within-class substitutions, with "fourteen" and "seventeen" accounting for 76% of the errors. The morphological decomposition hypothesis would interpret these results to mean that AT is substantially impaired in accessing the phonological representation of the base morpheme /six/, such that she often retrieves /four/ or /seven/ instead.

On this interpretation, AT should be impaired to a comparable extent in the production of *six* and *sixty*, because production of these words also required retrieval of the base /six/. Further, the pattern of errors for *six* and *sixty* should closely match the pattern for *sixteen*. That is, if in attempting to retrieve the base /six/ AT often retrieves /four/ or /seven/ instead, she should frequently substitute "four" or "seven" for "six," and "forty" or "seventy" for "sixty."

The actual results for *six* and *sixty* stand in striking contrast to the pattern expected on the morphological decomposition hypothesis. As can be seen in Table 1.6, AT was 94% correct in production of "six," and 98% correct for "sixty." Both of these percentages are reliably higher than the 59% correct for *sixteen* (sixteen vs. six: $X^2[1,N = 1{,}219] = 169.7, p < .001$; sixteen vs. sixty: $X^2[1,N = 531] = 140.2, p < .001$).

Further, the pattern of lexical substitutions for *six* and *sixty* was very different from that for *sixteen*. Whereas "fourteen" and "seventeen" were the most common errors for *sixteen*, the word most commonly substituted for *six* was "eight"; "four" and "seven" were substituted far less frequently. For *sixty* there were very few errors overall, and "forty" was not among them.

Note that AT's error pattern also argues against a digit-encoding error interpretation. An encoding error interpretation cannot readily explain why misencoding would occur frequently for 6's corresponding to the word *sixteen* in the verbal form of a number, but not for 6's corresponding to the word *six* or *sixty*.

The results for *eight, eighteen*, and *eighty* are similar to those for *six, sixteen*, and *sixty*. AT was only 68% correct in the production of *eighteen*, yet she was 90% correct for *eight* ($X^2[1,N = 1{,}202] = 58.2, p < .001$), and 85% correct for *eighty* ($X^2[1,N = 530] = 19.5, p < .001$). Further, the pattern of errors was quite different for *eighteen* than for *eight* or *eighty*. For example, the most common substitutions for *eighteen* were *seventeen* and *nineteen*, but the word most frequently substituted for *eight* was *six*.

AT's results are, thus, very difficult to reconcile with the morphological productivity hypothesis. This hypothesis assumes that the production of

TABLE 1.7
Examples of JE's Errors in Reading Aloud Arabic Numbers

Stimulus	*Response*
5,012	five thousand one hundred two
7,900	seven thousand ninety
1,200	one thousand twenty
6,003	six hundred three
2,070	twenty thousand seventy
59,800	fifty-nine thousand eighty
45,010	forty-five thousand one hundred

corresponding ones, teens, and tens words (e.g., *six, sixteen, sixty*) involves a shared process—that of retrieving a phonological representation of a base morpheme (e.g., /six/). AT makes errors for *sixteen* and *eighteen* that require the hypothesis to assume that retrieval of the base for these words is impaired. Yet other words that also require retrieval of the same base (i.e., *six* and *sixty* in the case of *sixteen, eight* and *eighty* in the case of *eighteen*) do not show the errors expected if retrieval of the base is impaired.

Thus, the data strongly suggest that number words are retrieved from the phonological production lexicon in whole-word units. Given this assumption, retrieval of /sixteen/ could conceivably be disrupted, whereas /six/ and /sixty/ remain unimpaired (although the precise nature of a deficit that would yield such item-specific effects is not entirely clear).

In the following section, we discuss a subject who makes errors rather different from those produced by HY, JG, and AT.

SYNTACTIC FRAMES AND SEMANTIC REPRESENTATIONS

Subject JE is a right-handed male college graduate who suffered a left-hemisphere cerebrovascular accident in May, 1979, at the age of 42. Prior to his CVA, JE held positions requiring extensive use of numbers (e.g., high school science teacher, senior administrator in medicaid programs). JE was tested for a period of 4 months in 1985. During the testing period, he read aloud 848 Arabic numbers of one to five digits, with an error rate of 6.4%.

Approximately one fourth of JE's errors were within-class lexical substitutions (e.g., stimulus 5,097, response "five thousand ninety-*five*"). The remaining three fourths of the errors were quantity shift errors, in which a quantity associated with one power of 10 in the Arabic stimulus number was associated with another power of 10 in the verbal response. For example, in response to the stimulus 8,900, JE said "eight thousand ninety." Thus, the nine hundreds in the stimulus became nine tens in the response. Other examples of quantity shift errors are presented in Table 1.7. Note that most of these errors are not interpretable as lexical substitutions in which an incorrect word was retrieved in place of a correct word, because the incorrect responses usually contained a different number of words than the corresponding correct responses. For example, the correct response to the stimulus 5,012 contains three words, but JE's response—"five thousand one hundred two"—included five.

To determine whether JE's errors could have resulted from a deficit in comprehension of the Arabic stimulus numbers, we presented him with several tasks chosen to probe Arabic number comprehension. One task involved plastic chips with "values" of 1, 10, 100, 1,000, and 10,000. The value of a chip was indicated by its color and by Arabic and verbal number labels on the chip. For example, the chips representing 100 were yellow, with *100* and *One Hundred* written on them. In the chips task, JE was presented with an Arabic number and asked to select the corresponding chips (e.g., five thousands chips and six tens chips for the stimulus 5,060). Over several testing sessions, 234 Arabic numbers of one to five digits were presented, and JE selected the correct combination of chips for all of the stimuli. JE was also 100% correct (40/40) in judging which of two single- or multidigit Arabic numbers was larger. These results strongly suggest that JE's ability to comprehend Arabic numbers is intact, and thus that his errors in the number-reading task reflect a disruption of the verbal number production process.

JE's lexical substitution errors (e.g., stimulus 7,000, response "*nine* thousand"), like those of HY, may be interpreted as the result of a mild impairment in addressing the appropriate within-class position during the retrieval of phonological number word representations from the production lexicon. However, the quantity shift errors (e.g., stimulus 8,600, response "eight thousand sixty") require a different interpretation.

The number production model we have described assumes that the production process involves the construction of a syntactic frame that specifies abstractly the sequence of to-be-produced number words. Given this assumption, we may explain JE's quantity shift errors in terms of a deficit in syntactic frame processing. More specifically, we assume on the basis of JE's perfect performance on tests of Arabic number comprehension that he is unimpaired in generating a semantic representation from an Arabic stimulus number. His impairment, we suggest, involves the use of the power of 10 specifications in the semantic representations to generate the appropriate syntactic frame and to assign semantic quantity representations to the appropriate slots in a frame.

Consider, for example, the stimulus 5,012, to which JE responded "five thousand one hundred two." For this stimulus, the Arabic number comprehension process should generate the semantic representation {5}10EXP3,{1}10EXP1,{2}10EXP0, and from this semantic representation the verbal number production process should create the following syntactic frame:

[ONES:{5}] MULT:T [[ONES:___] MULT:H TENS:{1} ONES:{2}]
"10EXP3" "10EXP2" "10EXP1" "10EXP0"

Assume, however, that in the process of filling the syntactic frame the 10EXP1 specification associated with the quantity {1} in the semantic representation is misinterpreted as 10EXP2. The result would be assignment of the {1} representation not to the correct 10EXP1 slot in the syntactic frame, but rather to the 10EXP2 slot:

[ONES:{5}] MULT:T [[ONES:{1}] MULT:H TENS:___ ONES:{2}]
"10EXP3" "10EXP2" "10EXP1" "10EXP0"

This error in filling the syntactic frame would lead to the incorrect response "five thousand one hundred two."

This interpretation can also account for the quantity shift errors in which JE's response was of a different order of magnitude than the correct response (e.g., stimulus 602, response "six thousand two"). Our model assumes that a syntactic frame is generated on the basis of the largest power of 10 in the to-be-produced number. For example, from the semantic representation of the number 602—{6}10EXP2,{2{10EXP0—the following frame should be generated:

[[ONES:___] MULT:H TENS:___ ONES:___]
"10EXP2" "10EXP1" "10EXP0"

If, however, the power of 10 specification 10EXP2 is misinterpreted as 10EXP3, then an incorrect frame would be generated:

[ONES:___] MULT:T [[ONES:___] MULT:H TENS:___ ONES:___]
"10EXP3" "10EXP2" "10EXP1" "10EXP0"

Assuming that the quantity representation associated with the largest power of 10 is routinely assigned to the leftmost slot in the frame, the filled frame would take the following form, resulting in the production of "six thousand two" in place of the correct response "six hundred two".

[ONES:{6}] MULT:T [[ONES:___] MULT:H TENS:___ ONES:{2}]
"10EXP3" "10EXP2" "10EXP1" "10EXP0"

Semantic Representations. JE's performance also bears in an interesting way on our assumption that the inputs to the verbal number production process are semantic representations of numbers. Examination of the quantity shift errors reveals that when a shift occurred to a power of 10 included in the stimulus number, that power of 10 was virtually always associated with a zero in the stimulus. For example, in JE's response of "six thousand three hundred" to the stimulus 6,030, the quantity {3} moved to the hundreds position, which was occupied by a zero in the Arabic stimulus. JE virtually never made shift or transposition errors in which a quantity moved to a position occupied by a nonzero digit in the stimulus number (e.g., stimulus 6,530, response "six thousand three hundred" or "six thousand three hundred fifty").

Why did quantities shift only to positions occupied by zeros in the stimulus number? Within the framework of our model, these positions are special in that they correspond to empty slots in the syntactic frame. This special status is a consequence of the assumption that the inputs to the number production process take the form of semantic representations that include only those powers of 10 associated with nonzero quantities in the stimulus number. Consider, for example, the number 6,030. We assume that this number is represented as {6}10EXP3,{3}10EXP1, and not as {6}10EXP3,{0}10EXP2,{3}10EXP1,{0}10EXP0.[3] Thus, when the syntactic frame is filled with the quantity values from the semantic representation, the 10EXP2 and 10EXP0 slots remain empty:

[ONES:{6}] MULT:T	[[ONES:___] MULT:H	TENS:{3}	ONES:___]
"10EXP3"	"10EXP2"	"10EXP1"	"10EXP0"

If, then, the 10EXP1 specification associated with {3} in the semantic representation is misinterpreted as 10EXP2, the quantity {3} may be assigned to the 10EXP2 slot, which would otherwise be empty.

Consider in contrast the number 6,530. For this number, the 10EXP2 slot does not remain empty; rather, this slot is filled with the quantity representation {5}. Thus, if the 10EXP1 specification associated with the quantity {3} is subsequently misinterpreted as 10EXP2, the error may be detected (and corrected) when the 10EXP2 slot is found to be already filled with the {5} representation. (Note that this argument does not depend on assumptions about the order in which quantities are assigned to slots in the syntactic frame. If the {3} representation is mistakenly assigned to the 10EXP2 slot before the {5} representation is assigned, the error may be detected when an attempt is made to assign the {5} to the already filled 10EXP2 slot.)

The critical assumption underlying this interpretation is that the verbal

---

[3]The assumptions about zeros are not arbitrary. The need for the digit 0 in the Arabic number system arises from the arabic system's use of position to indicate the power of 10 associated with each quantity in a number. For example, a 6 represents six tens if it is in the second position from the right, and six thousands if it is in the fourth position. To maintain the appropriate placement of digits, all positions corresponding to powers of 10 smaller than the largest power in the number must be filled, even if some of these powers of 10 are not represented in the number. For example, the number *six hundred four* cannot be written as 64; the tens position must be filled, even though there are no tens in the number. The digit 0 serves this place-holding function. In representational schemes that do not use position to indicate the power of 10 associated with a quantity, there is no need for a place-holding element. The semantic representations we have postulated do not use a positional system; each quantity representation of explicitly associated with a representation of the appropriate power of 10. Hence, there is no motivation for including {0}'s in the semantic representations.

number production process operates on semantic representations of numbers (and more specifically, on semantic representations that specify only those powers of 10 associated with nonzero quantities). It is by virtue of this assumption that syntactic frame slots corresponding to zeros in the stimulus number remain empty when the frame is correctly filled, so that erroneous assignments of quantities to these slots may go undetected. Thus, JE's error pattern supports our assumptions about the nature of the inputs to the verbal number production process.

If we assume a number-reading process that does not involve generation of a semantic representation, the error pattern cannot readily be explained. Consider, for example, a model assuming that Arabic numbers are read aloud through a process that does not compute a semantic representation, but simply inserts digit representations into a syntactic frame and then uses this frame as a basis for retrieving the appropriate phonological word representations. Thus, for example, the filled frame for the stimulus 6,030 would take the following form:

[ONES: 6] MULT:T [[ONES: 0] MULT:H TENS: 3 ONES: 0]

This sort of model cannot explain why quantity shifts occurred only into positions corresponding to zeros in the stimulus number. The quantity shift errors would be interpreted as transpositions involving a zero and a nonzero digit (e.g., a transposition of 0 and 3 for the response of "six thousand three hundred" to the stimulus 6,030). However, the model cannot then explain why JE made no responses interpretable as transpositions of two nonzero digits. The model accords zero no special status, and therefore provides no basis for arguing that a zero and a nonzero digit may be transposed, whereas two nonzero digits may not.

Further support for the assumption that the number production process operates on semantic representations comes from JE's performance on a task in which numbers were presented in written verbal form, and JE was asked to read the numbers aloud (e.g., stimulus *six thousand thirty*, response "six thousand thirty"). Interpretation of the results is complicated by the fact that JE is severely impaired in comprehension of written words. He reported that he relied heavily on the initial letter of a word in attempting to interpret it, and his performance bears out this claim. For example, the word *seven* was variously read as "six," "sixteen," "sixty," "seven," "seventeen," and "seventy." Thus, many of JE's errors undoubtedly resulted from his difficulty in comprehension of the words in the stimuli.

However, several of the errors cannot be interpreted in terms of an impairment in comprehension of individual words, because the stimulus and JE's response contained different numbers of words. These responses took the form of quantity shift errors. For example, in response to the stimulus *one thousand eighty*, JE said "one thousand eight hundred."

The occurrence of responses containing a different number of words than the corresponding stimuli clearly suggests that JE did not simply retrieve and produce a phonological representation for each individual word. Instead, it appears that the stimulus numbers were subjected to a verbal number comprehension process that generated a semantic representation of a number as a whole. The semantic representations were then apparently processed by the verbal number production process to yield the spoken responses, leading to quantity shift errors of the sort that occurred in the Arabic number-reading task.

WRITTEN VERSUS SPOKEN VERBAL NUMBER PRODUCTION

Thus far, we have focused on spoken production of verbal numbers. However, the nature of production mechanisms we have postulated suggests that some of these mechanisms may be shared by written number production as well. Our model assumes that the initial step in the production process is the construction of a syntactic frame that specifies the to-be-produced number words in abstract lexical-semantic form (e.g., TENS:{4}, ONES:{8}). At this abstract planning level, neither the representations nor the processes that compute these representations are tied specifically to the spoken production mode. Consequently, we might expect the initial planning stage to be shared by spoken and written number production.

Written and spoken production may diverge, however, at the lexical retrieval stage. In the case of spoken production, phonological number word representations must be retrieved from a phonological production lexicon. Written production, in contrast, presumably requires retrieval of graphemic representations (e.g., a representation of the grapheme sequence e-i-g-h-t) from a graphemic production lexicon.

These assumptions about the architecture of the verbal number production system lead to predictions about patterns of performance that may be observed in subjects with verbal number production deficits. If the process of generating and filling a syntactic frame is shared by spoken and written number production, then we would expect any deficit implicating the construction of the syntactic frame to manifest itself in both production modes. In contrast, if spoken and written verbal number production diverge at the lexical retrieval stage, we might expect to observe dissociations in which lexical retrieval is impaired for one production mode but not the other. In this section we describe a brain-damaged subject who presents with both a syntactic association and a lexical dissociation in spoken versus written verbal number production. (See Sokol & McCloskey, 1988, for a more detailed discussion).

JS is a college-educated right-handed man who suffered a left-hemisphere cerebrovascular accident in July, 1979, at the age of 44. Prior to his

CVA, JS worked as an army staff sergeant in charge of payroll. He reports that before his accident he had no difficulties with numbers or calculation. Studies of JS's language processing (Caramazza, Berndt, & Basili, 1983; Martin & Caramazza, 1982) characterize JS as a fluent aphasic with a marked impairment in auditory comprehension resulting from a deficit in phonological coding.

JS was tested with two tasks chosen to contrast spoken and written production of verbal numbers. The stimuli in both tasks were Arabic numbers of one to nine digits. In the spoken production task, JS was asked to read the stimulus number aloud, whereas in the written task JS was asked to write the number in verbal form (e.g., given 34, write *thirty-four*). Over several testing sessions, 246 Arabic numbers were presented in the spoken production task and 242 in the written production task. JS's overall error rate was 27.2% in the spoken production task, and 18% in the written production task.

On tests of Arabic number comprehension, JS showed excellent performance. In particular, he was 100% correct (61/61) in judging which of two Arabic numbers was larger, and 100% correct (28/28) in selecting plastic chips corresponding to an Arabic stimulus number. (See pp. 19 for a description of the chips task.) These results suggest that JS's errors in the spoken and written verbal number production tasks reflect an impairment in production of the verbal responses, and not in comprehension of the Arabic stimuli.

In the spoken production task (i.e., reading aloud Arabic numbers), JS presented with two distinct types of errors. For 13.4% of the stimuli, he made lexical substitutions of the sort evidenced by HY, JG, and AT (e.g., stimulus 309, response "*six* hundred nine"). All but two of these lexical substitutions were within-class errors. The lexical substitutions may be interpreted as reflecting a deficit in retrieval of phonological number word representations from the phonological production lexicon.

In addition to the lexical substitution errors, JS made syntactic errors for 17.1% of the stimuli. The syntactic errors involved incorrect arrangements of multiplier words in the spoken response. For example, JS read aloud the stimulus 407,013 as "*four hundred thousand seven* thirteen." Interestingly, the syntactic errors occurred only for six- through nine-digit stimuli, and were in fact limited to either the hundred thousands or hundred millions part of a response (i.e., the unit correctly produced as ONES hundred TENS ONES thousand, such as four hundred sixty-seven thousand, or ONES hundred TENS ONES million, such as three hundred fifty-nine million).

We refer to these units (i.e., the hundred thousands and hundred millions parts of numbers) as *compound multiplier units*, because these units involve multiplication of basic number word values by more than one multiplier. For example, in the unit *three hundred forty-seven thousand*, three is multiplied by both hundred and thousand. (More specifically, hundred multiplies three, and thousand multiplies the entire unit three hundred forty-seven.)

JS made three different types of syntactic errors for the six- to nine-digit stimuli. The most common was one in which he realized compound multiplier units as ONES hundred thousand TENS ONES, or ONES hundred million TENS ONES (e.g., stimulus 146,359; response "*one hundred thousand forty-six*, three hundred fifty-nine"). The second type of syntactic error was one in which JS realized the compound multiplier units as ONES thousand TENS ONES, or ONES million TENS ONES (e.g., stimulus 509,362,490; response "*five million nine, three thousand sixty-two*, four hundred ninety"). Finally, JS also produced syntactic errors in which he realized these units as ONES TENS ONES thousand, or ONES TENS ONES million (e.g., stimulus 799,970; response "*seven ninety-nine thousand*, nine hundred seventy"). Other examples of each type of syntactic error are presented in Table 1.8.

According to our assumptions about the architecture of the verbal number production system, the process of creating a syntactic frame is common to spoken and written production. Hence, we would expect any syntactic errors observed in the spoken production task to occur in equal proportion in the written production task. This was in fact the case. In writing the verbal numbers corresponding to Arabic stimulus numbers, JS made syntactic errors for 17.8% of the stimuli. The difference between this error proportion and the proportion of syntactic errors produced in the spoken production task (i.e., 17.1%) is of course not statistically reliable ($X^2[1, N = 488] = .05$).

Furthermore, as shown in Table 1.8, the types of syntactic errors in the written production task were identical to those in the spoken production task, and again occurred only for six- through nine-digit stimulus numbers. For example, in response to the Arabic number 570,990, JS wrote "*five hundred thousand seventy* nine hundred ninety"; in response to 209,712, he wrote "*two thousand nine* seven hundred twelve"; and in response to 230,561,317, he wrote "*two thirty million five sixty one thousand* three hundred seventeen." This pattern of results—that is, the occurrence of the same proportion and types of syntactic errors in both spoken and written production tasks—supports the assumption of a syntactic processing component that is shared between spoken and written number production.

JS's performance also supports the claim that spoken and written production diverge at the lexical retrieval stage. Whereas JS made lexical substitution errors for 13.4% of the stimuli in the spoken production task, he made no lexical errors in the written production task. The difference in rate of lexical substitutions over the two tasks is highly reliable ($X^2[1, N = 488] = 33.24$, $p < .001$). This dissociation may be interpreted by assuming that JS is impaired in retrieval of phonological number word rep-

TABLE 1.8
Examples of Syntactic Errors in JS's Verbal Number Production

Stimulus	Response
Spoken Production	
407,013	*four hundred thousand seven* thirteen
146,359	*one hundred thousand forty-six* three hundred fifty-nine
4,258,631	four million *two thousand fifty-eight* six hundred thirty-one
509,362,490	*five million nine three thousand sixty-two* four hundred ninety
799,970	*seven ninety-nine thousand* nine hundred seventy
349,258,107	*three forty-nine million two fifty-eight thousand* one hundred seven
Written Production	
Stimulus	*Response*
106,230	*one hundred thousand six* two hundred thirty
358,916	*three hundred thousand fifty-eight* nine hundred sixteen
209,712	*two thousand nine* seven hundred twelve
6,304,500	six million *three thousand four* five hundred
230,561,317	*two thirty million five sixty-one thousand* three hundred seventeen
681,423,609	*six eighty-one million four twenty-three thousand* six hundred nine

resentations from the phonological production lexicon, but not in retrieval of graphemic number word representations from the graphemic production lexicon.

Thus, the syntactic association and the lexical dissociation evidenced by JS are consistent with the general conception of verbal number production as comprising an initial planning stage that is modality independent, and then a lexical retrieval stage that is modality specific.

SUMMARY AND CONCLUSIONS

In this chapter, we presented results from several brain-damaged subjects in support of a model of verbal number production. According to the model, the production process accepts as input a semantic representation of a to-be-produced number, and from this input generates a syntactic frame that constitutes a plan for the production of the appropriate sequence of words. The syntactic frame, filled with quantity values from the semantic representation, specifies each to-be-produced word in terms of number-lexical class, and position within class (e.g., TENS:{7}). The class/position-within-class specifications guide the retrieval of number word representations from a phonological or graphemic production lexicon in which the number words are partitioned into functionally distinct ones, teens, and tens classes.

The patterns of performance evidenced by the five subjects we discussed support the principal assumptions of the model. The patterns apparent in the lexical substitution errors of subjects HY and JG provide evidence in favor of the assumptions that number word representations in the phonological production lexicon are partitioned into ones, teens, and tens classes, and that to-be-retrieved words are specified in terms of class and position within class. Further, the striking dissociations evidenced by AT in spoken production of corresponding ones, teens, and tens words (e.g., *six, sixteen, sixty*) suggest that, as we assumed, the lexical retrieval processes accesses whole-word representations of number words in the phonological production lexicon.

The quantity shift errors made by subject JE are consistent with the assumption that the verbal number production process involves the creation of a syntactic frame, and also support the assumption that the inputs to the production process are in the form of semantic representations. Finally, the association for syntactic errors and the dissociation for lexical errors evidenced by JS in spoken versus written production of verbal numbers supports the claim that verbal number production involves an initial modality-independent planning stage, and a subsequent modality-specific lexical retrieval stage.

Broader Implications

Thus far, we have focused specifically on number processing. However, our findings also have several broader implications.

The Lexicon and Lexical Retrieval. In our verbal number production model, the planning of the to-be-produced word sequence is carried out in terms of classes of words: ones words, teens words, tens words, multiplier words. The error patterns of subjects HY and JG strongly suggest that these lexical class distinctions are reflected in the organization of the number word representations in the production lexicon, and in the processes that retrieve these representations.

It is not a foregone conclusion that this principle applies to language in general. At the least, however, our results suggest that lexical class distinctions relevant to language comprehension and production processes are reflected in the structure of the lexicon and in lexical access procedures. Recent evidence suggests that this may indeed be the case, both for the distinction between open- and closed-class words (see Caramazza & Berndt, 1985, for a review), and also for distinctions within the set of open-class words (e.g., the distinction between nouns and verbs; see Miceli, Silveri, Villa, & Caramazza, 1984).

Lexical Morphology. We argued on the basis of AT's performance that retrieval of number word representations from the phonological production lexicon involves accessing whole-word units, and not a process of assembling a base (e.g., /six/) and an affix (e.g.,–/ty/). Obviously, the extension of this conclusion to words in general would be unjustified. The number words comprise a small closed set that includes several irregular words (e.g., *eleven, twelve*). Other sets of lexical items—especially those that are larger, more open, and more regular morphologically—may behave differently. Nevertheless, our results suggest that the production lexicon stores whole-word representations for at least some polymorphemic words that are regular both semantically and phonologically, and further that whole-word retrieval may occur even in instances where information about morphological structure is available in the cognitive system.

Levels of Representation. The model we have proposed embodies the general claim (e.g., Garrett, 1980) that language production involves a progression through several levels of representation, each of which is required to support a particular type of computation (e.g., the planning of the syntactic form of an utterance; the selection of particular lexical items). Although once again caution must be exercised in generalizing from numbers to language in general, our results can reasonably be taken as support for this claim. It would certainly be surprising if multiple levels of representation were required in the production of verbal numbers, which have a relatively straightforward lexical and syntactic structure, but not in the production of sentences, which are vastly more complex.

Cognitive Research with Brain-Damaged Subjects

A detailed discussion of the rationale for using the performance of brain-damaged subjects to develop and evaluate cognitive theories is beyond the scope of this chapter. However, several points are worth mentioning briefly.

Functional Level of Analysis. It has long been recognized that studies exploring relationships between cognitive deficits and lesion loci can offer insights concerning the implementation of cognitive processes in the brain. However, the research strategy illustrated in this chapter involves the analysis of acquired cognitive deficits at a purely functional level. The aim is to draw conclusions about cognitive processes, not about brain–cognition relationships. Further, the conclusions are drawn on the basis of subjects' performance on cognitive tasks, and not from neurophysiological or neuroanatomical data (e.g., lesion localization data). Finally, the characterization of a subject's deficit, which plays a central role in linking theory and data, is stated in functional and not neurological terms. For example, we related HY's impaired number-reading performance to our number production model by positing an impairment in retrieval of number word representations from a phonological production lexicon. The fact that HY's brain lesion was in the left temporal and parietal lobes did not enter into our interpretation.

Analysis of Individual Cases. In using data from brain-damaged subjects to develop and test cognitive models, the appropriate methodology is that of the single case study. Brain damage may disrupt a cognitive system in a variety of different ways, and thus may lead to a variety of different patterns of impaired performance. Differences in performance among brain-damaged subjects consequently cannot be dismissed as noise, and averaging data across subjects is usually not justified. In fact, the research strategy is powerful in large measure because it capitalizes on the heterogeneity of cognitive deficits, by requiring that a model of a normal cognitive system be capable of accounting for each of the many diverse patterns of impairment that may result from damage to the system.

It is important to point out that the use of a single-case study methodology does not mean that a different model is developed for each subject. To the contrary, the same model of the normal system must be used in interpreting the data from each subject; only the assumptions about what components of the system are damaged can vary across subjects. As we illustrated in this chapter, the aim is to bring data from many different subjects to bear on a single model of the normal system, by specifying damage to the system that would result in the particular pattern observed for each individual subject.

Advantages of Research with Brain-damaged Subjects. It is a truism in cognitive science that errors made in performing a task are often extremely informative about the underlying cognitive processes. However, many cognitive functions, including number comprehension and production, are carried out by normal subjects with very low error rates. Furthermore, a corpus of errors collected from a normal subject may often represent a mixture of several different error types, each resulting from the occasional malfunctioning of one of the processes involved in the task. For example, were we to ask normal subjects to read aloud Arabic numbers, error rates would undoubtedly be very low, and the observed incorrect responses would probably include digit encoding errors, digit transpositions, errors in generating or filling a syntactic frame, lexical retrieval errors, and so forth. Although it might be possible to make inferences about number processing from such an error corpus, the mixing of errors from several sources would certainly complicate the process of interpretation.

Manipulations to induce errors in normal subjects may often be useful. However, some component processes may not be readily susceptible to selective disruption through manipulations that can be carried out on normal subjects. For example, it is unclear how in studies of normal subjects one could selectively disrupt the processes that were impaired by brain damage in subjects HY and JG (i.e., retrieval of number word representations from the phonological production lexicon). Certainly, we could induce errors in the Arabic number-reading task by presenting stimuli tachistoscopically, by introducing a filled retention interval of several minutes between presentation of an Arabic stimulus and production of the verbal response, or simply by placing subjects under extreme speed pressure. However, it is questionable whether any of these manipulations would selectively disrupt the verbal number production process, much less the subprocess of lexical retrieval. Tachistoscopic presentation and the introduction of a retention interval would presumably produce errors not by impairing the verbal number production process, but rather by disrupting other cognitive processes (i.e., encoding of the Arabic stimuli in the case of tachistoscopic presentation, and maintenance of a number representation in memory in the case of the retention interval). Further, the effects of the speed pressure manipulation would probably be nonselective—that is, speed pressure would probably disrupt several of the processes involved in performing the task (and the disrupted processes might or might not include verbal number production processes).

The advantages attached to the use of brain-damaged subjects stem from the fact that brain damage may selectively impair particular components of a cognitive system, including components that are difficult to disrupt selectively in studies of normal subjects. Thus, it is often possible to accumulate a large corpus of errors reflecting the disruption of a particular cognitive process. Analyses of such a corpus may reveal in a clear and sometimes even dramatic fashion the form of the representations on which the disrupted process operates, and the nature of the operations performed on these representations. Thus, the study of several brain-damaged subjects with various types of disruption to the different components of a cognitive system will often lead to rapid progress in the development of a well-articulated model of that system.

ACKNOWLEDGMENTS

This research was supported by NIH Grants NS21047 and NS07851. Scott Sokol was supported by a National Science Foundation Graduate Fellowship. We thank Sarah Raskin, Lisa Ijiri, and Samira Saliba for testing subjects and conducting data analyses. We also thank William Badecker for his helpful comments.

REFERENCES

Ashcraft, M. H., & Battaglia, J. (1978). Cognitive arithmetic: Evidence for retrieval and decision processes in mental addition. *Journal of Experimental Psychology: Human Learning and Memory, 4*, 527–538.

Boller, F., & Grafman, J. (1983). Acalculia: Historical development and current significance. *Brain and Cognition, 2*, 205–223.

Caramazza, A (1984). The logic of neuropsychological research and the problem of patient classification in aphasia. *Brain and Language, 21*, 9–20.

Caramazza, A. (1986). On drawing inferences about the structure of normal cognitive systems from the analysis of patterns of impaired performance: The case for single-patient studies. *Brain and Cognition, 5*, 41–66.

Caramazza, A., & Berndt, R. S. (1985). A multicomponent deficit view of agrammatic Broca's aphasia. In M.-L. Kean (Ed.), *Agrammatism* (pp. 27–63). New York: Academic Press.

Caramazza, A., Berndt, R. S., & Basili, A. G. (1983). The selective impairment of phonological processing: A case study. *Brain & Language, 18*, 128–174.

Deloche, G., & Seron, X. (1982a). From one to 1: An analysis of a transcoding process by means of neuropsychological data. *Cognition, 12*, 119–149.

Deloche, G., & Seron, X. (1982b). From three to 3: A differential analysis of skills in transcoding quantities between patients with Broca's and Wernicke's aphasia. *Brain, 105*, 719–733.

Deloche, G., & Seron, X. (1984). Semantic errors reconsidered in the procedural light of stack concepts. *Brain and Language, 21*, 59–71.

Fuson, K. C., Richards, J., & Briars, D. J. (1982). The acquisition and elaboration of the number word sequence. In C. J. Brainerd (Ed.), *Children's logical and mathematical cognition* (pp. 33–92). New York: Springer-Verlag.

Garrett, M. (1980). Levels of processing in sentence production. In B. Butterworth (Ed.), *Language production, Volume 1: Speech and talk* (pp. 177–120). London: Academic Press.

Gelman, R., & Gallistel, C. R. (1978). *The child's understanding of number*. Cambridge, MA: Harvard University Press.

Hurford, J. R. (1975). *The linguistic theory of numerals*. Cambridge: Cambridge University Press.

Levin, H. S., & Spiers, P. A. (1985). Acalculia. In K. M. Heilman & E. Valenstein (Eds.), *Clinical neuropsychology* (pp. 97–114). New York: Oxford University Press.

Martin, R. C., & Caramazza, A. (1982). Short-term memory performance in the absence of phonological coding. *Brain and Cognition, 1*, 50–70.

McCloskey, M., & Caramazza, A. (1987). Cognitive mechanisms in normal and impaired number processing. In G. Deloche & X. Seron (Eds.), *Mathematical disabilities: A cognitive neuropsychological perspective* (pp. 201–219). Hillsdale, NJ: Lawrence Erlbaum Associates.

McCloskey, M., Caramazza, A., & Basili, A. (1985). Cognitive mechanisms in number processing and calculation: Evidence from dyscalculia. *Brain and Cognition, 4*, 171–196.

McCloskey, M., Sokol, S. M., & Goodman, R. A. (1986). Cognitive processes in verbal number production Inferences from the performance of brain-damaged subjects. *Journal of Experimental Psychology: General, 115*, 307–330.

Menninger, K. (1969). *Number words and number symbols: A cultural history of numbers*. Cambridge, MA: M.I.T. Press.

Miceli, G., Silveri, M. C., Villa, G., & Caramazza, A. (1984). On the basis for the agrammatic's difficulty in producing main verbs. *Cortex, 20*, 207–220.

Miller, K., Perlmutter, M., & Keating, D. (1984). Cognitive arithmetic: Comparison of operations. *Journal of Experimental Psychology: Learning, Memory, & Cognition, 10*, 46–60.

Power, R. J. D., & Longuet-Higgins, H. C. (1978). Learning to count: A computational model of language acquisition. *Proceedings of the Royal Society of London: B, 200*, 391–417.

Seron, X., & Deloche, G. (1983). From 4 to four: A supplement to 'From three to 3'. *Brain, 106*, 735–744.

Seron, X., & Deloche, G. (1984). From 2 to two: An analysis of a transcoding process by means of neuropsychological evidence. *Journal of Psycholinguistic Research, 13*, 215–236.

Shallice, T. (1979). Case study approach in neuropsychological research. *Journal of Clinical Neuropsychology, 1*, 183–211.

Siegler, R. S., & Robinson, M. (1982). The development of numerical understandings. In H.

Reese & L. Lipsitt (Eds.), *Advances in child development and behavior* (Vol. 16, pp. 241–312). New York: Academic Press.

Sokol, S., & McCloskey, M. (1988). Levels of representation in verbal number production. *Applied Psycholinguistics, 9*, 267–281.

2 Phonological Deficits in Aphasia: Theoretical Perspectives

Sheila E. Blumstein
Brown University

Neurolinguistics is an area of research that is of critical importance to the understanding of normal human language and cognition. The ultimate aim of this research is to understand and explicate the principles of language, delineate the mechanisms and processes implicated in language use, and specify their neurological instantiation.

Much of the study of neurolinguistics has been guided by theoretical principles derived from linguistic theory. For example, Roman Jakobson provided one of the first indications that phonological impairments in aphasia break down in lawful ways, lawful only if certain assumptions are made about the primitives and structural principles of the phonological system (Jakobson, 1968). Even descriptive studies that claim to simply observe patterns of impairment are not theory neutral. The descriptive vocabularies of such studies effectively make theoretical claims and statements. For example, if a study investigating sentence production in aphasia analyzes or classifies the patient's productions in terms of traditional parts of speech such as noun, verb, adjective, and so forth, then a theoretical claim has been made. In particular, there is an implicit assumption about the nature and organization of the vocabulary used in sentence production. If, instead, the researcher analyzed the same data in terms of the frequency of occurrence of each word produced, irrespective of its syntactic role, then a different theoretical claim has been made.

Nevertheless, neurolinguistic investigations need not always be derivative to linguistic theory. The study of aphasia may in itself importantly inform linguistic theory. On the one hand, it may provide evidence that confirms particular theories of language. Such evidence is not trivial, as it provides converging information using different research methodologies and different sources of data than those used in theoretical studies. In addition, the study of language in aphasia may provide critical evidence for distinguishing among theories of language. In particular, data may be provided that confirm one theory, while disconfirming another. Perhaps most importantly, evidence from aphasia may constrain theories of language in critical ways, and, in this sense, uniquely inform linguistic theory. On the one hand, studies of aphasia may provide insights not afforded by theoretical investigations or studies of normal language processing. On the other hand, they may suggest theoretical explications that have not been formally incorporated into current theoretical models.

In this chapter, we consider how the analysis of the patterns of language dysfunction in aphasia can inform and constrain theories of normal language processing. To this end, we focus on the phonological component of the linguistic grammar, and particularly consider how the studies of speech production and speech perception in aphasia speak to current phonetic/phonological theories. The issues we address include the nature of the primitives in the phonological component, their organization and structure, and the neural instantiation of this component of the grammar, particularly as it may constrain theories of the modularity of language (Fodor, 1983).

THE PRIMITIVES OF PHONOLOGICAL REPRESENTATION: THEIR ORGANIZATION AND STRUCTURE

Linguistic theory makes a distinction between *phonology*, the study of the sound systems and sound patterns of human language, and *phonetics*, the study of the speech sounds themselves, and the nature of their physical (articulatory and acoustic) properties. Both phonology and phonetics form the phonological component of the linguistic grammar. The distinction between phonetics and phonology is translated for models of language processing in terms of two distinct stages of processing required for speech production, and two distinct stages of processing required for speech perception. It is generally assumed that the representation of words in the lexicon is defined in terms of abstract phonological attributes such as segments and phonetic features. To produce a word requires access to this representation (phonological planning) and ultimately the conversion of such a representation into articulatory commands (articulatory implementation). Conversely, to perceive a word requires converting a continuous acoustic signal into a discrete phonetic-phonological representation for lexical access.

The facts of aphasia basically support the dichotomy between a phonetic and phonological level of representation, particularly with respect to the basis of speech production deficits in two distinct clinical types of aphasia—Broca's and Wernicke's aphasia. Nevertheless, as we discuss later, this dichotomy may not be as clear-cut as current models and theoretical claims would suggest. Before considering the dichotomy between phonetic and phonological levels of representation in aphasia, we review the evidence from aphasia that addresses the nature of the primitives in phonological representation, as well as their organization and structure.

Nearly all current phonological theories consider the segment and particularly the phonetic feature to be the basic primitives of sound structure (Chomsky & Halle, 1968; Clements & Keyser, 1983; Jakobson, Fant, & Halle, 1956). Phonetic features are, in theory, the vocabulary of lexical representation. They correspond to acoustic-articulatory attributes or properties that occur together to uniquely define a particular segment in the language inventory. For example, the segment [d] is defined in terms of a bundle of phonetic features—it is a consonant in contrast to a vowel, [+consonantal]; it is made with a complete closure in the mouth in contrast to a production with a different release characteristic, [-continuant]; the closure is made with the blade of the tongue at the alveolar ridge in contrast to the lips or velum, [+coronal]; and vocal cord vibration begins in the vicinity of the stop release in contrast to beginning well after the release [+voiced].

Evidence from aphasia is generally consistent with the view that lexical items are stored at some level of representation in terms of phonetic features. In speech perception, aphasic patients, regardless of lesion site or clinical type, show deficits in discriminating stimuli as a function of their phonetic feature distance. In particular, they show greater difficulty in discriminating stimulus pairs distinguished by one phonetic feature, either *voice* or *place of articulation*, than two phonetic features, *voice* and *place of articulation*. Moreover, within single feature contrasts, *place of articulation* contrasts are harder to discriminate than *voice* contrasts. These results obtain regardless of whether the stimuli are real words or nonsense syllables or whether the phonetic contrast occurs initially or finally in one-syllable words or initially or medially in two-syllable words (Baker, Blumstein, & Goodglass, 1981; Blumstein, Baker, & Goodglass, 1977).

Perhaps the strongest evidence for the phonetic feature is found in investigations of speech production impairments in aphasia. Nearly all aphasics, regardless of clinical type, manifest some phonological difficulties in speech output. Although a broad array of phonological errors may occur, they can be reduced to four descriptive categories (Blumstein, 1973): phoneme substitution errors in which a phoneme is substituted for another, for example, *teams* → [kimz]; simplification errors in which a phoneme or syllable is deleted, for example, *green* → [gin]; addition errors in which an extra phoneme or syllable is added, for example, *see* → [sti]; and environment errors in which a particular phoneme occurs that can be accounted for by the influence of the surrounding phonological context. These environment errors include metatheses, for example *degree* → [gədriz], and progressive and regressive assimilations, for example, *Crete* → [krik] and *Crete* → [trit], respectively. The stability of these patterns is evidenced by their occurrence among different phonological systems in varying languages—French (Bouman & Grünbaum, 1925; Lecours & Lhermitte, 1969), German (Bouman & Grünbaum, 1925; Goldstein, 1948), English (Blumstein, 1973; Green, 1969), Turkish (Peuser & Fittschen, 1977), Russian (Luria, 1955), and Finnish (Niemi, Koivuselka-Sallinen, & Hanninen, 1985).

Consideration of the nature of phoneme substitution errors speaks directly to the critical importance of the phonetic feature. The question basically centers on whether segments are organized as unanalyzable wholes or in terms of phonetic features. If segments are represented as indissoluble units, then phoneme substitution errors should occur randomly—any phoneme should theoretically be substituted for any other phoneme. In contrast, if segments are defined in terms of underlying properties or phonetic features, then one might expect a systematic relation between target phoneme and substitution error. In particular, substitution errors may more likely occur between phonemes separated by a single phonetic feature than between phonemes separated by more than one phonetic feature. Results of a number of studies show that this is indeed the case. Although the particular occurrence of a phoneme substitution error cannot be predicted, the direction of such errors can be (Blumstein, 1973; Lecours & Lhermitte, 1969). When patients substitute one sound segment for another, the substituted sound is usually different by one phonetic feature from that of the attempted or target sound. For example, patients may make voicing errors, such as, *doll* → [tal]; place of articulation errors, *teams* → [kimz]; but they rarely make errors involving both voicing and place of articulation errors in the same sound substitution (*doll* → [kal]). Nearly all aphasics show this same pattern of errors.

It is important to note that although there have been some challenges to these generalities, they are difficult to evaluate. Research methodologies have varied across studies, as have classification schemas for the various error types (Burns & Canter, 1977; Canter, Trost, & Burns, 1985; Kohn, 1985; Martin, Wasserman, Gilden, & West, 1975; Nespoulous, Joanette, Beland, Caplan, & Lecours, 1984; Trost & Canter, 1974). Perhaps most importantly, researchers have often used different phonetic feature systems, and some have based their analyses on a comparison of fully specified feature matrices, whereas others have used partially specified matrices. Thus, for example, a place of articulation substitution change from [b] → [g] involves a two-feature change in Chomsky and Halle's (1968) feature system, whereas it involves a one-feature change in Jakobson et al's. (1956) feature system. Further, a change from [d] → [g] involves a three feature change in Chomsky and Halle's (1968) feature system using a fully specified matrix, whereas it involves a one feature change in Jakobson et al.'s (1956) feature system using a partially specified matrix. As it turns out, place of articulation errors are among the most common type of phoneme substitution error. Thus, the different results in these studies may be misleading, as they may reflect the different feature systems used rather than actual conflicting findings.

Interestingly, these discrepancies turn out to be more apparent than real when the organization and structure of the feature system is considered in terms of current linguistic theory. As discussed earlier, theories of phonology using phonetic features as primitives have treated the analysis of segments in terms of bundles of phonetic features (Chomsky & Halle, 1968; Jakobson et al., 1956). This bundle constitutes a specification of all feature values appropriate to the particular segment. Nevertheless, what this approach fails to capture is that there are intrinsic relations *among* the phonetic features characterizing the sounds of speech. Some features are mutually interdependent, whereas others are mutually dependent. For example, place of articulation features such as [anterior] and [back] are not independent. A speech sound cannot be both [+ anterior] and [+ back]. Similarly, a sound that is [+ coronal] (i.e., produced with the blade of the tongue) cannot also be [+ back] (i.e., produced with the body of the tongue retracted). Laryngeal features, representing various states of the larynx, are largely interdependent in their articulatory manifestations. In contrast, other features are mutually independent. Features such as [continuant] or [delayed release] correspond to the nature of the release characteristics of a consonant, and these features are largely independent of laryngeal features and place of articulation features.

More recent phonological models have attempted to formally characterize this internal structure of phonetic features (Clements, 1985). Mutually independent features are represented as separate feature tiers. These include *laryngeal features* corresponding to states of the larynx, *nasal features* corresponding to the degree of closure of the velum, *manner features* corresponding to the degree and type of closure and release in the supralaryngeal vocal tract, and *place of articulation features* corresponding to the point in the vocal tract where the particular constriction occurs.

If we consider the aphasic data in terms of this model, it is clear that the predominance of phoneme substitution errors reflects feature changes *within* a single tier rather than *across* tiers. Thus, errors may involve voicing, place, or manner and are less likely to involve both voicing and place or voicing and manner. Although this approach is similar to those that simply counted the number of feature changes in a phoneme substitution error, it differs in one crucial respect. It formally distinguishes between feature changes that, by definition, are interdependent from those that are not. Thus, the place of articulation changes discussed previously from [b] → [g] and [d] → [g] are single-tier changes, despite the fact that [b] is distinguished from [g] by the features [anterior] and [back], and [d] is distinguished from [g] by the features [coronal], [anterior], and [back]. [b] is

[– coronal], [+ anterior], and [– back]; [d] is [+ coronal], [+ anterior], and [– back]; and [g] is [– coronal], [– anterior], and [+ back]. Note that the discrepancies that emerged in the feature analyses of phoneme substitution errors, particularly as they involved place of articulation errors, now disappear.

Further analysis of the patterns of phoneme substitution errors reveals that there are other constraints on the occurrence of these errors. In particular, over 77% of consonant phoneme substitution errors occur when the target phoneme is in a singleton position; that is, when a single consonant (C) precedes a vowel (V), (CV), when it is in intervocalic position (VCV), or when it follows a vowel (VC) (Blumstein, 1973, 1978). Few substitutions occur when the consonant is part of a consonant cluster. Thus, phoneme substitution errors are sensitive to the syllable structure of the target word. That is, there seems to be a sharp distinction between the effects of consonants and vowels on the articulatory programming of syllable-sized units. The juxtaposition of two consonants seems to form a more cohesive programmed articulatory sequence than does the juxtaposition of a consonant followed by a vowel.

There is no formal means by which generative phonology can account for these data, as a lexical item is represented as a linear string of consecutive segments with each segment consisting of a bundle of phonetic features (Chomsky & Halle, 1968). However, more recent approaches to phonology have given independent status to the syllable and to the hierarchical structure of the segments C and V. It is beyond the scope of this chapter to consider the motivations and details of the theoretical arguments and solutions surrounding the construct of the syllable. Suffice it to say, however, that in this view the phonological representation of words includes not only their segmental structure and phonetic feature structure, but also their syllable structure (Clements & Keyser, 1983; Goldsmith, 1976; Lass, 1984).

For example, as shown in Fig. 2.1, a syllable is a hierarchical branching structure consisting of an onset (0) and a rhyme (R). The rhyme is further delineated in terms of a nucleus (N) and a coda (C). These nodes dominate categories like C and V, which in turn dominate segments and their features. Examples of the structures of the words *seat* and *street* are shown in Fig. 2.2 and Fig. 2.3.

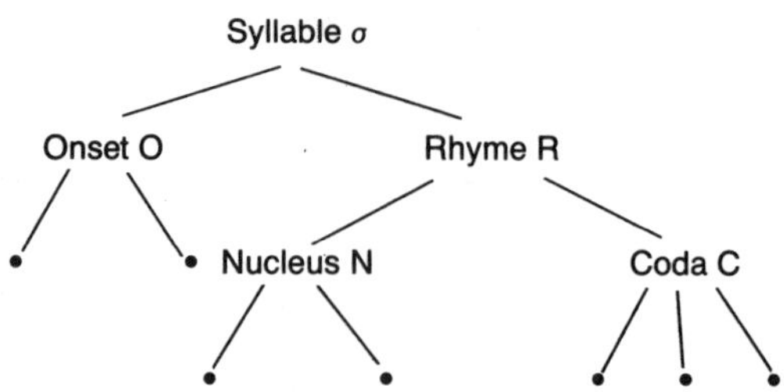

FIG. 2.1.

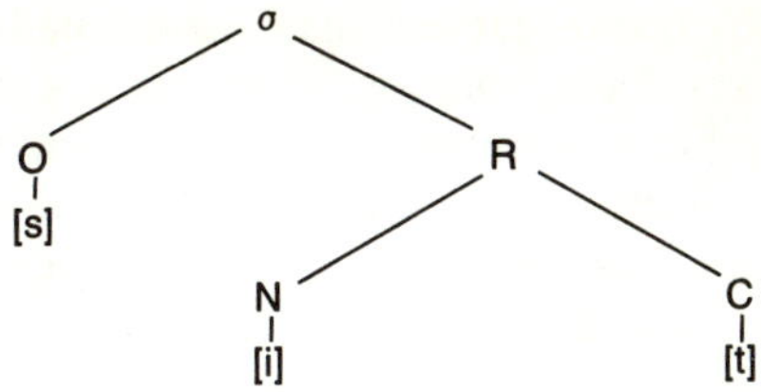

FIG. 2.2.

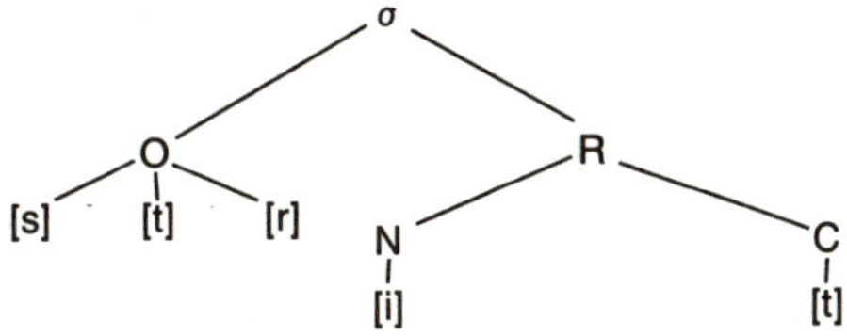

FIG. 2.3.

Turning now to constraints on phoneme substitution errors, it is clear that consonant clusters in an onset or a coda form a level of representation or unit of analysis distinct from the nucleus. Thus, at this level of representation, two contiguous consonants form a more cohesive unit than does a consonant followed by a vowel or a vowel followed by a consonant. The fact that the aphasic data can be accounted for within this theoretical framework lends support to this theory and weakens a theoretical model that has no formal means of capturing syllable structure in lexical representation.

The critical importance of syllable structure in the pattern of phonological errors also emerges in considering simplification errors and addition errors in aphasia (Blumstein, 1973, 1978). Even stronger support for a theoretical framework that incorporates syllable structure as a level of representation comes from analyses of assimilation errors across word boundaries. Basically, such assimilation errors preserve syllable structure relations between the contaminating and assimilated phoneme. If the contaminating phoneme is in the onset, so is the assimilated phoneme; for example, *history books* → [bIstri bUks], *green beret* → [brin bəre]. If the contaminating phoneme is in the coda, so is the assimilated phoneme; for example, *roast beef* → [rof bif]. These results indicate that syllable structure must be represented in the lexical structure of words and must be marked as such when lexical items are accessed and organized in some type of a planning buffer for sentence production. Otherwise, such syllabic constraints would not emerge across word boundaries.

In sum, the nature of phonological deficits in aphasia provides constraints on the form of the phonological representation of words. The pattern of deficits indicates a structural richness to this representation. In particular, the data are consistent with theories in which phonetic features are primitives in phonological representation. The nature of the feature errors that occur, however, suggests that there is internal structure to the organization of phonetic features. Such structure is characterized by a tier system in which those features that are mutually independent are represented on separate tiers, whereas those features that are mutually interdependent are represented on the same tier. Moreover, lexical entries must not only contain phonetic features but also syllable structure representations. The aphasic data thus disconfirm those phonological theories in which the minimal unit of sound structure is the segment (Bloomfield, 1933), those theories in which phonetic features are represented as undifferentiated bundles of phonetic features (Chomsky & Halle, 1968; Jakobson et al., 1956), and those theories in which lexical entries are represented solely in terms of a linear organization of segments and features (Chomsky & Halle, 1968).

DICHOTOMY BETWEEN PHONOLOGICAL PLANNING AND PHONETIC IMPLEMENTATION

Whereas deficits at the phonological level of representation (i.e., phonological planning) affect the sound patterns and sound structure of language, deficits at the phonetic level of representation (i.e., articulatory implementation) affect the physical properties of speech sounds. Numerous studies have shown that patients with anterior brain damage, and particularly Broca's aphasics, manifest phonetic impairments in speech production. Nevertheless, to ascribe these patients' deficit to a particular level of representation (e.g., phonetic level or level of articulatory implementation) provides no explanation of the nature of the disorder. As we will see, acoustic analyses of the speech production of these patients have revealed an interesting pattern of impairments that uniquely characterizes the nature of articulatory implementation deficits in aphasia. Most importantly, the results of these studies suggest that phonetic impairments in aphasia do not reflect a pervasive impairment affecting all speech sounds. The particular patterns that emerge suggest that there are separate subsystems contributing to articulatory implementation, and that some of these subsystems can be selectively impaired, whereas others remain relatively preserved.

Investigations of the phonetic patterns of speech have primarily used acoustic measurements of the speech produced by patients to infer the nature of their impairments (Alajouanine, Ombredane, & Durand, 1939; Kent & Rosenbek, 1983; Lehiste, 1968). More direct measures of articulation using fiberoptics (Itoh, Sasanuma, & Ushijima, 1979), computer-controlled X-ray microbeams (Itoh, Sasanuma, Hirose, Yoshioka, & Ushijima, 1980), and electromyography (Shankweiler, Harris, & Taylor, 1968) have also been made.

The phonetic attribute that has received the most attention is that of voice-onset time (VOT). VOT is a critical attribute to the voiced-voiceless phonetic distinction. It reflects the timing relation between the release of a stop consonant and the onset of glottal pulsing or voicing. Results of numerous studies have revealed that Broca's aphasics are significantly impaired in their production of VOT. Unlike normal subjects, Broca's aphasics show impairments in maintaining the category distinction between voiced and voiceless stops. As a result, the VOT production of many target voiced and voiceless stops shows overlap, particularly at the category boundary. These patterns emerge not only in English and Japanese, for which VOT serves to distinguish voiced and voiceless phonetic categories (Blumstein, Cooper, Goodglass, Statlender, & Gottlieb, 1980; Blumstein, Cooper, Zurif, & Caramazza, 1977; Freeman, Sands, & Harris, 1978; Hoit-Dalgaard, Murray, & Kopp, 1983; Itoh, Sasanuma, Tatsumi, Murakami, Fukusako, & Suzuki, 1982; Shewan, Leeper, & Booth, 1984); but also in Thai, for which VOT serves as a three-category distinction for prevoiced, short lag, and voiceless aspirated stops; for example, [b], [p], [ph], respectively (Gandour & Dardarananda, 1984a).

Similar problems have also been shown in the production of nasal consonants (Itoh et al., 1979). In particular, Broca's patients show impairments in the timing of the opening of the velum and the release of the oral closure in the production of nasal consonants; for example, [m] or [n].

Nevertheless, a series of studies investigating other acoustic attributes have failed to find significant impairments. In several analyses of vowel production, it has been shown that although Broca's aphasics are more variable than normals, the formant frequencies of their vowels are within normal limits (Ryalls, 1986). And although the absolute durations of their vowel productions differ from normals, results seem to vary across studies (Collins, Rosenbek, & Wertz, 1983; Duffy & Gawle, 1984; Ryalls, 1986). Importantly, Broca's aphasics maintain the distinction between intrinsic vowel duration in English (e.g., [u] in *who'd* is longer than [U] in *hood*) and contrastive vowel duration (e.g., [i] in *heed* is longer than [i] in *heat* [Duffy & Gawle, 1984]). They also show preserved phonemic length in Thai; for example, [bot] *to grind* versus [boot] *temple* (Gandour & Dardarananda, 1984b).

A number of studies have explored consonant production in Broca's aphasics. These studies have explored the production of fricative consonants and the production of place of articulation in stop consonants. With respect to fricatives, no significant impairments have emerged in analyses of the duration of fricative noise before vowels or in consonant clusters (Harmes et al., 1984). The only problems that have shown up for Broca's aphasics involve the voicing of fricatives, in particular, in the onset of voicing relative to the onset of frication noise (Harmes et al., 1984; Kent & Rosenbek, 1983).

Acoustic analyses of stop consonants have explored the phonetic dimensions of place of articulation by investigating the spectral characteristics at the release of the stop closure. Results showed that spectral patterns of the stop consonants [p t k b d g] produced by Broca's aphasics could not be distinguished from normals (although Broca's did show some impairments in the production of alveolar stops), suggesting that on balance these patients were able to get their vocal tract into the appropriate configuration for production of place of articulation (Shinn & Blumstein, 1983). And finally, Broca's aphasics show relatively normal coarticulation effects in the transitions between consonants and vowels (Katz, 1988), although these effects might be somewhat delayed in time (Ziegler & Von Cramon, 1985).

The results of all of these studies suggest that clear-cut impairments in articulatory implementation emerge in Broca's aphasics only in those productions requiring the timing of two independent articulators; for example, VOT, nasal consonants, and frication noise relative to voicing onset. Thus, the articulatory implementation disorder of Broca's aphasics seems to be predominantly a timing one—but only as it involves the timing of articulators that can be separately implemented. Note that intrinsic and contrastive durations of vowels and overall durations of vowels and fricatives are relatively normal. This pattern of results is consistent with the model we have elaborated in the previous section, in which phonetic features are represented on tiers, with features representing independent articulatory maneuvers instantiated on separate tiers, and features representing interdependent articulatory maneuvers instantiated on the same tier. Segmental impairments seem to arise as a result of an impairment in the implementation of the timing of these separate tiers. Thus, the articulatory implementation impairment affecting segmental production is not a pervasive one, but rather involves a subsystem relating to the timing characteristics of the feature bundle contributing to a particular sound segment. A great deal more research will be necessary to determine whether other phonetic attributes contributing to the production of sound segments are impaired in Broca's aphasics and to ascertain whether such impairments are consistent with this view.

Nevertheless, although the correct timing of the attributes of features comprising a sound segment is critical to normal articulation, speech production is not merely the implementation of a linear concatenation of sound segments. Normal speech has its own prosody, and as with other attributes of language, different patterns typify different languages. Speech prosody involves both the melody and rhythm of language. The melody of speech relates to the fundamental frequency characteristics of words, phrases, and sentences. The rhythm of speech relates to the stress pattern and timing of syllable structure. From a linguistic point of view, prosody is a part of the phonological component of the grammar, and although theories of grammar have attempted formally to characterize particular aspects of prosody such as stress and pitch (Chomsky & Halle, 1968; Goldsmith, 1976), a full treatment of all aspects of prosody within the linguistic grammar has not as yet been realized.

Recent evidence suggests that speech prosody forms a separate subsystem of the phonological component of the grammar, and this subsystem can be selectively impaired with the remainder of the phonetic/phonological system intact. This evidence comes from a fairly rare syndrome called the *foreign accent syndrome*. The major presenting feature of this syndrome is the emergence of what seems to be a foreign accent in speech subsequent to a lateralized brain lesion. What is curious is that to the listener the speech output of the patient is not pathological, but rather sounds like a foreigner speaking English (or whatever language is native to the patient). To date there are only seven reported cases in the literature (Blumstein, Alexander, Ryalls, Katz, & Dworetzky, 1987; Graff-Radford, 1986; Monrad-Krohn, 1947; Pick, 1919; Schiff, Alexander, Naeser, & Galaburda, 1983; Whitaker, 1982; Whitty, 1964).

In a recent case study, we explored the acoustic characteristics of a number of aspects of the speech production of a patient presenting with the foreign accent syndrome (Blumstein et al., 1987). This patient was born and raised in a city in New England, had no experience with foreign languages, and had not traveled to any foreign country. Acoustic analyses revealed that there was a constellation of features that were produced normally. Voiceless stops were aspirated, the stops [t] and [d] were produced as alveolars, and vowel quality and intrinsic vowel duration were characteristic of native English speakers.

Nevertheless, there was a constellation of acoustic features that were not characteristic of English. Initial voiced stops were produced with unusually long prevoicing, and at times, an epenthetic vowel was produced prior to the release of the stop. Monosyllabic CVC utterances were often produced with a final epenthetic vowel added to the end of the utterance. Prestressed alveolar stops were produced as full stops rather than flaps. Vowels were more tense than normal. And fundamental frequency patterns were quite abnormal, with uncharacteristic rising pitch contours at the terminal elements, even for simple declarative sentences and wh-questions.

All of these anomalous acoustic features can be linked to a common underlying deficit in speech prosody. The fundamental frequency impairments clearly implicate a prosodic disorder. The particular anomalous segmental features are also consistent with an impairment in prosody, and, in particular, with an impairment in speech rhythm or speech timing. A change in speech rhythm from stressed-timed, as in English, to syllable-timed, would affect specific phonetic characteristics of segmental features while leaving others intact. Those features could include changes in syllable structure, with the introduction of epenthetic vowels, the emergence of full stops instead of flaps for alveolar consonants, and tensing of vowels. That many elements of segmental production were absolutely normal in this patient, including voicing and place of articulation in stop consonants and vowel quality, indicates that there is no deficit in the production of the intrinsic segmental properties of speech. Instead, there are a few highly specific segment production anomalies that seem to be secondary to a basic disturbance in prosody. The selectivity of this disorder is consistent with the view that prosody is a subsystem of the phonological component and that it may be instantiated by separate neural mechanisms other than those involved in other subsystems of the phonological component.

In sum, phonetic impairments described in this section indicate that there is a distinct level of representation having to do with the articulatory implementation of speech. This level is distinct from phonological planning, in which the selection or organization of the features comprising lexical entries are affected in very particular ways, as described in the previous section. At the level of articulatory implementation, the physical properties of sound structure are affected. This level of representation, however, seems to be characterized by a set of subsystems. At least two have been identified thus far. One concerns the implementation of the timing of the tiers of phonetic features comprising segments, and the other concerns the implementation of speech prosody. Other subsystems may well emerge as further research on the phonetic properties of aphasic speech is conducted.

NEURAL INSTANTIATION OF THE PHONETIC/PHONOLOGICAL COMPONENT

Recent theories of language processing have suggested that language is modular. That is, it is suggested that the processing of language turns on mechanisms that are specialized for language and that are, in essence, apart from those mechanisms subserving higher cortical functions. More importantly, the claim that language is modular requires that the language system be comprised of a specialized working vocabulary or set of primitives and a highly constrained set of operations dictated by theoretical principles inherent to language. There are a number of versions of a modular theory of language. Perhaps the strongest and most constrained are those of Fodor (1983), Forster (1979), and Garrett (1979), who hypothesized that language consists of submodules or autonomous subsystems, each with its own vocabulary and each with a restricted domain of analysis and processing.

One of the characteristics that Fodor considered critical to modular systems is that they be associated with distinct neural structures. He elaborated this view by stating that a modular system is hard-wired "in the sense of being associated with specific, localized, and elaborately structured neural systems. . . ." (1983, p. 37). In a broad-stroke view, he is correct in that the aphasias are associated with distinct neural structures. That is, aphasia in right-handers is usually the consequence of left hemisphere pathology, and damage to different areas of the left hemisphere generally results in distinct clinical syndromes (Damasio, 1981; Goodglass & Kaplan, 1983; Naeser, 1985).

However, the claims of modularity are much stronger than that, because the subsystems of language are themselves proposed to be modular, and thus neurally distinct as well. As we discussed earlier, the phonetic/phonological component seems to be comprised of various subsystems relating to speech perception, on the one hand, and speech production, on the other. What is less clear is whether these subsystems are associated with specific, localized areas of the brain. A number of neurolinguistic models have made fairly strong claims in this regard (Darley, Aronson, & Brown, 1975; Mlcoch & Noll, 1980; Rosenbek, Kent, & LaPointe, 1984). However, the data derived from speech perception and speech production studies are not consistent with such a strictly localizationist view.

Turning first to speech perception in aphasia, nearly all aphasic patients show deficits in perceiving the sounds of speech. Such studies have focused on the perception of phonemic or segmental contrasts. Results have shown that aphasics do evidence deficits in processing segmental contrasts in tasks requiring them to determine if two naturally spoken real words or nonsense syllables are the same or different (e.g., *bait* versus *date* or [beip] versus [deip]) or to point to an appropriate picture of an auditorily presented target word given a picture array containing phonologically similar words; for example, target *pea* with pictures of a *pea*, *T*, *key* (Baker et al., 1981; Blumstein, Baker, & Goodglass, 1977; Jauhiainen & Nuutila, 1977; Miceli, Caltagirone, Gainotti, & Payer–Rigo, 1978; Miceli, Gainotti, Caltagirone, & Masullo, 1980). In terms of the feature relations of the consonants, subjects are more likely to make discrimination errors when the test stimuli contrast by a single phonetic feature than when they contrast by two or more features (Baker et al., 1981; Blumstein et al., 1977a; Miceli et al., 1978; Sasanuma, Tatsumi, & Fujisaki, 1976). Further, discrimination errors on place of articulation contrasts are more common than are errors on voicing contrasts (Baker et al., 1981; Blumstein, Baker, & Goodglass, 1977; Miceli et al., 1978).

Nevertheless, although the quantity of errors may vary, these patterns of impairment emerge across types of aphasia. None of these studies has shown selective impairments in processing the sounds of speech as a function of type of aphasia or lesion site. In fact, studies that have attempted to determine if performance on speech perception tasks relates in any way to auditory language comprehension have failed to show any systematic or strong correlations (Basso, Casati, & Vignolo, 1977; Blumstein, Baker, & Goodglass, 1977; Boller, 1978; Jauhiainen and Nuutila, 1978; Lesser, 1978; Miceli et al., 1980).

Further studies investigating speech perception have explored aphasic patients' sensitivity to the acoustic parameters contributing to phonetic contrasts. They have investigated whether the failure to perceive the phonetic dimensions of speech reflects an impairment in converting the acoustic parameters of speech into their discrete phonetic representations. To pursue this question, researchers have explored the phenomenon of categorical perception in aphasia. If normal listeners are presented with a continuum of stimuli in which the endpoint stimuli contain acoustic parameters appropriate to two different phonetic categories, and the remaining stimuli vary in equal steps along a particular acoustic dimension, a very particular relation obtains between their ability to label and discriminate the stimuli (Liberman, Cooper, Shankweiler, & Studdert-Kennedy, 1967). Namely, subjects perceive the stimuli as belonging to discrete categories and show a fairly sharp change in the identification of the categories at a particular stimulus along the continuum. When asked to discriminate the stimuli, they discriminate at a high level of accuracy only those stimuli that they label as two different phonetic categories. Those stimuli labeled as members of the same phonetic category are discriminated only slightly better than chance.

The studies exploring categorical perception in aphasia have focused on two phonetic dimensions—voicing (Basso et al., 1977; Blumstein, Cooper, Zurif, & Caramazza, 1977b; Gandour & Dardarananda, 1982; Itoh et al., 1986) and place of articulation (Blumstein, Tartter, Nigro, & Statlender, 1984). The parameters investigated included voice-onset time, relating to the phonetic feature for voicing, and the spectral characteristics at the onset of stop consonants, relating to the phonetic features for place of articulation. Results of all of these studies have shown that aphasic patients have particular difficulties in labeling the test stimuli. Interestingly, in those studies comparing labeling and discrimination, there were some patients who were unable to label the stimuli or produced abnormal labeling functions and yet were able to discriminate the stimuli (Blumstein, Cooper, Zurif, & Caramazza, 1977; Blumstein et al., 1984; Gandour & Dardarananda, 1982). Most importantly, the discrimination functions were generally similar in shape and crossover boundary to those of normals. Nevertheless, there seemed to be no relation between performance on the categorical perception tasks and lesion site or type of aphasia.

These results challenge the view that the perception of the auditory properties of speech or their categorization into phonetic dimensions is selectively impaired in aphasia, and, moreover, that these processes are subserved by distinct neural subsystems (Mlcoch & Noll, 1980). Thus, damage to anterior portions of the left hemisphere is as likely to result in deficits in speech perception as is damage to the left temporal regions, the site where the auditory association areas are located. We consider the implications of these results for theories of the modularity of language after we discuss speech production deficits in aphasia.

As we discussed earlier, there is fairly clear-cut evidence for the dichotomy between phonological planning and articulatory implementation in speech production. In particular, there seem to be two distinct levels of representation, one having to do with accessing the phonological representation of a word from the lexicon and the other having to do with converting this representation into articulatory commands. A number of neurolinguistic models have suggested that this dichotomy is reflected in neurologically distinct areas. It has been hypothesized that articulatory implementation deficits are found in patients with anterior lesions, particularly Broca's aphasics or patients with apraxia of speech, and phonological planning deficits are found in patients with posterior lesions, particularly Conduction and/or Wernicke's aphasics (Alajouanine et al., 1939; Darley et al., 1975; Itoh et al., 1982; Kohn, 1985; Mlcoch & Noll, 1980; Monoi, Fukusako, Itoh, & Sasanuma, 1983; Nespoulous et al., 1984). However, the data from studies of speech production in aphasia do not support such models. As we show, although Broca's aphasics clearly do have a disorder affecting articulatory implementation, their patterns of production implicate phonological planning deficits as well. Conversely, although the speech production deficits of posterior patients seem to be primarily phonological in nature, they also display subtle phonetic impairments.

Let us first consider the evidence for phonological disturbances in anterior aphasics. There is a subset of phonological errors that can not be explained in terms of a deficit in articulatory implementation. These include the pattern of phoneme substitution errors as well as metathesis and assimilation errors. With respect to phoneme substitution errors, there is some difficulty in interpreting the basis for those single-feature substitution errors in which the phonetic feature change can be defined on a continuous scale. This is especially the case for those features that define a timing relation between two independent articulators. Thus, consonant voicing errors, defined by VOT, or consonant nasal errors, defined by the opening of the velum relative to the release of the stop closure, could either reflect an articulatory implementation error or a phonological planning error. When the timing characteristics of the utterances are completely abnormal and do not represent the appropriate timing characteristic for either phonetic category, (e.g., voiced or voiceless), then those errors have been considered articulatory implementation errors. However, in those productions in which the timing characteristics are appropriate for one phonetic category but the target production is for the other phonetic category, the interpretation becomes more problematic. Some researchers have considered the possibility that such patterns might reflect underlying phonological planning as well as articulatory implementation errors, with, for example, abnormal VOT patterns reflecting articulatory implementation errors and correct VOT values but for the wrong target category reflecting phonological planning errors (Blumstein et al., 1980). Others, however, have chosen to interpret the VOT patterns obtained as reflecting only articulatory implementation errors (Itoh et al., 1982).

Nevertheless, there are many other types of phoneme substitution errors that do not present such ambiguities. In particular, it is difficult to see how place of articulation errors such as [p] → [t], [k] → [t], or [p] → [k] can reflect an articulatory implementation error. That is, the category errors are discrete, as are the articulatory gestures and the acoustic patterns underlying these productions. Given the structure of the human vocal tract and the acoustic patterns that follow from articulatory configurations, it is impossible to produce a consonant that is a midvalue along a continuum between a labial stop and an alveolar stop. A labial articulation with a closure at the lips represents a completely different articulatory gesture than an alveolar stop with a closure made by the tip of the tongue at the alveolar ridge. Similarly, an alveolar stop is different from a velar stop, where, in the latter case, the tongue body rather than the tongue tip is making the closure. These phoneme substitution error types require that the wrong articulatory gesture is made, and, as a result, the error is one of phonological planning and not articulatory implementation. It is, of course, possible for articulatory implementation errors to occur in the production of place of articulation. As we discussed in the previous section, such deficits have not emerged strongly in aphasic patients, although there is some indication that Broca's aphasics do have difficulties in producing alveolar stops (Shinn & Blumstein, 1983).

Turning to metathesis and assimilation errors, neither of these error types can be accounted for in terms of articulatory implementation errors. Both require that the utterance be incorrectly preplanned. In metathesis errors, the order of phonemes is incorrect (e.g., *degree* → [gədriz]), not their phonetic realization. Assimilation errors are of two types: progressive and regressive assimilations. In progressive assimilation errors, the target phoneme is assimilated to a previously occurring phoneme (e.g., *duck* → [dəd]). In regressive assimilation errors, the target phoneme is assimilated to one that occurs later in the sequence (e.g., *doll* → [lal]). As we indicated earlier, assimilation errors occur not only within words but across word boundaries. Regressive assimilation errors, both within and across word boundaries, are by far a more common error than progressive assimilation errors (Blumstein, 1973). The fact that a phoneme is replaced by one that occurs later in the sequence indicates that the articulatory program determining the specific ordering of the utterance must be modified before the patterns of articulatory movement can be implemented.

Although there has been some debate in the literature as to whether all aphasics have exactly the same distribution of these error types, all aphasics, including Broca's and other anterior aphasics, produce metathesis and regressive assimilation errors (Blumstein, 1973; Burns & Canter, 1977; Canter et al., 1985; Nespoulous et al., 1984). Thus, a phonological planning deficit is clearly implicated, and the full range of speech production impairments in these patients cannot be accounted for solely in terms of articulatory implementation errors.

Turning to Wernicke's aphasics, there has been increasing evidence that these patients display a subtle phonetic impairment. Such findings are unexpected given that clinically these patients present with well-articulated fluent speech, and to the listener the phonetic characteristics of their speech seem quite normal. Nevertheless, a number of recent studies suggest that this is not the case. The first observation of potential impairments came from Blumstein et al. (1980), who noted in their analysis of VOT production that Wernicke's aphasics tended to prevoice their voiced stops. Although prevoicing is not abnormal in English, it was surprising that all of the Wernickes tested showed this pattern. Nevertheless, as these researchers indicated, results could have reflected a subtle phonetic deficit or sampling error. Further studies, however, have shown systematic differences between Wernicke's aphasics and normals in the phonetic attributes of speech sounds. In particular, Ryalls (1986) found that although Wernicke's aphasics maintained the distinction between the intrinsic duration of the vowels of English (e.g. the vowel in *heed* is longer than that in *hid*), the overall durations of the vowels were longer than normals. Moreover, these patients showed greater variability in the formant frequency and durations of English vowels than did normals. And finally, the fundamental frequency of their vowels tended to be higher than that of normals. Interestingly, similar patterns of vowel production were found in Broca's patients. Duffy and Gawle (1984), investigating vowel duration in contexts where duration cues final consonant voicing (e.g., *beet* versus *bead*) also noted some abnormalities in vowel duration in their group of fluent aphasics (Tuller, 1984). In a recent study, Baum, Blumstein, Naeser, and Palumbo (1989) explored duration characteristics of both vowel and consonant productions in Broca's and Wernicke's aphasics. Their findings for the vowel analysis generally replicated the aforementioned results. Although they found no evidence for VOT impairments in their Wernicke's aphasics, they did show impairments in the production of fricative consonants. In particular, although Wernicke's aphasics maintained the intrinsic duration of the fricative consonants [f θ s š], their overall fricative durations were longer than normal. Moreover, the Wernickes patients failed to maintain the duration distinction between voiced and voiceless fricative consonants in the contrast between [f]–[v] and [s]–[z]. As with the results of Ryalls (1986), the pattern of results obtained for Wernicke's were similar to those obtained for Broca's aphasics. The results from all of these studies suggest that Wernicke's aphasics display a subtle phonetic impairment that implicates a deficit at the level of articulatory implementation.

The findings that Broca's aphasics manifest phonological impairments and Wernicke's aphasics display phonetic impairments run counter to those claims of a theory of modularity that requires that modular systems be strictly localizable. The issue of concern is whether these results argue against a theory of modularity itself or rather suggest that the condition that modular systems be associated with specific localized neural structures is too strong. Although at this time it is impossible to choose between these alternatives, we favor the latter, for several reasons. First, the other characteristics of modular systems proposed by Fodor (1983, p. 21) have not been disconfirmed. Second, whereas the phonetic/phonological system does not seem to be represented in strictly localized areas, the speech/language system clearly is. Damage to the left hemisphere does affect language in ways that damage to the right hemisphere does not. Moreover, the breakdown of language use does vary as a function of lesion site. However, what is emerging from neuroanatomical studies is that the architecture of the brain and its relation to structure and function is much more complicated than originally viewed. For example, the motor/articulatory system is not solely innervated from anterior brain structures. There are, in fact, projections from auditory cortex to deep white matter motor structures. Damage to posterior portions of these white matter structures can produce a phonetic output disorder (Damasio, Damasio, Rizzo, Varney, & Gersh, 1982). Much more research will be necessary to map out the neural systems underlying language and speech. Suffice it to say that the neural architecture of the brain subserving the phonological component of the grammar seems to reflect complex neural systems that may be fairly diffusely localized in the language dominant hemisphere.

ACKNOWLEDGMENTS

Many thanks to Shari Baum and Susan Behrens for many helpful discussions and for their comments on an earlier draft of this chapter. This research was supported in part by NS 22282 to Brown University and NS 06209 to the Boston University School of Medicine.

REFERENCES

Alajouanine, T., Ombredane, A., & Durand, M. (1939). *Le syndrome de la désintégration phonétique dans l' aphasie* [The syndrome of phonetic disintegration in aphasia]. Paris: Masson.

Baker, E., Blumstein, S. E., & Goodglass, H. (1981). Interaction between phonological and semantic factors in auditory comprehension. *Neuropsychologia, 19*, 1–16.

Basso, A., Casati, G., & Vignolo, L. A. (1977). Phonemic identification defects in aphasia. *Cortex, 13*, 84–95.

Baum, S., Blumstein, S. E., Naeser, M. A., & Palumbo, C. (1989). Temporal dimensions of consonant and vowel production: An acoustic and CT scan investigation of aphasic speech. Manuscript submitted for publication.

Bloomfield, L. (1933). *Language*. New York: Holt, Rinehart & Winston.

Blumstein, S. E. (1973). *A phonological investigation of aphasic speech*. The Hague: Mouton.

Blumstein, S. E. (1978). Segment structure and the syllable in aphasia. In A. Bell and J. B. Hooper (Eds.), *Syllables and segments* (pp. 189–200). Holland: North-Holland Pub. Co.

Blumstein, S. E., Alexander, M. P., Ryalls, J. H., Katz, W., & Dworetzky, B. (1987). On the nature of the foreign accent syndrome: a case study. *Brain and Language, 31*, 215–244.

Blumstein, S. E., Baker, E., & Goodglass, H. (1977). Phonological factors in auditory comprehension in aphasia. *Neuropsychologia*, 15, 19–30.

Blumstein, S. E., Cooper, W. E., Goodglass, H., Statlender, S., & Gottlieb, J. (1980). Production deficits in aphasia: A voice-onset time analysis. *Brain and Language, 9*, 153–170.

Blumstein, S. E., Cooper, W. E., Zurif, E., & Caramazza, A. (1977). The perception and production of voice-onset time in aphasia. *Neuropsychologia, 15*, 371–383.

Blumstein, S. E., Tartter, V. C., Nigro, G., and Statlender, S. (1984). Acoustic cues for the perception of place of articulation in aphasia. *Brain and Language, 22*, 128–149.

Boller, F. (1978). Comprehension disorders in aphasia: A historical review. *Brain and Language, 5*, 149–165.

Bouman, L., & Grünbaum, A. (1925). Experimentell-psychologische Untersuchungen sur Aphasie und Paraphasie [Experimental psychological investigation of aphasia and paraphasia]. *Zeitschrift fur die gesamte Neurologie und Psychiatrie, 96*, 481–538.

Burns, M. S., & Canter, G. C. (1977). Phonemic behavior of aphasic patients with posterior cerebral lesions. *Brain and Language, 4*, 492–507.

Canter, G. J., Trost, J. E., & Burns, M. S. (1985). Contrasting speech patterns in apraxia of speech and phonemic paraphasia. *Brain and Language, 24*, 204–222.

Chomsky, N., & Halle, M. (1968). *The sound pattern of English*. New York: Harper & Row.

Clements, G. N. (1985). The geometry of phonological features. *Phonology Yearbook, 2*, 225–252.

Clements, G. N., & Keyser, S. J. (1983). *CV phonology: A generative theory of the syllable*. Cambridge, MA: MIT Press.

Collins, M., Rosenbek, J. C., & Wertz, R. T. (1983). Spectrographic analysis of vowel and word duration in apraxia of speech. *Journal of Speech and Hearing Research, 26*, 224–230.

Damasio, H. (1981). Cerebral localization in aphasia. In M. T. Sarno (Ed.), *Acquired aphasia* (pp. 27–65). New York: Academic Press.

Damasio, A. R., Damasio, H., Rizzo, M., Varney, O., & Gersh, F. (1982). Aphasia with nonhemorrhagic lesions in the basal ganglia and internal capsule. *Archives of Neurology, 39*, 15–20.

Darley, F. L., Aronson, A. E., & Brown, J. R. (1975). *Motor speech disorders*. Philadelphia: Saunders.

Duffy, J. R., & Gawle, C. A. (1984). Apraxic speakers' vowel duration in consonant-vowel-consonant syllables. In J. C. Rosenbek, M. R. McNeil, & A. E. Aronson (Eds.), *Apraxia of speech: Physiology, acoustics linguistics, management* (pp. 167–196). San Diego: College-Hill Press.

Fodor, J. A. (1983). *The modularity of mind*. Cambridge, MA: MIT Press.

Forster, K. I. (1979). Levels of processing and the structure of the language processor. In W. E. Cooper & E. C. T. Walker (Eds.), *Sentence processing*, (pp. 27–85). Hillsdale, NJ: Lawrence Erlbaum Associates.

Freeman, F. J., Sands, E. S., & Harris, K. S. (1978). Temporal coordination of phonation and articulation in a case of verbal apraxia: A voice-onset time study. *Brain and Language, 6*, 106–111.

Gandour, J., & Dardarananda, R. (1982). Voice onset time in aphasia: Thai. I. perception. *Brain and Language, 17*, 24–33.

Gandour, J., & Dardarananda, R. (1984a). Voice onset time in aphasia: Thai II. production. *Brain and Language, 23*, 177–205.

Gandour, J., & Dardarananda, R. (1984b). Prosodic disturbance in aphasia: Vowel length in Thai. *Brain and Language, 23*: 206–224.

Garrett, M. (1979). Levels of processing in sentence production. In B. Butterworth (Ed.), *Language production* (pp. 177–220). London: Academic Press.

Goldsmith, J. A. (1976). *Autosegmental phonology*. Bloomington, IN: Indiana University Linguistics Club.

Goldstein, K. (1948). *Language and language disturbances*. New York: Grune & Stratton.

Goodglass, H., & Kaplan, E. (1983). *The assessment of aphasia and related disorders*. Philadelphia: Lea & Febiger.

Graff-Radford, N. R., Cooper, W. E., Colsher, P. L., & Damasio, A. R. (1986). An unlearned foreign "accent" in a patient with aphasia. *Brain and Language, 28*, 86–94.

Green, E. (1969). Phonological and grammatical aspects of jargon in an aphasic patient: A case study. *Language and Speech, 12*, 103–118.

Harmes, S., Daniloff, R. G., Hoffman, P. R., Lewis, J., Kramer, M. B., & Absher, R. (1984). Temporal and articulatory control of fricative articulation by speakers with Broca's aphasia. *Journal of Phonetics, 12*, 367–385.

Hoit-Dalgaard, J., Murray, T., & Kopp, H. G. (1983). Voice onset time production and perception in apraxic subjects. *Brain and Language, 20*, 329–339.

Itoh, M., Sasanuma, S., Hirose, H., Yoshioka, H., & Ushijima, T. (1980). Abnormal articulatory dynamics in a patient with apraxia of speech. *Brain and Language, 11*, 66–75.

Itoh, M., Sasanuma, S., Tatsumi, I. F., Murakami, S., Fukusako, Y., & Suzuki, T. (1982). Voice onset time characteristics in apraxia of speech. *Brain and Language, 17*, 193–210.

Itoh, M., Sasanuma, S., & Ushijima, T. (1979). Velar movements during speech in a patient with apraxia of speech. *Brain and Language, 7*, 227–239.

Itoh, M., Tatsumi, I. F., Sasanuma, S., & Fukusako, Y. (1986). Voice onset time perception in Japanese aphasic patients. *Brain and Language, 28*, 71–85.

Jakobson, R. (1968). *Child language, aphasia, and phonological universals* (A. R. Keiler, Trans.) The Hague: Mouton.

Jakobson, R., Fant, G., & Halle, M. (1956). *Preliminaries to speech analysis*. Cambridge, MA: MIT Press.

Jauhiainen, T., & Nuutila, A. (1977). Auditory perception of speech and speech sounds in recent and recovered cases of aphasia. *Brain and Language, 4*, 572–579.

Katz, W. (1988). Anticipatory coarticulation in aphasia: Acoustic and perceptual data. *Brain and Language, 35*, 340–368.

Kent, R. D., & Rosenbek, J. C. (1983). Acoustic patterns of apraxia of speech. *Journal of Speech and Hearing Research, 26*, 231–249.

Kohn, S. (1985). *Phonological breakdown in aphasia*. Unpublished doctoral dissertation, Tufts University.

Lass, R. (1984). *Phonology: An introduction to basic concepts*. London: Cambridge University Press.

Lecours, A. R., & Lhermitte, F. (1969). Phonemic paraphasias: Linguistic structures and tentative hypotheses. *Cortex, 5*, 193–228.

Lehiste, I. (1968). *Some acoustic characteristics of dysarthria*. Switzerland: Biblioteca Phonetica.

Lesser, R. (1978). *Linguistic investigations of aphasia*. London: Arnold.

Liberman, A. M., Cooper, F. S., Shankweiler, D. P., & Studdert-Kennedy, M. (1967). Perception of the speech code. *Psychological Review, 74*, 431–461.

Luria, A. R. (1966). *Higher cortical functions in man*. New York: Basic Books.

Martin, A. D., Wasserman, N. H., Gilden, L., & West, J. (1975). A process model of repetition in aphasia: An investigation of phonological and morphological interactions in aphasic error performance. *Brain and Language, 2*, 434–450.

Miceli, G., Caltagirone, C., Gainotti, C., & Payer-Rigo, P. (1978). Discrimination of voice versus place contrasts in aphasia. *Brain and Language, 6*, 47–51.

Miceli, G., Gainotti, G., Caltagirone, C., & Masullo, C. (1980). Some aspects of phonological impairment in aphasia. *Brain and Language, 11*, 159–169.

Mlcoch, A. G., & Noll, J. D. (1980). Speech production models as related to the concept of apraxia of speech. In N. J. Lass (Ed.), *Speech and language: Advances in basic research and practice* (Vol. 4, pp. 201-238). New York: Academic Press.

Monoi, H., Fukusako, Y., Itoh, M., & Sasanuma, S. (1983). Speech sound errors in patients with Conduction and Broca's aphasia. *Brain and Language, 20*, 175–194.

Monrad-Krohn, G. H. (1947). Dysprosody or altered "melody of language." *Brain, 70*, 405–415.

Naeser, M. A. (1985). Quantitative approaches to computerized tomography in behavioral neurology. In M. M. Mesulam (Ed.), *Principles of behavioral neurology* (pp. 363-383). New York: F. A. Davis.

Nespoulous, J. L., Joanette, Y., Beland, S., Caplan, D., & Lecours, A. R. (1984). Production deficits in Broca's and conduction aphasia: Repetition vs. reading. Paper presented at Symposium of Motor and Sensory Language Processing, Montreal, Quebec, Canada.

Niemi, J., Koivuselka-Sallinen, P., & Hanninen, R. (1985). Phoneme errors in Broca's aphasia: Three Finnish cases. *Brain and Language, 26*, 28–48.

Peuser, G., & Fittschen, M. (1977). On the universality of language dissolution: The case of a Turkish aphasic. *Brain and Language, 4*, 196–207.

Pick, A. (1919). Uber anderungen des sprachcarakters als begleiterscheinung aphasischer störungen [On changes in speech sounds accompanying aphasic disturbances]. *Zeitschrift fur de Gesamte Neurologie und Psychiatrie, 45*, 230–241.

Rosenbek, J. C., Kent, R. D., & LaPointe, L. L. (1984). Apraxia of speech: An overview and some perspectives. In J. C. Rosenbek, M. R. McNeil, & A. E. Aronson (Eds.), *Apraxia of speech: Physiology, acoustics, linguistics, management* (pp. 1–72). San Diego: College-Hill.

Ryalls, J. H. (1986). A study of vowel production in aphasia. *Brain and Language, 29*, 48–67.

Sasanuma, S., Tatsumi, I. F., & Fujisaki, H. (1976). Discrimination of phonemes and word accent types in Japanese aphasic patients. *XVIth International Congress of Logopedics and Phoniatrics*, 403-408.

Schiff, H. B., Alexander, M. P., Naeser, M. A., & Galaburda, A. M. (1983). Aphemia: Clinico-anatomic correlations. *Archives of Neurology, 40*, 720–727.

Shankweiler, D. P., Harris, K. S., & Taylor, M. L. (1968). Electromyographic study of articulation in aphasia. *Archives of Physical Medicine and Rehabilitation, 49*, 1–8.

Shewan, C. M., Leeper, H. A., & Booth, J. C. (1984). An analysis of voice onset time (VOT) in aphasic and normal subjects. In J. Rosenbek, M. McNeil, & A. Aronson (Eds.), *Apraxia of speech: Physiology, acoustics, linguistics, management* (pp. 197–220). San Diego: College-Hill Press.

Shinn, P., & Blumstein, S. E. (1983). Phonetic disintegration in aphasia: Acoustic analysis of spectral characteristics for place of articulation. *Brain and Language, 20*, 90–114.

Trost, J. E., & Canter, G. J. (1974). Apraxia of speech in patients with Broca's aphasia: A study of phoneme production accuracy and error patterns. *Brain and Language, 1*, 63–79.

Tuller, B. (1984). On categorizing speech errors. *Neuropsychologia, 22*, 547–558.

Whitaker, H. (1982). Levels of impairment in disorders of speech. In R. N. Malatesha & L. C. Hartlage (Eds.), *Neuropsychology and cognition* (Vol. 1, pp. 168–207). The Hague: Nijhoff.

Whitty, C. W. M. (1964). Cortical dysarthria and dysprosody of speech. *Journal of Neurology, Neurosurgery, and Psychiatry, 27*, 507–510.

Ziegler, W., & von Cramon, D. (1985). Anticipatory co-articulation in a patient with apraxia of speech. *Brain and Language, 26*, 117–130.

3 Neuropsychology of Sentence Parsing

Marcia C. Linebarger
Paoli Research Center
Unisys Corporation

INTRODUCTION

This chapter explores the question of how evidence from language pathology may constrain theories of sentence parsing. The discussion focuses on two points of contact between aphasiology and the investigation of linguistic performance in the normal case: evidence for modularity, and evidence about language procession.

Evidence for Modularity

We consider first the possibility that the patterns of language breakdown in neurologically impaired subjects can provide support for one particular set of claims about language processing: the thesis of linguistic modularity. To what extent is the process of sentence comprehension carried out by autonomous processing systems, in the sense that, minimally, each performs distinct mental operations over a distinct computational vocabulary? And, more specifically, to what extent do the neuropsychological data provide support for the claim that the syntactic structure of sentences is analyzed by an autonomous subcomponent of the language processor?

We argue that the patterns of selective preservation and loss observed in brain-damaged subjects provide support for, at the very least, gross modularity: for the distinctness of linguistic processing from cognitive processes generally, and, within the language system itself, for the distinctness of lexical, syntactic, and semantic computations.

Evidence About Language Processing

Beyond this general support for modularity, aphasiological data may complement the psycholinguistic investigation of normals in providing quite specific information about receptive language processing. Two such arguments from aphasia are considered: first, the claim (Bradley, Garrett, & Zurif, 1980) that the performance of agrammatic aphasic patients provides support for a model of language processing in which the closed-class vocabulary plays a distinct and central role in sentence processing; and, second, a suggestion that the receptive language function of certain agrammatic patients provides support for a two-stage model of sentence processing.

Before considering these issues,, however, it is worthwhile to review the nature (and limitations) of the evidence from language pathology.

The neuropsychological data are of three basic types: selective loss, selective preservation, and exposed encoding (Marin, Saffran, & Schwartz, 1976). If brain damage can in some instances render a subject incapable of performing mental operation *X* (selective loss) but capable of performing operation *Y* (selective preservation), then this dissociation between *X* and *Y* suggests that they may be carried out by functionally distinct mechanisms, especially if one also finds the converse dissociation: ability to perform *X* but not *Y*. Furthermore, if the output of the preserved subcomponent would normally be subject to further processing by the impaired subcomponent, then the loss of these further operations may provide us with a window on the functioning of the preserved subcomponent (exposed encoding).

The logic of the argument from neuropsychological data seems quite straightforward at first glance: selective preservation, selective loss, exposed encoding. However, the strategy of arguing from pathological dissociations to cognitive mechanisms underlying normal performance requires a number of strong assumptions. In particular, we must assume that brain damage does, in at least some cases, "fractionate the cognitive system along psycholinguistically significant lines" (the "fractionation assumption" of Caramazza, 1984, p. 10); that is, we must assume that in at least some cases the symptoms reflect the impairment of one or more components of the system. Furthermore, we must assume (the transparency hypothesis) that the performance of brain-injured patients reflects fairly straightforwardly the normal system minus the impaired subcomponent(s). Clearly, this need not be the case: It might be that complex adaptations arise in the injured brain, bearing no relation to operations in the normal system.

Furthermore, the inference from symptoms to impaired subcomponents is by no means straightforward. The same symptom, for example, may follow from impairments to quite different subcomponents. The interpretation of a given patient's performance can only be interpreted in the context of his or her other impaired and preserved capacities. Because, as has been emphasized in the recent literature (see, e.g., Caramazza, 1984; Schwartz,

1984), the standard classification of aphasic syndromes does not reflect a sufficiently fine-grained analysis of psycholinguistic function, the following discussion focuses largely on arguments from dissociations observed in specific patients, rather than on large-scale group comparisons with patients defined in terms of the classical syndromes.

Other difficulties arise in the interpretation of apparent loss and preservation of function. True double dissociations of language function are rare or nonexistent, and single dissociations are more difficult to interpret.

For example, if a subject can perform a set of operations *X* but can no longer perform a different set of operations *Y*, we must establish that the operations in *Y* are not intrinsically more difficult than those of *X*. A dissociation is interesting only if there is no obvious disparity between the intrinsic difficulty of the two processes.

Even if the two sorts of computation do seem comparable in this way, their dissociation under brain damage may not be simple to interpret. Perhaps the operations of *X* are more highly automatized than those of *Y*, because they are employed more frequently. Need *X* and *Y* be distinct subsystems? Perhaps *X* and *Y* are a single system, and *Y* simply comprises the less commonly employed operations.

Or perhaps the computations of *X* are less likely to be affected by a short-term memory deficit than those of *Y*, simply because the input to *Y* must remain available for some interval, whereas *X* operates over the input as soon as it becomes available. Need *X* and *Y* be distinct subsystems? *X* and *Y* might be performed by the same subprocessor, with *Y* simply representing all the storage-dependent operations; a deficit of short-term verbal memory might prevent the patient from carrying out the operations of *X* but not those of *Y*.

To argue from the one-way dissociation between *X* and *Y* to distinct psychological subprocessors, then, we must establish that the computations in *X* and *Y* are, at least intuitively, of equal difficulty; that they are comparable in the extent to which they require a record of the input; and that each represents computations that might plausibly be performed by a single module (it must be plausible, for example, to conceive of the set of operations within a subprocessor as employing the same code).

As a final caveat, the focus in the following discussion is psycholinguistic. Inference from patterns of language pathology to neuroanatomical localization of subcomponents of the language processing system is a theoretically separable issue and is not addressed here (but see, e.g., Caplan, 1981; Kertesz, 1979).

EVIDENCE FOR MODULARITY

The investigation of language pathology discloses a variety of sometimes counterintuitive dissociations between different kinds of language processing. This section examines the extent to which these dissociations reveal distinct modules, subprocessors dedicated to specific kinds of computations in the mapping from sound to semantic interpretation.

It is uncontroversial to claim that the mechanism(s) involved in speech recognition are likely to be distinct from those involved in syntactic analysis, given the dissimilarity of the codes over which these computations are performed. That is, it is simply implausible to believe that there are psychological operations that effect a direct mapping between raw phonetic input and some mental representation of syntactic structure or of meaning, without some intermediate segmentation into units such as phonemes, morphemes, or words. This is because, for example, phonemes are unquestionably distinct from syntactic objects such as verb phrases and noun phrases, and from semantic objects such as denotations of predicates and arguments.

On the other hand, the distinctness of syntactic and semantic information is not so uncontroversial; syntactic and semantic units have not struck all investigators as apples and oranges. And so the primary focus of investigations of linguistic modularity has been the issue of autonomous syntactic processing.

In the section on "Autonomous Syntax" we attempt to spell out this notion of autonomous syntactic processing in sufficient detail to support the discussion in following sections. In the section on "Agrammatism as an Argument for Modularity" we present a classic neuropsychological argument for the autonomy of syntactic processing: The claim that the linguistic performance of at least some agrammatic Broca's aphasic patients is most plausibly characterized as a selective loss of the ability to perform syntactic processing. We argue that the data do not support such a selective loss argument; but that, instead, this symptom-complex does provide a selective preservation argument for autonomous syntax. In the section on "Selective Preservation of Syntax: Lexical Disorders" we review the evidence that the ability to process word meaning and the ability to process syntactic structure dissociate strikingly in certain disorders, suggesting to many investigators that these phenomena provide a selective preservation argument that syntactic structure is computed by an autonomous subcomponent of the language processing system.

Autonomous Syntax

We begin the attempt to clarify this notion with a brief examination of its roots in formal grammar.

The Autonomous Systems Approach in Linguistic Theory. An issue of long standing in generative grammar is the question of whether language as a formal system is independent of the meanings that it expresses.

Many linguists, of course, have argued that it is not. Generative semanticists, for example, argued emphatically against such a distinction between linguistic form and content. And the essential claim of the linguistic theory built on the work of Richard Montague is that there is a quite thoroughgoing parallelism between syntactic and semantic processes.

But the mainstream of generative grammar holds what Hale (1976) termed the autonomous systems view:

> A language consists of a number of distinct systems, each possessing inherent principles of organization which are utterly independent of factors relating to any other linguistic system, or to extralinguistic factors. (p. 120)

On this view, elaborated in Chomsky (1977a) and elsewhere, the linguistic system as a whole operates autonomously of other cognitive systems, and the subcomponents of the linguistic system are autonomous with respect to one another.

This claim is simple to express within the classical model of transformational grammar (that is, the model developed in Chomsky, 1965): the three subcomponents of the grammar—phonology, syntax, and semantics—are characterized in terms of different primitives, and the primitives of one subcomponent may not enter into the functioning of the others, except at the periphery. (That is, the systems interact only to the extent that the output of one system is the input to another.) The syntactic component consists of context-free rewriting rules that express the basic phrasal geometry of a given language (under universal constraints such as *X*-bar theory), and transformations, which operate on these deep structures in various ways. The standard theory of transformational grammar has the structure depicted in Fig. 3.1.

The autonomy of syntax thesis in this model forbids semantic constraints on syntactic processes; the passivization transformation, for example, may not be restricted on the basis of animacy (Hale, Jeanne, & Platero, 1977).

There are, of course, quite systematic connections between syntactic structure and semantic function. Subcategorization restrictions mirror semantic structure closely if imperfectly: It is no accident that *punch* may be followed by an NP (Noun phrase) but not by an S (clause), or that *happen* is intransitive. After all, *punch* expresses a relation between a puncher and a punchee, neither of which is likely to be expressed by a clause. But this isomorphism between syntactic and semantic form is at the periphery: Deep structure (in the classical model) is the input to semantic interpretation, and its raison dêtre is to provide a transparent structural representation of thematic structure. That clauses tend to express propositions and noun phrases tend to express arguments such as *agent*, *patient*, *goal* follows from the fact that the language system is embedded in other cognitive systems; that sentences are used to express meaning. The autonomy thesis sim-

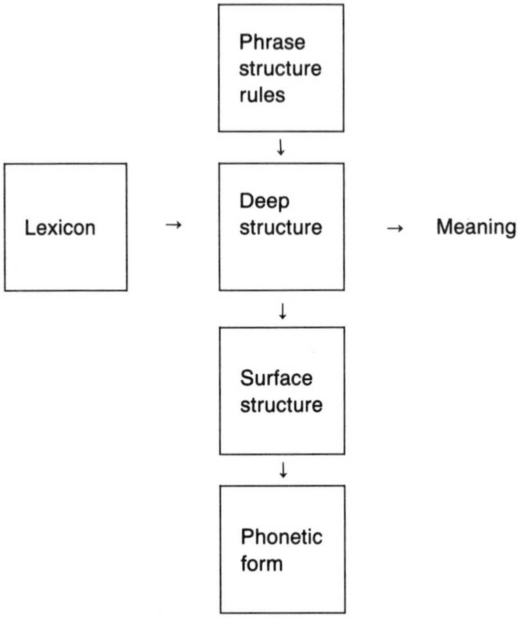

FIG. 3.1 Classical model of transformational grammar.

ply insists that semantic notions do not play a role in the internal workings of the language system. In a model of transformational grammar, such as that in Figure 3.1, this requirement is simple to express: Syntactic processes are expressed as rules, and these rules must operate over a purely formal code.

Chomsky (1981) argued for a still further degree of modularity. Chomsky suggested that formal grammar may best be characterized in terms of modular subsystems associated with grammatical processes such as the binding of anaphors, Case assignment, assignment of thematic roles, locality conditions on movement rules, control of phonologically null pronouns, and so forth; these subsystems, which do not correspond to the traditional subcomponents of the grammar, interact with each other but are characterized by their own principles and parameters (fixed in the course of language acquisition). They can be compared to highly specialized subroutines, whose computations are far removed from native speakers' intuitions about the processes of their language.

The abstractness of these principles—that is, their purely formal nature—is striking. The sentences in example 1, which follows, are both ungrammatical for the same reason (they are violations of the Case filter, the requirement that all noun phrases be marked for abstract Case, despite the almost total absence of morphological case-marking in English); and the sentences in example 2 are both violations of a principle of the binding theory which requires that anaphors—a category that includes both reflexive pronouns and also the empty position left by a noun phrase moved by the transformation *NP movement*—be bound quite locally. However, it is virtually certain that nonlinguist native speakers would be most unlikely to regard examples 1.a. and 1.b., or 2.a. and 2.b., as violations of the "same" type.

1.a. *The photograph Louise is very nice.
(Compare: The photograph of Louise is very nice.)
b. *It is certain John to go.
(Compare; It is certain that John will go.)
2.a. *John told Mary to invite himself.
(Compare: John told himself to invite Mary.)
b. *John seems that Mary likes __.
(Compare: Mary seems to like John;
It seems that Mary likes John.)

If this theory of grammar (generally referred to as *government-binding theory*, or *GB theory*, is correct, then it can be concluded that grammatical systems do, in fact, operate autonomously of meaning to a considerable extent. As the preceding comparison with grammatical sentences of similar form suggests, there is simply no way to derive such abstract principles as Case theory or the binding theory directly from meaning; syntax is not just a subcase of thinking applied to groups of words, but is a separate module (or set of modules) with its own primitives and principles. (In earlier models of transformational grammar, sentences such as those in examples 1 and 2 are ungrammatical because there are simply no transformations or phrase structure rules that would generate them; such misapplications do not need to be explained further by grammatical principles.)

Despite its thoroughgoing modularity, this more recent model of grammar complicates the traditional characterization of syntactic autonomy. For one thing, the focus has shifted from rules to representations. The properties of a given construction (e.g., passive or the wh-question) are no longer expressed by means of a transformational rule deriving this construction from an underlying phrase marker. Rather, the transformational component has been simplified, in recent approaches (e.g., Chomsky, 1973, 1977b), to the single-rule schema 'move alpha'; that is, 'move anything anywhere'. The massive overgeneration that results from this reduction of the transformational component shifts the emphasis from rules to representations. Well-formedness constraints are no longer built into the rules themselves, but are rather expressed as conditions on representations. And, because (in the Revised Extended Standard Theory, or REST, of Chomsky and others) these representations are ultimately the input to interpretive processes, the characterization of a given violation as unsyntactic or unsemantic becomes blurred, and it becomes correspondingly more difficult to disprove (and hence, to prove) the autonomy thesis.

A related complication for the autonomy thesis is that the line between grammar and meaning is drawn somewhat differently now than in the classical model. It has been argued by Chomsky and others that there is a level of grammatical representation at which those aspects of meaning that are strictly determined by sentence grammar are expressed. This level of logical form (LF) expresses such syntactico-semantic information as quantifier scope, anaphoric binding, and thematic relations. Despite the fact that such semantic phenomena are represented at LF, LF is still a grammatical object, not an interpretation: It contains lexical items, not representations of meaning; and phenomena such as scope are represented by means of the same grammatical devices (configuration, co-indexation) that express pure syntactic processes. In fact, much of the motivation for LF as a level of linguistic representation is the evidence that logical elements such as quantifiers are subject to the same constraints as overtly moved elements, such as relative pronouns (Chomsky, 1977; Kayne, 1981; May, 1977; Rizzi, 1982a).

Because it is a transparent expression of certain logical properties of sentences, LF functions as the input to interpretive processes; it is the interface between grammar and other cognitive systems. This model (Chomsky & Lasnik, 1977) is presented in Fig. 3.2.

Note, incidentally, that this model differs in certain other respects from that presented in Fig. 3.1. The level of S-structure represents the output of the transformational component; it is more abstract than surface structure (the phonetically specified labeled bracketing of the sentence that is the output of the phonological component) in that the effects of certain stylistic and deletion rules are 'undone' at S-structure, and certain empty categories are expressed at S-structure but not at surface structure. LF, which expresses all and only those aspects of meaning that are strictly determined by sentence grammar, is derived algorithmically from S-structure, and is itself the input to further (extragrammatical) interpretive processes.

But how does this level of LF fit into the characterization of syntax as autonomous of meaning? That is, does LF count as meaning or as syntax?

If it counts as meaning, then the thesis of the autonomy of syntax is stripped of content. In this model of grammar, LF bears much of the burden of distinguishing grammatical from ungrammatical sentences. Under the view that the transformation component massively overgenerates, applying almost without constraint, the ill-formedness of its output must in many cases be ruled out by constraints on this quasi-semantic grammatical level of LF. Thus, it would be incoherent to maintain the autonomy of syntax thesis if LF is treated as meaning rather than syntax.

And so the line of demarcation in this model has shifted; it is now drawn

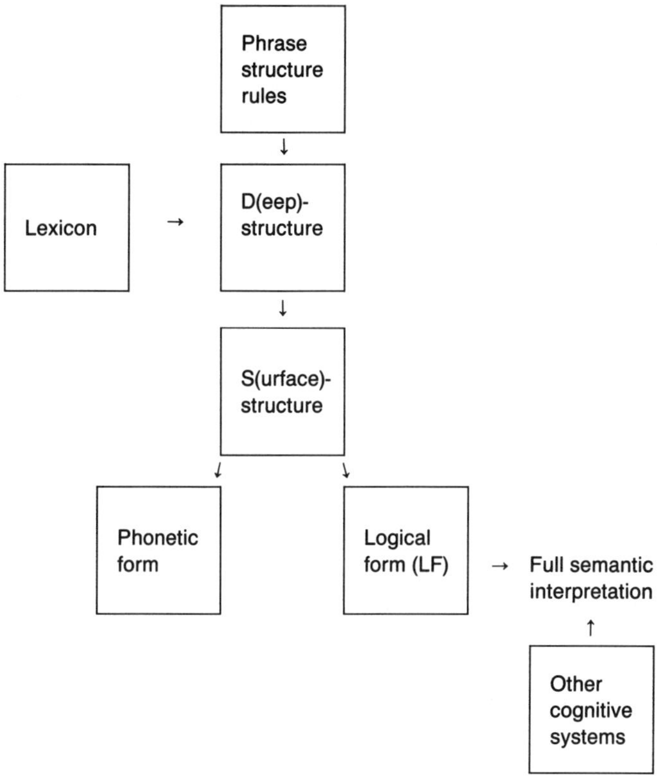

FIG. 3.2 Revised extended standard theory (REST).

between grammatical and extra grammatical processes; the term *syntax* has become correspondingly less clear-cut. According to Chomsky (1982),

> The term syntax can be used in many ways. What we might mean by syntax is the system of rules and representations of the language faculty, including representations that many people call "semantic"; also phonology. . . . In fact, a better term for it might just be the computational component of the language faculty. . . . The thesis of the autonomy of syntax would say that this system is pretty well self-contained. (pp. 114–115)

In line with this fluidity, the term *syntax* is used with the same underspecification throughout much of the following discussion, with some reconsideration of the matter later. The crucial distinction is between grammatical representation and semantic/pragmatic interpretation. Syntax represents the properties of the code as distinct from the properties of the message.

Summary

The autonomous systems approach in linguistics represents a theory about the relationships among different kinds of linguistic and extralinguistic information. The thesis of the autonomy of syntax claims, broadly, that linguistic form and content are not interdefinable. The still more fine-grained modularity of some recent approaches to generative grammar (e.g., Chomsky, 1981) extends this notion further: Grammatical processes are decomposed into subroutines carried out by distinct and highly specialized subcomponents of the grammar. In this model, the autonomy thesis lives on as a claim that the computation of grammatical form need not be carried out in the same way, by means of the same rule systems, as the computation of meaning. Even if certain aspects of meaning are expressed grammatically (at LF), this distinction holds: Properties of the code are not interdefinable with, or derivable from, properties of the message.

But these are claims about the structure of a possible human grammar (and hence, about the nature of language acquisition) rather than about the psychological operations carried out in the course of language comprehension and production. The issue of whether this distinction also characterizes the psychological mechanisms responsible for language processing is, of course, a central issue in the psychology of language.

Autonomous Syntactic Processing

The autonomy of syntax thesis claims that language is not a unitary mapping between sound and meaning, but rather is decomposable into quite distinct subsystems. It is, of course, a claim about competence—that is, about native speakers' tacit awareness of the grammatical patterns of their language—rather than about performance. We may ask: Given the complexity of possible relations between grammars and parsers, is there any reason to assume that the modularity of grammatical systems is reflected in language processing? Does the autonomy thesis have a psychological reflex?

It is widely agreed[1] that grammatical models such as those expressed in Fig. 3.1 and 3.2 make very few predictions about the temporal course of language comprehension; in particular, they do not compel a serial model of language comprehension in which full syntactic analysis of a sentence precedes semantic interpretation. However, because these grammatical models distinguish syntactic information from semantic or pragmatic information, they do predict that language processing would maintain this distinction in some form. If it were possible to demonstrate that the distinction played no role whatsoever in language processing, then we

[1]See, for example, Berwick and Weinberg (1983), Bresnan (1978), Fodor, Bever, and Garrett (1974), and Forster (1979).

might well question whether these modular theories of grammar represented anything other than a convenient shorthand for summarizing grammars.

But the question of whether there is autonomous syntactic processing is central to psycholinguistics apart from any confirmation or disconfirmation of theories of grammar. It is the focus of the modularity hypothesis about language processing. This question may be decomposed (nonexhaustively) into the following three questions.

Input Autonomy. Does the language processor perform computations that respond specifically to syntactic properties of the input: to form-class, word order, the lexical identities of those elements that are identified as grammatical morphemes within a given theory, and so forth? Evidence that such computations are in fact performed would support (although not compel) the claim that there is a psychological mechanism, a module, devoted to such operations. Note that the claim that there is input autonomy does not specify the subsequent use to which syntactic information is put.

Output Autonomy. Do listeners build syntactic representations? If we assume input autonomy, and thereby claim that certain processing operations respond selectively to syntactic features of the input, we may now ask: Do these computations build as their output representations that are also purely syntactic? Under a particularly transparent incorporation of a grammar into a language processor, for example, we might say that the different levels of grammatical representation are themselves the targets of distinct subprocessors (Fodor, Bever, & Garrett, 1974).

However, there are other plausible accounts of the process of language comprehension that specifically deny that such representations are built. Such accounts need not deny input autonomy; that is, they need not deny that there are psychological computations that respond specifically to syntactic information.

For example, one could conceive of processing operations that respond only to syntactic features of the input (input autonomy), but that respond to this syntactic information by triggering certain semantic interpretive processes. A subprocessor dedicated to such computations might take as input the fact that the string *the gray cat* is a determiner followed by an adjective followed by a noun; its response might be to call a particular semantic interpretive subroutine that looks up the meanings of the component morphemes and constructs a semantic interpretation of the entire noun phrase on the basis of the internal structure of the NP. In this case, the fact that this string is an NP is realized only insofar as it calls the appropriate interpretive subroutine.

On such an account, then, the hierarchical syntactic structure of a sentence merely reflects the semantic operations that must be applied in building up an interpretation compositionally from the meanings of its elements. The fact that *killed the snake* is a verb phrase in the sentence *The man killed the snake* is not expressed directly in any mental representation of the sentence; rather, the position of *the snake* in the phrase marker signals to the processor to build an interpretation in which the entity denoted by *the snake* is the patient (given the lexical properties of the verb) rather than the agent of the action denoted by *kill*. Thus, syntactic information is crucial to the recovery of thematic roles, on this account, but syntactic structure is expressed only by virtue of its effect on semantic interpretation.

Such an account has been proposed by a number of investigators. The Semantic Transition Network (STN) described in Johnson–Laird (1978) responds to both syntactic and semantic properties of the input (hence, input autonomy is also denied) to build a direct semantic interpretation. Unlike the Augmented Transition Network (ATN), the STN

> no longer produces an explicit analysis of syntactic relations, but is simply responsive to them in building up a semantic representation. This principle can be epitomized in a variant of Occam's razor: if you can read the signposts, you don't need a map. Parsing a sentence is, indeed, like following a set of signposts: you can reach your destination without having to keep a record of the directions in which they point. To adopt a metaphor of Davies and Isard (1972), once you reach your destination, it is quite unnecessary to thread your way through the labyrinth again. (Johnson–Laird, 1978, p. 114)

Similarly, Ades & Steedman (1982) proposed a model of (Montague) grammar that, they argued, is easily translatable into a theory of sentence comprehension:

> Because there is a one-to-one correspondence between rules of grammar and rules of semantics, [this model] does not require that the processor build autonomous syntactic representations, however temporary, for subsequent semantic interpretation. According to this model, syntax is something that a speaker or hearer *does* in getting from strings to meanings, or vice versa, not something that is built. (p. 550)

This view of the role of syntactic information in sentence processing seems to make a clear prediction: Syntactic structure cannot be computed without a corresponding computation of semantic structure. That is, to recognize *The man was killed by the snake* as a passive sentence is just to interpret the subject NP *the man* as the thematic patient rather than agent (given the lexical specification of *kill*). We should not expect to find sensitivity to the syntax of the passive construction without an appreciation of its semantic consequences. The syntactic structure makes itself felt only by virtue of the fact that it guides semantic interpretation.

This is a strong and therefore interesting prediction: Sensitivity to syntactic structure ought to manifest itself only where there is a concomitant appreciation of its semantic consequences. We should never find pure parsing, the computation of syntactic structure in the absence of semantic interpretation.

Certain potential objections arise to this direct interpretation model. First, the very fact that linguists draw tree diagrams shows that the notion of syntactic form as distinct from meaning is not incoherent. But under this direct interpretation model, phrase markers represent a history of the semantic operations to be applied in interpreting the sentence. Or, alternatively, one could simply attribute speakers' explicitly syntactic intuitions to general problem-solving skills rather than the mechanisms responsible for language comprehension and production.

Along the same lines, one might point to the ability to recover the syntactic structure of jabberwocky such as *The clemp zurked the tegs*. If syntactic structure simply guides semantic interpretation, then why is it that listeners seem to parse such meaningless strings? Again, one could answer this objection in a variety of ways; for example, one could argue that *clemp*, *zurk*, and *teg* all share the meaning *nonsense*. In a sense, then, the string does receive a syntactically guided semantic interpretation.

Is there evidence in support of this model? In his discussion of the direct interpretation approach, Cooper (1983, p. 10) pointed to the reports that listeners are often able to recall the meaning but not the precise syntactic structure of sentences. But of course the long-term memory representation of a sentence can tell us very little about the representations constructed during sentence processing; and, unfortunately, it is a formidable experimental task to reveal the nature of intermediate levels of linguistic encoding (but see Tanenhaus, Carlson, & Seidenberg, 1985, for an ingenious and promising approach).

Early Versus Late Interaction. A third major issue associated with the role of syntactic processing in language comprehension is the question of at what point syntactic computations are influenced by semantic/inferential information.

In the voluminous discussion of this matter (see, e.g., Forster, 1979; Marslen-Wilson & Tyler, 1980; Tyler & Marslen-Wilson, 1977) the question of early versus late interaction seems to reduce to the question: Is there any evidence that information about the semantic/pragmatic plausibility of alternative syntactic analyses is not used as soon as it is available? That is, is there evidence that the parser ignores potentially disambiguating information about the relative plausibility of several possible analyses?

It would be misleading to phrase this question as, Do semantic/pragmatic factors influence syntactic analysis? The answer is a priori yes, they do, at the end of the sentence. Even if the parser blindly computes syntactic structure, at the end of the sentence the semantic consequences are computed and an implausible interpretation will force the parser to reanalyze the sentence, or to choose between multiple already constructed analyses. Thus, at this point, syntactic analysis is indubitably responsive to meaning. Similarly, the answer to the question, Do semantic/pragmatic factors influence syntactic analysis? is a priori no, they do not, in the very early stages of the processing of the sentence: Even if semantic/pragmatic information is used to decide among alternate syntactic analyses, the syntactic alternatives must still (presumably) be initially computed without regard for their semantic consequences, a point that is argued with particular clarity in Forster (1979, p. 54).

Thus, the distinction between an early-interactive and a late-interactive model is apparent only at choice points prior to the end of the sentence, junctures at which alternate syntactic analyses could be profitably evaluated on the basis of their semantic consequences. According to the late-interactive model, the parser does not use semantic/pragmatic plausibility in order to decide between alternate syntactic analyses at these points. Instead, the parser uses only structural information and structure-based strategies, computing many different syntactic analyses in parallel or computing one, subject to later backtracking if it fails (either because it leads to syntactic ill-formedness or because it leads to a semantically or pragmatically anomalous interpretation). In contrast, under the late-interactive account such semantic considerations influence syntactic decisions prior to the end of the sentence; although, as noted, the initial structural analyses represent "pure" syntactic analysis.

Both of these positions are compatible with the autonomous systems approach within linguistic theory (e.g., Berwick & Weinberg, 1983; Forster, 1979). Clearly, the late-interactive model would provide strong evidence that the grammatical characterization of autonomous syntax is psychologically real, because it is most unlikely that such a distinction would characterize the processor dedicated to implementing a nonmodular grammar. And, as observed in Forster (1979), the late-interactive model is the stronger, and therefore the more interesting, theory. However, the question of whether syntactic processing is carried out by a distinct psychological mechanism does not turn exclusively on this question.

Summary

In the preceding discussion, the question of autonomous syntactic processing was decomposed into three distinct questions: (a) Input autonomy: Do listeners perform computations that respond only to syntactic features of the input? (b) Output autonomy: Do listeners build syntactic representations, or does syntactic structure make itself felt only insofar as it guides semantic interpretation? and (c) Late interaction: Is semantic/pragmatic information that would resolve syntactic ambiguities ever ignored?

Of the three positions defined by affirmative answers to these questions, input autonomy seems to be the weakest position, and late interaction seems to be the strongest position. Otherwise, the three positions are independent of one another to a considerable degree. Although it would result in an implausible model of language processing to deny that there is input autonomy while asserting either output autonomy or late interaction (why would the processor respond initially to nonsyntactic information only to subsequently ignore it?), it is reasonable to deny output autonomy and simultaneously maintain late interaction: The processor may directly compute all the possible semantic interpretations in parallel, and choose among them at the end. And it is widely argued (Berwick & Weinberg, 1983; Forster, 1979) that to assert early interaction is not to deny input or output autonomy. But one can assert input autonomy while simultaneously denying output autonomy: if the processor responds to syntactic features of the input but uses this information to build an interpretation directly, as in the Ades and Steedman (1982) and Johnson-Laird (1978) models discussed previously.

In the following sections, several sources of neuropsychological evidence bearing on these issues are examined. We consider an argument for input autonomy: The apparent insensitivity to specifically syntactic information found in agrammatic Broca's aphasics has suggested to many investigators that there is a psychological mechanism dedicated to the retrieval of syntactic structure, as evidenced by its apparent loss in this syndrome. Although this argument is rejected, the same symptom-complex gives rise to an argument for output autonomy, based on the apparent phenomenon of parsing in the absence of semantic interpretation. A different argument for input autonomy is also examined: The dissociation of lexical and syntactic knowledge at least suggests that—psychologically as well as formally—linguistic information is far from homogeneous; sensitivity to syntactic information may be preserved even in the face of severe impairments of lexical and (in some cases) more general cognitive processing.

Agrammatism as an Argument for Modularity

We consider first a well-known neuropsychological argument for modularity: the claim that syntactic processing must be autonomous because the psychological mechanism(s) by which it is carried out may be selectively disrupted by brain damage. It has been argued on the basis of the asyntactic comprehension deficit observed in certain agrammatic Broca's aphasics that focal brain damage can selectively impair the ability to perform syntactic computations.

Before considering the specifics of this claim, we ask what exactly could be concluded from a selective loss of syntactic capacities. If we could demonstrate that sensitivity to syntactic structure can be impaired independently of sensitivity to other linguistic phenomena, then we would have an argument for input autonomy. However, a loss of syntactic capacity would not provide evidence in support of output autonomy: If these patients are unresponsive to syntactic structure, then there is no way to determine whether the language processor's response to syntactic structure is to build a syntactic representation or to map the input directly onto a representation of meaning. Similarly, these phenomena do not bear on the question of late interaction: If syntactic analysis is not performed at all, then there is no way to determine when it would be influenced by semantic or pragmatic considerations in the normal case.

Agrammatism

Agrammatic Broca's aphasia, associated with lesions in the anterior portion of the dominant hemisphere, is characterized by a distinctive nonfluency of speech: Grammatical affixes and function words are omitted or misselected, phrase length is greatly reduced, and syntactic structure is generally impoverished; verbs are frequently omitted or nominalized.[2] Following are the attempts of five agrammatic patients to describe a picture of a girl giving flowers to a teacher, cited in Saffran, Schwartz, and Marin (1980).

> The girl is flower the woman.
> The girl is. . .going to flowers.
> The girl is giving. . .giving the teacher. . .giving it teacher.
> The young. . .the girl the little girl is. . .the flower.
> The girl is. . .is roses. The girl is rosin'.

As these samples demonstrate, agrammatism cannot be described simply as a stripping away of function words and affixes; there is also in some cases a failure to express grammatical relations by means of the order of open class items (Saffran, Schwartz, & Marin, 1980), as well as a tendency to omit verbs. Furthermore, the definite article and progressive suffix –ing, both closed class elements, are fixtures of agrammatic output. However, the omission of closed class elements is still a major feature of agrammatic speech; note, for example, the failure of four of the patients to produce the dative preposition *to*.

As noted, terms such as *agrammatism* remain pretheoretic and potentially misleading heuristics. Given the great variety of speech patterns la-

---

[2]The term *Broca's aphasia* is usually applied to patients with lesions in Broca's area and nonfluent expressive language deficits, whose speech is not necessarily agrammatic; that is, characterized by the omission and misselection of closed class elements, syntactically impoverished, and so forth. Thus, the term *agrammatism* is used here, to apply specifically to this subset of Broca's aphasics.

beled as agrammatic, it remains an open question whether it is appropriate to group patients on the basis of the clinical impression of agrammatism. (See, e.g., Badecker & Caramazza, 1985).

In the last 15 years, a parallel comprehension deficit has been reported (Caramazza & Zurif, 1976; Heilman & Scholes, 1976; Parisi & Pizzamiglio, 1970; Schwartz, Saffran, & Marin, 1980, Zurif & Blumstein, 1978) in at least a subset of these patients. This deficit, known as *asyntactic comprehension*, is characterized by a failure to utilize syntactic cues such as morphology and word order. Asyntactic comprehenders perform poorly on sentence–picture matching tasks involving semantically reversible sentences such as the following (a) sentences.

3. Relative clause:
   a. The cat which the dog is biting is black.
   b. The apple which the boy is eating is red.
4. Passive:
   a. The boy is chased by the girl.
   b. The apple is eaten by the boy.

The same subjects demonstrate markedly superior comprehension with nonreversible materials such as the preceding (b) sentences, suggesting an ability to build up a plausible scenario on the basis of open-class lexical content. It is only when syntactic structure alone provides crucial cues to meaning that these patients' often severe comprehension impairment comes to light.

The frequent co-occurrence of asyntactic comprehension with agrammatic speech led a number of investigators to argue for a characterization of agrammatism as a central syntactic disorder, an impairment of syntactic knowledge (or of the psychological mechanisms responsible for syntactic processing—a distinction to be considered more closely later, one that is revealed in all modalities of language use.

But this interpretation of asyntactic comprehension and agrammatic production as manifestations of a central syntactic disorder has been rejected by some investigators (e.g., Caramazza & Berndt, 1985; Goodglass & Menn, 1985) on the basis of double dissociations between agrammatic production and asyntactic comprehension.

On the one hand, asyntactic comprehension occurs in the absence of agrammatic production: Caramazza, Basili, Koller, and Berndt (1981), Caramazza and Zurif (1976), Heilman and Scholes (1976), and Saffran and Marin (1975) reported that conduction aphasics, who are not agrammatic in production, also demonstrate this failure to respond to syntactic structure in sentence comprehension tasks. Furthermore, asyntactic comprehension has also been reported in mild Wernicke's aphasics (Blumstein, Goodglass, Statlender, & Biber, 1983; Heeschen, 1980).

The converse dissociation, agrammatic production without asyntactic comprehension, has also been reported: Kolk, van Grunsven, and Keyser (1985) and Miceli, Mazzucchi, Menn, and Goodglass (1983) reported cases of agrammatism in speech in the absence of asyntactic comprehension.

Such dissociations are not outright counterexamples to the interpretation of agrammatic production and asyntactic comprehension as features of a central syntactic disorder, but they may render it uneconomical. It is not implausible to posit different sources for asyntactic comprehension: The comprehension impairment observed in conduction aphasics, for example, has been ascribed to a limitation of phonological working memory rather than to the breakdown of a central syntactic processor (e.g., Saffran & Marin, 1975; Warrington & Shallice, 1969). And the reported cases of agrammatic speech without asyntactic comprehension do not in themselves disprove the central disorder hypothesis. It may be that these patients were simply less severely impaired than those agrammatic patients who comprehend asyntactically. Certainly Miceli et al.'s (1983) patients diverge from more "typical" agrammatics in many respects: Case 1 was able to repeat and read aloud without agrammatism, and Case 2 showed normal fluency and normal phrase length.

Thus, dissociations such as the aforementioned do not in themselves render the central disorder hypothesis untenable; further investigation of the production and comprehension impairments of these different populations would be required to resolve the matter. Is the language production of agrammatic aphasics without asyntactic comprehension different in kind from that of agrammatic aphasics with asyntactic comprehension? And is the comprehension impairment in conduction aphasia qualitatively distinct from the asyntactic comprehension observed in agrammatic Broca's aphasics?

The question of whether the co-occurrence of asyntactic comprehension and agrammatism reflects a central syntactic disorder is clearly important, because it bears directly on the question of whether expressive and receptive language processing involve distinct mechanisms in the normal case. It is not, however, critical to the selective loss argument for autonomous syntactic processes in language comprehension. For the purposes of the following discussion, therefore, it is assumed that the asyntactic comprehension observed in agrammatic Broca's aphasics is fully dissociable from agrammatism of speech; more generally, it is assumed that language production and comprehension, although possibly drawing on—or developing out of—a common data base of tacit grammatical knowledge, are nevertheless carried out by distinct psychological mechanisms. (For further discussion of this matter, see Schwartz, Linebarger, & Saffran, 1985).

What is required for the selective loss argument is the demonstration that the mechanism(s) responsive to syntactic structure can break down independently of other mechanisms involved in language comprehension. The pattern of asyntactic comprehension observed in some agrammatic aphasics offers the possibility of providing this demonstration.

Whether in fact it does is considered next. In the following discussion, the term *agrammatic comprehension* refers to this comprehension disorder in cases where it co-occurs with agrammatism of speech. This usage implies no claim about its relation to patterns of asyntactic comprehension in other aphasic populations.

Agrammatic Comprehension as a Selective Loss Argument: Counterevidence

The hypothesis that agrammatism represents a specific impairment of syntactic knowledge or of syntactic processing capability represents a strong and interesting claim about modularity, because it constitutes a selective loss argument that syntactic processing is performed by a distinct subprocessor that can be selectively disrupted under brain damage.

As previously observed, agrammatism need not be construed as a central deficit in order to furnish a selective loss argument for autonomous syntactic processing. All that is needed is evidence that focal brain damage may selectively impair the ability to perform syntactic analysis, if only receptively. But in order for a selective loss argument to go through, it is imperative to demonstrate that agrammatic comprehenders simply cannot carry out the necessary computations for the retrieval of syntactic structure. If there are any circumstances under which syntactic analysis can in fact be performed, then asyntactic comprehension in these or any other aphasic patients cannot be attributed to a selective impairment to the psychological mechanisms responsible for syntactic processing.

Evidence of preserved syntactic abilities in agrammatic comprehenders, that is, agrammatic aphasics with asyntactic comprehension, has come from a variety of sources. Goodglass, Gleason, Bernholtz, and Hyde (1972) argued that the self-corrections of agrammatic speakers point toward a preserved syntactic sensitivity that is not revealed in the same patients' production, which raises the possibility that agrammatic aphasics' grammatical abilities might also be underrepresented in their frequently poor performance on comprehension tasks. Friederici (1982) reported that agrammatic patients performed well in judging the grammatical well-formedness of dependencies between verbs and obligatory prepositions despite poor performance on such prepositions in other tasks. And Linebarger, Schwartz, and Saffran (1983a) reported that four agrammatic Broca's aphasics with severely asyntactic comprehension were able to perform at a very high level of accuracy on most conditions of a grammaticality judgment task.

I briefly examine the results of this study. Representative test sentences are given; percentage figures represent the mean percent correct of six agrammatic aphasics (the original four and two subsequently tested), all of whom demonstrate the classic comprehension deficit. All six performed at chance or worse than chance (for example, on comprehension tasks involving simple passive sentences); and three of the six performed at chance also on simple actives. (See Table 3.5 for fuller subject data.) The data are presented as percent correct, for ease of presentation; but see Linebarger et al. (1983a) for an argument that single detection analysis provides a more sensitive measure of their performance. The procedures, stimuli, and data analysis are discussed in Linebarger et al. (1983a).

5. Subject-auxiliary inversion (87.5%)
   a. Was the girl enjoying the show?
   b. *Was the girl enjoy the show?
6. Incomplete extractions (85.4%)
   a. Which records are you going to give to Louise?[3]
   b. *Which are you going to give records to Louise?
7. a. They stood in the line very patiently.
   b. *They stood the line in very patiently.
   c. We broke in the engine very carefully
   d. We broke the engine in very carefully.
8. Empty elements (83.7%)
   a. Frank thought he was going to get the job.
   b. *Frank thought __was going to get the job.
   c. That's who Frank thought__was going to get the job.
   d. *Who__thought__was going to get the job?
9. Phrase structure (90.4%)[4]
   a. The starving man is hungry for food.
   b. *The starving man is hungry food.
10. Subcategorization (81.2%)
    a. The man sat on the new sofa.
    b. *The man sat the new sofa.
11. Gapless relative clauses (84.2%)
    a. Bill dropped a plate that__was too hot.
    b. *Bill dropped a plate that the stove was too hot.

This disparity between good performance on a grammaticality judgment task and impaired comprehension has recently been reported for two Hebrew-speaking agrammatics with asyntactic comprehension (Baharav,

---

[3]Most, but not all, of the violations in this condition represent violations of the left branch constraint.

[4]The violations in this condition were fairly heterogeneous, turning on one or another impermissible sequence of syntactic categories. Obviously, the grammatical explanations for the ill-formedness of sentences in this condition will be equally heterogeneous. The test reported in Linebarger et al. (1983a) was quite intentionally theory-neutral.

1985), and for Serbo-Croatian agrammatic patients (Lukatela, Crain, & Shankweiler, 1985).

The good performance of agrammatic subjects on sentences such as these demonstrates that they are capable—at least under the circumstances of the grammaticality judgment tasks—of syntactically analyzing auditorily presented sentences. Their good performance indicates more than simply that they appreciate the well-formedness constraints at issue in this task. More importantly, they could not have performed well unless they were, in fact, able to parse the test sentences.

This conclusion is discussed at some length in Linebarger et al. (1983a, 1983b), who argued that the task requires considerable sensitivity to closed-class elements, along with the ability to recover hierarchical phrase structure and to handle long-distance dependencies. A reliance on semantic/pragmatic cues, and on open-class lexical heuristics, could not have enabled subjects to perform the tasks; for example, there is no clear semantic strategy capable of distinguishing the foregoing ill-formed example 5.b. from its well-formed counterpart. The impossibility of performing the task on the basis of purely prosodic information is also discussed in Linebarger et al. (1983a).

It has been objected (Zurif & Grodzinsky, 1983) that because this grammaticality judgment was not necessarily performed on-line by our subjects, their good performance may be dismissed as irrelevant to the question of what underlies their asyntactic comprehension. In fact, however, Crain, Shankweiler, and Tuller (1984) reported that six agrammatic aphasics (four of whom are a subset of the six just described) were in fact able to make similar judgments on-line.

But even if this were not the case, we cannot dismiss the judgment results as irrelevant, under the assumption that the task does not tap those psychological mechanisms that are normally employed in sentence processing. This objection might save the selective loss argument by attributing the good performance of these agrammatic comprehenders to some off-line system that is not the "real" syntactic processor, the latter having been selectively impaired. But there are many problems with this objection, discussed in greater length in Linebarger et al. (1983b). (One problem, of course, is the proliferation of syntactic analyzers that we are forced to postulate: one for on-line sentence parsing and one for grammaticality judgments. But how would such an auxiliary parser come to exist? Surely not for the making of grammaticality judgments. And because all the comprehension tasks that have established the existence of the agrammatic comprehension deficit are themselves off-line, why couldn't this off-line parser by employed in these tasks?)

These findings, then, appear to provide very strong counterevidence against the claim that agrammatism represents a selective loss of syntactic capacity, whether as a central deficit involving all modalities of language use or as a purely receptive impairment

Asyntactic Comprehension as a Selective Preservation/Exposed Encoding Argument for Modularity

However, the same data that undermine the selective loss argument for autonomous syntactic processing are nevertheless quite suggestive of a *selective preservation* or an *exposed encoding* argument for modularity.[5] This is because the performance of these subjects reveals a totally unexpected—one might say counterintuitive—dissociation between parsing and sentence interpretation.

Consider, for example, five of these subjects' ability to process passive sentences. All five, as noted, performed at chance on a variety of comprehension tasks involving simple passive sentences. In a series of further grammaticality judgment tasks (Linebarger, Schwartz, & Saffran, 1983c), these subjects performed at a very high level of accuracy (89.1% correct) on sentences such as the following:

12. John has finally kissed Louise.
13. *John was finally kissed Louise.
14. The boy was followed by the girl.
15. *The boy was followed the girl.
16. The boy was following the girl.

The violations in this condition all contain a passive verb followed by a direct object. Note that a simple morphological change (-ed → -ing) would render these sentences acceptable, as would a substitution of *has* for *was*.

These results are certainly incompatible with the claim that agrammatic subjects' difficulties with passive sentences stem from a lack of appreciation of passive morphology. These subjects are quite sensitive to the structural consequences of passive morphology, however we wish to capture these consequences (as a loss of Case-assigning properties, for example; or as a different subcategorization, stated lexically for passive verbs.)

It appears, then, that the structural and interpretive consequences of the passive construction are dissociable. In order to perform well on the judgment task, subjects must respond differently to passive than to active forms of the verb, and they must appreciate the structural consequences of passive

[5]Whether the parsing/interpretation disparity provides a selective preservation argument for a syntactic subprocessor would seem to depend on the correctness of the mapping hypothesis: Have these subjects lost the capacity to map from syntactic structure onto semantic interpretation (selective preservation); or do other factors simply prevent them from doing so, thereby revealing the output of the parser (exposed encoding)?

morphology; that is, its intransitivizing effect. Thus, in some sense they know that the sentence is passive. In the comprehension task, by contrast, they make no consistent use of the passive morphology.

The same dissociation between asyntactic comprehension and excellent performance on grammaticality judgments has recently been reported in a patient with a short-term memory impairment (Saffran, 1985). Saffran's subject TI demonstrates the asyntactic comprehension pattern that has been reported elsewhere for patients with specific impairments of verbal short-term memory. In contrast to his asyntactic comprehension, however, TI performs exceptionally well on grammaticality judgments.

Again, we see a striking dissociation between sensitivity to the structural and the semantic consequences of passive morphology; and, more generally, an apparent dissociation between parsing and interpretation.

The reasons for this dissociation are not obvious, and may differ for the two types of patients. We consider here the question of what follows from the fact that the two kinds of processing dissociate as they do.

First of all, these results appear to argue against any model of sentence comprehension in which hierarchical syntactic structure is not mentally represented per se, but functions simply to guide interpretation. This is the claim made for the semantic parsers discussed previously; these models embody the view that "a parser for a natural language [should] be a pairing between phrases and semantic interpretation directly, without overtly defining a pairing between phrases and syntactic structure" (Cooper, 1983, p. 10). Or recall the statement of Johnson-Laird, who argued for a model of sentence processing that does not build "an explicit analysis of syntactic relations, but is simply responsive to them in building up a semantic representation" (Johnson-Laird, 1978, p. 114). Such views seem incompatible with the agrammatic data: What is sensitivity to syntax, on their account, but the ability to use syntactic structure to recover meaning? To parse without arriving at a semantic interpretation should be as paradoxical (in their metaphor) as to follow the signposts correctly and yet not arrive at one's destination.

This dissociation, therefore, seems to lend strong support to a view of sentence processing in which syntactic structure is computed as a level of representation distinct from semantic/pragmatic representation. These results, then, argue for an affirmative answer to the question of output autonomy: Do listeners construct representations of syntactic structure? Whatever the reasons for the failure to perform further interpretive processing in these two patient groups—whether this failure is the result of an STM deficit or of a specific inability to perform the necessary interpretive operations—the fact remains that syntactic analysis can be performed independently of interpretation.

It should also be observed that both patient groups perform well on comprehension tasks utilizing nonreversible sentences. Thus, they are clearly capable of building up semantic representations by combining the meanings of open-class lexical items; it cannot be claimed that the syntactic analysis they demonstrate on the judgment task did in fact come about in the course of a semantic parse, the structure of the input having directed them to the appropriate semantic operations that they were subsequently unable to perform. They seem unimpaired in their ability to arrive at the meaning of a sentence on the basis of compositional semantic operations on open-class items. It is only when syntax must point the way that they fail, for whatever reasons.

What of the question of late versus early interaction between syntactic and semantic/pragmatic processing? Clearly, these data cannot address the issue directly, because the semantic information in question is unavailable to these patients (whatever the reason, it should be reiterated). But this is an area that deserved further investigation. One possible account of the comprehension/judgment dissociation would explain the apparent superiority of syntactic processing over semantic interpretation of the same structures by claiming that the syntactic operations (even those involving long-distance dependencies over the entire sentence) precede the interpretive ones, and are thereby less affected by memory limitations. Such an account would tend to support late interaction. Furthermore, if sentence comprehension is as interactive as is claimed by the proponents of early interaction, then one might expect parsing to be disrupted in patients who are deprived of the semantic/pragmatic feedback that normally (on this view) guides parsing. At choice points, they should flounder. More generally, they should perhaps be unable to turn off their semantic processing of the input—and given the effortful and generally unsuccessful nature of their sentence comprehension, their performance on the grammaticality judgment task should perhaps be disrupted by attempts to interpret, if interpretation is such an integral part of the comprehension process. However, this is pure speculation. And given the difficulty of investigating the interaction of noninteraction between syntactic analysis and unavailable information about the semantic consequences of syntactic analyses, this autonomy question is perhaps the least likely to yield to neuropsychological evidence.

But, as argued, the question of when semantic information is utilized need not be construed as the central question about modularity within the language processing system. Evidence that listeners represent pure syntactic structure, that is, an affirmative answer to the question of output autonomy, would represent quite strong evidence that computation of syntactic structure is a distinct process from semantic interpretation. And the dissociation between parsing and interpretation previously discussed appears to provide support for this view. It is, in a sense, a neuropsychological counterpart to much of the work of Forster and his colleagues (Forster, 1979), who documented the distinctness of these processes under a variety of experimental conditions.

So far we have not considered closely the cause of this disparity. Do the comprehension failures of these six agrammatic subjects reflect failure to interpret a relatively accurate syntactic parse, or is parsing itself disrupted when processing demands are high? If the former, then the performance of these subjects may provide exposed encoding evidence about the early stages of sentence processing which is not easily available from the investigation of language processing in normals. After all, it is likely that in the normal case syntactic analyses are input to interpretive operations so rapidly as to render the initial parse unavailable for introspection and resistent to all but the most ingenious on-line investigation. We argue later that these subjects' language processing does, in fact, provide such evidence about the initial stages of sentence comprehension.

Before addressing these issues, however, we consider briefly another set of neuropsychological phenomena that provide a strong argument for linguistic modularity: disorders in which syntactic processing remains unimpaired in the face of lexical breakdown.

Selective Preservation of Syntax: Lexical Disorders

A variety of otherwise heterogeneous disorders have been characterized as disorders of lexical processing, because comprehension (as well as production) of single words is severely impaired. Included in this category of lexical impairments are Wernicke's aphasia, characterized by fluent but empty and neologistic speech output; transcortical sensory aphasia, resembling Wernicke's aphasia with the exception that the transcortical sensory aphasics demonstrate a striking ability to repeat sentences, despite an inability to generate coherent speech or to comprehend it; and, finally, dementia. Patients with diffuse cerebral pathology in which cognitive processing generally is impaired have been reported to demonstrate a striking dissociation between preserved syntax and severely impaired lexical semantics.

It is clearly not a straightforward matter to establish such a dissociation in receptive language function. If subjects are unable to comprehend the open-class items in a sentence, how can their appreciation of the relationships between these words be communicated? Suppose that a patient is able to use either some residual knowledge of the form class of open-class items (or else is able to derive this information from the closed-class items, in the worse case mimicking the Thorne, Bratley, and Dewar (1968) parser, which contained no open-class lexicon at all), and is able to build a syntactic representation of the sentence on the basis of this information and the information carried by function words and affixes. It is not clear how such preserved capacities could be demonstrated. Confronted with a picture-matching task involving *The man follows the woman*, for example, the patient might indeed appreciate that *the man* is the grammatical subject of the sentence, and that *the woman* is the direct object; but without an appreciation of what these nouns mean, he or she will be unable to choose between the correct sentence and a syntactic distractor like *The woman follows the man*.

Nevertheless, there are a few studies that suggest that the dissociation between syntactic and lexical processing, which characterizes the speech of these three groups, may also characterize their receptive language processing.

Wernicke's Aphasia

The speech of Wernicke's aphasics is frequently neologistic; unrecognizable or empty or inappropriate open-class items are linked together with closed-class items so that the effect is sentential, as in the following sample of written but characteristic jargon:

> His wife saw the wonting to wofin to a house with the umbledor. Then he left the wonding then he too to the womin and to the umbella upstairs. . . . (Goodglass & Kaplan, 1972, p. 59).

The semblance of syntactic coherence is in striking contrast to this patient's very limited control of the open-class lexicon. But, as noted, it is not easy to test the receptive appreciation of syntactic structure in isolation from awareness of the meanings of lexical items, even if we assume that such patients are capable of recovering form-class information about lexical items or are able to infer this information from the closed-class context.

One potential source of evidence about receptive syntactic processing might be furnished by the grammaticality judgment paradigm. The judgment task discussed in Linebarger et al. (1983a) has been administered to one Wernicke's aphasic (Pate, 1985); this subject's performance on this and even simpler judgment tasks was very poor, in contrast to that of the agrammatics. No dissociation has yet emerged between this patient's performance on lexically based conditions such as subcategorization and on conditions that could be performed on the basis of the closed-class vocabulary alone. (**The man was chased the woman* is an example of the latter sort.)

Another approach is the sentence anagram task. Von Stockert & Bader (1976) administered a sentence anagram task to a group of German-speaking aphasics. The Wernicke patients, all of whom demonstrated severely impaired comprehension for written material, nevertheless arranged two NPs around a verb with great consistency: the nominative NP preceded the verb and the accusative NP followed the verb, in accordance with canonical word order in German. They were able to perform this task well even when the morphology dictated a semantically implausible interpretation (as in *der hase/schiesst/den jaeger*, in which they demonstrated no awareness of the anomaly), and performed equally well on structured nonsense strings.

Thus, the data are currently quite sparse on whether the receptive language processing of Wernicke's aphasics is characterized by the selective preservation of syntax that their output suggests.

Sentence Comprehension in Dementia

The apparent preservation of syntactic abilities even in very late stages of progressive dementing disease has been widely reported (Geschwind, Quadfasel, & Segarra, 1968; Goldstein, 1948; Irigaray, 1973; Schwartz, Maring, & Saffran, 1979; Whitaker, 1976). In language production, syntactic complexity may remain long after lexical breakdown has reduced the patient's speech to near-empty lexical content and neologistic jargon. The selective preservation of syntactic processing in receptive language function is, as noted, difficult to demonstrate. One source of evidence comes from spontaneous corrections during repetition, to be discussed in the following section.

A particularly suggestive report of the persistence of complex syntactic processing in the face of general cognitive impairment (as well as lexical breakdown) is found in Schwartz et al.'s (1979) case study of a demented patient. This patient's language production revealed a classic dissociation between lexical impairment and preserved syntactic capacity: Her repertoire of open-class words shrank almost to the single item *shopping center*, but her empty productions retained an elaborated syntactic structure.

This dissociation was reflected in her receptive langauge processing as well. Presented with a sentence-picture matching task involving simple active and passive sentences, she performed virtually without error on sentences containing nouns that she recognized. (Thus, presented with a sentence *The man is chased by the woman*, she was able to select the picture depicting this activity and to reject the syntactic distractor, a picture in which a man chases a woman.) However, her processing of sentences containing nouns that she did not recognize was quite interesting. On the picture-matching task, her performance was, of course, random. In a subsequent task, however, Schwartz et al. (1979) presented these same sentences to her along with a single picture. In half of the trials, the picture and sentence matched; in the other half, the picture used was the syntactic distractor, representing the same activity and participants but with reversed thematic roles. She was then asked, for example: "This is a picture of a cat being chased by a dog. Which one is the cat?" (In half the trials, this instruction was, of course, an incorrect description of the picture.) Although her lexical impairment was so severe that she no longer recognized either of these nouns, she nevertheless employed a strategy that revealed her preserved ability to assign thematic roles on the basis of syntactic structure and the lexical properties of verbs. What she did was simply to point to the animal or object that was playing the thematic role assigned by grammatical principle to that NP. Thus, her responses to the pictures that matched the sentence were correct, whereas her responses to the mismatching pictures were systematically incorrect.

She adopted this strategy with adjectives and prepositions as well as verbs, demonstrating sensitivity to argument structure even when she no longer recognized the nouns denoting the arguments.

This pattern illustrates once again the striking nonhomogeneity of linguistic processing. How could a patient unable to differentiate between *cat* and *dog* nevertheless perform the appropriate mapping from syntactic function to thematic role? It is as if nouns are treated as free variables. One might conceive a view of sentence processing in which the syntactic module computes argument structures (e.g., CHASE(x,y)), a first step in the interpretation of such structures being the instantiation of the variables with the meanings of the nouns. But the meanings of the nouns, on this account, are accessed in parallel with, but independently of, the construction of this thematic frame. This view of sentence processing has an echo in the special status accorded to NPs in Montague grammar: The meaning of an NP need not be incorporated into the meaning of the sentence at the point at which the NP occurs; rather, the NP may be stored and its meaning combined with the meanings of the other elements at some higher point in the sentence. This notion of storage, intended to account for certain facts about scope and intensionality, reflects the same independence of nominals from the structures in which they occur as is found in these disorders in which access to nouns breaks down independently of the ability to compute other aspects of sentence meaning. In such an account, nouns represent the link between grammatical and extragrammatical analysis, between parsing (construed broadly) and interpretation.

Repetition in Dementia and Transcortical Sensory Aphasia

It has been widely observed that transcortical sensory aphasics and patients suffering from progressive dementing disease often make spontaneous corrections during repetition of ill-formed sentences (Davis, Foldi, Gardner, & Zurif, 1978; Geschwind et al., 1968; Whitaker, 1976). These same patients demonstrate virtually no language comprehension; in some cases, repetition becomes compulsive (echolalia).

Whitaker (1976) and Davis et al. (1978) reported that the spontaneous corrections of these patients tend to be almost purely syntactic. In the Davis et al. study, factually incorrect sentences and semantically anomalous sentences were generally repeated verbatim. On the other hand, violations of pronoun case (**The boy gave she a present*) and number agreement violations (**The maids sweeps the floor*) were generally corrected. Whitaker's patient also corrected number agreement violations but not semantic anomaly; she distinguished between noun and verb stress patterns on words like *permit*, changing *perMIT* to *PERmit* in the context, *My permit has expired*.

This spontaneous correction of syntactic but not semantic or factual anomalies is found even in patients without general cognitive impairment. Thus, insensitivity to the anomaly of these sentences cannot be attributed to a failure to appreciate the anomaly at a conceptual level.

This dissociation between form and content is perhaps the most striking in the literature, and points toward a view of language as an autonomous system, distinct from other cognitive systems. Although the highly syntactic nature of the corrections would seem to support a claim for further modularity within the language processor, that is, for a specifically syntactic subprocessor, one could argue otherwise. It might be claimed, for example, that these subjects are able to map from sound to a grammatically computed model-theoretic interpretation of the input sentence and that they are unable to evaluate this representation against the world, given the neuroanatomical isolation of the language areas of the brain. However, this baroque possibility does not weaken the force of the argument for the independence of language from other cognitive systems.

Summary

The findings reviewed in this section all point toward a selective preservation argument for autonomous syntactic processing. Linguistic processing seems dissociable, under brain damage, from general cognitive processing, as we see from the preserved syntactic capacities of demented patients. Furthermore, there is considerable evidence for nonhomogeneity within the linguistic system, given the preservation of complex syntactic processing in patients with severe lexical impairment, and, specifically, impaired access to nouns. The fact that a patient who can no longer distinguish between *cat* and *dog* is nevertheless capable of mapping from syntactic function to thematic role raises the possibility that nouns are semantically encapsulated, that the meanings of nouns are not as intrinsic to structural computations as are, for example, the meanings of verbs and other predicates.

EVIDENCE ABOUT LANGUAGE PROCESSING

In the preceding discussion, we reviewed the most convincing neuropsychological evidence for linguistic modularity. Despite the limitations of a selective loss of syntax argument for input autonomy on the basis of asyntactic comprehension in agrammatism, there seems to be considerable neuropsychological evidence in support of autonomous syntactic processing. The dissociation between parsing and interpretation found in both agrammatic Broca's aphasics and conduction aphasics—regardless of the ultimate sources of this dissociation in the two cases—argues strongly for the view that the computation of syntactic structure is a distinct psychological process from the computation of its semantic consequences. As noted, this dissociation mirrors the findings of Forster and his colleagues (Forster, 1979; Forster & Olbrei, 1973), which document, in a variety of experimental tasks, the distinctness of the two processes. And the evidence of preserved syntactic processing in the face of severe lexical-semantic breakdown lends considerable support to the modularity thesis.

In addition to this evidence for the dissociability of syntactic and semantic processing, neuropsychological phenomena also represent a rich source of evidence about receptive language processing generally. In this section, we consider in greater detail the sentence processing capacities of agrammatic comprehenders, patients who show the co-occurrence of agrammatism of speech and asyntactic comprehension. In particular, we examine two points of contact between the aphasiological data and studies of language processing in the normal case.

Role of the Closed-class Vocabulary. A number of psycholinguistic studies (notably Garrett, 1975, 1976, 1980) have suggested that function words and grammatical affixes play a pivotal role in normal sentence processing. It has been suggested, therefore, that the asyntactic comprehension deficit found in patients with agrammatism of speech may reflect a parallel impairment in receptive language processing: Under the strongest (and therefore most interesting) version of the closed-class hypothesis, the co-occurrence of asyntactic comprehension and agrammatic production is the manifestation of a modality-neutral impairment to the processing of function words and inflectional morphology (Bradley et al., 1980; Kean, 1977).

Early Stages of Sentence Processing. Are there temporally distinct stages in sentence interpretation? And if (as previously argued) listeners do construct specifically syntactic representations, what is the nature of these representations? The latter question presents a considerable methodological challenge, as observed in Tanenhaus et al. (1985): Even if speakers do build syntactic representations, these representations may be very rapidly transformed into full semantic interpretations. Investigations of on-line sentence processing in normal speakers, such as those proposed in Tanenhaus et al. (1985), may prove to be a rich source of evidence about these matters. In addition, however, it may be that neuropsychological data can be brought to bear on this question. Aphasic deficits are of interest not merely because they indicate what processes are dissociable, and hence may be assumed (under the aforementioned assumptions) to represent distinct psychological processes; in addition, there may be evidence from language pathology about the nature of intermediate levels of encoding. Recall, for example, the parsing-interpretation disparity discussed previously. If these agrammatic patients are constructing syntactic representations that they are unable subsequently to interpret—one possible explanation for the disparity—then these unexploited representations may have consequences for behavior that are not manifest in the normal case.

The discussion of these issues begins with a consideration of the symptom-complex of agrammatic comprehension; we then discuss the closed-class hypothesis about agrammatic comprehension; and finally, report on some further investigations of agrammatic sentence processing that may reveal something about the early stages of grammatical encoding.

Agrammatic Comprehension

We previously argued that agrammatic comprehension—that is, asyntactic comprehension co-occurring with agrammatic production—cannot be attributed to a loss of implicit syntactic knowledge nor to a loss of the ability to perform the mental operations involved in syntactic analysis. Why, then, do these agrammatic subjects comprehend asyntactically? Because this section focuses on the implications of agrammatic language processing for models of normal function, it may prove useful to review briefly the range of explanations that have been proposed to account for this pattern of impaired comprehension.

The explanations fall into three groups. First, there are the explanations that invoke a syntactic deficit, a possibility we have already rejected. Next are the explanations that also attribute agrammatic comprehension to the failure to perform syntactic analysis, but do not represent this failure as reflecting an inability to perform the syntactic computations per se; rather, syntactic analysis is prevented by the unavailability of crucial input, or by a memory deficit, or by a loss of efficiency of the parser itself or of other systems. A final alternative is the mapping hypothesis, which claims that syntactic analysis is reliably performed by these agrammatic comprehenders, and that their comprehension failures result from the failure to perform further interpretive processing of the syntactic analysis that has been achieved.

As indicated, a number of investigators have argued that the source of agrammatic comprehension is a disability specific to the grammatical affixes and function words that are typically omitted or misselected in agrammatic speech. This closed-class hypothesis concerning agrammatic comprehension has numerous variants.

Agrammatic Comprehension as Reflecting Inability to Perform Particular Syntactic Computations

Loss of Syntactic Knowledge Base. Under one set of assumptions about the structure of the language processing system, comprehension and production draw on a common data base of grammatical knowledge, whatever additional, task-specific routines may also be employed. Thus, one possible account of agrammatic comprehension is that it reflects the loss of this common data base. Such an account was implicit in the conclusion of Caramazza and Zurif (1976) that agrammatic comprehension represents a loss of algorithmic as distinct from heuristic operations.

Loss of Parsing Routines. Another hypothesis is that agrammatic comprehension reflects impairment of the psychological mechanisms responsible for receptive syntactic analysis. Despite a possibly unimpaired syntactic knowledge base, the agrammatic comprehender is no longer able to retrieve the syntactic structure of spoken sentences. No claims need be made, under this approach, about the extent to which comprehension and production share a common knowledge base or common functional machinery; it is only to the extent that the impaired mechanisms are utilized in both comprehension and production that agrammatic comprehension is predicted to co-occur with agrammatic speech.

Agrammatic Comprehension as Reflecting Failure to Perform Syntactic Analysis Despite the Ability to Do So

Loss of Crucial Input. Another source of agrammatic comprehension might be the inability to access lexical items that play a crucial role in syntactic analysis. For example (considering here the most straightforward version of the closed-class hypothesis) experimentally masking all the determiners, auxiliaries, inflectional affixes, and other closed-class elements while sparing open-class expressions such as nouns and verbs might be expected in some cases to render normal subjects asyntactic in sentence comprehension, despite their ability to build up syntactic structures on the basis of these expressions. Of course, a general breakdown of all lexical access would also prevent comprehension of reversible sentences such as *The man follows the woman*, but the pattern of asyntactic comprehension would not emerge, as performance would also suffer on nonreversible sentences such as *The woman eats the apple.*

However, the good performance of agrammatic subjects on grammaticality judgment tasks that turn crucially on closed-class elements (Baharav, 1985; Friederici, 1982; Linebarger et al., 1983a, 1983c; Lukatela, Crain, & Shankweiler, 1985) argues strongly against the hypothesis that agrammatic comprehension reflects a simple insensitivity to closed-class elements.

Memory Deficit. Another account of agrammatic comprehension attributes the disorder to a restriction in working memory. It has been widely proposed that language comprehension is supported by some form of phonological short-term memory store in the normal case (Baddeley & Hitch, 1974; Clark & Clark, 1977; Glanzer, 1972; Kleiman, 1975); the processing of long or syntactically complex sentences may require a verbatim record of surface structure. And a number of investigators (Caramazza, Berndt, Basili, & Koller, 1981; Saffran & Marin, 1975; Vallar & Baddeley, 1984a, 1984b; Warrington & Shallice, 1969) have proposed that the asyntactic comprehension observed in conduction aphasics results from an impairment to verbal working memory. On this account, subjects are unable to maintain a phonological trace of the input long enough to parse syntactically complex sentences. (There are, of course, other accounts of how such a deficit would impair sentence comprehension; this question is taken up again later.)

Because there is a similar and well-documented restriction of immediate memory span in Broca's aphasia (Goodglass, Gleason, & Hyde, 1970; Heilman, Scholes, & Watson, 1976), it is not unreasonable to extend this explanation to agrammatic comprehenders. On this account, then, the asyntactic comprehension observed in both conduction and agrammatic Broca's aphasics has a common source, and no disruption specific to the parser is invoked.

Loss of Efficiency of Parser. Another possible account of agrammatic comprehension is that these patients are in principle capable of carrying out syntactic analysis, but that syntactic computations are performed with diminished efficiency. It is this diminished efficiency, rather than the unavailability of critical input, that accounts for asyntactic comprehension.

A less efficient parser might create excessive demands on the verbal working memory store. The failure to very quickly chunk incoming material by carrying out an initial phrasal analysis could have the effect of preventing syntactic analysis altogether, simply because it is not possible to maintain the unanalyzed input string in working memory. Thus, syntactic processing would be possible in principle, but only under the idealization of unlimited working memory.

Alternatively, the loss of efficiency might cause the parser to compete with semantic interpretive operations for processing resources. This was termed the *trade-off hypothesis* in Linebarger, Schwartz, and Saffran (1983a). Thus, it would still be possible for agrammatic comprehenders to perform syntactic analysis, but at the cost of semantic interpretation. In this case, patients confronted with a comprehension task might not even attempt syntactic analysis (although retaining the capacity to perform the necessary computations on tasks that make fewer semantic demands), restricting themselves to open-class lexical heuristics.

An explanation along these lines is proposed in Blumstein and Milberg (1983), who suggested that the language processing in agrammatic Broca's aphasics is no longer automatic.

Loss of Efficiency of Other Systems. On this account, agrammatic comprehension derives from a loss of efficiency not specific to the parser. A decrease in the efficiency of open-class lexical access routines, semantic interpretive processes, or information processing generally might create excessive demands on memory resources and prevent parsing, even under the assumption that there are no memory or parsing impairments per se.

Grodzinsky, Swinney, and Zurif (1985) put forth an explanation along these lines; they raised the possibility that agrammatic comprehension might result in part from a disruption to domain-general routines for "automatized, rapid exhaustive searches of memory" (p. 79).

Agrammatic Comprehension as Reflecting Failure to Exploit Syntactic Analyses

Interpretive Mapping Deficit. Another possible explanation for agrammatic comprehension is what may be termed the mapping hypothesis: These subjects are able to compute a full and accurate syntactic analysis, but are unable to map from syntactic to semantic representation. (The term *semantic representation* is left underspecified here; it may be taken to cover any representation of meaning along the continuum from a purely grammatical level such as logical form to a full specification of the truth conditions and pragmatic force of the sentence.)

The possibility that asyntactic comprehension might reflect an inability to map from syntactic to semantic representation is suggested in Caramazza and Berndt (1985), Linebarger et al. (1983a), Rizzi (1982b), Schwartz, Saffran, and Mann (1980), and Schwartz et al. (1985). It might be, for example, that the thematic consequences of syntactic roles such as subject or object are not computed, and therefore subjects are unable to match reversible test sentences with the appropriate pictures.

Mapping Failure Due to Memory or Resource Limitations. Another possibility is that the failure to perform this mapping arises from memory or resource limitations of the sort just discussed, rather than from a specific inability to perform the mapping operations.

In summary, then, it is clear that a number of distinct factors may underlie agrammatic comprehension, even if we set aside the possibility of a genuine syntactic deficit or a failure to parse. But this failure to exploit syntactic analyses may stem from either a loss of the capacity to do so, or from memory or resource limitations that prevent semantic interpretation.

The following section concerns a further set of explanations for agrammatic comprehension, under which the aforementioned explanation types are formulated in accordance with the hypothesis that agrammatic sentence processing represents a disability specific to the closed-class vocabulary.

Agrammatic Comprehension and the Closed-Class Vocabulary

An important set of hypotheses about agrammatic comprehension focuses on the set of vocabulary items most regularly omitted from agrammatic speech: function words and affixes, which comprise the closed-class vocabulary (so named because of its low rate of lexical turnover). The closed-class hypothesis represents a particularly suggestive point of contact between neuropsychological data and psycholinguistic studies, because these elements have also been claimed to pay a distinctive role in normal sentence processing.

The Role of the Closed Class in Sentence Processing

Although grammarians have considered the matter for perhaps two millenia, agreement has yet to be reached about the precise nature of the distinction between open- and closed-class elements. Nevertheless, it is clear that natural languages tend to contain two quite different sorts of morphemes, those that are primarily of the world, and those that are primarily of the grammar. The closed class is most naturally conceived of in terms of what it does not contain: nouns, verbs, and adjectives, primarily. Thus, in English this class is generally taken to include prepositions, determiners, degree adverbs, pronouns, conjunctions, auxiliaries, inflectional affixes, and a variety of other expressions. Recent attempts to provide a unifying linguistic characterization of this heterogenous class include Carlson and Tanenhaus (1984), Kean (1977), and Lapointe (1983). In contrast, Fronek (1982) argued that the open–closed class distinction represents a continuum, and that, for example, the word *thing* functions as a member of both classes.

Despite the lack of agreement about its linguistic status, it is unquestionable that the closed-class vocabulary plays an important role in sentence parsing. It almost certainly provides crucial cues about syntactic structure, particularly information about the grammatical category of open-class items.

This predictive role of closed-class items has been incorporated into machine parsing models such as that of Thorne, Bratley, and Dewar (1968), which contained no open-class lexicon at all (apart from a list of inflectional red herrings such as B*ed*, len*s*, and so forth); and into Augmented Transition Networks (Wanner & Maratsos, 1978; Woods, 1970).

Psycholinguistic studies have provided support for this distinction. The work of Garrett (1975, 1976, 1980) strongly suggests that closed-class elements are computationally distinct from the open-class vocabulary in sentence production. On the basis of speech error patterns, Garrett argued that closed-class elements provide a syntactic frame into which open-class items are inserted in the course of sentence production.

Function words have also been argued to play a pivotal role in sentence perception, comparable to their predictive role in machine parsing models. Garrett (1978) suggested that closed-class expressions "provide a basis for the grammatical classification of open-class items *prior* to lexical lookup" (p. 620). Because open-class words tend to be ambiguous with respect to form class (*major*, for example, can function as a noun, verb, or adjective), the information provided by closed-class items could greatly reduce the search space in lexical lookup; or, given the findings of Tanenhaus, Lieman, and Seidenberg (1979) that both noun and verb meanings of ambiguous open-class words are initially accessed even in sentential disambiguating contexts, it is plausible to credit the closed class for the very rapid postaccess decision reported by these authors.

But in addition to facilitating lexical access, the closed-class vocabulary shares with word order the burden of expressing hierarchical syntactic structure above the single-word level; one need only consider the distinction between active and passive sentences, or the role of determiners as NP-introducers in sentences such as the following (from Heilman et al., 1976):

17. He showed *her* baby *the* pictures.
18. He showed *her the* baby pictures.

Evidence for the computational distinctness of the closed-class vocabulary in receptive language processing appeared to be furnished by the report in Bradley (1978) that normal subjects performed differently on open- and closed-class items in a lexical decision task; only the open-class items showed frequency sensitivity, for example. The differing performance on the two types of lexical items led Bradley to propose that they are retrieved by two quite distinct access systems in the normal case, the existence of these two access systems being assumed to facilitate the initial retrieval of syntactic structure during sentence comprehension.

In line with this hypothesis about the parsing function of a closed-class retrieval system, the performance of Broca's aphasics on this task differed from that of normals: The Broca patients showed no difference in frequency sensitivity to the two classes (Bradley, 1978; Bradley, Garrett, & Zurif, 1980). However, Bradley's findings about the frequency sensitivity of both normals and aphasics have been widely challenged (Gordon & Caramazza, 1982, 1983; Segui, Mehler, Frauenfelder, & Morton, 1982). Nevertheless, the hypothesis that there is a distinct access system for the closed class, and that agrammatic comprehension may reflect impaired processing of this element, remains interesting and plausible. Next we review the evidence concerning this claimed impairment to receptive processing of the closed-class vocabulary; then we consider the question of how such an impairment might affect the sentence processing of agrammatic subjects.

Processing of the Closed Class by Broca's Aphasics: Word Monitoring Studies

Despite the difficulties associated with Bradley's lexical decision study, it has led to an increased interest in the role of closed-class elements in the receptive language processing of both normal and agrammatic subjects. A variety of chronometric studies have attempted to track the processing of these elements during on-line sentence processing.

Studies utilizing word monitoring tasks have uniformly revealed that agrammatic Broca's aphasics recognize open-class items faster than closed-class items, whereas normal subjects show the reverse effect.

Swinney, Zurif, and Cutler (1980) reported that agrammatic subjects responded more quickly to open-class words than to closed-class words, regardless of stress; they also made significantly more errors on closed-class effect. Normal subjects, in conrast, displayed no significant word class effect. Friederici (1983), utilizing the same paradigm of word monitoring in the context of auditory sentence comprehension, found agrammatic Broca's aphasics slower to respond to closed-class words than to open-class words (although their error rate for both word classes was low); in contrast, normal subjects were faster to respond to closed-class than to open-class words.

These word monitoring studies have been interpreted as evidence that agrammatic Broca's aphasics process closed-class items differently than open-class items in the course of on-line sentence processing; the longer latencies for closed-class words were interpreted by both Swinney et al. (1980) and Friederici (1983) as evidence for an on-line processing deficit involving the closed-class vocabulary; one which, in their view, underlies the asyntactic comprehension found in these same patients. That may, indeed, be the correct interpretation of these findings. However, we need not draw this conclusion.

Perhaps it is more difficult for agrammatic subjects to retain closed-class items in memory, a requirement specific to the monitoring task. Although the high degree of accuracy reported for the agrammatic subjects in the Friederici (1983) study demonstrates that they were, in fact, able to retain these items, it may have been quite difficult for them.

If this is the case (whatever the reason), then the longer latencies for the closed-class items might simply reflect a greater overall processing load during the presentation of sentences containing closed-class targets. That is, on the trials in which the target was a closed-class word, the subjects may have had diminished resources to allocate to the task generally, and hence responded more slowly to the target.

The fact that subjects had the target word written in front of them throughout the (auditory) presentation of the sentence does not remove these possible alternative interpretations. Even under the assumption that none of these subjects was deep dyslexic, the reading of function words is often difficult for agrammatic subjects.

And if, in fact, closed-class words are particularly difficult for these subjects to retain, due to some disability specific to their processing of the closed-class vocabulary, such a disability might have no impact whatsoever on the use of closed-class elements in on-line sentence parsing, despite its effects in the word monitoring task.

These results, then, are suggestive but do not force the conclusion that agrammatic subjects are specifically impaired in the on-line processing of the closed-class vocabulary.

Closed-class Hypotheses About Agrammatic Comprehension

If agrammatic comprehenders are, in fact, impaired in their processing of the closed-class vocabulary, then we must ask how this disability brings about agrammatic comprehension, under the assumption that difficulty with function words represents a cause rather than simply an effect of disrupted parsing.

Clearly an outright excision of these items from the lexicon would account for asyntactic comprehension: Without auxiliaries and prepositions, for example, there is no way to distinguish active from passive sentences. Hence, an otherwise unimpaired syntactic analyzer would still fail to construct a syntactic analysis of any sentence in which the identity of a closed-class item is critical. But an explanation of this type, a variant of the loss of crucial input explanation discussed previously, would not account for the report in Bradley (1978) that agrammatic subjects were able to identify closed-class items as words of their language, or for the relatively high level of accuracy displayed by agrammatic Broca's aphasics in monitoring for closed-class items reported in Friederici (1983), or for the good performance of agrammatic comprehenders on grammaticality judgment tasks reported in previous sections. Nor would it be able to account for the finding of Schwartz, Saffran, and Marin (1980) that agrammatic subjects' comprehension errors in sentences with prepositions involved misassignment of arguments around the preposition rather than insensitivity to the actual semantic content of the preposition (*behind*, *in*, *on*, etc.). Thus, an account of agrammatic comprehension as the simple loss of closed-class items cannot be maintained.

Another suggestion is that agrammatic comprehenders are unable to retrieve closed-class elements rapidly enough to facilitate the assignment of constituent structure on-line. The function of the specialized closed-class retrieval system, on this account, is to allow for differentially rapid access to these items, before the phonological trace of the input is lost. According to Kean (1981):

> The initial hypothesis behind the study of normals was that a special access system for clitics [closed class elements] would aid in parsing since the rapid retrieval of clitics would make available a rich source of information for making initial hypotheses as to local syntactic structure. . . . If, as the aphasia data [Bradley's lexical decision findings] indicate, the agrammatic subjects have an impairment which precludes rapid clitic access, then under the hypothesis they should have, derivatively, a syntactic deficit. . . . Any apparent syntactic deficit would, under this view, be a by-product of the accessing impairment, that is, the mechanisms of syntactic processing are themselves intact, but they are unable to function normally due to the lack of a central class of inputs. (p. 195)

This account is a hybrid of explanation due to loss of crucial input and loss of efficiency to systems other than those responsible for carrying out syntactic computations. It assumes that agrammatic comprehenders retain the capacity to perform syntactic analysis, and remain cognizant of closed-class elements and their syntactic consequences. Under ideal circumstances, syntactic analysis would in fact be carried out. But these ideal circumstances rarely occur, because the delayed recognition of closed-class items slows down the initial chunking of the input and thereby prevents parsing. Again, the grammaticality judgment data argue against such an account, as they suggest that agrammatic comprehenders are able to parse under certain circumstances.

A third possibility is that the retrieval system for closed-class elements does not exist merely to speed up access to this set of critical items. Rather, to access a closed-class item via this retrieval system is to retrieve the structure-building operations that are associated with it. To retrieve the preposition *into* by this route, for example, is to retrieve the rule for constructing a prepositional phrase with *into* as its head. (Marcus, 1982, described the closed class as "hard-wired" into the grammar.) Semantic information about these elements is accessed through the routines that are shared with open-class elements; the ability of agrammatics to access closed-class items via this second, shared, route is consistent with the greater likelihood that agrammatics will produce the lexical semantic prepositions reported in Friederici (1981), and the sensitivity (reported in Berndt, Caramazza, & Zurif, 1983; and Zurif, 1984) that agrammatics demonstrate to the semantic/pragmatic force of the definite/indefinite articles. This view seems implicit in Zurif (1980, 1984) and is summarized in Berndt et al. (1983):

> By hypothesis, the special closed-class access route, which the Broca's aphasics seemed unable to exploit [in the Bradley lexical decision task], serves a syntactic function. As input to a parser, the closed-class items signal, for example, the introduction of a noun phrase, the distinctions between main and subordinate clauses, the difference between active and passive sentences, and so on.
>
> This then, for the moment, provides an explanation for the Broca's aphasics' inability to use the closed-class elements as syntactic place-holders, and correspondingly, for their agrammatic comprehension. . . . Since Broca's aphasics recognized the closed-class elements as items in their language, yet failed to treat them differently from open-class items, it seems reasonable to suppose that in addition to the special closed-class route, grammatical morphemes can also be accessed—along with open-class vocabulary items—via the frequency-sensitive system, and further that this frequency-sensitive system complements the parsing function of the closed-class route by contacting semantic information.

Under this account, then, a great many structure-building procedures of the parser are accessible only through closed-class items. Due to the failure of the specialized retrieval system, certain parsing procedures (i.e., the structure-building routines associated with closed-class elements) can no longer be carried out, even under ideal conditions of unlimited memory and resources.

Again, however, the grammaticality judgment data are problematic. If there are any circumstances under which subjects are able to parse sentences built up out of closed-class elements, then we cannot attribute asyntactic comprehension to parsing failures linked to impaired processing of these items.

Another possibility, to be considered in the following section, is that impaired processing of closed-class elements does contribute to these agrammatics' comprehension impairment, but at a stage of sentence processing subsequent to the initial structural analysis.

Early Stages of Language Comprehension: Exposed Encoding Evidence from Agrammatic Sentence Processing

We argued earlier that the sentence processing capabilities of certain agrammatic subjects provide an argument for output autonomy, given the rather surprising disparity between these subjects' asyntactic comprehension and their good performance on a grammaticality judgment task. Syntactic analysis, it appears, can be carried out independently of semantic interpretation. It may be, therefore, that the output of the parser can be observed with particular clarity in the performance of these agrammatic patients. In this section, we consider further the possibility that the language processing of agrammatic comprehenders may provide exposed encoding evidence about the nature of listeners' syntactic representations in the normal case.

One place to look for clues to the source of this disparity between grammaticality judgment and comprehension is in the details of performance on the judgment task itself. In particular, it may be worthwhile to examine closely any grammatical constructions that these subjects are insensitive to on this task, as this insensitivity may arise from the same source as their asyntactic comprehension.

This section concerns a pattern of performance that has emerged within the grammaticality judgment task. This pattern provides suggestive evidence in support of the claim that these agrammatic subjects are able to perform a first-pass parse, a highly structural analysis perhaps informationally equivalent to the recovery of S-structure, which they are unable to exploit for further syntactic and semantic interpretive processing.

Patterns of Performance Within the Grammaticality Judgment Task

In contrast to their generally good performance on sentences such as those discussed earlier, the performance of these agrammatic subjects on the other three conditions of the judgment task was considerably less impressive:

19. Tag questions/subject copying (62.1% correct)[6]
    a. The blonde woman is outside, isn't she?
    b. *The blonde woman is outside, isn't it?
20. Tag questions/auxiliary copying (63.7%)
    a. John is very tall, isn't he?
    b. *John is very tall, doesn't he?
21. Reflexives (64.2%)
    a. The famous man himself attended the ceremony.
    b. *The famous man itself attended the ceremony.
    c. The girl fixed herself a sandwich.
    c. *The girl fixed himself a sandwich.

These failures on the tag and reflexive conditions are intriguing. What is it that makes these constructions more difficult for the agrammatic subjects to assess, at least in this task? Does this difficulty have the same source as their asyntactic comprehension? It must be acknowledged, of course, that poor performance on a given task is considerably more difficult to evaluate

[6]See following sections for data on individual subjects' performance. All six subjects were not available for testing on every condition; for simplicity, the figures in the text summarize the performance of all subjects tested on any given condition.

than good performance. (See, e.g., Kolk & van Grunsven, 1984, for discussion of this issue.) Nevertheless, the contrast with their generally good performance on the other conditions of the task is quite striking and suggests that their poor performance on these three conditions might in fact prove revealing about their language processing generally. This possibility is strengthened by some further grammaticality judgment data from agrammatic comprehenders (recall that this term is used here to refer to patients with agrammatic language production and asyntactic comprehension, with all the aforementioned provisos).

The conditions explored in these further studies (certain of which are reported in Linebarger et al., 1983c) fall into three groups: (a) conditions involving pronouns of various sorts; (b) conditions involving auxiliaries; and (c) conditions involving wh-elements.

The performance of our subjects on these three sets of conditions is outlined following.

Pronoun Conditions. The finding of apparently deficient processing of reflexives echoes other reports in the literature on agrammatism. Blumstein et al. (1983), for example, reported insensitivity to the reflexive-antecedent relationship in their agrammatic subjects. The most revealing data on this score are provided by the two pretests administered to provide a baseline score on the appreciation of reflexive and personal pronouns. In the first of these, the pronoun pretest, subjects were asked to point to *him*, *her*, or *them*, presented on each trial with the sam set of three pictures of a man, a woman, and a couple. The Broca's aphasics performed without error on this test. In the second pretest, the reflexive pretest, subjects were presented with sentences like the following in a picture-matching task:

22. She washed her.
23. She washed herself.

On this test, the Broca patients' performance dropped to 68.4%

This is an interesting contrast. The good performance on the pronoun test suggests that these subjects are able to distinguish the various pronominal forms, at least on the basis of gender. Blumstein et al. (1983) suggested that the same subjects' poor performance on the reflexive test stems from the fact that *-self*, which distinguishes reflexives from personal pronouns, is a closed-class element. (Note, however, that because the personal pronouns themselves are generally regarded as belonging to the closed class, and behave phonologically like clitics, it is not clear why subjects should be sensitive to, for example, the distinction between *he* and *her*, but not to the distinction between *him* and *himself*.)

However, an inability to distinguish reflexive from personal pronouns is not the only possible explanation for these subjects' differing performance on the two pretests. The reflexive pretest requires subjects to apply structural constraints on anaphora in determining the meanings of the test sentences. Thus, subjects must demonstrate an appreciation of the fact that the pronoun in the foregoing sentence 22 cannot be interpreted as coreferential with the subject (in the binding theory of Chomsky, 1981, this is expressed by the requirement that personal pronouns not be locally bound to an antecedent). As the following sentence demonstrates, other configurations do permit coreference between the subject and a nonreflexive pronoun to its right; thus, detection of the violation requires an appreciation of structure rather than simply of linear order.

24. *She* wanted them to invite *her*.

Thus, Blumstein et al.'s reflexive pretest requires subjects to determine whether two pronouns can be coindexed in a given syntactic structure. Their ability to discriminate among personal pronouns in the pronoun pretest suggests that they might well be sensitive to the distinction between personal pronouns and reflexives, although it is unclear how one might test this distinction in isolation.

The most natural interpretation of their poor performance on the reflexive pretest is that it follows from a failure to handle properly the relation between reflexives and their antecedents in a given structure. Despite the differing task demands, this failure on the reflexive pretest seems analogous to the poor performance of the agrammatic subjects on sentences like the foregoing sentence 21 in the Linebarger et al. (1983a) grammaticality judgment test. (The reflexive condition of this task contains gender, number, and person mismatches between reflexives and their antecedents; no difference was found in subjects' performance on these three types of mismatch.)

Another report of difficulty with reflexive pronouns in an agrammatic patient is found in Baharav (1985). On a grammaticality judgment task, one of Baharav's two subject's errors were concentrated almost entirely on sentences involving reflexive-antecedent relationships equivalent to the foregoing sentence 21. However, it remains unclear from this report whether the subject could distinguish among different reflexive pronouns in other conditions.

Thus, the reflexive-antecedent relationship seems to be problematic not only for the subjects studied in Linebarger et al. (1983a, 1983c) but also for Blumstein et al.'s (1983) subjects, and possibly also for one of Baharav's (1985) subjects. These data alone do not pinpoint the reason for subjects' failures with reflexives. Acceptance of a sentence like **The woman cut himself* might represent insensitivity to the requirement that reflexives be locally bound, or inability to distinguish between reflexives and personal pronouns, or insensitivity to the semantic anomaly arising out of the grammatically required coindexation of *the woman* and *himself*, and so forth.

Two further conditions explore these subjects' processing of pronominals and reflexives. In the case condition, violations involved personal pronouns in the wrong case, as in sentences 25.b. and 26.b., following. In addition, one fourth of the violations involved reflexive pronouns as subjects of tensed clauses, as in sentence 27.b.; these may be regarded as double violations of case and anaphoric binding. They are violations of case marking, because the reflexive forms are a morphological complex of the objective forms of the pronouns followed by *-self*; and they are violations of reflexive binding, because the reflexive is not bound to an antecedent within the clause. These contrasts were included as a gross check to confirm that subjects were, in fact, sensitive to the distinction between reflexives and personal pronouns, and to the fact that there are restrictions on the occurrence of reflexives.

25.a. We are always glad to see you.
b. *Us are always glad to see you.
26.a. We will send them a letter.
b. *We will send they a letter.
27.a. They obeyed the speed limit.
b. *Themselves obeyed the speed limit.

A second condition, the SAI/case condition, contained violations such as those in sentences 28(a) and (b); the subject pronoun has been inverted and now follows the auxiliary. Despite its postverbal position, the pronoun must be marked nominative rather than objective. The purpose of these contrasts was to rule out the possibility that subjects in the case condition were employing a simpleminded heuristic such as "a pronoun may be nominative only if it is claus-initial."

28.a. Can they speak German very well?
b. *Can them speak German very well?

Our subjects' performance on all the pronoun conditions administered (including those in the Linebarger et al., 1983a study) is given in Table 3.1. The incompleteness of the data in the cases noted is due to the fact that two of the original six subjects (EB and EG) are no longer available.

The performance on the two case conditions is excellent without exception and contrasts in most cases with much poorer performance on the reflexive and tag conditions. Sensitivity to violations of morphological

TABLE 3.1
Pronoun Conditions

Easy conditions						
		Case			*SAI/case*	
Subject	*HR*	*FAR*	*% correct*	*HR*	*FAR*	*% correct*
L.S.	1.00	.10	95	.80	.00	90
A.T.	1.00	.05	97.5	1.00	.00	100
F.M.	.80	.10	85	.73	.13	80
V.S.	1.00	.00	100	1.00	.00	100
E.B.	N/A	—	—	N/A	—	—
E.G.	.80	.10	85	N/A	—	—
Difficult conditions						
		Reflexive			*Tag/subject*	
Subject	*HR*	*FAR*	*% correct*	*HR*	*FAR*	*% correct*
L.S.	1.00	.70	65	.80	.35	72.5
A.T.	1.00	1.00	50	.85	.30	77.5
F.M.	.65	.65	50	.20	.15	52.5
V.S.	.95	.10	92.5	.05	.00	52.5
E.B.	95	.70	62.5	.95	.60	67.5
E.G.	.80	.50	65	.50	.50	50

Note. HR (hit rate): "good" responses to well-informed sentences. FAR (false alarm rate): "good" responses to ill-formed sentences. Subjects E.B. and E.B. are no longer available. Data for E.G. in Case condition reflect performance on earlier version of test.

case-marking among agrammatic patients was also reported by Grossman and Haberman (1982).[7]

Thus, it is not likely that the poor performance on the two difficult conditions emerged involving pronouns can be attributed to a simple inability to distinguish among different forms of pronouns. After all, nominative/objective contrasts such as *he/him* are no more phonologically obvious than gender contrasts such as *her/him*. Of course, the fact that different features are at issue in the easy and difficult conditions (case in the former, gender and number in the latter) may be important. This is discussed further later.

Auxiliary Conditions. Five subjects performed poorly on the Tag question/auxiliary condition. Again we ask: Do they fail to respond to mismatches between auxiliaries in the matrix clause and the tag question (as in the foregoing sentence 20.b.) because they cannot discriminate among auxiliaries and verb affixes? Three new conditions involving auxiliaries were therefore developed. The first was a revision of the original subject-aux inversion

[7]Grossman and Haberman also reported that their agrammatic subjects' detection of case violations declined in passive sentences, an interesting finding that deserves further investigation.

condition. In the original subject-aux inversion condition (henceforth, *SAI-1*), a third of the violations involved fronting of an auxiliary and the main verb, or of two auxiliaries or the main verb alone (as in sentence 29); these violations could be detected by a subject who was unable to discriminate among the various auxiliaries and verb affixes. Therefore, a new condition (*SAI-2*) was developed that contains only contrasts such as those in sentences 30(a) and (b).

29. *Is eating the little girl her breakfast?
30.a. Have you done the homework problem?
b. *Have you do the homework problem?
c. Will you do the math problem?
c. *Will you do the math problem?
d. *Will you done the math problem?

A second auxiliary condition involved the passive construction, described earlier. Recall that this condition contained sentences like 31 through 33, following. Clearly, the correct judgments in this condition require attention to the specific identities of verbal affixes and auxiliaries.

31.a. The car was following the truck.
b. *The car was followed the truck.
32.a. The teacher was disliked by the students.
b. *The teacher was disliked the students.
33.a. The bird has noticed the cat.
b. *The bird was noticed the cat.

Finally, the verb phrase deletion condition contained contrasts such as those in sentences 34(a) and (b), in which the mismatch between the auxiliaries and verb affixes violates the requirement (given a certain intonational contour), or at least the strong expectation, that the antecedent of the elliptical verb phrase is that in the first conjunct. This condition is thus very close to the tag/auxiliary condition, because both involve verb phrase anaphora.

34.a. George was angry, and so was Bill.
b. *George was angry, and so did Bill.

As demonstrated by Table 3.2, a pattern of easy and difficult conditions emerged and the passive condition was generally at least 20 percentage points higher than performance on the VP deletion and tag/auxiliary conditions.

Wh-Conditions. Two conditions involving wh-words elicited a very clear pattern of performance. One condition, *wh-moved subcategorization*, con-

TABLE 3.2
Auxiliary Conditions

Easy conditions						
	Passive			*SAI*		
Subject	*HR*	*FAR*	*% correct*	*HR*	*FAR*	*% correct*
L.S.	.80	.00	90	.93	.03	95
A.T.	.90	.15	87.5	.975	.30	83.8
F.M.	.75	.05	85	.95	.325	81.3
V.S.	1.00	.00	100	.95	.05	95
E.B.	.95	.10	92.5	N/A	—	—
E.G.	1.00	.10	95			
Difficult conditions						
	Tag/auxiliary			*VP deletion*		
Subject	*HR*	*FAR*	*% correct*	*HR*	*FAR*	*% correct*
L.S.	.65	.30	67.5	1.00	.60	70
A.T.	.70	.65	52.5	1.00	.95	52.5
F.M.	.10	.20	45	.90	.60	65
V.S.	.00	.00	50	.90	.05	92.5
E.B.	95	.10	925	N/A	—	—
E.G.	.55	.50	75	.90	.60	65

Note. HR (hit rate): "good" responses to well-informed sentences. FAR (false alarm rate): "good" responses to ill-formed sentences. Subjects E.B. and E.B. are no longer available. Data for LS, VS, AT, and FM in Subject-aux inversion condition reflect averaging of the two SAI conditions (SAI-1 and SAI-2).

tained contrasts such as those in sentences 35a and b: The category of a fronted wh-word must be attended to in order for subjects to appreciate whether there is a subcategorization violation comparable to that in sentence 35.c. (Half of the good counterparts were of the form of sentence 35.a., half of the form of sentence 35.b.) Simple counterparts such as those in sentences 36a and b were also included in the test, so that we could determine whether subjects were sensitive to the subcategorization requirements in structures without wh-movement.

35.a. Who did the teacher smile at?
 b. When did the teacher smile?
 c. *Who did the teacher smile?
36.a. The teacher smiled at the student.
 b. *The teacher smiled the student.

Wh-head agreement, the other wh-condition, also required attention to the identity of a wh-expression, but of a semantic nature. In the unacceptable sentences, the inanimate head of a relative clause is followed by the rela-

TABLE 3.3
WH Conditions

Easy conditions			
	WH-moved subcategorization		
Subject	*HR*	*FAR*	*% correct*
L.S.	.95	.00	97.5
A.T.	.65	.00	82.5
F.M.	.75	.35	70
V.S.	.90	.25	82.5
Difficult conditions			
	Wh-head agreement		
Subject	*HR*	*FAR*	*% correct*
L.S.	1.00	.85	57.5
A.T.	1.00	.90	55
F.M.	.40	.10	65
V.S.	.90	.40	75

Note. F.M.'s relatively low score in wh-moved subcategorization condition is no lower than his score on the baseline subcategorization condition. HR (hit rate): "good" responses to well-informed sentences. FAR (false alarm rate): "good" responses to ill-formed sentences. Subjects E.B. and E.B. are no longer available.

tive pronoun *who*. (Unacceptable sentences are marked with *, with no claim implied about whether these are ungrammatical as distinct from semantically anomalous or improbable.)

37.a. I like the bookshelf which Mary saw.
b. *I like the bookshelf who Mary saw.

As is clear from Table 3.3, the wh-moved subcategorization condition proved considerably easier than the wh-head agreement.[8] For subject LS in particular, the difference between performance on the two conditions is striking.

We see, then, that these agrammatic subjects' performance within the grammaticality judgment task varies systematically across conditions. This pattern is summarized following:

Easy conditions:
38. *John gave she a new dress. *Case*
39. *Who did the principal frown? *Wh-moved subcategorization*
40. *The man was helped the clerk. *Passive*

[8]Note, incidentally, that subjects' errors on the wh-moved subcategorization condition consisted almost entirely of false acceptances; thus their poor performance on this condition does not bear on the *who/whom* distinction currently disappearing from English.

41. *Was the old man enjoy the view? *SAI-2-*
42. *Can them speak German very well? *SAI/case*

Difficult conditions:

43. *The woman dressed himself quickly. *Reflexive*
44. *The blonde woman laughed, didn't it? *Tag/pronoun*
45. *The pencil who you brought is nice. *Wh-head agreement*
46. *John is here, and so does Bill. *VP deletion*
47. *John is very tall, doesn't he? *Tab/auxiliary*

This pattern is of interest because it cannot be attributed to difficulty with particular lexical items such as pronouns, auxiliaries, or wh-words per se; rather, it appears that certain grammatical computations involving these elements are performed easily by these subjects, whereas others are not.

Explanations for the Pattern

What, then, are we to make of this pattern of performance within the grammaticality judgment task? Is it possible that it has the same source as asyntactic comprehension? No hint of this pattern has been found in normal subjects, nor in the single Wernicke aphasic to whom the original grammaticality judgment task has been administered (Pate, 1985), nor in brain-damaged control subjects.

Before considering the implications of the pattern, it may be useful to reject several plausible, but unsatisfactory, explanations for it.

Closed-class Insensitivity. Note that all 11 conditions—the easy as well as the difficult ones—turn crucially on closed-class elements (auxiliaries, affixes, wh-words, quantificational particles, pronouns). Thus, we cannot account for the pattern by pointing to the fact that the difficult conditions revolve around closed-class elements. A suggestion along these lines is made in Zurif and Grodzinsky (1983), who proposed what is termed here the *closed-class insensitivity* hypothesis. Based on the report in Grodzinsky (1984) that Hebrew-speaking agrammatic aphasics tend to misselect (rather than omit) closed-class elements, Zurif and Grodzinsky suggested that the four agrammatics studied in Linebarger et al. (1983a) may have been capable of recovering categorial information about closed-class elements, but insensitive to their lexical identities. This suggestion does account for the fact that the reflexive and tag/pronoun conditions were difficult for these subjects, because they turn on the distinctions among different forms of personal and reflexive pronouns. And it similarly accounts for the subsequently poor performance of these and other agrammatic subjects on the wh-head agreement and VP deletion conditions, because these conditions also require sensitivity to the distinct forms of closed-class elements. But it does not account for their good performance on the case, SAI-2, and pas-

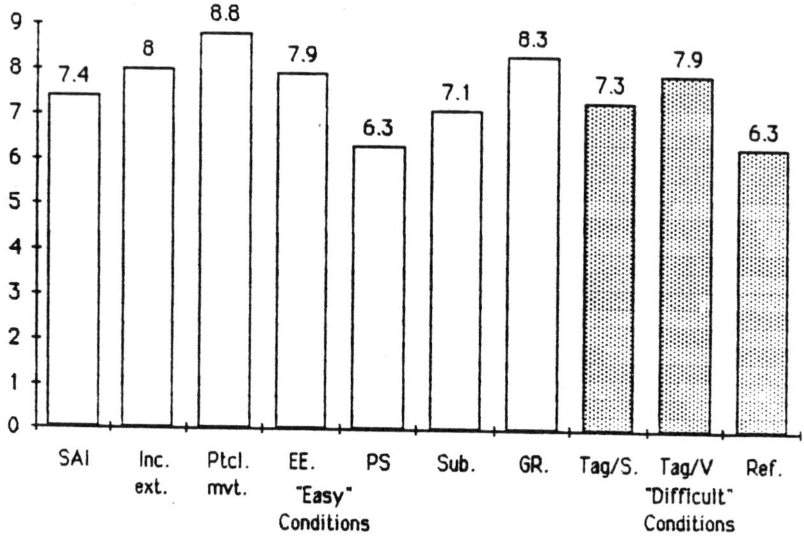

FIG. 3.3 Sentence length

sive conditions, which likewise turn on distinctions among different elements of the same category. In fact, the distinction between the passive and SAI-2 conditions, on the one hand, and the VP deletion and tag/auxiliary conditions on the other hand, demonstrates conclusively that subjects are capable of distinguishing between the very same items in certain conditions but not in others.

Sentence Length. Another explanation that can be ruled out is that the difficult conditions are simply longer than the easy conditions. As a casual examination of the foregoing sentences 38 through 47 reveals, the difficult conditions are in some cases (auxiliary, wh-conditions) longer than the easy conditions. However, this is not invariably so, as in the number agreement conditions; and, within the pronoun conditions, the reflexive and SAI/case conditions are of equal length. There are other reasons to believe that sentence length is not the determining factor. First, Fig. 3.3 demonstrates that sentence length was clearly not a determinant in the Linebarger et al. (1983a) study.

Reflexive, for example, was among the shortest conditions, despite subjects' poor performance on these sentences. And within particular conditions there is no indication that subjects' errors are concentrated on the longer sentences.

Distance Between Critical Elements. Another possibility that has been suggested is that the difficult conditions turn on long-distance dependencies between (nonadjacent) elements in the sentence, whereas the easy conditions involve no such interval. In several of the difficult conditions, however, the two elements are immediately adjacent (in the intensifier reflexives, wh-head agreements, Q-float); and some of the easy conditions involve long-range dependencies (as in, e.g., SAI-2 and wh-subcategorization).

Correctibility. Another possibility to consider is that the difficult conditions are more correctible and hence less easily noticed. However, the easy and difficult conditions do not seem to differ on this dimension: Because they all turn on the choice of a single item, they would all seem to be equally correctible.

Implications of the Grammaticality Judgment Pattern

It appears, then, that the dissociation between asyntactic comprehension and good performance on most conditions of the grammaticality judgment task is echoed by a distinctive pattern of performance within the judgment task itself. The hypothesis that I wish to explore here is that this pattern of performance on the grammaticality judgment task reflects the structural preoccupations of the parser during a first-pass parse. The poor performance of these subjects on the difficult conditions, as well as their asyntactic comprehension, reflects, on this view, a failure to exploit an initial structural analysis for further processing.

This notion of an initial structure-building stage of sentence processing has been proposed by a number of psycholinguists (see, e.g., Forster, 1979; Frazier, Clifton, & Randall, 1983; Holmes, 1979) on the basis of a variety of experimental tasks with normal subjects. Frazier et al. (1983), for example, argued for "a view of sentence processing in which processing operations involving constraints on the permissible indexing (or evaluation) of structures lag behind the processor's structure-building operations" (p. 188).

On this account, then, listeners *do* in fact "thread [their] way through the labyrinth again" (Johnson–Laird, 1978, p. 114). Sentence processing is not a direct mapping from sound to meaning, guided by syntax; rather, an initial structural analysis is computed and is only subsequently interpreted. It is this subsequent interpretation that Johnson–Laird and others dismissed as an unparsimonious rethreading of the labyrinth; and which, on the hypothesis under consideration here, is not performed by these agrammatic subjects.

Several features of the judgment pattern suggest this view. There are three very general lines along which the easy and difficult conditions seem to diverge.

Anaphora Between Lexical Items. The difficult conditions all turn on the match or mismatch between a pronoun or elliptical VP and some coreferential element earlier in the sentence. The easy conditions, although in most cases they involve dependencies between elements similarly distant from one another, do not turn on such anaphoric mismatches. Rather, the dependencies involve, for example, a fronted wh-word and the VP from which it has been moved (in the wh-subcategorization condition) or a fronted auxiliary and its original position. Determining the position in the sentence with which a fronted element has been associated has immediate consequences for constituent structure, whereas the anaphoric relation between full lexical items does not; anaphora therefore might well be ignored during an initial structure-building stage of parsing.

Predictiveness. In the reflexive condition, there is no warning that the subject NP is to be the antecedent of a reflexive pronoun; in the two tag question conditions, there is no warning that the main clause will be followed by a tag question that must agree with certain features of the subject or auxiliary; in the wh-head agreement condition, there is no warning that a relative clause will follow a given noun, whose semantic features will determine the acceptability of *who* versus *which.*

In contrast, dependencies in the easy conditions are more predictable. The presence of a fronted auxiliary (in the SAI condition) severely constrains the form of the auxiliary and verb that will occur several words downstream; the presence of a passive verb predicts that there will be no direct object; fronted wh-elements signal an upcoming gap of the same category (NP, adverb, PP, etc.); case-marking violations are generally apparent *in situ*, on the basis of the pronoun's surface structure position alone. Such predictability might well be exploited early on by a parsing mechanism seeking to reduce the number of possible analyses to be matched against the input.

Semanticity. The distinctions that the difficult conditions require subjects to make frequently, although not invariably, involve semantic features such as gender and animacy, as in the tag question/pronoun, wh-head agreement, and reflexive conditions. And some of the difficult pronoun conditions involve mismatches of number, which have frequently been treated as syntactic, because grammatical number is not predictable from real-world knowledge alone (as demonstrated by the ungrammaticality of sentences like **The crowd are noisy*). The grammatical status of all of these features is not resolved, particularly for a language like English in which they are not systematically expressed and in which grammatical gender coincides with real-world gender.

It is not clear at this point which, if any, of these three properties are predictive of the agrammatic pattern. Taken together, however, they suggest that the difficult conditions test relationships that might safely be ignored by a sentence processing mechanism devoted to the retrieval of constituent structure but little or nothing else.

The hypothesis under consideration, then, is that subjects who demonstrate asyntactic comprehension and the aforementioned judgment pattern are capable of performing an initial structural analysis but fail to exploit this first-pass parse for further interpretive processing.

Thus, the distinction between the easy conditions and the difficult conditions within the judgment task mirrors a corresponding division of labor within the language processor. For reasons explored later, only the former (on this account) are carried out by these agrammatic subjects.

Recall from the introductory discussion, however, the various caveats that must be considered before inferring psychological mechanisms from one-way dissociations of this type. To argue, for example, that a set of operations *X* is psychologically distinct from another set *Y*, we must be satisfied that (a) the operations in *Y* are not simply harder in some intuitive sense; (b) the operations in *Y* do not simply require more storage of input than those in *X* (ignoring any claims about special mechanisms by which *X* is able to overcome such storage requirements); and (c) the operations in *X* are not simply more frequently employed than those in *Y*.

Consider again the dissociation between preserved sensitivity to the structural consequences of passive morphology, as demonstrated by the ability to detect violations such as **The man is watched the woman*, in conjunction with chance performance on comprehension tasks involving equally simple passive sentences, or—in the case of truncated passives such as *The man is watched*—even simpler sentences than those employed in the judgment task. What is perplexing about this dissociation is that exploiting the semantic consequences of the passive does not seem intrinsically more difficult than computing its syntactic consequences, and yet subjects break down only on the former task. And the disparity is even greater when we consider some of the long-distance dependencies that must be computed in other conditions of the judgment task; in the empty elements condition, for example, or the wh-moved subcategorization condition. It seems difficult to explain the disparity between these two sets of operations on the grounds that one is intrinsically more difficult than the other.

Similarly, the two sets of operations do not seem to be distinguishable on the basis of storage requirements. In the judgment task, both the easy and difficult conditions involve long-distance dependencies; and some of the difficult conditions involve dependencies between adjacent elements. Similarly, the storage requirements for the comprehension of a truncated passive *The man is watched* seem no greater than, for example, the wh-moved subcategorization condition *Who did the girl smile__?*), because there is not even the requirement to maintain the relative ordering of two NPs (although, under the REST analysis of the passive construction, there are two

NP positions in the sentence: the subject position, and the empty postverbal position from which the NP originates).

And, finally, it does not seem likely that the processing operations required by the easy conditions represent more frequently applied computations than either the computations required by the difficult conditions or by sentence interpretation. The reflexive, for example, is a staple of English grammar.

Thus, it seems reasonable to consider the possibility that the pattern within the judgment task may represent a genuine division of labor within the language processor. Of course, the precise nature of this claim turns to a large extent on the reason why these further interpretive processes are not performed. Therefore, we examine this hypothesis in connection with what seem to be the two most plausible families of explanations for agrammatic comprehension: the mapping explanation and explanations invoking deficiencies of short-term memory.

The First-Pass Parse Hypothesis Under a Mapping Deficit Account of Agrammatic Comprehension

If, for example, there is a selective loss of the ability to perform these further computations (the mapping hypothesis discussed in Caramazza & Berndt, 1985; Linebarger et al., 1983a, 1983b, 1983c; Schwartz et al., 1980, 1985) then the first-pass parse hypothesis represents a claim that there is a selective preservation argument for the psychological distinctness of syntactic and semantic processing, because syntactic operations are preserved but interpretive operations are impaired.

The explanation for asyntactic comprehension in this case is clear-cut: Subjects are simply unable to perform the relevant computations. What about the judgment pattern? Under the mapping account, the easy conditions define the operations performed by the intact syntactic processor. Any sentence processing operations that there subjects fail to perform in the judgment task are assumed to fall under the category of impaired mapping operations. There is, in a sense, no need to explain the pattern, because the pattern merely reflects the division of labor within the language processor. The performance of these agrammatic comprehenders, on this account, provides evidence about what counts psychologically as syntactic.

The mapping hypothesis is compatible with agrammatic comprehension and with the good performance of agrammatics on the judgment task, but it would be undermined by any demonstration that agrammatic comprehenders are capable of performing semantic interpretation over syntactic structure. As yet, such evidence is lacking. However, there are suggestions in the literature that agrammatic comprehenders do not suffer from such an absolute, qualitative disability, even for complex structures such as passives. For example Smith and Mimica (1984) reported that the convergence of morphological, order, and semantic reversibility cues seems to play an important role in agrammatic sentence comprehension, suggesting that the agrammatic comprehension deficit may be a function of processing limitations rather than of inability to perform specific mapping operations. Finally, Baharav (1985) reported that two agrammatic subjects' comprehension performance was greatly affected by task demands, a finding that seems to argue against the mapping hypothesis in its absolute form.

These findings, although preliminary, tend to argue against any simple variant of the hypothesis that agrammatic comprehenders have specifically lost the ability to perform interpretive operations over syntactic structures. Less absolute variants of this account—appeals to partial impairment of the ability to perform these operations—remain to be explored.

The First-pass Parse Hypothesis Under an STM Account of Agrammatic Comprehension

To consider another major family of possibilities, if the failure to perform further interpretive operations on the output of an initial parse follows from an inability to maintain this structure in short-term memory, then the easy conditions are those that, for some reason, are less affected by the STM limitation.

On this account, we expect to find the grammaticality judgment pattern not only in agrammatic comprehenders but also in conduction aphasics who demonstrate asyntactic comprehension; the two groups, on this account, share a common source for their asyntactic comprehension. Thus, any evidence that there are distinct patterns of receptive language processing in the two groups, given comparable STM capacities, would tend to argue against this proposal. And, in fact, Saffran (1985) reported an STM patient, TI, with asyntactic comprehension, whose excellent performance on the grammaticality judgment tasks just described does not reflect this pattern of easy and difficult conditions. Although TI has yet to be studied fully, the initial report in Saffran (1985) does suggest some differences with agrammatic comprehenders.

One difference that might plausibly be invoked has to do with the closed-class vocabulary, which appears to present particular difficulties to the agrammatic patients. Thus, one possible account of the agrammatic comprehenders' receptive language processing is that these agrammatic listeners carry out an accurate initial retrieval of closed-class elements, and are sensitive to their structural consequences, but find it difficult to retain these items in working memory. On this account, one might expect to find sensitivity to the closed class only in tasks that require no retention of closed-class elements beyond the first-pass parse.

In the judgment task, all of the difficult conditions involve dependencies between a closed-class item and some later element. So, of course, do the easy conditions; thus we would need some way to explain why the dependencies in the easy conditions are computed in the first-pass parse and the dependencies in the difficult conditions are not.

Under the STM account, the easy dependencies are easy because the structure of the parser somehow protects the first element from the limitations imposed by the STM impairment. But the crucial question here is: What are these limitations? That is, how exactly would an STM impairment bring about the pattern within the judgment task (and, under the assumption of a common source) the asyntactic comprehension pattern as well? Saffran (1985) observed that the specific role of STM in language comprehension has not been spelled out. One possibility is that a phonological buffer might be required to store the input string during parsing; however, this account predicts poor performance of STM patients on grammaticality judgment tasks. And the STM patient studied in Saffran (1985) performed exceptionally well on grammaticality judgment tasks.

A second possibility is that the phonological buffer plays a crucial role at the stage of semantic interpretation, by indexing elements of an abstract syntactic representation to the lexical content of the input string. According to Saffran (1985):

> Consider another possibility: that the phonological buffer does indeed perform a critical indexing function, not at the parsing stage but subsequently, at the point where syntactic structure guides semantic interpretation. Why?, you might ask, since the output of the parser—if it is anything like the tree structures drawn by linguists—should contain all the information, lexical as well as syntactic, that is required for semantic interpretation: syntactic function is marked by location on a tree, whose nodes are specified for particular lexical items. Suppose, however, that the parser represents structure more abstractly—that, to use the tree structure analogy again, the terminal nodes contain category information rather than specific lexical information. . . . If this were the case, then there would have to be some way to link structural to lexical information, and this is where indexation of category nodes to an order-preserving phonological representation could come into play. (p. 17)

On this account of sentence processing, the lexical identities of elements in the string must be maintained independently of the syntactic analysis built up by the parser. Interpretation requires the integration of lexical and structural information. Although there are other possibilities, we consider how the judgment pattern might emerge under this model.

The difficult conditions of the judgment task require access to the lexical identities of elements in the string, and this information is hypothesized, under the STM account, to be subject to severe degradation. The antecedent elements of the easy dependencies, however, are somehow protected from this decay of the memory trace. This protection might be implemented in any of the following ways, to select among the multiplicity of possibilities.

One possibility is that the easy conditions turn on information that is computed early on in sentence processing, while the antecedent elements of the dependencies are still available. On this account, then, the first-pass parse hypothesis represents a claim about the temporal structure of sentence processing: Constituent structure is worked out in some detail before interpretive operations are applied. This is not to deny that lexical semantic processing may be performed during the first-pass parse, only that interpretation over structure is deferred, and hence that such processing is differentially vulnerable to STM limitations.

Another possibility is that the easy dependencies are in a sense built into the parser: The presence of a fronted wh-word, for example, alters the internal state of the parser by triggering a search for a gap of a certain category. The parser is not, on this account, holding the fronted wh-word in STM in the wh-moved subcategorization condition; rather, it is now executing a search for an NP or adverbial gap.[9] In the easy subject-auxiliary inversion condition, the presence of a fronted auxiliary triggers expectations about the form of the aux and verb downstream; the particular lexical item, for example, *has*, is not retained in working memory. Similarly, the passive verb morphology leads the parser to anticipate that there will be no direct object; the very fact that the head of the VP is a passive verb (as distinct from an intransitive but active verb) may not be explicitly stored by the parser.

These expectations might be implemented in a variety of ways. An intransitive or passive verb might lead the parser to label the current phrase under construction as an intransitive VP; or NP might be excised from the set of possible analyses of the constituent following the verb. A wh-word, as noted, might lead the parser to call a subroutine (SEEK gap).

In contrast, the difficult dependencies do not, on this account, trigger specific expectations in the parser, however these expectations are implemented. That is, the presence of an NP does not create the expectation that there will be a relative pronoun or personal pronoun or reflexive pronoun with matching features; the presence of an auxiliary does not set up expectations for a tag question or elliptical *and so* tag. Hence, any mismatch between the antecedent and an element later in the sentence can be evaluated only by reaccessing the antecedent. And, for patients with limited STM, any processing that requires reaccess of lexical items will be subject to the severe limitations in these patients' ability to retain verbal material; if the agrammatic patients are specifically impaired in their ability to retain closed-class elements, then such a reaccess will prove especially difficult.

This account does not necessarily appeal to any inherently greater predic-

[9]Of course, there need not be a wh-word in relative clauses (e.g., *The cheese the mouse ate was old*).

TABLE 3.4
Flagged Reflexive Condition

Subject	*HR*	*FAR*	*% correct*
L.S.	.90	.70	60
A.T.	1.00	.70	65
F.M.	.70	.70	50
V.S.	.80	.90	45
E.G.	.90	.70	60

tiveness of the easy conditions. Certain difficult dependencies may be equally predictive. For example, a reflexive pronoun may precede its antecedent in English, in sentences such as the following:

48.a. Pouring herself coffee, she sat down.
b. *Pouring herself coffee, he sat down.
49.a. It was himself that the old man blamed.
b. *It was herself that the old man blamed.

It might be that a subject presented with such sentences would set up a specific expectation for a coreferential NP antecedent for the reflexive pronoun.[10] However, five of our subjects performed quite poorly on a set of such sentences, as shown in Table 3.4.

Furthermore, Baharav (1985) reported that the agrammatic subject who performed poorly on grammaticality judgments of sentences with reflexives performed equally poorly in those cases in which the reflexive preceded its antecedent, as occurs freely in Hebrew.

So it is not a question of whether subjects could set up some prediction, given the information available to them, that distinguishes the easy from the difficult conditions, on this account. Rather, the claim is that the pattern of easy and difficult conditions reflects the structure of the parser and provides evidence about what kinds of dependencies are protected from decay of the memory trace (under the STM account) simply because they are built into the parsing mechanism. The initial elements of the easy dependencies are remembered only through their guidance of the parser.

A third possibility is that in the easy dependencies the parser itself puts the lexical identity of the first element into a short-term store so that it will be available throughout the first-pass parse (see footnote 9). Recall, for example, the HOLD mechanism in Wanner and Maratsos' (1978) account of the parsing of relative clauses in an ATN model. Elements not specifically

[10]In sentence 48, the relationship between the reflexive pronoun and the coreferential pronoun to its right is indirect, because the pronoun is bound to the phonetically null subject of *pouring*, which is itself obligatorily bound to the subject of the matrix clause.

maintained by the parser would compete with other elements in the phonological buffer, and would be less likely to be preserved than those singled out by the parser for preservation during the first-pass parse.

Summary

Under this account, then, the pattern of easy and difficult conditions on the judgment task reflects the initial structure-building operations of the syntactic processor. On the STM deficit account of agrammatic comprehension, the dependencies that must be computed in order to perform either sentence interpretation itself or the assessment of grammaticality in the difficult conditions require maintenance of a record of the input to a degree that taxes the impaired capacities of both agrammatic and conduction aphasic subjects. In contrast, assessment of grammaticality in the easy conditions turns on dependencies that are computed during the first-pass parse and that are protected from this STM limitation: Either the first-pass parse occurs early enough that the antecedent elements of the dependencies are still available, or the antecedent elements are somehow carried along as alterations of the internal state of the parser, or the parser "knows" to store the phonological shapes of these items.

Finally, the possibility has been raised that distinct patterns may emerge for agrammatic and conduction aphasic patients on this constellation of tasks. Perhaps these different populations are characterizable in terms of the kinds of lexical material that they find it difficult to retain: The agrammatics, for example, may be differentially impaired in their ability to retain elements of the closed-class vocabulary, an impairment that might well be tied to their impaired production of the same items.

The First-pass Parse and Levels of Grammatical Representation

What is the nature of this initial structural analysis? Is it possible to identify the information crucial to the easy conditions of the judgment task with information specifically available at any linguistic level of representation? Clearly, this need not be the case; positing levels of grammatical representation is a way of representing the points of contact among distinct rule systems, but the distinctness of rule systems might well be expressed psychologically in some other way than in the construction of temporally isolable levels of representation corresponding to the levels defined in formal grammar.

Nonetheless, the possibility is worth exploring. Looking at the easy conditions just discussed, and at the seven conditions of the original task on which these agrammatic subjects performed well, we may summarize the properties of this initial structural representation:

1. Hierarchical constituent structure is represented.
2. Subcategorization frames of specific lexical items are satisfied.
3. Despite suggestions in the literature (e.g., Tyler, 1985) that agrammatic aphasics' syntactic processing is quite local, it appears from the judgment data that nonlocal dependencies are computed (see, e.g., the SAI and wh-moved subcategorization conditions).
4. Specifically, it appears (given their good performance on the wh-moved subcategorization condition) that these subjects are able to determine the relation between a fronted wh-word and its original location, a result that is compatible with (although not a compelling argument for) generalized phrase structure grammar, because it treats the wh-word/gap relation as part and parcel of initial structure-building operations.
5. Finally, certain aspects of the binding theory are enforced: the distinctions among *Who hoped__to win?*,* *Who hoped__would win?*, *That's who I hoped__would win*, and **John was expected__would win*, presented in the empty elements condition of Linebarger et al. (1983a), require an appreciation that the missing subject of a tensed clause cannot be PRO or NP-trace, as well as that the subject, in English, cannot simply be missing altogether. Thus, we see some sensitivity to binding conditions on the admissibility of gaps in certain positions.

But it remains entirely unclear whether the representations that the judgment data allow us to impute to these subjects are equivalent to any levels of grammatical representation proposed within linguistic theory. Given the sensitivity to binding conditions involved in detecting contrasts such as the aforementioned, we might look to a level more abstract than the phonological surface structure. On the other hand, subjects' poor performance on reflexives, and on other conditions that turn on mismatched, but obligatorily coindexed, elements might be interpreted as indicating an insensitivity to coindexation generally, and to constraints postulated by the binding theory in particular.

But this raises the obvious problem: We cannot know why subjects reject or accept sentences, correctly or incorrectly. A subject who accepts **The old man cut herself* might not appreciate principle A of the binding theory of Chomsky (1981), that such anaphors must be bound quite locally. On the other hand, he or she might appreciate this restriction, and coindex the reflexive with the NP subject; such a subject's false acceptance of the sentence might follow instead from a failure to interpret this coindexed structure, even if individual lexical items were interpreted. That is, it might be that the semantic consequences of this coindexation are never evaluated.

In fact, the possibility that a full LF representation is computed (but not interpreted) cannot be dismissed. For example, it is not unreasonable to consider the possibility that subjects assign thematic roles to NP arguments,[11] but that this structure is not interpreted. Thus, subjects confronted with a passive sentence like *The boy is kicked by the girl* in a comprehension task might in fact associate the subject with the thematic role of patient and the NP following *by* with the thematic role of agent; but, given the failure to maintain the input string phonologically, the structure on which these assignments are expressed is never input to semantic interpretive processing.

On this interpretation, then, subjects do in fact assign thematic roles to NPs, and do associate antecedents and anaphors in accordance with the binding theory; their failures on the reflexive and other conditions, and on comprehension tasks, reflect a failure to carry sentence interpretation to the further point at which the semantic anomaly or implausibility that results from, for example, coindexing an NP denoting a female being with a masculine pronoun, becomes evident. In this case, the failure is located at the point of interpretation rather than at the point of coindexation.

Alternatively, perhaps neither coindexation nor thematic roles are computed during the first-pass parse; they are not critical to the determination of constituent structure. In this case, a level with the properties of logical form (LF) is too abstract to be associated with the first-pass parse.

One potential source of evidence on these matters is the study of anaphora resolution in normal sentence processing. It has been reported (see, e.g., Erlich, 1983; Tanenhaus et al., 1985) that normal subjects appear to assign referents to pronouns on-line. One might ask whether evidence that this is in fact the case would be problematic for the first-pass parse/STM-deficit version. (Under the mapping version, the agrammatics are simply unable to perform such interpretive operations, and no claim is made about the point in sentence processing at which such assignments are made.) It would, but only if there were evidence that this anaphoric assignment respected grammatical constraints on coindexation, rather than simply applying to isolated lexical items. Thus, for example, if cross-modal priming or eye-fixation studies indicated that *herself* had been associated with *the woman* in a sentence such as *The woman washed herself*, then the claim that difficult conditions such as the reflexive condition represent second-stage processes might be suspect. On the other hand, one would need evidence that such anaphoric associations do in fact respect purely grammatical constraints on coindexation; that is, that they apply over structures. Thus, one would also need evidence that an anaphoric link is not established between *the woman* and *her* in, for example, *The woman washed her*, as the grammar does not permit coindexation between these two elements. If on-line anaphora resolution is shown to respect such restrictions, then this account of agrammatic subjects' failures on the reflex-

[11]As noted earlier, we need not assume that the semantic content of thematic roles is expressed at LF.

ive condition is undermined. On the other hand, evidence that anaphora resolution is initially blind to such grammatical constraints would support this version of the first-pass parse hypothesis.

Summary

The good performance of agrammatic aphasics on most conditions of the grammaticality judgment task of Linebarger et al. (1983a) provides strong evidence that these subjects are in fact capable of retrieving the syntactic structure of spoken sentences. However, this good performance is in striking contrast to the poor performance of these same subjects on sentence comprehension tasks and on other conditions within the grammaticality judgment paradigm. One possible account of these facts is that the locus of the agrammatic comprehension impairment is not a failure to retrieve syntactic structure, on-line or off-line; rather, it may reflect an inability to build on this early syntactic analysis.

A number of possibilities have been considered for this inability. One important possibility is that the use of syntactic structure to support sentence interpretation requires the maintenance of a representation of the sentence in some form of short-term storage that is disabled in certain aphasic populations; specifically, in both agrammatic and conduction aphasic subjects who perform asyntactically in sentence comprehension tasks. The possibility that the judgment pattern may be specific to agrammatic comprehenders also suggests that the appeal to an STM deficit may require further specification o the kinds of lexical items that are difficult for a given population to retain; the agrammatic subjects may experience particular difficulty in retaining closed-class items in short-term memory, despite their ability to utilize these elements in the retrieval of syntactic structure.

On the other hand, one might wish to invoke some disability more specific to the linguistic operations involved, some inability to integrate syntactic and semantic information. This account (the mapping hypothesis) seems plausibly applicable only to agrammatic comprehenders; and, even for this population, there are some suggestions in the literature that an absolute disability cannot be demonstrated.

Many interesting questions arise. For example, are gender and number mismatches noticed more reliably by agrammatic subjects whose native language is characterized by a richer system of morphological agreement, in which grammatical gender is distinguished from semantic gender? Will this same pattern emerge in normals if the grammaticality judgment task is embedded in a dual task paradigm? Are there in fact distinct patterns among agrammatic and conduction aphasic subjects?

However these questions are resolved, it appears that these patterns may provide evidence about the functional architecture of the human parser, providing a window on the early stages of grammatical analysis.

CONCLUSIONS

The investigation of language pathology offers a variety of evidence about language processing in the normal case.

The neuropsychological data would appear to provide quite unequivocal support for the modularity thesis. The dissociability of linguistic processing and general cognitive function indicates that language represents an autonomous system, subject to breakdown in patients who are otherwise unimpaired and preserved in the face of general cognitive decline. And there are strong suggestions of modularity within the language processor, dissociations among lexical processing, syntactic analysis, and the semantic interpretation of syntactic structures.

The foregoing discussion has focused on the receptive language processing of certain agrammatic aphasics who are able to parse sentences that they cannot interpret; and whose performance, it appears, may furnish exposed encoding evidence about the nature of listeners' syntactic representations.

ACKNOWLEDGMENTS

Preparation was aided by NIH grant NS21566. I wish to thank Eleanor Saffran, Harold Pashler, Richard Larson, Gary Milsark, Myrna Schwartz, and Muffy Siegel for commenting on an earlier version of this manuscript.

TABLE 3.5
Subject Information—Six Agrammatic Aphasics

Subject	*Age*	*Sex*	*Years Post-cva*	*Comprehension performance*	
				Actives	*Passives*
L.S.	51	F	10	20/24	15/24*
A.T.	40	F	11	15/24*	7/24**
F.M.	42	M	3	12/24*	13/24*
V.S.	60	F	14	22/24	15/24*
E.B.	45	F	3	16/24*	13/24*
E.G.	40	F	1	19/24	8/24*

Note. See Schwartz, Saffan, & Marin (1980) for details of this comprehension test. *Chance performance. **Performance significantly worse than chance.

REFERENCES

Ades, A., & Steedman, S. (1982). On the order of words. *Linguistics and Philosophy*, *6*, 517–558.

Badecker, W., & Caramazza, A. (1985). *On considerations of method and theory governing the use of clinical categories in neurolinguistics and cognitive neuropsychology: The case against agrammatism*. Unpublished manuscript. Department of Psychology, The Johns Hopkins University.

Baddeley, A. D., & Hitch, G. J. (1974). Working memory. In G. H. Bower (ed.), *The psychology of learning and motivation: Advances in research and theory* (Vol. 8, pp. 47–90). New York: Academic Press.

Baharav, E. (1985). *Aspects of speech production and speech comprehension in Hebrew agrammatism of speech: Two case studies*. Unpublished doctoral dissertation, Boston University.

Berndt, R. S., Caramazza, A., & Zurif, E. (1983). Language functions: Syntax and semantics. In S. J. Segalowitz (Ed.). *Language functions and brain organization* (pp. 5–28). New York: Academic Press.

Berwick, R., & Weinberg, A. (1983). The role of grammars in language use. *Cognition*, *13*, 1–61.

Blumstein, S. E., Goodglass, H., Statlender, S., & Biber, C. (1983). Comprehension strategies determining reference in aphasia: A study of reflexivization. *Brain and Language*, *18*, 115–127.

Blumstein, S. E., & Milberg, W. (1983, October). *Automatic and controlled processing in speech/language deficits in aphasia*. Paper presented at symposium on automatic speech, Academy of Aphasia, Minneapolis, MN.

Bradley, D. (1978). *Computational distinctions of vocabulary type*. Unpublished doctoral dissertation, Massachusetts Institute of Technology, Cambridge, MA.

Bradley, D., Garrett, M., & Zurif, E. (1980). Syntactic deficits in Broca's aphasia. In D. Caplan (Ed.), *Biological studies of mental processes* (pp. 269–286). Cambridge, MA: MIT Press.

Bresnan, J. (1978). A realistic transformational grammar. In M. Halle, J. Bresnan, & G. A.Miller (Eds.) *Linguistic Theory and Psychological Reality*. Cambridge, MA: MIT Press.

Caplan, D. (1981). On the cerebral localization of linguistic functions: Logical and empirical causes surrounding deficit analyses and functional localization. *Brain and Language*, *14*, 120–137.

Caramazza, A. (1984). The logic of neuropsychological research and the problem of patient classification in aphasia. *Brain and Language*, *21*, 9–20.

Caramazza, A., Basili, A. G., Koller, J., & Berndt, R. S. (1981). An investigation of repetition and language processing in a case of conduction aphasia. *Brain and Language*, *14*, 235–271.

Caramazza, A., & Berndt, R. (1985). A multi-component deficit view of agrammatic Broca's aphasia. In M.-L. Kean (Ed.), *Agrammatism* (pp. 27–64). New York: Academic Press.

Caramazza, A., Berndt, R. S., Basili, A., & Koller, J. (1981). Syntactic processing deficits in aphasia. *Cortex*, *17*, 333–438.

Caramazza, A., & Zurif, E. (1976). Dissociation of algorithmic and heuristic processes in language comprehension: Evidence from aphasia. *Brain and Language*, *3*, 572–582.

Carlson, G., & Tanenhaus, M. K. (1984). Lexical meanings, structural meanings, and concepts. In J. Drago, V. Mishra, & D. Testen (Eds.), *Papers from the twentieth regional meeting of the Chicago linguistic society*. Chicago, IL: Chicago Linguistics Society.

Chomsky, N. (1965). *Aspects of the theory of syntax*. Cambridge, MA: MIT Press.

Chomsky, N. (1973). Conditions of transformations. In S. Anderson & P. Kiparsky (Eds.), *Festschrift for Morris Halle* (pp. 232–286). New York: Holt, Rinehart, & Winston.

Chomsky, N. (1977a). Questions of form and interpretation. In N. Chomsky (Ed.), *Essays on form and interpretation* (pp. 25–59). New York: North-Holland.

Chomsky, N. (1977b). On wh-movement. In P. W. Culicover, T. Wasow & A. Akmajian (Eds.), *Formal syntax* (pp. 71–132). New York: Academic Press.

Chomsky, N. (1981). *Lectures on government and binding*. Dordrecht: Foris.

Chomsky, N. (1982). *The generative enterprise: A discussion with Riny Huybregts and Henk van Riemsdijk*. Dordrecht: Foris.

Chomsky, N., & Lasnik, H. (1977). Filters and control. *Linguistic Inquiry*, *8*(3), 425–504.

Cinque, G. (1981). On Keenan and Comrie's primary relativization constraint. *Linguistic Inquiry*, *12*, 293–308.

Clark, H., & Clark, E. (1977). *Psychology and language*. New York: Harcourt Brace Jovanovich.

Cooper, R. (1983) *Quantification and syntactic theory*. Dordrecht: Reidel.

Crain, S., Shankweiler, D., & Tuller, E. (1984). *Preservation of sensitivity to closed class items in agrammatism*. Paper presented to the Academy of Aphasia, Los Angeles, CA.

Davis, L., Foldi, N., Gardner, H., & Zurif, E. (1978). Repetition in the transcortical aphasias. *Brain and Language*, *6*, 226–238.

Erlich, K. (1983). Eye movements in pronoun assignment: A study of sentence integration. In K. Rayner, (Ed.), *Eye movements in reading: Perceptual and language processes* (pp. 253–268). New York: Academic Press.

Fodor, J. A., Bever, T., & Garrett, M. (1974). *The psychology of language: An introduction to psycholinguistics and generative grammar*. New York: McGraw Hill.

Forster, K. (1979) Levels of processing and the structure of the language processor. In W. E. Cooper & E. C. T. Walker (Eds.), *Sentence processing: Psycholinguistic studies presented to Merrill Garrett* (pp. 27–86). Hillsdale, NJ: Lawrence Erlbaum Associates.

Forster, K., & Olbrei, I. (1973). Semantic heuristics and syntactic analysis. *Cognition*, *2*, 319–348.

Frazier, L., Clifton, C., & Randall, J. (1983). Filling gaps: decision principles and structure in sentence comprehension. *Cognition*, *13*, 187–222.

Friederici, A. (1981). Production and comprehension of prepositions in aphasia. *Neuropsychologia*, *19*, 191–199.

Friederici, A. (1982). Syntactic and semantic processes in aphasic deficits: The availability of prepositions. *Brain and Language*, *15*, 249–258.

Friederici, A. (1983). Aphasics' perception of words in sentential context: Some real-time processing evidence. *Neuropsychologia*, *21* 351–358.

Friederici, A., & Schoenle, P (1980). Computational dissociation of two vocabulary types: Evidence from aphasia. *Neuropsychologia*, *18*, 11–20.

Fronek, J. (1982). 'Thing' as a function word. *Linguistics*, *20*, 633–654.

Garrett, M. F. (1975). The analysis of sentence production. In G.H. Bower (Ed.), *The psychology of learning and motivation* (pp. 133–177). New York: Academic Press.

Garrett, M. F. (1976). Syntactic processes in sentence production. In R. Wales & E. Walker (Eds.), *New approaches to language mechanisms* (pp. 231–256). Amsterdam: North-Holland.

Garrett, M. F. (1978). Word and sentence perception. In R. Held, H. W. Leibowitz, & H.-L. Teuber (Eds.), *Handbook of sensory physiology, Vol. VIII, Perception* (pp. 611–623). Berlin: Springer.

Garrett, M. F. (1980). Levels of processing in sentence production. In B. Butterworth (Ed.), *Language production* (Vol. 1, pp. 177–220). New York: Academic Press.

Geschwind, N., Quadfasel, F. A., & Segarra, J. M. (1968). Isolation of the speech area. *Neuropsychologia*, *6*, 327–340.

Glanzer, M. (1972). Storage mechanisms in free recall. In G. H. Bower (Ed.), *The psychology of learning and motivation: Advances in research and theory* (Vol. 5, pp. 129–193). New York: Academic Press.

Goldstein, K. (1948). *Language and language disturbances*. New York: Grune & Stratton.

Goodglass, H., Gleason, J. B., & Hyde, M. R. (1970). Some dimensions of auditory language comprehension in aphasia. *Journal of Speech and Hearing Research*, *13*, 595–606.

Goodglass, H., Gleason, J. B., Bernholtz, N., & Hyde, M. R. (1972). Some linguistic structures in the speech of a Broca's aphasic. *Cortex*, *8*, 191-212.

Goodglass, H., & Kaplan, E. (1972). *The assessment of aphasia and related disorders*. Philadelphia: Lea & Febiger.

Goodglass, H., & Menn, L. (1985). Is agrammatism a unitary phenomenon? In M.-L. Kean (Ed.), *Agrammatism* (pp. 1-26). New York: Academic Press.

Gordon, B., & Caramazza, A. (1982). Lexical decision for open- and closed-class words: Failure to replicate differential frequency sensitivity. *Brain and Language*, *15*, 143-160.

Gordon, B., & Caramazza, B. (1983). Closed- and open-class lexical access in agrammatic and fluent aphasics. *Brain and Language*, *19*, 335-345.

Grodzinsky, Y. (1984). The syntactic characterization of agrammatism. *Cognition 16*, 99-120.

Grodzinsky, Y., Swinney, D., & Zurif, E. (1985). Agrammatism: Structural deficits and antecedent processing disruptions. In M. L. Kean (Ed.), *Agrammatism* (pp. 65-82). New York: Academic Press.

Grossman, M., & Haberman, S. (1982). Aphasics' selective deficits in appreciating grammatical agreements. *Brain and Language*, *16*, 109-120.

Hale, K. (1976). Linguistic autonomy and the linguistics of Carl Voegelin. *Anthropological linguistics*, *18*, 120-128.

Hale, K., Jeanne, L., & Platero, P. (1977). Three cases of overgeneration. In P. W. Culicover, T. Wasow & A. Akmajian (Eds.), *Formal syntax* (pp. 379-416). New York: Academic Press.

Heeschen, C. (1980). Strategies of decoding actor-object relations by aphasic patients. *Cortex*, *15*, 5-19.

Heilman, K., & Scholes, R. (1976). The nature of comprehension errors in Broca's, conduction, and Wernicke's aphasics. *Cortex*, *12* 258-265.

Heilman, K. M., Scholes, R., & Watson, R. T. (1976). Defects of immediate memory in Broca's and conduction aphasia. *Brain and Language*, *3*, 201-208.

Holmes, V. M. (1979). Some hypotheses about syntactic processing in sentence comprehension. In W. E. Cooper & E. Walker (Eds.), *Sentence processing: Studies presented to Merrill Garrett*. Hillsdale, NJ: Lawrence Erlbaum Associates.

Irigaray, L. (1973). *Le Langage des Dements* [Language in Dementia]. The Hague: Mouton.

Johnson-Laird, P. N. (1978). Psycholinguistics without linguistics. In N. S. Sutherland (Ed.), *Tutorial essays in psychology* (Vol. 1, pp. 75-135). Hillsdale, NJ: Lawrence Erlbaum Associates.

Kayne, R. S. (1981). Two notes on the NIC. In A. Belletti, L. Brandi, & L. Rizzi (Eds.), *Theory of markedness in generative grammar*. Pisa: Scuole Normale Superiore.

Kean, M.-L. (1977). The linguistic interpretation of aphasic syndromes: Agrammatism in Broca's aphasia, an example. *Cognition*, *5*, 9-46.

Kean, M.-L. (1981). Explanation in neurolinguistics. In N. Hornstein & D. Lightfoot (Eds.), *Explanation in linguistics* (pp. 174-208). London: Longman.

Kertesz, A. (1979). *Aphasia and related disorders*. New York: Grune & Stratton.

Kleiman, G. M. (1975). Speech recoding in reading. *Journal of Verbal Learning and Verbal Behavior 14*, 323-339.

Kolk, H. J., & van Grunsven, M. J. F. (1984). Metalinguistic judgments on sentence structure in agrammatism: A matter of task misinterpretation. *Neuropsychologia*, *22*(1), 31-39.

Kolk, H. J., van Grunsven, M. J. F., & Keyser, A. (1985). On the parallelism between production and comprehension in agrammatism. In M.-L. Kean (Ed.), *Agrammatism* (pp. 165-206). New York: Academic Press.

Lapointe, S. (1983). Some issues in the linguistic description of agrammatism. *Cognition*, *14*, 1-39.

Linebarger, M., Schwartz, M., & Saffran, E. (1983a). Sensitivity to grammatical structure in so-called agrammatic aphasics. *Cognition*, *13*, 361-392.

Linebarger, M., Schwartz, M., & Saffran, E. (1983b). Syntactic processing in agrammatism: A reply to Zurif and Grodzinsky. *Cognition, 15*, 207–213.

Linebarger, M., Schwartz, M., & Saffran, E. (1983c). *Patterns of syntactic processing in agrammatic aphasics*. Paper presented at the annual meeting of the Academy of Aphasia, Minneapolis, MN.

Lukatela, G., Crain, S., & Shankweiler, D. (1985, October). *Sensitivity to closed class items in Serbo-Croat agrammatism*. Paper presented to the Academy of Aphasia, Pittsburgh, PA.

Marcus, M. P. (1982). Consequences of functional deficits in a parsing model: Implications for Broca's aphasia. In M. Arbib, D. Caplan, & J. Marshall (Eds.), *Neural models of language processes* (pp. 115–133). New York: Academic Press.

Marin, O. S. M., Saffran, E. M., & Schwartz, M. F. (1976). Dissociations of language in aphasia: Implications for normal function. *Annals of the New York Academy of Sciences, 280*, 868–884.

Marslen–Wilson, W. D., & Tyler, L. (1980). The temporal structure of spoken language understanding. *Cognition, 8*, 1–71.

May, R. (1977). *The grammar of quantification*. Unpublished doctoral dissertation, Massachusetts Institute of Technology, Cambridge, MA.

Miceli, G. Mazzucchi, A., Menn, L., & Goodglass, H. (1983). Contrasting cases of Italian agrammatic aphasia with and without comprehension disorder. *Brain and Language, 19*, 65–98.

Parisi, D., & Pizzamiglio, L. (1970). Syntactic comprehension in aphasia. *Cortex, 6*, 204–215.

Pate, D. (1985, October). *The syntactic sensitivity of a Wernicke's patient: A case report*. Paper presented to the Academy of Aphasia, Pittsburgh, PA.

Rizzi, L. (1982a). Negation, wh-movement, and the null subject parameter. In (Ed.) *Issues in Italian syntax* (pp. 117–184). Dordrecht: Foris.

Rizzi, L. (1982b, June). *Two notes on the linguistic interpretation of Broca's aphasia*. Paper presented at the Syntax section of the Nans-les-Pins Sloan workshop, Nans-les-Pins, France.

Saffran, E. (1985, March). *STM and language comprehension*. Paper presented at the meeting on Cognitive Neuropsychology, Venice, Italy.

Saffran, E., & Marin, O. (1975). Immediate memory for words and sentences in a patient with deficient auditory short-term memory. *Brain and Language, 2*, 420–433.

Saffran, E., Schwartz., M., & Marin, O. (1980). The word order problem in agrammatism: II. Production. *Brain and Language, 10*, 263–280.

Schwartz, M., Saffran, E., & Marin, O. (1980). The word order problem in agrammatism: I. Comprehension. *Brain and Language, 10*, 249-262.

Schwartz, M. F. (1984). What the classical aphasia categories can't do for us, and why. *Brain and Language, 21*, 3-8.

Schwartz, M. F., Linebarger, M. C., & Saffran, E. (1985) The status of the syntactic deficit theory of agrammatism. In M.-L. Kean (Ed.), *Agrammatism* (pp. 83–124). New York: Academic Press.

Schwartz, M. F., Marin, O. S. M., & Saffran, E. S. (1979). Dissociations of language function in dementia: A case study. *Brain and Language, 7*, 277–306.

Segui, J., Mehler, J., Frauenfelder, U., & Morton, J. (1982). The word frequency effect and lexical access. *Neuropsychologia, 20*, 615–627.

Smith, S. D., & Mimica, I. (1984). Agrammatism in a case-inflected language: Comprehension of agent-object relations. *Brain and Language, 21*, 274–290.

Swinney, D., Zurif, E. G., & Cutler, E. (1980). Effects of sentential stress and word class comprehension in Broca's aphasics. *Brain and Language, 10*, 132–144.

Tanenhaus, M. K., Carlson, G. N., & Seidenberg, M. S. (1985). Do listeners compute linguistic representations? In D. Dowty, L. Karttunen, & A. Zwicky (Eds.), *Natural language parsing: Psychological, computational, and theoretical perspectives*. Cambridge: Cambridge University Press.

Tanenhaus, M. K., Leiman, J. M., & Seidenberg, M. D. (1979). Evidence for multiple stages in the processing of ambiguous words in syntactic contexts. *Journal of Verbal Learning and Verbal Behavior, 18*, 427–440.

Thorne, J., Bratley, P., & Dewar, H. (1968). The syntactic analysis of English by machine. In D. Michie (Ed.), *Machine intelligence* (Vol. 3, pp. 281–297). New York: American Elsevier.

Tyler, L. (1985). Real-time comprehension in agrammatism: A case study. *Brain and Language*.

Tyler, L. K., & Marslen-Wilson, W. P. (1977). The on-line effects of semantic context on syntactic processing. *Journal of Verbal Learning and Verbal Behavior, 16*, 683–692.

Vallar, G., & Baddeley, A. (1984a). Fractionation of working memory: Neuropsychological evidence for a phonological short-term store. *Journal of Verbal Learning and Verbal Behavior, 23*, 151–161.

Vallar, G., & Baddeley, A. (1984b). Phonological short-term store, phonological processing, and sentence comprehension: A neuropsychological case study. *Cognitive Neuropsychology, 1*, 121–141.

von Stockert, T., & Bader, L. (1976). Some relations of grammar and lexicon in aphasia. *Cortex, 12*, 49–60.

Wanner, E., & Maratsos, M. (1978). An ATN approach to comprehension. In M. Halle, J. Bresnan, & G. A. Miller (Eds.), *Linguistic theory and psychological reality* (pp. 119–161). Cambridge, MA: MIT Press.

Warrington, E., & Shallice, T. (1969). The selective impairment of auditory verbal short-term memory. *Brain, 92*, 885–896.

Whitaker, H. (1976). A case of the isolation of the language function. In H. Whitaker & H. A. Whitaker (Eds.), *Studies in neurolinguistics* (Vol. 2, pp. 1–58). New York: Academic Press.

Woods, W. (1970). Transition network grammar for natural language analysis. *Communications of the ACM, 13*, 591–606.

Zurif, E. (1980). Language mechanisms: A neuropsychological perspective. *American Scientist, 68*, 305–311.

Zurif, E. (1984). The use of data from aphasia in constructing a performance model of language. In M. Arbib & D. Caplan (Eds.),, *Neural models of language processes* (pp. 203–207). New York: Academic Press.

Zurif, E., & Blumstein, S. E. (1978). Language and the brain. In M. Halle, J. Bresnan, & G. A. Miller (Eds.), *Linguistic theory and psychological reality* (pp. 229–246). Cambridge, MA: MIT Press.

Zurif, E., & Grodzinsky, Y. (1983). Sensitivity to grammatical structure in agrammatic aphasia: A reply to Linebarger, Schwartz, and Saffran. *Cognition, 15*, 207–213.

4 Lexical Processing and Sentence Comprehension in Aphasia

Edgar Zurif
Brandeis University
and
Aphasia Research Center
Boston University School of Medicine

David Swinney
Graduate Center of City University of New York

Merrill Garrett
University of Arizona

We show in this chapter that selective aphasic deficits dissociate distinct language processing systems. To this end, we focus on disruptions of lexical access that appear to implicate initial stages of sentence comprehension.

The analyses we present turn on comparisons between agrammatic (Broca's) aphasic patients and paragrammatic (Wernicke's) aphasic patients. By the former we mean roughly, that type of aphasia in which complex syntactic structures and closed-class elements tend to be omitted in production and abnormally processed for comprehension purposes (Berndt & Caramazza, 1980; Zurif & Blumstein, 1978). Wernicke's aphasic patients, by contrast, present with an output that features misuse of grammatical devices—prepositions notably—and not telegraphic omission (Goodglass & Kaplan, 1972). Patients within this latter group also have sentence comprehension problems (Goodglass & Kaplan, 1972)—on some accounts, problems of the same sorts as those shown by the agrammatic patients (e.g., Goodglass & Menn, 1985; Shewan & Cantor, 1971). However, arguments for similarity in this respect rest on demonstrations that both groups fail to comprehend complex sentences. Without arguing the matter in detail, it is entirely possible that an apparently similar failure can have different antecedents (e.g., Friederici, 1983; Pastouriaux, 1984). Our group analyses are designed to explore this possibility.

A general feature of the analyses described here is that, unlike much work in neuropsychology, we do not translate freely between linguistic and processing theories. We do not distinguish, say, between a syntactic processing module and a phonological processing module simply in virtue of formal linguistic terminology. Rather, although we accept that processing modules are initially defined by linguistic information types, we seek evidence for their existence in terms of fixed and mandatory operating characteristics—that is, in terms of a functional architecture elaborated in real-time terms (Fodor, 1983; Pylyshyn, 1983). We return to this point in the context of the two experiments reported here.

GRAMMATICAL CLASS EFFECTS IN SENTENCE PROCESSING

The first of these studies turns on our efforts to characterize a sentence parsing device based on closed-class vocabulary elements and relatedly, to reconstruct features of agrammatic comprehension on the basis of a disruption to this device.

The initial line of observations supporting this set of possibilities stemmed from a number of lexical decision tasks—tasks in which subjects must decide if a letter string does or does not form a word in their language. Normal subjects were observed to respond in systematically different ways to open-class and closed-class items. Their reaction times for open-class words but not for closed-class words were found to be frequency sensitive. Also, they showed sensitivity to potential word formation processes for open-class items but not for closed-class items, this latter being manifested as an interference effect—an elevation in judgment time—for nonword judgments when the nonwords contained content word stems. So, for example, they took longer to classify *casterty* as a nonword than they did *nacherty*, *cast* but not *nach* being an open-class item. This interference effect did not occur, however, for nonwords in which the first syllable was a closed-class item: *sucherty* took no longer to be classified as a nonword than did *nacherty*. In effect, the closed class seemed to be contacted in some fashion that eliminates interference from a partial analysis as the input is being processed (Bradley, 1978).

Importantly, however, agrammatic patients did not show this insulation effect for the closed class. Nor did they show frequency insensitivity for closed-class recognition in the first mentioned task. In short, on both tasks, agrammatic patients treated closed-class items as they did open-class items (Bradley, 1978; Bradley, Garrett, & Zurif, 1980).

These observations were interpreted by Bradley et al. (1980) as evidence for a differential impairment of two normally distinct forms of word retrieval. By hypothesis, the closed-class access system was taken normally to provide essential input to a parser (i.e., to a device that assigns a syntactic analysis to the input), and the agrammatic patients' apparent inability to exploit this system was thus argued to provide a plausible account of their syntactic problems in comprehension. This argument was strengthened, moreover, by evidence that the failure to distinguish the two word classes on these tests was not a consequence of brain damage in general, but was tied to patients whose syntactic limitations demonstrably implicated elements of the closed class. Several mild Wernicke's (or possibly anomic) patients were tested with the same materials and they showed the normal dissociation patterns (Bradley et al., 1980).

Some aspects of these original observations have not been uniformly replicated. In particular, the general claim that closed-class access is not frequency sensitive is questionable (Gordon & Caramazza, 1982; Segui, Mehler, Frauenfelder, & Morton, 1982). For English language materials, it seems likely that item selection, word length, and range of frequency sampled are important factors in determining the experimental outcome (e.g., Egido & Garrett, 1981). Yet, although the status of claims for frequency based differences between open- and closed-class words in lexical decision tasks is thoroughly mixed, we have been impelled to a certain stubbornness in pursuing part of an account of agrammatic comprehension in terms of a disruption to the normal mode of contacting closed-class representations.

Our continued interest in this possibility has turned on a number of factors. There are, first of all, the observations that, whatever the nature of the antecedent disruption(s), agrammatic patients are unable to make normal use of closed-class items for comprehension (e.g., Berndt & Caramazza, 1980). And so far as normal processing is concerned, there remain a number of replicable and individually persuasive observations—apart from frequency effects—indicating that the features governing open-class access are different from those governing access of the closed class. This difference appears to implicate early, automatic (i.e., unconscious) mechanisms of word recognition. We have already cited the interference effect for nonword judgments in this respect (Bradley, 1978; Bradley et al., 1980). There are, in addition, a number of visual hemifield effects implicating open-closed class access differences—that is, observations that the two classes are treated differently in the right visual field but not the left (Bradley & Garrett, 1983; Shapiro & Jensen, 1986). And there is a general class of effects that indicate a difference between the two classes in their availability for conscious report (Garcia-Alba & Sanchez-Casas, 1983; Haber & Schindler, 1981; Healy, 1976; Mundie, 1980). It is this last set of effects—the so-called invisibility effects—that we have most recently used as a means of analyzing normal and aphasic performance and on which we report here. (See also Rosenberg, Zurif, Bownell, Garrett, & Bradley, 1985.)

The particular task that we used was a letter cancellation task. When neurologically intact subjects are faced with the requirement to cross out target letters in a text, they are more apt to notice and cancel the letters when they appear in open-class words than when in closed-class words. These experimental findings are informally confirmed by one's normal impression of proofreading experience in which inversions and repetitions of closed-class items seem more likely to be overlooked than similar errors involving open-class elements. In some sense, then, properties of closed-class items less readily intrude themselves into conscious attention—they tend toward invisibility. And clearly one plausible assumption is that this pattern arises because of differences in the way that the products of the open- and closed-class access routes relate to processes of sentence analysis and interpretation, and hence to processes of conscious report.

There are, of course, other possible assumptions. One such is that the normal pattern of detection failures is not a function of vocabulary type, but, rather, is influenced by frequency differences that are confounded with the vocabulary type contrast. Closed-class items are, after all, generally more frequent than open-class items, and it is possible that the higher the frequency of a letter sequence, the more likely the target letter embedded in that sequence is to be missed in a letter cancellation task (e.g., Drenowski & Healy, 1977; Healy, 1976).

Other questions relating to our assumption that the invisibility effect is intimately related to the operation of the closed-class route also compelled our consideration: First, even assuming that the detection difference could be accountable in terms of the open–closed class distinction, would this difference be altered by instruction? Specifically, could the extra closed-class errors be eliminated by alerting subjects to potential error in that class, as would be the case if the data reflected nothing other than some situation-specific scanning strategy? Or, as we were supposing, would the pattern prove to be intractable—the result, that is, of an unconscious and impenetrable processing mechanism, and in particular, the result of an automatic closed-class parsing device? Second, would the normal letter detection pattern emerge only for sentence material, that is, only in a situation in which the closed-class mechanism carries out its normal parsing function, or would the normal pattern also—and less explicably, from our perspective—be observed for nonsense or scrambled "prose"? Finally, what might be expected of aphasic patients' performance? Would those who speak and understand agrammatically—those who by our hypothesis no longer have access to a closed-class parsing route—notice and cross out target letters equally for the two vocabulary classes? That is, would they treat open- and close-class items similarly? And if so, would this effect be rooted specifically in agrammatism, or would it be observed as a consequence of brain damage in general? Clearly, Wernicke's patients also have sentence processing limitations, but to return to the question posed earlier, are these limitations of the same sort vis-à-vis unconscious lexical access processes as those in agrammatism?

To gain information on these questions we used the letter detection task, but with the following features incorporated: We prepared three normal prose passages typed in capital letters; the target in two of them was the letter *T*, in the third *A*. In two of these passages—one with an *A* target and one with a *T* target—we included sets of three target-bearing words such that the members of each set resembled each other phonologically and also bore a particular relation to each other in terms of frequency. These triplets were each comprised of one closed-class item (e.g., *BUT*), one high frequency open-class item (e.g., *PUT*), and one low frequency open-class item (e.g., *BAT*). In each such triplet, the closed-class item was approximately 10 times more frequent that the high frequency open-class item, which, in turn, was approximately 10 times more frequent than the low frequency open-class item. In addition to the three prose passages, we prepared a scrambled word version of one of the passages, in which the words within each sentence were randomly ordered.

We tested neurologically intact patients, agrammatic aphasic patients, and Wernicke's aphasic patients with this material. To minimize task-specific strategies, the patients were instructed to read each passage at normal speed and they were timed with a stopwatch to encourage them not to read more slowly than they do normally. Further, they were asked multiple choice questions in the middle and at the end of each of the passages to ensure that they were reading for meaning and not just scanning the letters. Finally, and as forecast, in order to determine how resistant the open–closed class difference is to attentional demands, we instructed a subset of the neurologically intact subjects to pay special attention to small words like *by* or *such*, as these are often neglected on the task.

The data we obtained are rather straightforward. First, the neurologically intact subjects: We confirmed previous reports that they are less able to detect target letters in closed-class items than in open-class items. In addition, we observed no effect of frequency per se on the error pattern. That is, when we considered performance for targets embedded in the triplets stepped in frequency, we found a significantly higher proportion of detection errors in the closed-class items than in the high and low frequency open-class items, but no significant difference between the high and low frequency items within the open class. We also found the normal open–closed class target detection difference to be significant in the prose condition but not in the scrambled condition, indicating that the invisibility of closed-class items is in some way dependent on sentence parsing and interpretation. And we noted no significant performance differences between subjects who were specifically instructed to attend to the closed class and those who were not forewarned, suggesting that the greater number of closed-class errors observed on this task reflects the operation of a normally automatic and impenetrable processing mechanism. Of course, a clear candidate for such a mechanism is the closed-class word retrieval system that we have described—the system that is, by hypothesis, in the service of a parser.

With respect to the aphasic patients, we found that for standard prose, the Wernicke's patients, like the neurologically intact patients, were less able to detect target letters in closed-class items than in open-class items, whereas the agrammatic aphasic patients detected targets with an almost equal facility in the two vocabulary classes. These data are also compatible with our functional analysis. Thus, the agrammatics' relatively equal number of errors on open- and closed-class targets may reasonably be viewed as reflecting a disruption of the structurally relevant closed-class access and analysis route. and as the Wernicke's data make clear, this processing problem is selectively tied to the overt features of agrammatism and not to the consequences of brain damage in general.[1]

It should be noted, however, that the Wernicke's patients did not perform entirely normally on these tasks either. The pertinent data in this respect are those obtained in the scrambled word condition: As already remarked, the normals showed much less of an open-closed class difference in this condition than they did with normal prose; by contrast, the Wernicke's patients showed very little shift from the pattern observed for them on the prose condition. Their closed-class access and parsing mechanism may, therefore, be hypothesized to be less than normally tied to the exigencies of interpretive systems. The effects of damage to the tissue implicated in Wernicke's aphasia may spare the ability to construct phrasal constituents (via the closed class route, at least), but these constructions cannot then be mapped normally onto semantically interpretable levels. Alternatively, one may suppose that for normals the mapping is effected and rejected on interpretive grounds, but that this feedback influence is lost for Wernicke's patients.

These last possibilities for Wernicke's raise the question: How can a device that provides input to a parser persist in its operation when faced with unparsable (scrambled prose) passages? The answer we think turns on the notion of impenetrability (Fodor, 1983; Pylyshyn, 1983): One facet of a form-driven or bottom-up device—of the sort that we characterized in our discussion of the closed-class route—is that it accesses lexical information, but does not evaluate the context in which the item appears (nor, relatedly,

---

[1]Two earlier studies by Ross (1983) and by Locke and Deck (1982) using the standard letter detection paradigm have been recorded in the literature. Our results differ from those of Ross, who reported the normal detection pattern for anteriorly lesioned patients; but our data are in agreement with those reported by Locke and Deck for a similar group. In both these other studies, however, the manner of patient classification makes the results difficult to interpret in relation to agrammatism. Both studies distinguish patients on the basis of lesion site—broadly, anterior versus posterior; and neither indicated the degree to which the behavioral features of agrammatism were present. It seems likely, then, that patient selection differences underlie the variations in the outcome of these studies.

In this respect, we cannot ignore the pitfalls of group research spelled out by Badecker and Caramazza (1985). They question agrammatism as a coherent psychological entity and claim, on this and other bases, that the only proper manner by which to reach an understanding of the mechanisms of language processing is to analyze exhaustively single aphasic cases. In our view, it seems somewhat premature to assume what theoretical processing distinctions ought to be applied in the evaluation of a coherent theoretical entity. Rather, our best hope of forming cognitively coherent categories—of bootstrapping our knowledge of agrammatism—is to form groups on the basis of specific behavioral features of presumed theoretical relevance. Still, as made abundantly clear by Badecker & Caramazza (1985), we can no longer afford to treat interlaboratory or even intragroup variability as a random effect of no theoretical significance.

the semantic force of the item). On this view, contextual constraints apply after the information has been accessed. Accordingly, initial access based on word forms may be spared in Wernicke's aphasia, but because patients presenting with this syndrome have an interpretation problem, they are unable to apply context—or more properly in the present instance, lack of context—to block local phrasal assignment efforts.

But to return to the closed-class access device, itself: The data to this point sustain a mechanistic account in terms of the operating characteristics of a specific word access system—characteristics that show the system to be distinguished normally from that underlying open-class access; and that show it to be unalterable, and cognitively impenetrable (as underlined by the Wernicke's patients performance). And on such an account, the agrammatic patients' failure to contact closed-class word representations is not seen as some failure of stored representations, but rather as a processing failure—as a failure, presumably, to make these elements available at the right time in the processing sequence.

EXHAUSTIVE LEXICAL ACCESS IN SENTENCE PROCESSING

In this section we continue to explore the impenetrability of lexical access. We do so now, however, in a more direct and encompassing fashion, bringing forth evidence that provides a somewhat different perspective on the agrammatics' failure to make normal use of a closed-class access and parsing device.

The study that we undertook—detailed elsewhere (Swinney, Zurif, & Nicol, 1989) and only summarized here—turned on the use of words with two or more meanings. These items provide a straightforward means of examining the effects of context on lexical access: Simply, sentence context can be rigged to make one or the other meaning of an ambiguous item relevant, and if lexical access were not contextually impenetrable, only the contextually relevant sense of that item should be accessed. If, however, access is impenetrable, then all meanings might be expected to be momentarily active. Clearly, this last claim is a time-dependent one. Context must eventually exert an effect—we do not normally experience entertaining contextually irrelevant meanings of such words. Accordingly, any investigation of impenetrability must depend on measures of lexical access as they unfold during the act of comprehension.

Such measures are termed *on-line* or *real-time* measures. They are not rooted in an assessment of the finished product, that is, in an assessment of ultimate success or failure of sentence comprehension. The letter detection measure, on these grounds, is one such. For the ambiguous word study to be reported, we made use of a different technique termed *cross modal lexi-*

cal priming (CMLP) (Swinney, Onifer, Prather, & Hirshkowitz, 1979). This technique depends on the effects of lexical priming, which is the facilitation in the processing of one word due to having heard just previously another related word. As an example of CMLP, consider the experimental situation in which a subject listens to, "The doctor decided to see his patients only on Monday," and, while listening, is required to make a lexical decision—that is, a word/nonword judgment—for a visually presented letter string. The priming effect is embodied in the finding that if the letter string is presented immediately on hearing *doctor*, lexical decisions are faster for words related to *doctor* (e.g., *nurse*) than for unrelated, control words. Such priming indicates that the meaning of the word in the sentence—*doctor*—has been activated or, somehow, contacted.

As forecast, the variation on this technique that is of interest here turns on the inclusion of ambiguous words in sentences. Specifically, in this situation priming is assessed for both meanings of the word in sentence contexts that are relevant to only one or the other of its meanings. So, for example, in the sentence, *The man saw several spiders, roaches, and other bugs in the corner of his room*, priming is assessed for both meanings of the word *bugs*—the contextually relevant insect sense and the contextually irrelevant espionage sense. In the first instance, the lexical decision time for the letter string *ANT* is charted; in the second instance, that for the string *SPY* is examined; and in each instance, the reaction time is compared to the lexical decision time for a letter string forming a word that is matched in frequency to the target (*SPY* or *ANT*) but unrelated to any sense of *bugs*.

Repeatedly, two phenomena are observed with neurologically intact subjects. The first is that when the letter string is flashed on the screen at a point immediately after the subject has heard the word *bugs* in the aurally presented sentence, there is priming for both of its interpretations, regardless of contextual information and regardless, also, of the a priori likelihood of the interpretations of the ambiguity. (In the example given, the insect sense of *bugs* is more usual than the spy sense.) The second phenomenon is that if the lexical decision probe is delayed—if the letter string does not appear until about one and a half seconds after the word *bugs* is heard—only the contextually relevant interpretation of the ambiguity shows a priming effect (again, independently of the a priori frequency of the interpretation) (Onifer & Swinney, 1981; Swinney, 1983).

These observations suggest that lexical access during normal sentence comprehension is an autonomous—contextually impenetrable—form driven process; that it involves the exhaustive retrieval of interpretations for a lexical candidate; and that contextual information has its effect on lexical processing only after access (Swinney, 1983). Presumably, the point of this design feature—of the temporary activation of all senses of a word—is not to be wasteful, but to provide efficiency in a situation that demands rapid processing—to provide, more particularly, a fully elaborated lexical data base for independent, (but, of course, unconscious) decision processes. The point is to avoid commitment to a wrong word sense that will require backtracking.

It was in the context of these findings and attendant speculation that we again examined our mechanistic account of agrammatism. The questions we posed were: Is the failure of agrammatic patients to access normally closed-class items a failure restricted to that domain? Or is the problem more pervasive, affecting properties of open-class access as well as closed-class access? Are they deficient, that is, in all language activities that demand rapid processing—not only in the rapid (possibly, simultaneous) access of closed-class items for the purpose of phrasal assignment, but also in the exhaustive access of ambiguous open-class items? And, again, if a disruption to such initial processing stages is found to occur, is it restricted to agrammatism or does it accompany aphasia in general?

Acting on these questions, we prepared sentences for aural presentation containing lexical ambiguities of the aforementioned type (indeed, including the example given); and we used the CMLP paradigm wherein the visually presented target items demanding a lexical decision appeared immediately after the ambiguous word in the sentence. We tested neurologically intact patients, agrammatic, and Wernicke's aphasic patients. And to buttress our instructions that they were not just to wait for the letter string, but to try also to understand each sentence, each subject was asked at several points during the experimental session to "say in your own words what you have just heard."

The neurologically intact patients showed priming for both senses of each ambiguous word. Their data, in short, uphold earlier indications that lexical access momentarily involves the exhaustive retrieval of interpretations of a lexical item and that such retrieval is not influenced by contextual information. More generally, these normal data sustain the notion of a language comprehension system organized in terms of encapsulated (autonomous) processesor modules, and they sustain its corollary, that contextual constraint is not introduced wherever potentially useful, but only after the access processes have done their work. That is, context is introduced as a means of selecting among competing representations provided by an independent processing device.

The fluent Wernicke's aphasic patients also showed priming for both senses of ambiguities. Again, as in the letter detection task, we found no compelling evidence of a disruption at initial stages in which form-based word retrieval processes are active. Rather, and now with some cumulative force, we are led to the conclusion that the Wernicke's limitation is to be located elsewhere, somehow involving either the formation of semantically interpretable structures based on data provided by the encapsulated lexical access system or the capacity to draw inferences from such structures.

The agrammatic patients, by contrast, did show a disruption at the stage of exhaustively accessing word meanings. Specifically, they showed priming only for the most frequent sense of the ambiguous word—regardless of context. Although this pattern is clearly aberrent, it cannot be construed as the consequence of an undifferentiated failure of automatic processing, at least not in the context of sentence interpretation.[2]

The data suggest, therefore, that lexical access in agrammatism remains context free—that is, is still informationally encapsulated (Swinney et al., 1989). One possible account of this is that the module can no longer sustain parallel access. This assumes that the normal access of ambiguous word meanings is correctly characterized as the consequence of a parallel engagement of representations. That is a plausible construal, but it is not the only possibility. We must consider also a second scenario: (a) that exhaustive access takes the form of an ordered activation or a serial search through the range of meaning candidates within the set defined by an ambiguous word; (b) that the order of this search or activation is controlled by frequency of meaning occurrence (e.g., Forster, 1979; Simpson, 1984); and (c) that when the number of candidates in the set is very limited, the activation or search is normally carried out at a rate too fast for us to measure with our existing techniques. On this view, the lexical module in agrammatism operates with a slower than normal rise time, and only the most frequent meaning representation is engaged within the time frame imposed by the on-line experimental paradigm. Pursuing this notion, the facilitation for all senses of an ambiguous word should eventually be shown, but at a point in the sentence that is noticeably later than that which is shown normally. We are currently investigating this possibility.

We cannot resolve this parallel-serial issue here. But whether the lexical access limitation in agrammatism is to be characterized as a failure to engage word meaning representation in parallel or as a slower than normal frequency controlled search or activation, the effect of the disruptions is the same: The sentence comprehension device is provided with an impoverished lexical data base for subsequent processing.

Earlier we forecast that these data would provide a different perspective on the closed-class processing problem. We now return to this forecast, emphasizing, first, what we do not mean by it. We do not think that the CMLP data in any way argue against the respective processing roles of thc

[2]Although we failed to find a normal priming pattern, we demonstrated some priming, namely priming for the most frequent senses of a word. Milberg and Blumstein (1981), by contrast, demonstrated no evidence of priming in agrammatic Broca's aphasia. Importantly, they employed an isolated word processing paradigm, where we assessed priming in the context of sentence processing. Whether it is this difference—that of examining normal language processing or of examining processing on a lexical task with which subjects have little familiarity—or some other difference that underlies their different observations is a problem currently under investigation.

open and closed vocabulary classes, or even against the use of this distinction to account in part for the agrammatics' parsing disruption. Rather, we refer to only the possibility that the agrammatic patients' closed-class accessing problem might be an instance—the most sensitive reflection—of their failure to access exhaustively any restricted lexical domain—an instance possibly attributable to an inability to sustain normally rapid processing.

This possibility is at present no more than intriguing. The several meanings of an ambiguous word constitute a very different sense of domain than that defined by the array of closed-class vocabulary items. The former is elaborated in terms of whatever it is that underlies meaning relations; the latter constitutes a domain in virtue of a common function, namely, that of parsing (see also, Grodzinsky, 1984, and Kean, 1982). But, granting that this difference need not correspond to a processing module distinction, it seems reasonable to suppose that information in both domains—that comprised of meaning representations in the one instance and of lexical forms with the same function in the other instance—is accessed in the same obligatorily exhaustive fashion. Clearly, the tasks of determining what counts as more forceful evidence for this notion and then gaining the relevant data remain before us. For the present, however, it does not seem unreasonable to suppose that the inability to engage multiple representations at a normal rate has implications for more than the processing of ambiguous items.

The possibility that we have raised can be extended to bear on another substantive—indeed, fundamental—question concerning the characterization of brain–language relations: Is the agrammatic patients' failure to engage exhaustively meaning representations indicative of an even wider based disruption of information access—of a disruption that extends even beyond language? Thus, although the disruption that we examined here clearly impacts on language comprehension, it is much less clear that the processing disruption, itself, is to be viewed as a diagnostic of a language-specific problem. It might well be the case that the agrammatics' inability to access lexical items in the normally exhaustive manner is but one reflection of a failure to show exhaustive computation in any domain. Relevant here are preliminary unpublished data gathered by Swinney and Prather that suggest that exhaustive access is also normally a feature of processing in the nonverbal, visual domain—that neurologically intact subjects automatically (and momentarily) elaborate all interpretations of an ambiguous visual form (e.g., a necker cube) even though they only become aware of a single interpretation (organization) at any one time. Whether such elaboration is shown also by agrammatic patients is an issue that we are currently addressing, for only by examining this phenomenon in language and other realms will we be able to distinguish domain-specific from domain-general problems in aphasia.

CONCLUSION

At the outset of this chapter we distinguished between the approach taken here and the more usual information processing analyses of language disorders. both share the usual assumptions: that the language faculty can be decomposed into a set of processing components or modules, some of which are disrupted by brain damage; that the spared components do not, themselves, perform differently when one or more of the other components are not functioning normally; and that the pathological performance will provide a basis for discerning which components or modules are disrupted (Caramazza, 1984). The difference between the two approaches turns on the manner by which each isolates the modules of the system. Information processing approaches to language disorder characterizations typically produce modules in line with relatively uncontroversial distinctions among information types specified in linguistic theory. So, generally, there are phonological, syntactic, lexical, and semantic components—each, often, with its own buffer. To these constituents additional components and access routes are provided as needed whether to explain modality differences in performance (auditory vs. visual input systems) or to account for linguistically related symptoms, such as the relative sparing of concrete as opposed to abstract nouns or of open-class items as opposed to closed-class items (e.g., Coltheart, Patterson, & Marshall, 1980, chapters and references therein).

By contrast, the approach exemplified by the two studies described in this chapter is not one of isolating modules as a direct reflection of partitions in linguistic theory, nor one of isolating modules (together with their functional lesions) solely as a means of redescribing the patterns of sparing and loss in aphasia. Rather, the evidence for modules in the present analyses emerges as the consequence of charting mandatory operating characteristics of the comprehension system. Thus, whatever the status of closed-class access, our demonstration of the impenetrability (autonomy) of lexical access in general is grounded in the finding that such access is momentarily uninfluenced by context. And, to the extent that we have shown that the agrammatic deficit is statable in terms of a disruption internal to this device and not to its absence—the module is not destroyed, it just works abnormally—we have provided a more suitable framework for evaluating variability and imprecision in aphasic performance. By contrast, functionally excising one or another box in an information flow diagram disallows any explanation for the often encountered pattern of suboptimal performance that is, nonetheless, above chance.

By not confusing modules with the linguistic objects they are intended to implement, and by, instead, measuring and ensuring the degree of encapsulation of any particular device in terms of on-line operating characteristics, we lessen the distance between the science of cognitive psychology and neuroscience—the distance between descriptions of the functional architecture of language and descriptions of its (presumably hardwired) neurological resources.

ACKNOWLEDGMENTS

The research reported in this chapter was supported in part by NS 11408 and NS 06209 to the Aphasia Research Center, Department of Neurology, Boston University School of Medicine, by NS 21806 to Brandeis University, and by a grant from the Sloan Foundation to the MIT Cognitive Science Center.

REFERENCES

Badecker, W., & Caramazza, A. (1985). On considerations of method and theory governing the use of clinical categories in neurolinguistics and cognitive neuropsychology: The case against agrammatism. *Cognition, 20,* 97–125.

Berndt, R. S., & Caramazza, A. (1980). A redefinition of the syndrome of Broca's aphasia: Implications for a neuropsychological model of language. *Applied Psycholinguistics, 1,* 225–278.

Bradley, D. (1978). Computational distinctions of vocabulary type. Unpublished doctoral dissertation, Massachusetts Institute of Technology, Cambridge, MA.

Bradley, D., & Garrett, M. (1983). Hemisphere differences in the recognition of closed and open class words. *Neuropsychologia, 21,* 155–160.

Bradley, D., Garrett, M., & Zurif, E. B. (1980). Syntactic deficits in Broca's aphasics. In D. Caplan (Ed.), *Biological studies of mental processes* (pp. 269–286). Cambridge, MA: MIT Press.

Caramazza, A. (1984). The logic of neuropsychological research and the problem of patient classification in aphasia. *Brain and Language, 21,* 9–20.

Coltheart, M., Patterson, K., & Marshall, J. (Eds.). (1980). *Deep dyslexia.* London: Routledge & Kegan Paul.

Drenowski, A., & Healy, A. (1977). Deletion errors on "the" and "and": Evidence for reading units larger than the word. *Memory and Cognition, 5,* 636–647.

Egido, C., & Garrett, M. (1981). Frequency contrasts for open and closed class words on auditory lexical decision. Unpublished manuscript, Massachusetts Institute of Technology, Psychology Department, Cambridge, MA.

Fodor, J. (1983). *The modularity of mind.* Cambridge, MA: MIT Press.

Forster, K. I. (1979). Levels of processing and the structure of the language processor. In W. Cooper & E. C. T. Walker (Eds.), *Sentence Processing.* Hillsdale, NJ: Lawrence Erlbaum Associates.

Friederici, A. D. (1983). Aphasics' perception of words in sentential context: Some real-time processing evidence. *Neuropsychologia, 21,* 351–358.

Garcia-Albea, J., & Sanchez-Casas, Y. R. (1983). Language processes: Comparative psycholinguistic studies in word recognition. Final Research Report for the Joint Spanish North American Committee for Cultural and Educational Exchange.

Goodglass, H., & Kaplan, E. (1972). *The assessment of aphasia and related disorders.* Philadelphia: Lea & Febiger.

Goodglass, H., & Menn, L. (1985). Is agrammatism a unitary phenomenon? In M. L. Kean (Ed.), *Agrammatism*. New York: Academic Press.

Gordon, B., & Caramazza, A. (1982). Lexical decision for open- and closed-class items: Failure to replicate differential frequency sensitivity. *Brain and Language, 15*, 143–160.

Grodzinsky, Y. (1984). The syntactic characterization of agrammatism. *Cognition, 16*, 99–120.

Haber, R. N., & Schindler, R. M. (1981). Error in proofreading: Evidence of syntactic control of letter processing. *Journal of Experimental Psychology: Human Perception and Performance, 7*, 573–579.

Healy, A. F. (1976). Detection errors on the word "the": Evidence for reading units larger than letters. *Journal of Experimental Psychology: Human Perception and Performance, 2*, 235–242.

Kean, M. L. (1982). Three perspectives for the analysis of aphasic syndromes. In M. A. Arbib, D. Caplan, & J. Marshall (Eds.), *Neural models of language processes*. New York: Academic Press.

Locke, J. L., & Deck, J. N. (1982). The processing of printed language by aphasic adults: Some phonological and syntactic effects. *Journal of Speech and Hearing Research, 25*, 314–319.

Milberg, W., & Blumstein, S. E. (1981). Lexical decision and aphasia: Evidence for semantic processing. *Brain and Language, 14*, 371–385.

Mundie, A. (1980). Detection errors on closed class words and open class words. Unpublished manuscript, Monash University, Psychology Department, Melbourne.

Onifer, W., & Swinney, D. (1981). Accessing lexical ambiguities during sentence comprehension: Effects of frequency-of-meaning and contextual bias. *Memory and Cognition, 9*, 225–236.

Pastouriaux, F. (1984). Les desordres des constructions syntaxiques chez les aphasiques de Broca et de Wernicke [ ]. Unpublished doctoral dissertation, University of Geneva.

Pylyshyn, Z. W. (1983). Syntax as an autonomous component of language. In M. Studdert-Kennedy (Ed.), *Psychobiology of language*. Cambridge, MA: MIT Press.

Rosenberg, B., Zurif, E. B., Brownell, H., & Garrett, M. (1985). Grammatical class effects in relation to normal and aphasic sentence processing. *Brain and Language, 26*, 287–303.

Ross, P. (1983). Phonological processing during silent reading in aphasic patients. *Brain and Language, 19*, 191–203.

Segui, J., Mehler, J., Frauenfelder, U., & Morton, J. (1982). The word frequency effect and lexical access. *Neuropsychologia, 20*, 615–628.

Shapiro, L., & Jensen, L. (1986). Processing open- and closed-class headed non-words: left hemisphere support for separate vocabularies. *Brain and Language, 28*, 318–327.

Shewan, R. M., & Cantor, G. (1971). Effects of vocabulary, syntax, and sentence length on auditory comprehension in aphasic patients. *Cortex, 7*, 209–226.

Simpson, G. B. (1984). Lexical ambiguity and its role in models of word recognition. *Psychological Bulletin*, 316–340.

Swinney, D. (1983). Theoretical and methodological issues in cognitive science: A psycholinguistic perspective. In W. Kintsch, J. Miller, & P. Polson (Eds.), *Methodology in cognitive science*. Hillsdale, NJ: Lawrence Erlbaum Associates.

Swinney, D., Onifer, W., Prather, P., & Hirshkowitz, M. (1979). Semantic facilitation across sensory modalities in the processing of individual words and sentences. *Memory and Cognition, 7*, 154–165.

Swinney, D., Zurif, E. B., & Nicol, J. (1989). The effects of focal brain damage on sentence processing: An examination of the neurological organization of a mental module. *Journal of Cognitive Neuroscience, 1*, 25–37.

Zurif, E. B., & Blumstein, S. E. (1978). Language and the brain. In M. Halle, J. Bresnan, & G. A. Miller (Eds.), *Linguistic theory and psychological reality*. Cambridge, MA: MIT Press.

5 Short-Term Memory Impairment and Language Processing

Eleanor M. Saffran
Temple University School of Medicine

INTRODUCTION

Normal subjects are able to repeat strings of about seven digits or five unrelated words immediately after hearing them. Brain damage can interfere with this auditory verbal short-term memory (STM) capacity, in some cases quite dramatically, leaving the patient with a span of only one or two items. The STM limitation can also be quite selective, occurring in patients who may appear to have no significant impairments in language function, other than certain difficulties in sentence comprehension that are consistently found to accompany the STM deficit. This chapter concerns the nature of STM impairments in brain-damaged subjects, their implications for theories of STM function, and the possible implications of reduced STM capacity for the processing of sentence materials.

Insofar as cognitive processes are concerned, the purview of this chapter is necessarily broad. To set our analysis of STM deficits within the framework of a model of STM function, we need to outline such a model, and hence to digress into the normal literature on STM. The discussion of sentence processing entails a different set of issues, also the subject of an extensive literature; this topic is only given cursory treatment here (for further discussion, see chapter 3).

With respect to neuropsychological data, however, our scope is relatively narrow. We focus on a small set of studies—most of them reports of single cases—in which the STM deficits, and in some instances, performance on sentence processing tasks, have been extensively investigated. Little consideration is given to studies that have dealt with STM and/or sentence processing deficits in groups of brain-damaged subjects, because most such investigations have failed to provide the detailed characterization of deficits that is required to address the processing issues of interest to us here.

DEFINING THE STM SYSTEM

Since the early 1970s, theoretical approaches to STM have followed two different courses. One, the more traditional approach, takes STM to be the function of a discrete cognitive subsystem dedicated to short-term information storage. The working memory model of Baddeley and Hitch (1974) is perhaps the most fully elaborated effort along these lines. An alternative view, proposed in 1972 by Craik and Lockhart, considers temporary storage to be a property of the systems (levels of processing) that process and represent that information, rather than of special-purpose mnestic devices. On this view, STM is not an isolable system but rather, as Monsell (1984) has suggested, an "umbrella term for a heterogeneous array (of) capacities for temporary storage . . . distributed over diverse cognitive subsystems" (p. 328). Empirical support for this view is provided by recent studies that indicate little commonality among the short-term storage capacities employed in different tasks, even where the tasks involve similar materials, as in the case of digit span and detection of a missing digit (Klapp, Marshburn, & Lester, 1983).

The view of STM that is developed in this chapter shares the basic assumptions of the levels of processing approach. In line with the task-specific view of STM, we focus on the capacities that underlie performance on a particular kind of task, namely, the memory span or immediate serial recall task that has served as the index of impaired STM function. Because this is obviously a verbal task, we assume that it involves capacities that can be specified in terms of linguistic processes and representations.[1] This is in contrast to the more traditional view, which has often appealed to constructs that are unspecified as to their representational characteristics; a common assumption of such models, for example, is that early list items are stored in long-term memory (LTM) (e.g., Glanzer, 1972). At this writing, there has been no serious attempt to develop an account of span performance that is closely tied to language processing models.[2] It is not the primary purpose of this chapter to provide such an account; however, in the interest of relating the neuropsychological data to a language-based model of STM function, it is necessary to make at least a preliminary effort in that direction.

---

[1]See Caplan, Vanier, and Baker (1986) for a somewhat different perspective on this issue.

[2]But see the paper by Barnard (1985), which appeared as this chapter was being written.

TABLE 5.1
Effects on Immediate Serial Recall Performance as a Function of Serial Position

	Serial Position		
	Beginning	*Middle*	*End*
	(Performance change relative to baseline condition: auditory presentation @ 1/sec)		
Rate of presentation—slow[a]	0/+	+	0
Articulatory suppression[b]	–	–	0
Phonemic similarity[c]	0	0	–
Word length[d]	0	0	0
Word frequency—low[e]	–	–	0
Suffix[f]	0	0	–
Visual presentation[g]	0	0	–

[a]Posner, 1964. [b]Campbell and Dodd, 1984. [c]Cheng, 1974. [d]Baddeley, Lewis, and Vallar, 1984. [e]Watkins and Watkins, 1977. [f]Crowder and Morton, 1969. [g]Murray, 1968.

Characteristics of Span Performance

Extensive studies of span performance in normal subjects have revealed a number of phenomena that must be taken into account in developing a model of STM function. We begin with a consideration of these phenomena.

The Serial Position Curve. Serial position curves for immediate serial recall (ISR) of strings that exceed subjects' capacity for verbatim reproduction show a U-shaped function, with superior recall of initial and terminal items compared with items in the middle of the list (the standard primacy and recency effects). The primacy and recency portions of the curve are differentially sensitive to a number of variables; these effects, summarized in Table 5.1, suggest that different capacities underlie the storage of items from early and late portions of the list. In particular, recall of items at the beginning of the list is influenced by factors like presentation rate and concurrent articulation, which would be expected to affect rehearsal; recall of late items is particularly sensitive to phonological similarity, implicating phonological processes in the maintenance of end-list information.

Modality Effects. ISR performance is influenced by the modality in which information is presented. In general, auditory presentation results in superior performance, particularly for the later portions of the list. The recall of visually presented materials can, however, be boosted to auditory levels by having subjects vocalize the items at presentation (Murray, 1968). Conversely, the auditory advantage can largely be eliminated by presenting a redundant item (suffix) at the end of the list (Crowder & Morton, 1969). The recency and suffix effects associated with auditory input have recently been found to occur, as well, with lip-read stimuli and with silent mouthing of lists presented visually (e.g., Campbell & Dodd, 1980; Greene & Crowder, 1984). These results imply that auditory input, as well as other sensory input that is speech-generated, provides additional information about terminal list items beyond that available from visual presentation, and that this information is vulnerable to interference from stimuli that immediately follow it.

A further distinction between auditory and visual presentation modes is that the retention of visual materials is more susceptible to interference from a concurrent articulatory task (e.g., Baddeley & Hitch, 1974). Moreover, whereas visual ISR is normally sensitive to phonological factors, such as word length and phonological similarity, which also affect performance on auditory lists, concurrent articulation reduces or eliminates the effects of these manipulations for lists presented visually (Baddeley, Thomson & Buchanan, 1975). Concurrent articulation also eliminates the effect of irrelevant auditory speech input, which normally interferes with visual ISR (Colle & Welsh, 1976; Salame & Baddeley, 1982). In contrast, ISR for auditory lists is less affected by concurrent articulation, particularly at recency positions (Campbell & Dodd, 1984), and its sensitivity to phonological parameters is largely unaffected by this manipulation (Baddeley, Lewis, & Vallar, 1984; Salame & Baddeley, 1982). These data have been interpreted to indicate that visual input gains access to phonological storage capacities via articulatory mediation.

Effects of Stimulus Materials. Span is a function of the nature of the items in the list. It is influenced by factors such as item familiarity and the size of the set from which the items are drawn; for example, digit span is greater than span for word lists, which in turn exceeds the span for nonsense syllable strings (Brener, 1940). These effects, along with the influence of word frequency on ISR performance (e.g., Watkins & Watkins, 1977), are indicative of lexical involvement in ISR. As noted, phonological similarity is a disruptive factor, in visual as well as auditory ISR (e.g., Conrad & Hull, 1964). The phonological similarity effect implicates speech-related capacities in the retention of both visually and auditorily presented materials.

These various effects suggest that serial recall draws on a number of information sources, including capacities related to speech perception and production, and to lexical representation.

Language Processing Capacities and STM

With these factors in mind, we begin our analysis of list recall, considered as a language task. On each trial, the subject is presented with a series of words, each word a discrete acoustic unit (unlike normal speech, where the speech stream must be segmented into words). Each unit is presumably identified as a word; that is, corresponding lexical representations become activated. At the termination of the list, the subject attempts to reproduce the items in order of their presentation.

The information processing requirements of this task entail the construction of several types of representations: The information in the input string is presumably encoded auditorily, phonologically, lexically, and, ultimately, in the form of a motor speech representation. To the extent that some or all of these representations persist for at least some brief period of time, they are potential sources of support for reproduction of the input string. The contributions of each will depend on factors such as decay constants, capacity limitations (i.e., the number of elements encompassed in a representation), and potential for regeneration of the information (via rehearsal). Our presumption is that subjects tend to draw on all available sources to reconstruct the stimulus list.

In the sections that follow, we consider each of these possible sources of information, and evidence, actual or potential, that might support their contribution to the serial recall task. Insofar as possible, postulated information sources are limited to constituents of language processing systems as they have been proposed in the existing literature. In line with this approach, our inventory of information retention devices emphasizes the utilization of existing representations (e.g., lexical and phonological units) as opposed to the construction of discrete, context-dependent (episodic) representations for each input string. Though some authors have invoked episodic representations in modeling related tasks such as repetition priming (e.g., Forster & Davis, 1984; Jacoby, 1983), their status remains controversial (e.g., Monsell, 1985), and we limit our use of this option here.

It becomes quickly apparent, however, that the task of mapping STM phenomena onto the language processing system is not an easy one. First, given the close (and, very likely, interactive) relationships among lexical, phonological, and articulatory representations, it is difficult to obtain evidence that unequivocally links a phenomenon to a particular level of representation. Second, because STM tasks have not been approached from a language processing perspective, critical data are often lacking; thus, whereas substitution errors are regarded as perhaps the richest source of data on the representations underlying language production (e.g., Garrett, 1975), errors in serial recall have not been given comparable attention. Finally, in some cases so little is known about the relevant language capacities that any assessment of their contribution to STM tasks must remain highly speculative. What follows should therefore be regarded as a preliminary attempt to project STM phenomena onto the language processing system.

A Lexical Contribution to ISR?

Persisting activation of lexical entries addressed by the list items is one possible mode of information storage in this task. Postaccess activation has been proposed as the mechanism for a variety of phenomena, including repetition priming, that is, the facilitatory effect of prior presentation on tasks such as word recognition and lexical decision (e.g., Monsell, 1985).

Effects of lexical status and word frequency provide direct evidence for lexical influences in serial recall. As compared with span for nonword lists, familiar words have a greater than two-item advantage (Brener, 1940). With supraspan (eight-item) lists, word frequency affects performance, except at the last two serial positions (Watkins & Watkins, 1977). The same pattern of frequency sensitivity across list positions also emerged in a study using mixed-frequency lists (Watkins, 1977); span was greater when the low frequency items occurred at the end of the list than at the beginning, indicating that lexical support is more important for early than for terminal items. Explanations for the interaction between frequency and position are considered later. Other evidence that can be taken to support the involvement of lexical activation in list recall includes the frequent intrusion of items from the immediately preceding list, terminal items being the most common source of such intrusions (Drewnowski & Murdock, 1980).[3]

But as the position-dependent frequency effect indicates, lexical factors do not provide a complete account of serial recall phenomena; other kinds of information must be contributing to the retention of items from the end of the list. Nor are lexical capacities likely to account for various other STM findings, such as modality differences and word length effects. Lexical activation is clearly but one of the sources of information that support list recall.

An Articulatory Contribution to ISR?

The standard span task engages the language production system, at least to the extent that the task requires a spoken response. Here we consider whether this system might serve a storage function in serial recall, as well as an output function. Ellis (1979) specifically made such a claim, arguing that "the *same* phonemic response buffer is involved in *both* short-term memory for phonemically-coded material *and* phonological storage in speech production" (p. 167). Such a mechanism could conceivably serve as a means of holding early list items as subsequent items are being received and processed.

The speech production system has a number of characteristics that could usefully be exploited in the short-term storage of list information. First, recent studies suggest that motor speech encoding of spoken input occurs effortlessly, at least at the single-word level; this is indicated by the fact that the translation to spoken output imposes very little cost on a concurrent

[3]This is not, however, the authors' interpretation of this result; they attribute the intrusions to auditory memory.

language task (e.g., Shallice, McLeod, & Lewis, 1985). Second, it is the function of the production system to construct representations consisting of linear arrays of lexical items; representations of this type are presumably required in the retention of list information. Third, the representations constructed by the speech production system are phonological in nature, and, as we have noted, phonological codes are implicated in STM phenomena.

Unfortunately, psycholinguistic studies provide little information that bears directly on the role of speech production processes in STM tasks. Thus, to evaluate the contribution of the production system to the retention of order information, it would be necessary to understand how multiword units are constructed. This issue has been addressed, but only with respect to the production of syntactically structured output; current models posit a slot-filler mechanism for the construction of phonological representations, where the sequence of slots designated to be filled by phonological segments is syntactically determined (e.g., Garrett, 1975). Speech error data, interpreted on these models, suggest that the computational unit spans a syntactic phrase (e.g., Garrett, 1975). It is not clear how the production of a string of unrelated words relates to these observations, though errors of a similar nature, implicating the programming of phonology over multiword units, have been obtained with short word lists in studies designed to elicit speech errors in laboratory settings (e.g., Baars, Motley, & MacKay, 1975). Preprogramming of multiword units for subsequent report also appears possible, at least under certain experimental conditions (Sternberg, Monsell, Knoll, & Wright, 1978). Thus, although there is no direct empirical or theoretical support for the maintenance of list information in the production system, the available evidence by no means rules out such a possibility. It might be possible, for example, to assemble the early list items in a form suitable for output and to hold them in that form until report can be initiated.[4]

Speech production mechanisms are more commonly implicated in memory tasks for their role in rehearsal, a process that employs motor speech activity to channel information back into the input system. Although it is generally assumed that subjects engage in rehearsal in serial recall tasks, the extent to which they do so is undetermined and, except where attempts are made to interfere with it, uncontrolled. The precise nature of the information supplied by rehearsal activity also remains unspecified.

The contribution of motor speech processes, including rehearsal, to serial recall tasks has been investigated by manipulating factors that would be expected to interfere with these operations. For example, rapid presentation of stimulus lists (e.g., at rates greater than two words per second) should limit subjects'

---

[4]Such a strategy would, however, preclude rehearsal of subsequent list items in articulatory form. It might therefore be more useful under conditions of rapid presentation, where rehearsal is difficult.

ability to rehearse, though it should not prevent encoding of the items by the production system. Increasing the presentation rate has a detrimental effect on recall of items in the middle of the list, and, in the case of long lists (e.g., 10 words), on the primacy portion as well (Jahnke, 1968; Posner, 1964); early- and middle-list items presumably stand to benefit more from rehearsal. Requiring subjects to articulate unrelated material during presentation would be expected to interfere with motor speech encoding generally, and hence also with rehearsal. There is some evidence that this manipulation, too, interferes with auditory ISR primarily at prerecency positions (Campbell & Dodd, 1984). Thus, it appears that the contribution of production processes to auditory span tasks primarily involves early- and middle-list information.

With visual input, the effects of concurrent articulation are more damaging, and extend to items at the end of the list (e.g., Campbell & Dodd, 1984). As noted, motor speech processes are strongly implicated in the phonological encoding of visual materials.

A Phonological Contribution to ISR?

Phonological representations are widely employed in the language system, both in the processing of speech input (e.g., Bierwisch, 1983) and the generation of speech output (e.g., Garrett, 1980). The detrimental effects of phonological similarity on serial recall, found with visual as well as auditory lists, clearly implicate phonological processes in STM. However, given the multiple possibilities for phonological representation in a task that involves speech input as well as output, it is not an easy matter to isolate the source, or sources, of these effects.

Recent work of Baddeley and his colleagues has attempted to distinguish between phonological storage capacities directly related to speech input and the role of a rehearsal process dependent on the speech output system. Two types of evidence implicate input-related phonological capacities in serial recall. In one set of studies, concurrent articulation (e.g., rapid recitation of a digit sequence) was used to interfere with rehearsal; this manipulation failed to eliminate the detrimental effects of phonological similarity on auditory ISR, indicating that these effects must derive, at least in part, from nonarticulatory phonological processes (Baddeley et al., 1984). A second form of evidence comes from effects of auditory input on visual ISR. The finding that task-irrelevant acoustic stimulation, unattended speech in particular, interferes with ISR for visually presented material, indicates that graphemic input is held in a system obligatorily accessed by spoken stimuli (e.g., Salame & Baddeley, 1982). This system is assumed to be a phonological store that receives auditory input directly, and graphemic input via articulatory mediation.

The properties of this phonological store remain largely unspecified, however, due in large part to the difficulty of isolating input phonology from output phonology. The attempt to identify the nature of capacity constraints on span performance is a case in point. Studies by Baddeley and his colleagues (Baddeley et al., 1984; Baddeley et al., 1975) have established that span is inversely related to word length. At issue is the locus of the length effect, which these investigators attribute to articulatory rehearsal. The evidence for this claim comes from the Baddeley et al. (1984) study, which showed that word length effects obtained with auditory presentation could be made to disappear if articulatory suppression was sustained during (written) recall as well as during list presentation. On the basis of these results, the investigators argued that word length effects reflect articulatory activity, and that phonological storage on the input side of the system is immune to such effects. This implies that the capacity of an input phonological store is not defined segmentally, but rather in terms of lexical units; in other words, the phonological store must involve postlexical, rather than prelexical, representations. One problem with this notion is that it is unclear why articulatory mediation should be required in the storage of visually presented lists, because written words appear to have direct access to lexical phonology (e.g., Morton & Patterson, 1980). It may be that lexical effects were exaggerated in the Baddeley et al. (1984; 1975) studies, in which the stimulus lists were drawn from a small pool of items (8 to 10); familiarity with the item pool could have reduced the necessity to maintain full segmental specifications for the list items.

Relatively little work on serial recall has been done with nonword materials, which would be expected to rely heavily, if not exclusively, on storage capacities of a phonological nature. The available evidence indicates that the ability to reproduce nonwords is a function of recency of presentation. Thus, in a study conducted with nonsense syllable lists, Watkins (1914) found that when given five- and six-item monosyllable strings, subjects had a tendency to begin with the last two or three items, which were "quickly and almost mechanically repeated, whereas the remainder are reproduced with considerable effort" (p. 337), if at all. As will become apparent, however, the basis for recency effects may not be entirely phonological; auditory information may also help to support the retention of items at the end of the list.

An Auditory Contribution to ISR?

Acoustic input to the language system is initially encoded auditorily. Evidence for modality differences in serial recall suggests that an auditory storage capacity contributes to STM.

As noted, there is a clear advantage to auditory presentation, particularly for retention of the latter part of the list (Table 5.1), but this advantage disappears if the visual items are vocalized at presentation. Because the benefit of vocalization is removed by masking the voice by noise, it must derive from auditory input and not from articulation (Murray, 1966). Additional evidence for auditory involvement comes from analyses of intrusion errors in serial recall. In comparing errors across auditory and visual presentation conditions, Drewnowski and Murdock (1980) found that auditory input was more likely to result in errors that were acoustically similar to the target word. The pattern of feature overlap between target and error also differed as a function of stimulus modality: Whereas errors that preserved the initial and final phonemes of target words occurred with equal frequency in the two conditions, errors preserving the stressed vowel arose more often in the auditory condition. It may be that steady-state vowel cues can be maintained in an auditory trace, in contrast to the transient frequency shifts that carry consonant information, which are likely to undergo rapid degradation. The finding that strings consisting of stop consonant syllables that share the same vowel (*pa*, *da*, *ba*, etc.) do not show the usual auditory advantage in STM (e.g., Crowder, 1971) is consistent with this view.

Given the evidence for phonological mediation in visual ISR tasks, auditory superiority effects cannot simply be equated with phonological encoding. It is necessary to assume either that phonological representations generated by graphemic input are in some way inferior to those produced by auditory input, or that additional information is supplied by an auditory record of the input string, at least of its terminal portion. Evidence for poststimulus persistence of speech sounds (e.g., Darwin, Turvey, & Crowder, 1972) provides some support for the latter view.

Those familiar with the STM literature will recall that a storage capacity of an auditory nature was explicitly postulated by Crowder and Morton (1969), who termed it a Precategorical Acoustic Store (PAS). They regarded this auditory, but speech-related, storage mechanism as the source of the enhanced recency effect with auditory presentation; also attributed to it was the suffix effect, the tendency for postlist stimuli to reduce or eliminate the recency effect in auditory lists. The auditory basis for these phenomena has since come into question, following demonstrations that similar effects are produced by lip-read and other nonacoustic speech (e.g., Campbell & Dodd, 1980; Nairne & Walters, 1983) and language stimuli, including American Sign Language (ASL) (Shand & Klima, 1981). Evidence that suffix effects are greatest when the postlist stimulus conforms with the rhythm of the stimulus list and is produced by the same speaker suggests that the salience of the terminal item may have to do with the perceptual grouping of speech input (Frankish & Turner, 1984). Thc representational nature of the storage capacity that gives rise to these effects remains unclear, though it is evidently speech-related.

It may be that auditory speech input produces an analog representation that preserves the rhythmic and prosodic characteristics of the input string, as well as some vowel information, with perhaps some additional acoustic information about items at the end of the string. Some support for this notion is provided by data from the Drewnowski and Murdock (1980) study. With item scores equated across presentation modality, serial position scores were higher in the auditory condition, suggesting that auditory presentation promotes the retention of serial order information. Input from lip-read or mouthed stimuli would presumably create the same kind of rhythmic envelope; in these cases, however, the auditory information contained within it would have to be generated rather than derived directly from the input signal.

Other Factors

To this point, our discussion of possible information sources in list recall has focused on capacities that might contribute to any language processing task involving auditory input. There are certain cognitive factors, however, that are peculiar to this experimental paradigm. Subjects are surely cognizant of the general features of the task, and must be encoding information about the task into memory: for example, that they are required to repeat lists consisting of a certain number of words, uttered in a certain voice, and so on. Among the contextual features registered by the subject must be that of current trial. It is possible that this information becomes linked to the lexical information corresponding to the first item for that trial. Such an association could provide the basis for the extremely robust primacy effects in ISR (see Table 5.1). Thus, for example, recall of the first item suffers only a 10% decrement when the subject is under instructions to produce the last four items of an eight-item list prior to recalling the first four items; in contrast, recall of the second item decreases by about 40% under these conditions (Posner, 1964). The fact that the primacy effect, unlike the recency effect, is modality-independent is consistent with this suggestion, as is evidence that primacy diminishes with unfamiliar stimulus materials, like nonsense words (Watkins, 1914).

Synthesis and Problems

Let us assume that all of the aforementioned information sources do, in fact, contribute to performance in ISR tasks. An account of list recall, based on these information sources (ignoring for present purposes the likelihood of feedback loops between various levels of representation), would go something like this: On the strength of the evidence from nonsense syllable lists, the information in the phonological representation, reinforced by auditory information, would appear to be sufficient for reproduction of two or three items from the end of the list. The contextual activation of the first item, together with lexical activation, contributes about two additional items; hence, the typical auditory word span of about five items (e.g., Brener, 1940). For lists longer than five items, performance is no longer entirely accurate. The items most likely to drop out are those from the middle of the list; the first word is supported by its contextual link and the last couple of items by their continued representation, phonologically and auditorily, as well as by residual lexical activation. The support that the terminal items receive from these additional sources accounts for their lack of dependence on the frequency parameter, which affects recall at earlier list positions. Intrusion errors reflect partial information in the auditory and phonological representations, as well as activity in the lexicon; items from the end of the just-previous list would be expected to remain somewhat activated for example.

Given the number of information sources postulated here, and the opportunities they present for interaction and strategic modification, it is not surprising that the list repetition task has spawned a vast literature, yet has resisted full understanding. It is also not surprising, in view of the number of processes that potentially could be disrupted, that span limitations are common in language-impaired patients, and that they occur in association with a wide range of aphasic disturbances (e.g., Heilman, Scholes, & Watson, 1976; Ostergaard & Meudell, 1984).

BRAIN DAMAGE AND STM FUNCTION

We move, finally, to a consideration of the STM deficits found in brain-damaged subjects. The fact that these deficits occur in association with several different forms of language impairment is consistent with the multicomponent view of short-term storage that we have adopted here. More importantly, the study of STM processes in patients with different underlying deficits provides a potentially powerful means of isolating the various components of STM performance. In this section, we first review evidence from studies that have focused on the relationship between STM function and specific forms of language impairment, and then turn to a particularly interesting group of patients, those characterized principally by their STM deficits.

Expressive Deficits and STM Function

Though span limitations are demonstrable in a wide range of language-impaired patients, there is one group in which STM performance seems to be spared. Several investigators have examined the STM capacities of brain-damaged patients with severe articulatory disorders (anarthria), some of them incapable of producing any speech at all (Baddeley & Wilson, 1985; Nebes, 1975; Vallar & Cappa, 1987). Auditory digit span, assessed by a pointing task, was found to be within normal limits in these subjects. Assuming that rehearsal plays a critical role in span tasks, these results indicate that it can be carried out without peripheral motor involvement. On visual STM tasks, these patients performed normally, showing the usual sensitivity to factors such as word length and phonological similarity that are thought to depend on articulatory mediation As in the case of rehearsal, the fact that phonological recoding processes are not disrupted by this relatively peripheral speech disorder suggests that these processes do not require the motor enactment of the speech program. These results also imply that the basis for the detrimental effects of concurrent articulation on visual ISR (e.g., Murray, 1968) is unlikely to be its interference with articulatory activity per se. The observations in anarthric patients further indicate that if STM does indeed depend on information held in the production system, it must be possible to access this information without converting it, via speech, to kinesthetic or auditory form.

Other production disorders, which presumably involve more central aspects of speech planning, do appear to be associated with impairment in STM tasks. The effects of speech dysfluency on STM were the subject of a study by Martin (1987), who examined the span performance of six nonfluent aphasics (three of whom were agrammatic) and four patients with fluent aphasias. As in the studies with anarthrics, a pointing response was used. Both sets of patients showed reduced spans relative to a matched group of normal subjects, the nonfluents performing somewhat worse than the fluents. The effects of word length (one- vs. two-syllable words) and articulatory complexity (indexed by the presence of consonant clusters) were significantly correlated with fluency. On the basis of this result, Martin attributed the STM deficits in the nonfluents to the disruption of inner rehearsal processes. This group therefore presents an interesting contrast with the anarthric patients, whose more peripheral deficits in speech production did not interfere with span.

STM and Lexical Impairment

As noted earlier, evidence from normal studies suggests that lexical structures contribute to the short-term retention of list information, particularly of items at preterminal positions. One would therefore expect lexical disturbances to result in impaired performance on STM tasks. A case study carried out in our laboratory provides evidence on this point (Martin & Saffran, 1987).

The patient, ST, had a lexical/semantic disturbance that seriously limited her ability to produce coherent speech on her own. In contrast to her spontaneous speech, which was semantically incoherent, perseverative, and neologistic, her performance on oral reading and repetition tasks was remarkably well preserved. (Those familiar with aphasia typology will recognize this as a case of transcortical sensory aphasia.) On list repetition tasks, her performance was sensitive to word frequency, suggesting some reliance on lexical information. Characteristics of her repetition performance indicated, however, that her ability to retrieve list items was strongly dependent on recent phonological input. Thus, in serial recall, she nearly always produced the last two items of the list correctly, often reporting them at the beginning of the output string. With lists of more than three items, she also showed a tendency to initiate recall with neologisms that consisted largely of phonemes derived from targets at later positions; for example, the string *spider harp arrow* was repeated as "/spaI-ro/ /haUp/ /hæ-ro/"; *cigarette candle lamp table* as "/kæm-bəl/ /læm-pəl/ table lamp table." ST's ability to recall early list items was not facilitated by a repetition priming procedure (i.e., the Hebb [1961] paradigm, which involves repeated presentation, every fourth trial, of the same list). It appeared that she was relying on a phonological (or auditory) trace that provided enough information to support the reproduction of terminal list items but not of items earlier in the list.

The performance pattern of this lexically impaired patient is entirely consistent with the notion that lexical structures contribute to the maintenance of early list information, as suggested by the pattern of frequency effects across serial positions in normals. ST showed reduced primacy with shorter lists and reported only the last two items from supraspan lists, which is exactly the pattern predicted by the normal data. ST's ability to reproduce the terminal items was based primarily on auditory/phonological information; in normals, the availability of this information for the terminal items presumably decreases reliance on the lexical structures that appear to support retention of the earlier items. ST's pattern also parallels the performance of normals on nonword lists, where they, too, lack adequate lexical support; in both cases, performance is biased toward terminal list items.

"Pure" Deficits in STM Function

In the cases discussed thus far, reduction in span occurred in the context of significant disruption of speech or language capacities. Here we focus on a group of patients with relatively mild or, in some cases, negligible language disturbances who are also impaired in STM tasks. These patients are sometimes classified as conduction aphasics because a disturbance in the repetition of spoken materials is a major feature of that clinical syndrome (e.g., Goodglass & Kaplan, 1972); they do not, however, produce the literal paraphasias that are classically associated with conduction aphasia, at least not with any great frequency. Shallice and Warrington (1977) argued for the need to distinguish between a repetition problem that has its origin in the language production system, which they termed a reproduction disorder, and one that originates in the input system, which they designated a true repetition disorder. It is the latter disturbance that is of interest to us here.

Warrington and Shallice (1969) were the first to characterize the repetition disorder as an impairment of STM. They studied a patient (KF) whose severely impaired performance in STM tasks could not be accounted for by

TABLE 5.2
Characteristics of STM Patients

	Auditory Span:			*Visual Span:*			
Patient	*Numbers*	*Letters*	*Words*	*Recency*	*Numbers*	*Letters*	*Words*
KF[a]	2.3	1.8	2.3	absent	3.0	3.1	—
KF[b]	3.5	2.5	3.0	absent	>4	3.5	—
JB[b]	4.0	3.0	3.0	absent	>4	>4	—
WH[b]	3.0	2.5	2.3	—	—	—	—
IL[c]	3.6	2.0	2.5	absent	>5	—	—
MC[d]	1.8	—	1.9	absent	>3	—	3.0
PV[e]	4.0	1.8	2.8	absent	4.5	4.5	5.5
EA[f]	<2	<2	<2	absent	2.4	—	—
EE[g]	—	—	<3	absent	—	—	—
TI[h]	3.5	—	1.9	absent	3.5	—	2.7

[a]Warrington and Shallice, 1969. [b]Warrington, Logue and Pratt (1971). [c]Saffran and Marin, 1975. [d]Caramazza, Basili, Koller, and Berndt, 1981. [e]Vallar and Baddeley, 1984a. [f]Friedrich, Glenn, and Marin, 1984. [g]Berndt, 1985a, 1985b. [h]Saffran, 1985. [i]Span defined as string length at which 50% of strings are repeated correctly.

any evident disturbance in receptive or expressive language function. For example, KF's ability to identify particular targets in the speech stream was found to be well preserved, a result that argued against a perceptual deficit as the source of his span limitation. The STM deficit was demonstrable in probe memory and pointing span tasks, and therefore appeared to be unrelated to the speech production requirements of the standard list repetition paradigm. KF's span was found to increase with visual presentation of the stimulus list (Warrington & Shallice, 1969, 1972), a pattern that contrasts with the auditory superiority found in normals (e.g., Murray, 1966). In auditory STM tasks involving nonlinguistic stimuli, KF was, however, unimpaired (Shallice & Warrington, 1974). Similar findings were subsequently reported in two additional patients (Warrington, Logue, & Pratt, 1971).

The essential features of these cases have since been demonstrated in a number of patients studied in other laboratories (Basso, Spinnler, Vallar, & Zanobio, 1982; Berndt, 1985a, 1985b; Caramazza, Basili, Koller, & Berndt, 1981; Friedrich, Glenn, & Mann, 1984; Saffran, 1985; Saffran & Marin, 1975). In addition to the reduction in span in the context of relatively preserved language function and the reversal in the modality effect,[5] other consistent features include absence of the recency effect normally found with auditory presentation and some degree of impairment in sentence comprehension. The characteristics of reported cases are summarized in Table 5.2.

In contrast to the STM impairments discussed earlier, the span limitations in these patients are not clearly linked to language deficits that might

[5]TI (Saffran, 1985) is an exception in this regard; he performed no better with visual than with auditory presentation.

indicate the source of the STM problem (though this point has been disputed by Allport, 1984). For the most part, hypotheses have come, instead, from models of STM function.

One possibility, suggested by Baddeley (1976) and by Ellis (1979), is that the deficit involves STM capacities associated with the speech production system (i.e., the articulatory response buffer). A limitation on response buffer capacity would be expected to restrict the size of speech programming units, resulting in slower speech rates and more frequent pauses; such abnormalities have not, however, been found in STM patients (Allport, 1984; Shallice & Butterworth, 1977; Vallar & Baddeley, 1984a).

An alternative locus for the deficit, involving a speech-related storage capacity in the input system, has been proposed by several investigators. To account for the loss of recency and the reversed modality effect, Saffran and Marin (1975) suggested that the deficit involves the Precategorical Acoustic Store that Crowder and Morton (1969) proposed as the source of the recency and modality effects in normal ISR. As noted earlier, this capacity is assumed to be specific to speech but pre-phonological in its representational mode. Others have proposed that the deficit involves a phonologically based storage capacity that may be accessed directly by auditory input, and indirectly, via articulatory encoding, by visual information (Caramazza et al., 1981; Shallice, 1979; Vallar & Baddeley, 1984a, 1984b).

For the most part, these two hypotheses generate similar predictions, at least with respect to performance on auditory lists. Both, for example, predict loss of the normal recency effect. The two are most clearly differentiated in their implications for visual STM performance: Because visual ISR normally involves phonological capacities, a deficit in phonological storage should affect performance with visual lists, whereas an auditory limitation should not.

The use of phonological capacities in visual ISR tasks has been investigated by examining the effects of phonological similarity. PV, the patient studied by Vallar and Baddeley (1984a, 1984b), showed an effect of phonological similarity when consonant strings were presented auditorily, but not with visual presentation. Her visual STM performance, which was quite good (see Table 5.2), was also unaffected by other factors normally detrimental to visual ISR, such as word length and articulatory suppression. PV therefore appeared not to be using phonological capacities in visual span tasks, though she had no speech production impairment that might impede the phonological encoding of graphemic input. On the basis of these observations, Vallar and Baddeley (1984a) attributed PV's STM deficit to a limitation on a phonological store; she demonstrated no phonological effects in visual tasks, they argued, because she did not store this material phonologically. A non-brain-damaged adult with an STM disorder studied by Campbell and Butterworth (1985; Butterworth, Campbell, & Howard, 1986) also failed to show a phonological similarity effect, with auditory as well as with visual lists.

Another observation that suggests a phonological basis for the STM deficit comes from the study by Friedrich et al. (1984). These authors noted that whereas the total number of items correctly repeated by patient EA remained relatively constant over strings of one to four words (roughly, one item), her performance on lists of nonsense syllables declined markedly, by the same index, as string length increased. For example, EA repeated 16 of 20 nonsense syllables correctly when given only one item per trial, but only 10 of 40 when two-syllable strings were presented, and 4 of 80 in the case of four-item strings. Familiar materials, like digits and letters, behaved similarly to words, except that the absolute (constant) span over two- to four-item strings was slightly greater (approximately 1.5 items repeated correctly). These data indicate that EA's capacity to retain information in phonological form was extremely limited, and that her performance on familiar materials must have depended primarily on other forms of information storage (see Saffran & Marin, 1975, for a similar argument). Data from Saffran and Marin's (1975) patient IL, whose span was, in general, somewhat greater than EA's, are indicative of similar effects: IL was 20 of 20 correct on single nonsense words, 20 of 40 on two-item, and 18 of 60 on three-item strings. In contrast, with letter and word lists he showed at least a 50% increment in the total number of items recalled from two- as compared with one-item strings, and a constant span across lists of two to four items.

Additional support for a phonologically based STM deficit comes from evidence that at least some of the STM patients are impaired on other types of phonological tasks. Allport (1984) proposed, in fact, that the retention deficit is the product of a more basic impairment in phonological encoding. He studied three patients with limited auditory spans, one of whom (JB) was the subject of previous reports by Warrington and Shallice (Shallice & Butterworth, 1977; Warrington et al., 1971) (see Table 5.2). All of these patients were found to be impaired on auditory lexical decision and phoneme discrimination tasks. Allport took these deficits to be indicative of "reduced distinctiveness in phonological coding" and argued that the coding problem is the source of the STM impairment. Evidence for an impairment in phoneme discrimination was also obtained by Friedrich et al. (1984) in their study of EA. In addition to mild abnormalities in phoneme discrimination and more serious deficiencies in phoneme categorization tasks (the latter involving synthetic speech sounds), EA was impaired in tests of word segmentation and in the recognition of written homophones. Deficits in phonological processing have also been demonstrated in the developmental case (RE) studied by Campbell and Butterworth (1985; Butterworth et al., 1986). RE performed normally on a test of speech perception, but was impaired on tasks involving the parsing and manipulation of phonological segments in words (tasks similar to the childhood game of Pig Latin). However, Vallar and Baddeley's (1984b) patient, PV, performed normally on tests of phoneme discrimination (involving natural speech sounds) and on other phonological tasks such as rhyme matching. Berndt's (1985a, 1985b) patient EE was also unimpaired on a battery of speech perception tests.

It is difficult to know what to make of these data. Because the tasks used to assess phonological capacities differ considerably from one study to another, it cannot be concluded with any certainty that any of these patients are free of deficits demonstrated in others. In some cases, furthermore, it is unclear how the phonological requirements of the task (e.g., written rhyme matching) relate to phonological processes involved in short-term memory; in others (e.g., A–X phoneme discrimination paradigms, where there is an interval between the two stimuli), it is debatable whether the task should properly be considered a perceptual measure or a measure of short-term memory. Nevertheless, in suggesting a diminished capacity for phonological representation, these data do lend additional support to a phonological account of the STM deficit.

In the model sketched earlier (p. 147), phonological information served primarily to maintain items occurring toward the end of the list. Without this information, recall should be biased toward early list items, which it is in these patients, both in serial (Caramazza et al., 1981; Friedrich et al., 1984; Saffran & Marin, 1975) and in free recall (Basso et al., 1982; Shallice & Warrington, 1970; Vallar & Papagno, 1986). The evidence from free recall is particularly compelling, because this is a task in which normal subjects tend to produce the most recent items first (e.g., Postman & Phillips, 1965). The model can account for retention of the early list items by means of contextual-lexical association and encoding within the speech production system. Reliance on lexical information is indicated by evidence of word frequency effects on span performance; of the STM cases in which this parameter has been examined, one patient (IL) showed a substantial frequency effect (Saffran & Marin, 1975), and another (MC) an effect with four-item though not with three-item lists (Caramazza et al., 1981). Effects of form class on MC's serial recall performance also suggest dependence on lexical information; this patient performed much better with concrete nouns than with functors.

The most problematic aspect of the data, from the standpoint of the model, is the apparent lack of contribution from an auditory store. Postulated in large part to account for the auditory superiority in STM, this store should supply some information about the most recent items beyond that available from phonological sources. One way to reconcile the patient data with the model is to propose that the STM patients have deficiencies in both phonological and auditory storage capacities; while multiple-deficit accounts may not be the preferred theoretical option, it is to be expected that neuropsychological data will sometimes require them (e.g., Shallice &

Warrington, 1980). Alternatively, because residual auditory information contributes to performance indirectly, via phonological encoding, it may be that the phonological deficit limits the usefulness of this source of information. A third possibility is that these two information sources are not as distinct as thus far suggested.

From an empirical standpoint, the most serious difficulty for the phonological account of the STM deficit is posed by the reversed modality effect demonstrated by the STM patients. In view of the significant role of phonological processes in normal visual STM performance, the STM patients might be expected to show at least as much impairment with visual presentation as they do with spoken materials. Unless information can be maintained in a visual or orthographic representation of the input string, their performance on visual lists should be based on the same sources of information available to them in the auditory task, minus the auditory contribution—namely, phonological, lexical, and motor speech processes. Evidence from normal subjects suggests that the use of visual capacities in the retention of graphemic input is quite limited. Thus, normals perform poorly in visual ISR tasks involving phonologically similar but visually distinctive lists; for example, span for completely homophonic lists of Chinese logographs was found to be less than three items (Zhang & Simon, 1985). How, then, do we account for the fact that the visual spans of the STM patients exceed their auditory spans, and in some cases (PV, IL, JB; see Table 5.2) even approach normal levels? (Note in Table 5.2 that some patients were examined only on list lengths sufficient to demonstrate the visual superiority; the limits of visual ISR were not tested.)

It is possible that impaired phonological mechanisms, which are automatically engaged by auditory but not by visual presentation, provide misleading information in the auditory condition; hence the reversal of the superiority effect. It may also be that, out of exigency, the STM patients learn to make better use of their visual capacities than normals typically do. Thus, Warrington and Shallice (1972) found evidence of visual similarity effects in KF; normals show little evidence of such effects in visual span tasks, though they are observed in deaf subjects (e.g., Conrad & Hull, 1964). The developmental STM patient studied by Campbell and Butterworth (1985; Butterworth et al., 1986) also appeared to be relying on visual memory capacities, even in auditory tasks.

Though an account of the STM impairment in terms of a phonological deficit leaves a good deal still to be explained, it is nevertheless a reasonable supposition that the reduction in span reflects some limitation in the representation and/or maintenance of phonological information. Whether the underlying deficit is perceptual in nature, as Allport (1984) suggested, remains an open issue; clearly, the phonological capacities of STM patients will have to be examined more carefully in future studies. The possible involvement of speech-related auditory capacities also merits further consideration.

It may be, as Allport (1985) argued, that an adequate understanding of the STM deficit will require a more radical shift in conceptual orientation. He suggested that neuropsychological impairments like the STM deficit, which are characterized by "'graceful degradation' of performance, whereby particular linguistic functions are impoverished, slowed, subject to increased equivocation and error, rather than simple, all-or-none loss of function" (p. 57), are best accounted for in terms of connectionist/parallel distributed processing models. This approach, applied to speech perception by McClelland and Elman (1986), makes no sharp distinction between perceptual and mnestic processes. Connectionist models also offer the possibility of providing an explicit account of short-term retention in terms of the interaction of several information sources, each providing partial information. The need for an interactive approach in modelling STM function has been implicit in our discussion here.

SENTENCE COMPREHENSION DEFICITS IN STM PATIENTS

Evidence for Comprehension Deficits

As noted earlier, all of the STM patients studied thus far have shown some degree of impairment in sentence comprehension. The specifics of comprehension testing in these patients vary widely. Nevertheless, there is general agreement that the comprehension problem centers on syntactic information. Thus, these patients tend to have difficulty with reversible sentences, like the following one, where interpretation is not highly constrained by lexical content and depends critically on structural information.

1. The cat that the dog chased was black.

The implication drawn from these observations is that the STM limitation is the source of the sentence processing problem. We examine the basis for this claim in some detail here.

The early studies of STM patients, which were directed primarily at memory questions, did not examine language comprehension in any detail. Thus, the only sentence comprehension data reported for Warrington et al.'s (1971) three STM patients are for performance on a short (15-item) version of the Token Test, a clinical measure that evaluates patients' ability to carry out commands such as the following:

2. Pick up the white circle after you pick up the red rectangle.

All three patients were impaired on this task, as more recently studied cases have been as well (Basso et al, 1982; Friedrich et al., 1984).

Saffran and Marin (1975) did not examine comprehension explicitly in patient IL, but looked at repetition performance as an index of sentence understanding. IL was generally unable to repeat sentences longer than five or six words verbatim. With longer sentences, he usually produced the first two or three (open-class) words accurately, a pattern that resembled his performance in list repetition, where he showed primacy but no recency effects. He did not, however, lose the rest of the sentence entirely. In most instances, his response would be considered an adequate paraphrase of the original sentence; for example, *The residence was located in a peaceful neighborhood* was "repeated" as *The residence was situated in a quiet district*. It was clear that for this patient, the attempt at reproduction involved regeneration of the sentence on the basis of a semantic interpretation of the input string. The finding of most interest was that the adequacy of these reconstructions depended on the structure of the sentence. Thus, IL made many errors in attempting to repeat semantically reversible passives in which thematic role assignment was not constrained by the first few words, which he was able to retain veridically; for example, *The two men, George and Carl, were closely watched* was repeated as *The two men, George and Carl, watched them closely*. Friedrich, Martin, and Kemper's (1985) patient EA showed a similar pattern in repetition tasks, preserving semantic relations in her responses to 81% of semantically constrained sentences but only 54% of semantically reversible sentences.

More recent investigations have examined comprehension performance more systematically, primarily by means of sentence-picture matching tasks. MC, the patient studied by Caramazza et al. (1981), was 81% correct on nonreversible sentences, but only 44% correct on semantically reversible sentences, which included several different structural types (actives, passives, subject- and object-relative clause constructions). Of the errors on the reversible condition, the majority (55%) were to reverse-role rather than lexical distractors; performance was not, however, broken down with respect to syntactic type. EA (Friedrich et al., 1985) showed a similar pattern; she made no errors at all on a comprehension task with lexical distractors (e.g., for *The boy was splashed by the dog*, a picture of a car splashing a boy), but had difficulty with similar sentences when the choice was a reversed-role distractor (a picture of a boy splashing a dog); in this task, EA scored 94% correct on actives and 67% on passives. She was also impaired (75% correct) on locative sentences (e.g., *The square is outside the circle*) tested with reversed-role distractors.

PV, extensively studied by Vallar and Baddeley (1984a, 1984b), showed a milder comprehension impairment. This patient scored within the normal range on a sentence–picture matching test comprised of semantically reversible sentences of various structural types (Parisi & Pizzamiglio, 1970). Vallar and Baddeley (1984b) suggested that PV's lack of impairment on this task may reflect the lesser severity of her STM deficit, as compared with the other STM patients (see Table 5.2); most of the sentences in the test were, in fact, within her six-word sentence repetition span. Vallar and Baddeley (1984b) challenged her further using longer sentences in an anomaly detection paradigm, contrasting sentences in which the anomaly depended on a semantic mismatch between two lexical items, as in sentence 3.a., with sentences in which the mismatch was dependent on structural factors, as in sentence 3.b.:

3.a. Lettuce is the kind of person that one rarely meets in a schoolroom.
b. One could reasonably claim that sailors are often lived on by ships of various kinds.

For comparison, they included short sentences containing lexical anomalies, but none with anomalies of the structural type. PV performed normally on the short sentences and on the long sentences in the lexically based condition; she was, however, impaired on the long sentences in the structure-based condition (61% correct, which is statistically at chance). The authors concluded from these results that "comprehension is disrupted only when the abnormally reduced capacity of the phonological short-term store is exceeded by material which has to be preserved in its superficial structure" (p. 138). This conclusion is weakened by their failure to include short versions of these structurally based anomalies in this study.

Berndt (1985a, 1985b) explored the relationship between comprehension impairment and sentence length more systematically. Her patient, EE, was 88% correct on reversible actives (length was six words) and only 25% correct on reversible passives (seven-word length). On locatives (e.g., *The barrel is above the box*) she was 100% correct; however, when an adjective, irrelevant to the picture-matching task, was added to the sentence, her performance declined markedly; she was 38% correct when the adjective occurred in the subject HP (*The red barrel is above the box*) and 88% correct when it occurred in the VP (*The barrel is above the red box*). Berndt (1985a) suggested that "the additional requirement of maintaining one extra word apparently undermined interpretation of the relationship between the noun and the preposition, even though it did not occur *between* the two relevant items" (p. 22)

However, the effects of sentence length on the performance of an STM patient studied in our laboratory are less clear cut (Saffran, 1985; Saffran & Martin, in press). In a sentence–picture matching task, TI did show an effect of adding irrelevant material to the end of a simple active sentence; his performance, which was 92% correct when an adverbial phrase (e.g., *in the forest*) preceded the kernel sentence (*the bird watched the brown squirrel*), declined to 58% when the adverbial phrase followed the critical material. TI's performance on this task was not simply a function of sentence length, however. The shortest sentences in this task (five words in length) were truncated passives (*The brown squirrel was watched*); TI found these sentences extremely difficult (33% correct), as difficult, in fact, as the longer (eight-word) full passives, despite the fact that he was able to repeat them verbatim. Moreover, in a subsequent study in which semantic anomaly judgments were used to assess sentence comprehension, TI failed to demonstrate length effects (Schwartz, Linebarger, Saffran, & Pate, 1987). TI was 78% correct on the base sentences in this study, simple active declarative sentences in which the anomaly depended on syntactic structure (e.g., *The worm swallowed the bird*). His performance was not significantly affected by "padding" the base sentences with additional lexical material, a manipulation that significantly increased the distance between critical thematic role-bearing elements (e.g., *As the sun rose, the worm in the cool wet grass swallowed the bird quickly and went away*); on these considerably longer sentences, he was 74% correct. On the other hand, his performance was affected by increasing the complexity of the critical thematic role-bearing structures; he was 66% correct on syntactically complex versions of the base sentences, such as passive and cleft object constructions (e.g., *It was the bird that the worm swallowed*). Note that these sentences were shorter than the sentences in the padded condition. In TI's case, then, length is not the critical parameter in the interpretation of syntactically encoded information.

To summarize, all of the STM patients reported in the literature have shown some impairment in syntactic aspects of sentence comprehension, though the degree of impairment varies widely among them. The implication drawn from these data is that the STM deficit limits the patients' ability to process syntactic information. If so, one might expect length to be a significant factor in their performance. Evidence on this point, however, is inconsistent.

Before attempting to resolve these inconsistencies, we need to give more careful consideration to the issue of how a restriction on span might impinge on the processing of syntactic information.

STM in Sentence Processing: Where is it Needed?

To understand a sentence, it is presumably necessary to store the partial products of various analyses (lexical, syntactic, semantic) until a full interpretation can be constructed. Sentence processing therefore entails memory capacity at several levels. Because the comprehension difficulties of STM patients appear to be structurally based, our discussion focuses on the possible role of STM capacities in the processing of syntactic information.

At the level of extracting structural information from the input string (or parsing), two types of storage capacities are required. To make structural assignments, the parser needs to be able to look ahead over some number of successive items; this entails the capacity to store a linear array of lexical items. There must also be some means of storing structures that are not yet complete, to which additional material can subsequently be attached. Recent parsing models assign this function to a "push-down stack" (e.g., Marcus, 1980).

Do these capacities bear any relation to the information stores utilized in standard memory span tasks? The span-related capacities maintain information sufficient to specify the phonological form and linear order of roughly five lexical items. To the extent that structure-building operations depend on access to a linear array of lexical items, there would seem to be some commonality between the storage capacities that underlie span performance and those required in the computation of syntactic structure. It must be recognized, however, that the parser does not deal with phonological representations but rather with form class information and other syntactic characteristics of lexical items. The parser could not, therefore, be looking directly at information displayed in a phonological buffer.

It is nevertheless conceivable that the phonological representation provides support for the syntactic information that is read by the parser. In particular, a phonological record could serve a place-holding function, ensuring that order information is maintained despite differences in the rate at which items are processed by the lexical system. (Introspection provides an extreme example along these lines: When a word in a sentence cannot be immediately identified, it does not seem to undergo displacement.) The phonological record could conceivably serve as a sort of order template for other representations of the input string, much as the separately extracted features of visual input (color, shape, movement, etc.) are thought to be indexed to spatial location in vision (e.g., Marr, 1982)

If this notion is correct, limiting the phonological record would be expected to affect parsing operations—but only to the extent that the parser requires access to a linear array that exceeds the capacity of the limited record. The look-ahead capacity of current parsing models is, in fact, quite minimal (two to three items), and does not exceed the limited spans of most STM patients (e.g., Berwick & Weinberg, 1984; Marcus, 1980). Thus, the STM patient should not be at a disadvantage even if phonological support is required in parsing.

A direct test of the STM patient's ability to recover syntactic structure was carried out in TI (Saffran, 1985; Saffran & Martin, in press) by means of the grammaticality judgments task previously used to demonstrate preservation of syntactic abilities in agrammatic aphasics (Linebarger, Schwartz, & Saffran, 1983). His good performance on this task (93% correct) indicates that he was not, in fact, having difficulty at the level of parsing. TI was also tested on padded versions of a subset of the original sentences, in which as many as seven words intervened between the critical elements, as in the following sentences:

4. **Has* the little girl with brown curly hair *has* eaten her breakfast yet?
5. *He *let* a friend of his from out of town *to* drive the new car.
6. **How many* do you think that she and her husband actually have *friends* in Philadelphia?

TI again had little difficulty, performing at a level (85% correct) that was within the range of right-hemisphere controls. We conclude, on the basis of these results, that limited span is not an impediment to the structural operations required in the grammaticality judgment task. Nor, if we consider the matter carefully, would we expect it to be. To detect the violations in these strings, it is not necessary to look directly at a linear array containing both critical elements; detection must be based, rather, on the parser's inability to assimilate the anomalous element to the structure it has already built. Similar considerations apply in the more usual sorts of sentence processing tasks. If there is need for a verbatim record in sentence processing, it does not appear to be at the level of parsing.

Elsewhere, my colleagues and I suggested that the locus of the comprehension difficulty, for agrammatic aphasics as well as for patients like TI, is in the mapping from syntactic to semantic (thematic role) information (Schwartz et al., 1987; see also chapter 3). This argument rests on the finding that the patients' level of performance on comprehension tasks is related to the transparency of the mapping between grammatical role and thematic role; a nontransparent mapping is one that deviates from the canonical relationship between the grammatical subject and the agent role. Thus, the patients tend to have relatively little difficulty with the transparent reversible active sentences, but, perform at chance, or in some cases significantly below chance, on noncanonical structures such as passives and object relatives.

Is there a role for span capacities in the mapping process? This question is difficult to answer without specifying the representational form of the parser's output. If the parser delivers a representation on the order of a tree structure with lexically labeled terminal nodes, it should be possible to make thematic role assignments on the basis of this information alone. However, if the structural information is represented more abstractly, as in the case of a tree structure with unlabeled terminal nodes, there would need to be some way to link lexical items to structural locations. It is conceivable that the phonological representation could serve the same sort of indexing function here that was suggested earlier, linking structural constituents (e.g., NP, VP) to corresponding lexical items. If the linkages could not be maintained due to loss of the phonological record, errors could arise, particularly in cases where the thematic role of the subject NP remains indeterminate for some distance into the sentence, as in the following sentence:

7. The cat that the dog had been chasing was black.

For the STM patient, who runs more than the usual risk of losing information unless it is rapidly encoded into semantic form (e.g., Saffran & Marin, 1975), it may be beneficial to adopt a "quick and dirty" approach to thematic role assignment, which relies on local syntactic information, heuristics, and pragmatics. On this scenario, the patient is unlikely to wait for full syntactic specification of the pivotal agent role but will take the first plausible NP to be the agent. This strategy is likely to serve the patient reasonably well under normal circumstances, where discourse context serves to constrain role assignment. These constraints are, of course, lacking in the laboratory tasks in which the comprehension failures are manifested. Further difficulty may arise from the fact that the patient is unable to refer to a verbatim record in revising an interpretation contraindicated by information that comes later in the sentence.

The notion is, then, that the STM patient is likely to have difficulty in circumstances where there is—or optimally should be—some lag between the receipt of information and its semantic interpretation. One such circumstance is the one we have already considered, which involves certain syntactic structures; there may well be others, involving bottlenecks at the level of semantic processing, which have yet to be explored. To deal with the structural impediments to rapid semantic encoding, it is suggested that the patient relies excessively on pragmatics and heuristics. Such strategies are likely to vary from patient to patient, and differences in comprehension performance across patients are therefore to be expected. This complicates matters for researchers who are trying to make sense of these behavior patterns. But there is also a more positive implication: If sentence processing is as strategy-dependent as has been suggested, it is possible that such patients could be taught to make better use of the syntactic information that is available to them (see Byng, 1986, for a successful effort along these lines in agrammatic aphasics). Perhaps it is because these processes are so open to strategic modification that the developmental STM case, RE, demonstrated no evident impairment in sentence comprehension (Butterworth et al., 1986).

Unfortunately, the literature on normal sentence processing is of little help in resolving the issues we have been considering here. The few studies that would appear to implicate span capacity in sentence processing are open to alternative interpretations. Thus, although it has been shown that concurrent list memory and comprehension tasks are mutually interfering (Savin & Perchonock, 1965; Wanner & Maratsos, 1978), it is not clear that the limiting resource is a span-type capacity common to the two tasks. Other evidence that is presumed to be relevant to the role of STM in sentence processing comes from studies of phonological effects in written sentence comprehension. It has been reported, for example, that concurrent articulation is detrimental to performance on sentence processing tasks, presumably because it interferes with the phonological encoding of written materials (e.g., Baddeley & Lewis, 1981). This interpretation has been challenged on the grounds that the performance decrements associated with concurrent articulation could reflect general processing demands of the secondary task rather than effects specific to phonological interference (Waters, Komoda, & Arbuckle., 1985). In one study that attempted to control for general processing demands, White (1985) contrasted the effects of syllable shadowing with those of a nonverbal task, tone shadowing, on various sentence processing tasks. Although both shadowing tasks produced decrements in performance, syllable shadowing was particularly detrimental in tasks requiring the use of syntactic information.

The conclusion that emerges from the work on written sentence comprehension is that normal subjects benefit from phonological information in processing these materials. As Patterson and Coltheart (1987) pointed out, this is probably because linguistic systems primarily intended for speech input are addressed most efficiently via a phonological code. This special compatibility between phonological input and syntactic and semantic processing mechanisms may have to do with the strict sequencing afforded by a phonological code, as well as prosodic cues to constituent structure. To the extent that such capacities also contribute to performance in STM tasks, the data from these studies of written sentence comprehension support a link between sentence processing and STM.

CONCLUSION

The basic finding of an association between sentence comprehension deficits and span limitations in the STM patients stands, and remains provocative. Spelling out the nature of the relationship between STM and sentence processing proves to be no easy matter, however. Though much of the evidence points toward a relationship between STM deficit and syntactic aspects of sentence processing, consideration of the informational requirements of the parsing process, together with data from grammaticality judgment tasks, suggests that veridical preservation of the input string is not essential for the recovery of syntactic structure per se. The comprehension difficulties of these patients may lie, rather, in their failure to make adequate use of syntactic information in constructing a semantic interpretation of the input string. The risk of rapidly losing semantically unencoded information may force the STM patients into a mode of developing a semantic representation quickly, and often prematurely, on the basis of lexical, pragmatic, and local structural information.

As to the nature of the deficit that underlies the span limitations in STM patients, this, too, remains uncertain, though the available evidence does implicate capacities involved in the generation or maintenance of auditory/phonological representations. Recent evidence from normals that suggests that such representations are important in grouping information in input strings (Frankish & Turner, 1984) points to a line of investigation worth pursuing in these patients, one that might bridge the gap between language processing and processes traditionally considered to lie in the domain of STM.

ACKNOWLEDGMENTS

Preparation of this chapter was supported by grant number NS18429 from the National Institutes of Health.

REFERENCES

Allport, D. A. (1984). Auditory-verbal short term memory and aphasia. In H. Bouma & D. G. Bouwhuis (Eds.), *Attention and performance X: Control of language processes* (pp. 313–325). Hillsdale, NJ: Lawrence Erlbaum Associates.

Allport, D. A. (1985). Distributed memory, modular subsystems and dysphasia. In S. Newman & R. Epstein (Eds.), *Current perspectives in dysphasia* (pp. 32–61). Edinburgh: Churchill Livingstone.

Baars, B. J., Motley, M. T., & MacKay, D. G. (1975). Output editing for lexical status from artificially elicited slips of the tongue. *Journal of Verbal Learning and Verbal Behavior*, *14*, 382–391.

Baddeley, A. D. (1976). *The psychology of memory*. New York: Academic Press.

Baddeley, A. D., & Hitch, G. (1974). Working memory. In G. H. Bower (Ed.), *The psychology of learning and motivation: Advances in research and theory* (Vol. 8, pp. 47–90). New York: Academic Press.

Baddeley, A. D., & Lewis, V. (1981). Inner active processes in reading: The inner voice, the inner ear and the inner eye. In A. M. Lesgold & C. A. Perfetti (Eds.), *Interactive processes in reading* (pp. 107–129). Hillsdale, NJ: Lawrence Erlbaum Associates.

Baddeley, A. D., Lewis, V., & Vallar, G. (1984). Exploring the articulatory loop. *Quarterly Journal of Experimental Psychology*, *36A*, 233–252.

Baddeley, A. D., Thomson, N., & Buchanan, M. (1975). Word length and the structure of short-term memory. *Journal of Verbal Learning and Verbal Behavior*, *14*, 575–589.

Baddeley, A. D., & Wilson, B. (1985). Phonological coding and short-term memory in patients without speech. *Journal of Memory and Language*, *24*, 490–502.

Barnard, P. (1985). Interacting cognitive subsystems: A psycholinguistic approach to short-term memory. In A. W. Ellis (Ed.), *Progress in the Psychology of Language* (Vol. 2, pp. 197–258). Hillsdale, NJ: Lawrence Erlbaum Associates.

Basso, A., Spinnler, H., Vallar, G., & Zanobio, M. (1982). Left hemisphere damage and selective impairment of auditory-verbal short-term memory. *Neuropsychologia*, *20*, 263–274.

Berndt, R. S. (1985a, March). *Working memory and auditory sentence comprehension*. Paper presented at the Second Venice Conference on Cognitive Neuropsychology, Venice.

Berndt, R. S. (1985b, October). *Phoneme discrimination, short-term memory deficit and sentence comprehension: Some dissociations*. Paper presented at Academy of Aphasia, Pittsburgh, PA.

Berwick, R., & Weinberg, A. (1984). *The grammatical basis of linguistic performance. Langauge use and acquisition*. Cambridge: MIT press.

Bierwisch, M. (1983). How on-line is language processing? In G. B. Flores D'Arcais & R. J. Jarvella (Eds.), *The process of language understanding* (pp. 113-191). New York: Wiley.

Brener, R. (1940). An experimental investigation of memory span. *Journal of Experimental Psychology, 26*, 467–482.

Butterworth, B., Campbell, R., & Howard, D. (1986). The uses of short-term memory: A case study. *Quarterly Journal of Experimental Psychology, 38A*, 705–737.

Byng, S. (1986). *Sentence processing deficits in aphasia: Investigation and remediation.* Unpublished doctoral dissertation, University of London.

Campbell, R., & Butterworth, B. (1985). Phonological dyslexia and dysgraphia in a highly literate subject: A developmental case with associated deficits of phonemic processing and awareness. *Quarterly Journal of Experimental Psychology, 37A*, 435–475.

Campbell, R., & Dodd, B. (1980). Hearing by eye. *Quarterly Journal of Experimental Psychology, 32*, 85–99.

Campbell, R., & Dodd, B. (1984). Aspects of hearing by eye. In H. Bouma and D. G. Bouwhius (Eds.), *Attention and performance X* (pp. 300–311). Hillsdale, NJ: Lawrence Erlbaum Associates.

Caplan, D., Vanier, M., & Baker, C. (1986). A case study of reproduction conduction aphasia II: Sentence comprehension. *Cognitive Neuropsychology, 3*, 129–146.

Caramazza, A., Basili, A. G., Koller, J. J., & Berndt, R. S. (1981). An investigation of repetition and language processing in a case of conduction aphasia. *Brain and Language. 14*, 235–271.

Colle, H. A., & Welsh, A. (1976). Auditory masking in primary memory. *Journal of Verbal Learning and Verbal Behavior, 15*, 17–32.

Conrad, R., & Hull, A. J. (1964). Information, acoustic confusion, and memory span. *British Journal of Psychology, 55*, 429–432.

Craik, F. I. M., & Lockhart, R. S. (1972). Levels of processing: A framework for memory research. *Journal of Verbal Learning and Verbal Behavior, 11*, 671–684.

Crowder, R. G. (1971). The sounds of vowels and consonants in immediate memory. *Journal of Verbal Learning and Verbal Behavior, 10*, 587–597.

Crowder, R. G., & Morton, J. (1969). Precategorical acoustic storage (PAS). *Perception and Psychophysics, 5*, 365–373.

Darwin, C. J., Turvey, M. T., & Crowder, R. G. (1972). An auditory analogue of the Sperling partial report procedure: Evidence for brief auditory storage. *Cognitive Psychology, 3*, 255–267.

Drewnowski, A., & Murdock, B. B. (1980). The role of auditory features in memory span for words. *Journal of Experimental Psychology: Human Learning and Memory, 6*, 319–332.

Ellis, A. W. (1979). Speech production and short-term memory. In J. Morton & J. C. Marshall (Eds.), *Psycholinguistics series 2. Structures and processes* (pp. 157–187). London: Elek.

Forster, K., & Davis, C. (1984). Repetition priming and frequency attentuation in lexical access. *Journal of Experimental Psychology: Learning, Memory and Cognition, 10*, 680–698.

Frankish, C., & Turner, J. (1984). Delayed suffix effects at very short delays. *Journal of Experimental Psychology: Learning, Memory and Cognition, 10*, 767–777.

Friedrich, F., Glenn, C., & Marin, O. (1984). Interruption of phonological coding in conduction aphasia. *Brain and Language, 22*, 266–291.

Friedrich, F. J., Martin, R., & Kemper, S. J. (1985). Consequences of a phonological coding deficit on sentence processing. *Cognitive Neuropsychology, 2*, 385–412.

Garrett, M. F. (1975). The analysis of sentence production. In G. Bower (Ed.), *The psychology of learning and motivation* (Vol. 9, pp. 133–177). New York: Academic Press.

Garrett, M. F. (1980). Levels of processing in sentence production. In B. Butterworth (Ed.), *Language production* (pp. 177–220). London: Academic Press.

Glanzer, M. (1972). Storage mechanisms in recall. In G. H. Bower & J. T. Spence (Eds.), *The psychology of learning and motivation* (Vol. 5, pp. 129–193). New York: Academic Press.

Goodglass, H., & Kaplan, E. (1972). *The assessment of aphasia and related disorders*. Philadelphia: Lea & Febiger.

Greene, R. L., & Crowder, R. G. (1984). Modality and suffix effects in the absence of auditory stimulation. *Journal of Verbal Learning and Verbal Behavior, 23*, 371–382.

Hebb, D. O. (1961). Distinctive features of learning in the higher animal. In J. F. Delafresnaye (Ed.), *Brain mechanisms and learning: A symposium* (pp. 37–51). Oxford: Blackwell.

Heilman, K., Scholes, R., & Watson, R. T. (1976). Defects of immediate memory in Broca's and conduction aphasia. *Brain and Language, 3*, 201–208.

Jacoby, L. L. (1983). Perceptual enhancement: persistent effects of an experience. *Journal of Experimental Psychology: Learning, Memory and Cognition, 9*, 21–38.

Jahnke, J. E. (1968). Presentation rate and the serial position effect of immediate serial recall. *Journal of Verbal Learning and Verbal Behavior, 7*, 608–612.

Klapp, S. T., Marshburn, E. A., & Lester, P. T. (1983). Short-term memory does not involve the "working memory" of information processing: The demise of a common assumption. *Journal of Experimental Psychology: General, 112*, 240–264.

Linebarger, M. C., Schwartz, M. F., & Saffran, E. M. (1983). Sensitivity to syntactic structure in so-called agrammatic aphasics. *Cognition, 13*, 361–392.

Marcus, M. (1980). *A theory of syntactic recognition for written language*. Cambridge: MIT Press.

Marr, D. (1982). *Vision*. San Francisco: Freeman.

Martin, R. C. (1987). Articulatory and phonological deficits in short-term memory and their relation to syntactic processing. *Brain and Language, 32*, 159–192.

Martin, N., & Saffran, E. M. (1987). *Factors underlying repetition performance in a transcortical sensory aphasic*. Unpublished manuscript.

McClelland, J., & Elman, J. L. (1986). The TRACE model of speech perception. *Cognitive Psychology, 18*, 1–86.

Monsell, S. (1984). Components of working memory underlying verbal skills: A "distributed capacities" view. In H. Bouma & D. Bouwhuis (Eds.), *Attention and performance X* (pp. 327–350). Hillsdale, NJ: Lawrence Erlbaum Associates.

Monsell, S. (1985). Repetition and the lexicon. In A. Ellis (Ed.), *Progress in the psychology of language* (Vol. 2, pp. 147–195). Hillsdale, NJ: Lawrence Erlbaum Associates.

Morton, J., & Patterson, K. (1980). A new attempt at an interpretation, or, an attempt at a new interpretation. In M. Coltheart, K. Patterson, & J. C. Marshall (Eds.), *Deep dyslexia* (pp. 91–118). London: Routledge & Kegan Paul.

Murray, D. J. (1966). Vocalization-at-presentation and immediate recall, with varying recall methods. *Quarterly Journal of Experimental Psychology, 18*, 9–18.

Murray, D. J. (1968). Articulation and acoustic confusability in short-term memory. *Journal of Experimental Psychology, 4*, 679–684.

Nairne, J. S., & Walters, V. L. (1983). Silent mouthing produces modality- and suffix-like effects. *Journal of Verbal Learning and Verbal Behavior, 22*, 475–483.

Nebes, R. N. (1975). The nature of internal speech in a patient with aphemia. *Brain and Language, 2*, 489–497.

Ostergaard, A. L., & Meudell, P. R. (1984). Immediate memory span, recognition memory for subspan series of words and serial position effects in recognition memory for subspan series of verbal and nonverbal items in Broca's and Wernicke's aphasia. *Brain and Language, 22*, 1–13.

Parisi, D., & Pizzamiglio, L. (1970). Syntactic comprehension in aphasia. *Cortex, 6*, 204–215.

Patterson, K., & Coltheart, V. (1987). Phonological processes in reading: A tutorial review. In M. Coltheart (Ed.), *Attention and performance XII* (pp. 421–447) Hillsdale, NJ: Lawrence Erlbaum Associates.

Posner, M. I. (1964). Rate of presentation and order of recall in immediate memory. *British Journal of Psychology, 55*, 303–306.

Postman, L., & Phillips, L. W. (1965). Short-term temporal changes in free recall. *Quarterly Journal of Experimental Psychology, 17*, 132–138.

Saffran, E. M. (1985, March). *Short-term memory impairment and language comprehension: Specifying the nature of the interaction.* Paper presented at the Second Venice Conference on Cognitive Neuropsychology, Venice.

Saffran, E. M., & Marin, O. S. M. (1975).Immediate memory for word lists and sentences in a patient with deficient auditory short-term memory. *Brain and Language, 2*, 420–433.

Saffran, E. M., & Martin, N. (in press). Short-term memory impairment and sentence processing: A case study. In G. Vallar, & T. Shallice (Eds.) *Neuropsychological Impairments of Short-Term Memory*. Cambridge: Cambridge University Press.

Salame, P., & Baddeley, A. (1982). Disruption of short-term memory by unattended speech: Implications for the structure of working memory. *Journal of Verbal Learning and Verbal Behavior, 21*, 150–184.

Savin, H., & Perchonock, E. (1965). Grammatical structure and immediate recall of sentences. *Journal of Verbal Learning and Verbal Behavior, 9*, 348–353.

Schwartz, M. F., Linebarger, M. C., Saffran, E. M., & Pate, D. S. (1987). Syntactic transparency and sentence interpretation in aphasia. *Language and Cognitive Processes, 2*, 85–113.

Shallice, T. (1979). Neuropsychological research and the fractionation of memory systems. In L. G. Nilsson (Ed.), *Perspectives in memory research* (pp. 257–277). Hillsdale, NJ: Lawrence Erlbaum Associates.

Shallice, T., & Butterworth, B. (1977). Short-term memory impairment and spontaneous speech. *Neuropsychologia, 15*, 729–735.

Shallice, T., McLeod, P., & Lewis, K. (1985). Isolating cognitive modules with the dual-task paradigm: Are speech perception and production separate processes? *Quarterly Journal of Experimental Psychology, 37A*, 507–532.

Shallice, T., & Warrington, E. K. (1970). Independent functioning of verbal memory stores: A neuropsychological study. *Quarterly Journal of Experimental Psychology, 22*, 261–273.

Shallice, T., & Warrington, E. K. (1974). The dissociation between short term retention of meaningful sounds and verbal material. *Neuropsychologia, 12*, 553–555.

Shallice, T., & Warrington, E. K. (1977). Auditory-verbal short-term memory impairment and conduction aphasia. *Brain and Language, 4*, 479–491.

Shallice, T., & Warrington, E. K. (1980). Single and multiple component central dyslexic syndromes. In M. Coltheart, K. E., Patterson, & J. C. Marshall (Eds.), *Deep dyslexia* (pp. 257–277). London: Routledge & Kegan Paul.

Shand, M. A., & Klima, E. S. (1981). Nonauditory suffix effects in congenitally deaf signers of American Sign Language. *Journal of Experimental Psychology: Human Learning and Memory, 7*, 464–474.

Sternberg, S., Monsell, S., Knoll, R., & Wright, C. (1978). The latency and duration of rapid sequential movement sequences: Comparisons of speech and typewriting. In C. Stelmach (Ed.), *Information processing in motor control and learning* (pp. 117–152). New York: Academic Press.

Vallar, G., & Baddeley, A. (1984a). Fractionation of working memory: Neuropsychological evidence for a phonological short term store. *Journal of Verbal Learning and Verbal Behavior, 23*, 151–162.

Vallar, G., & Baddeley, A. (1984b). Phonological short-term store. Phonological processing and sentence comprehension: A neuropsychological case study. *Cognitive Neuropsychology, 1*, 121–141.

Vallar, G., & Cappa, S. F. (1987). Articulation and verbal short-term memory: Evidence from anarthria. *Cognitive Neuropsychology, 4*, 55–77.

Vallar, G., & Papagno, C. (1986). Phonological short-term store and the nature of the recency effect. Evidence from neuropsychology. *Brain and Cognition*, *5*, 428–442.

Warrington, E. K., Logue, V., & Pratt, R. T. C. (1971). The anatomical localization of selective impairment of auditory verbal short term memory. *Neuropsychologia*, *9*, 377–387.

Warrington, E. K., & Shallice, T. (1969). The selective impairment of auditory verbal short-term memory. *Brain*, *92*, 885–896.

Warrington, E. K., & Shallice, T. (1972). Neuropsychological evidence of visual storage in short-term memory tasks. *Quarterly Journal of Experimental Psychology*, *24*, 30–40.

Waters, G. S., Komoda, M. K., & Arbuckle, T. Y. (1985). The effects of concurrent tasks on reading: Implications for phonological recoding. *Journal of Memory and Language*, *24*, 27–45.

Watkins, M. J. (1977). The intricacy of memory span. *Memory and Cognition*, *5*, 529–435.

Watkins, M. J., & Watkins, O. C. (1977). Serial recall and the modality effect: Effects of word frequency. *Journal of Experimental Psychology: Human Learning and Memory*, *6*, 712–718.

Watkins, S. H. (1914). Immediate memory and its evaluation. *Journal of Psychology*, *7*, 319–348.

White, E. A. (1985). *Phonological processing in the comprehension of written words and sentences.* Unpublished doctoral dissertation, The Johns Hopkins University, Baltimore, MD.

Zhang, G., & Simon, H. A. (1985). STM capacity for Chinese words and idioms: Chunking and acoustical loop hypothesis. *Memory and Cognition*, *13*, 193–201.

6 Image Generation in the Cerebral Hemispheres

Jeffrey D. Holtzman
Cornell University Medical School

Stephen M. Kosslyn
Harvard University

Visual mental imagery is not a unitary phenomenon. Indeed, individual differences in imagery correspond to variations in at least a half a dozen distinct processes (see Kosslyn, Brunn, Cave, & Wallach, 1985). These processes have different roles in information processing, and must be studied individually. In this chapter we explore one way of studying such processing, namely by investigating selective deficits in neuropsychological populations. This approach makes sense in part because there is good neuropsychological evidence that imagery is not a unitary phenomenon: In their reviews of the literature on the neuropsychology of imagery, Ehrlichman and Barrett (1983) and Farah (1984) found evidence for imagery's being a left hemisphere, right hemisphere, and bilateral event. The findings they reviewed are based on the results of different tasks, which presumably draw on different underlying processes, and there is reason to suspect that different imagery processes are localized differently in the brain. This chapter lends some credence to this interpretation of the literature.

One of the most basic observations about mental images is that we do not have them all of the time. For example, introspect as you try to answer the following questions: Do a German Shepard's ears stick above the top of its skull? Which is larger, a goat or a hog? Or, how would your sofa look against the opposite wall in your living room? Introspection suggests, and empirical results confirm (see chapters 6 and 9 of Kosslyn, 1980), that images are generated to answer questions like these. The images were not present until they became useful, at which point they were somehow generated on the basis of stored information. Although introspection can alert one to the fact that an object or scene is present in an image, it does not tell one how such images are created. In this chapter we illustrate ways in which neuropsychological data are especially well suited for answering questions about the mechanisms underlying image generation.

Any theory of image generation must be capable of accounting for three classes of empirical findings: First, although objects introspectively may seem to be imaged all at once, this is not so. Researchers have consistently found that the time to form an image increases proportionally for each additional part of an object or scene included in the image (e.g., Beech & Allport, 1978; Kosslyn, Cave, Provost, & Von Gierke, 1988; Kosslyn, Reiser, Farah, & Fliegel, 1973; Paivio, 1975). For example, the time to form an image of a geometric pattern increases when the pattern is composed of increasing numbers of units, when units are defined by the Gestalt laws of proximity, similarity, good continuity, and other factors (see Kosslyn, 1980, chapters 4 and 6 for a review of much of the relevant literature). These data suggest that images can be built up on the basis of separately stored encodings. This inference is particularly apparent in the finding that subjects can "mentally glue" together fragments that were originally presented sequentially, and later can form a composite image of the entire object (see Experiment 2 of Kosslyn et al., 1983).

Second, people can use descriptions of how parts are to be arranged to juxtapose parts correctly into a composite image. For example, Kosslyn et al. (1983) gave subjects descriptions that specified the directions and distances among objects in a scene; these subjects were asked to image scenes such as a frying pan floating 6 feet above a bicycle that is 6 feet to the right of a rabbit. Subjects had no difficulty in performing this task. This inference was justified in part by the finding that, once the image was formed, the time to scan between objects in it increased for objects that should be imaged farther apart (see also Beech & Allport, 1978).

Third, people can form images of objects at different subjective sizes (i.e., so they seem to subtend different visual angles). This finding was reported by Bundesen and Larsen (1975), Farah and Kosslyn (1981), Hayes (1973), and Kosslyn (1975). Less time is generally required to image objects at smaller sizes than larger sizes, presumably because parts of objects are omitted at smaller sizes because of a grain constraint in imagery (see chapter 5 of Kosslyn, 1980). A grain constraint, analogous to that on a TV screen, prevents high resolution when objects are imaged at small sizes. This idea is supported by the finding that more time is required to "see" a part of an object imaged at a small size than a large size; this finding is consistent with subjects' reports of having to "zoom in" to "see" parts at the smaller sizes (see Kosslyn, 1980).

These classes of empirical results can be explained if we assume that images are generated using three independent sets of processes. First, one set presumably is necessary to activate information stored in long-term memory. This information can be a visual memory of a single part or object. Second, if more than one part is integrated into an image, processes are necessary that can use descriptions of relations to arrange the parts together. Third, because objects can be imaged at different sizes, the locations of separate parts cannot be specified using absolute locations in space; they must be specified relative to other parts. It has been shown that subjects can form multipart images by using such descriptions (e.g., of the position of a frying pan relative to a rabbit). Thus, there must be processes that "look" for the location of another part that is already in the image. In short, a multipart image would be generated by (a) activating stored visual memories; (b) looking up a representation of how a part is connected to the previously generated one (e.g., the "forearm is connected to the upper arm") and extracting the reference part (upper arm) and relation (connected to); and (c) "looking" for and locating the reference part in the image, and then forming the image of the new part at the correct size and relative location. Descriptions of parts and relations are particularly useful in this process, given that they explicitly indicate how parts are arranged. Indeed, a computer simulation model has been built that uses these sets of processes, and this model is capable of accounting for the aforementioned empirical findings (see Kosslyn, 1980, 1987).

Functional Dissociations

These empirical findings tell us what subjects are able to do when asked to perform specific tasks. They do not tell us how images are ordinarily processed. A critical question is whether stored descriptions of spatial relations of parts are used, at least some of the time, in generating images even when no descriptions have been explicitly provided in advance. If there are distinct processes that interpret and use descriptions, then we might expect to find evidence of *functional dissociation* following brain damage. That is, some imagery tasks that require arranging parts together should require this sort of processing, whereas imagery tasks that do not require arranging parts should not require using stored descriptions. If we find that certain kinds of brain damage selectively disrupt performance only when stored descriptions of spatial relations should be used, we have evidence for the existence of two distinct sets of processes.

The experiments reported here all involve testing split-brain patients. Our hypothesis is that when one generates an image containing separate parts, a stored description of how the parts are arranged together is accessed in certain cases. In particular, when objects assume numerous configurations, a description of their structure may usefully abstract out the invariant aspects of the shape. For example, all uppercase versions of the letter *A* have an enclosed form with two, roughly equal, legs extending down at the sides. Such a description presumably is stored mentally in some kind of abstract, language-like code. The processes that look up and use such descriptions presumably manipulate symbolic representations. Many of the deficiencies in the right hemisphere can be considered to be deficiencies in manipulation of symbolic representations (e.g., Sidtis, Volpe, Wilson, Rayport, & Gazzaniga, 1981). Hence, we asked whether there is a selective deficiency in image generation in the right hemispheres of these patients. That is, we had no reason to expect any difference in tasks that involve forming images of single perceptual units; but if stored descriptions are used to form images of some types of multipart objects, then we expected a right hemisphere deficit in these tasks. At the time it was made, this was an especially interesting prediction because it was counterintuitive: The common wisdom has it that the right hemisphere, not the left, should be superior at forming and using mental images (e.g., Springer & Deutsch, 1981). Further details on the experiments and analyses are reported in Kosslyn, Holtzman, Farah, and Gazzaniga (1985).

A RIGHT HEMISPHERE IMAGERY DEFICIT

We began by attempting to demonstrate an imagery deficit in the right hemisphere for a task that we believed required accessing stored descriptions. Consider the following question: Which uppercase letters of the alphabet have only straight lines, and which have some curves? Introspectively, this task seems to require imagery, and in fact was used by Coltheart, Hull, and Slater (1975) to study sex differences in imagery. Letters are clearly composed of separate parts (strokes), and hence presumably would be perceptually parsed into parts (in accordance with the Gestalt laws of organization and the like), and these parts would be stored as separate units. Moreover, most adults have seen a very large number of letters (millions?), and the exemplars of each letter may vary considerably in font, weight, size, and so on. On seeing so many varied examples, we may come to abstract out and store a description of how parts are to be arranged into a prototypical image of the letter. Indeed, introspectively this task seems to involve images of a particular sort: Most people report that when they image an uppercase *A*, for example, they do not image a specific letter they once actually saw (e.g., on the front page of yesterday's *New York Times*). Instead, they report imaging a somewhat fuzzy, canonical, typical *A*, often floating free of any background or context. This sort of image makes sense if one uses a description of a general shape—and not a memory of a particular example actually seen—to form the image.

We began by giving the straight/curved letter classification task to a person who had previously undergone surgical transection of his corpus callosum as a therapeutic intervention for the control of otherwise intractable epilepsy. The subject stared straight ahead while lowercase letters were presented briefly to the left or right visual field, which ensured that only the right or left hemisphere perceived a letter on a given trial, respectively. After seeing a lowercase letter, the patient was to decide whether the corresponding uppercase version had only straight lines or included any curved lines.

The subject in the first set of experiments was JW, who has been extensively described elsewhere (Gazzaniga, 1983; Gazzaniga & Smylie, 1984; Sidtis et al., 1981). Briefly, JW is a right-handed 30-year-old male who suffered from intractable epilepsy since the age of 19, and underwent corpus collosumectomy in 1979. When he was given a neurological examination 8 months after the completed operation, JW was found to have a normal IQ. When we tested him he was oriented, alert, and conversed easily about present and past events. He had a good sense of humor and a quick wit. Following recovery from surgery, it was demonstrated that his left cerebral hemisphere was for all intents and purposes normal; his right hemisphere could comprehend most statements but could not speak. For present purposes, it is important to note that his right hemisphere can comprehend individual words as well as relatively sophisticated instructions: For example, the right hemisphere can classify named objects in terms of super- and subordination, can judge synonymy and antynomy, and can use a precue to direct his eye movements (see Holtzman & Gazzaniga, 1984; Sidtis et al., 1981).

Before we could infer that a relative difficulty in performing the task in his right hemisphere implicates an image generation deficiency, we had to rule out a host of counterexplanations. These counterexplanations rest on ascribing deficits to some other, nonimagery, component of the task. Thus, in order to document a deficit in image generation, we had to demonstrate that JW's hemispheres could perform all steps of the task except generating the image. The task can be decomposed into the following steps: (a) read the lowercase cue; (b) use the cue to access information about the uppercase version; (c) generate an image of the uppercase version; (d) maintain the image long enough to evaluate it; (e) inspect the image; (f) evaluate the lines in the uppercase letter, making a curved/straight judgment; and (g) respond appropriately. Furthermore, one must understand what the task requires and must be able to put these steps together to perform the task as a whole. Failure to perform the task well could reflect a deficit in any one or combination of these abilities.

The first set of experiments, then, were a systematic attempt to document a right hemisphere deficit in performing the task and then to eliminate the alternative explanations of the failure of JW's right hemisphere to perform the task well. After demonstrating the deficit, we considered the possibility that the right hemisphere is deficient at some component of the straight/curved task other than use of one (or more) of the imagery processes, and we assessed the right hemisphere's ability to use that component in another task.

The results of the first experiment revealed the expected deficit in the right hemisphere, with 70% accuracy and 100% accuracy for the right and left hemispheres, respectively. However, the right hemisphere also responded faster (1.216 vs. 1.476 sec for the left), which may indicate that it made more errors due to a speed–accuracy trade-off. Perhaps the right hemisphere simply did not understand what was required.

In the next experiment we asked our subject to perform a perceptual analogue of the imagery task. This task served as a control for the right hemisphere's understanding the nature of the classification task, and for its ability to encode letters, evaluate shapes, and make the proper response. The subject briefly saw uppercase letters and made the straight/curved judgment on the basis of what he actually saw. Immediately following this control task we repeated the letter cue imagery task, urging the subject to be accurate.

In contrast to the results from the previous experiment, both hemispheres did very well on the perceptual classification task. The left and right hemispheres had 100% and 97.5% accuracy, respectively, and the response times revealed the same pattern as did the error rates: There was no effect of hemisphere (.877 vs. .876 sec for left vs. right hemisphere).

Both hemispheres clearly understood the perceptual control task and clearly could perform it. We now had reason to expect that the right hemisphere would understand the imagery classification task, and hence we repeated it immediately after the control task. Performance in the imagery task was still severely impaired in the right hemisphere, 62% compared to 100% correct for the left hemisphere. In addition, there now was no significant difference between the response times of the two hemispheres (.973 and .949 for the left and right, respectively), belying a possible speed–accuracy trade-off.

Although the right hemisphere was impaired, its performance was still slightly above what would be expected if it were just guessing. We suspected that JW was making his judgments partly on the basis of the appearance of the lowercase cues themselves; indeed, all lowercase letters that are composed only of straight lines have corresponding uppercase versions that are composed only of straight lines, so this is not such a bad strategy. The next experiment was designed to eliminate this strategy.

In the next experiment we considered the possibility that the poor performance of the right hemisphere was an artifact of a Stroop-like phenomenon, where what JW saw interfered with image generation or response. Thus, in this experiment we used auditory presentation of the stimuli, eliminating the possibility of interference from the lowercase visual cue. Furthermore, the nature of the response was made compatible with the straight/curved judgment itself, which allowed us to rule out a Stroop-type response conflict.

In this experiment, the subject again began by staring at the fixation dot. Now, however, he heard the name of one of the letters. He was told to make his judgment and then to look for an *X O* or *O X* pair on the screen. If the imaged uppercase letter had only straight lines, he was to point at the location on the screen where the *X* had appeared; if the letter had any curves, he was to point where the *O* had appeared. The pair was presented for 150 msec to one side, so that even though both hemispheres heard the auditory cue, only one knew where to point.

The error rated revealed the now-familiar pattern: The left hemisphere did very well, making correct judgments on 95% of the trials, whereas the right hemisphere did very poorly, making correct judgments on only 52% of the trials. Thus, when the influence of the lowercase cues themselves was eliminated, performance in the right hemisphere was at chance. This is just as would be expected if images of letters simply cannot be constructed in this hemisphere.

Before we could infer an image generation deficit in the right hemisphere, we had to demonstrate that the right hemisphere could evaluate an image of uppercase letters. We were concerned that perhaps the right hemisphere could generate images but could not maintain them long enough to make the judgment. Or perhaps images are dimmer than percepts, and the "mind's eye" in the right hemisphere has less acuity than in the left hemisphere and so cannot effectively classify these dimmer patterns. Thus, in the next experiment we showed that JW's right hemisphere can perform the straight/curved judgment on images, except that the images he used in this task were not generated from long-term memory, but instead were simply retained from external input. That is, we assume that images can be evoked either by generating them from information stored in long-term memory, as has been discussed so far, or by briefly retaining on-line perceptual input.

The subject was tested in two conditions. The cue-before condition was intended as a baseline, given that this task contained all but the imagery components of processing. In this task, the subject was given the cue 1, 2, or 3 seconds before a three-letter word was presented. This cue told the subject that we wanted him to classify the first, second, or third letter of the word; all stimuli were uppercase three-letter words. Approximately one second after the cue was given verbally, a word was briefly presented to one visual field. The subject had to select the appropriate letter and classify it as having all straight lines or some curved lines, pressing buttons as usual. The cue-after condition differed only in that the cue was presented approximately two seconds after the word was presented. Thus, we assumed that the subject had to maintain an image of the word, which he then used to select the proper letter and make the classification (Kosslyn et al., 1985, defend this assumption). Note that even though the cues were given aloud, and hence were available to both hemispheres, lateralizing the words prevented both hemispheres from making the judgment.

There were no significant differences in accuracy in the analysis of the cue-before data, with accuracies of 95.8% versus 87.5% for the left and right hemisphere, respectively; in contrast, the analysis of response times revealed that the left hemisphere was faster than the right (1.646 vs. 2.265 sec). Similarly, in the cue-after data there were no significant comparisons in the analysis of the accuracy data, 95.8% versus 83.3%, for the left and right hemispheres; and the response times again were more sensitive to differences in the different conditions: Less time was required in the left hemisphere (4.018 vs. 4.769 sec; note that these times include the retention interval).

The critical analyses included both the cue-before and cue-after data. This was desirable because the cue-before task has all processing components in common with the cue-after task except those involved in imagery processing. Thus, the cue-before results provide a baseline against which we could discover the extent to which the ability to maintain or inspect an image might be affecting performance in the straight/curved imagery task. The important result was that the hemispheres performed equivalently in both conditions, with the same difference in error rates and response times occurring in both tasks. Thus, relative to the cue-before perceptual baseline, both hemispheres can perform the imagery task at equivalent levels.

To ensure that the right hemisphere had not suddenly gotten the idea of what we wanted, we administered the lower cue task immediately after the word evaluation tasks; indeed, the stimulus letters used here were identical to those used as target letters in the words. The results were as usual: The left hemisphere was more accurate than the right (100% vs. 60%), and, as before, the left was faster (1.318 vs. 2.032 sec).

These results are strong support for the inference that JW has a specific image generation deficit in his right cerebral hemisphere. When an image had to be maintained, both hemispheres performed the task as well, relative to the nonimagery baseline performance. But even after performing well in the image inspection task, he still could not perform the image generation task in his right hemisphere.

However, one might argue that the right hemisphere simply did not understand what we wanted it to do or that it was incapable of performing multistep tasks. Perhaps JW's right hemisphere is simply deficient at tasks that require more than one step. These concerns motivated us to perform another kind of perceptual control, which required the subject to view slides of pairs of letters. The upper- and lowercase versions of a letter were tachistoscopically presented side by side, and the subject was asked to pick out the uppercase version and to classify it as having all straight lines or some curves. Both versions were drawn at the same size, so size could not be used as a cue in the selection phase. This task, then, provided a control for several of the steps in the imagery task. First, both hemispheres had to understand what we meant in the instructions when we referred to uppercase letters. Second, both hemispheres had to select uppercase letters per se. Third, the judgment had to be made following selection of a stimulus. Thus, if the subject's difficulty in the imagery task is in fact due to confusion about the appearance of the uppercase letters, difficulties in making the judgment, or difficulty in integrating the two tasks together, then he should have difficulty in performing this task.

The analysis of accuracy rates revealed that the right hemisphere was actually more accurate than the left (93% vs. 80%), and there was no difference in the response times of the two hemispheres (2.439 sec vs. 2.238 sec for the left vs. right, respectively). Both hemispheres quickly caught on to what was required in the task and could select and evaluate the uppercase stimuli. Thus, these results demonstrate that JW's right hemisphere is capable of selecting the proper letter, evaluating it, and putting the two steps together.

Another remaining counterexplanation of the right hemisphere's failure on the straight/curved imagery task is that the right hemisphere simply did not understand what it was supposed to do when given the lowercase cue. In another experiment we first established baseline performance in the lowercase cue task. We then urged the subject to be cautious in responding and to consider his decisions carefully; following this, we provided feedback about accuracy of performance. The feedback provided the right hemisphere with examples of what we wanted, which in conjunction with the instructions should have made the nature of the task as clear as possible. The feedback procedure had the desired effect; by the fourth block of trials there was no significant difference in accuracy between the hemispheres, 100% for the left and 90% for the right. Finally, after we had the right hemisphere performing well, we switched to a new set of letters. If the improved performance following feedback was due to the subject's finally understanding what to image, and this was the only problem all along, then we expected that his ability to perform the task would transfer to the new letters. However, if the improved performance was merely the result of the right hemisphere's memorizing stimulus response pairs, then we would not expect transfer to new letters.

It is of interest, then, that when we switched to a new set of letters, there was virtually no transfer of practice in the right hemisphere: The overall accuracy of the two hemispheres was 95% and 66.7%, for the left and right, respectively. In addition, there was no overall difference in times for the two hemispheres in the initial trials, but we again found slower times for the right hemisphere when we switched to the new letters.

In summary, we demonstrated that JW's right hemisphere can encode letters; select uppercase versions of letters (as well as read a cue in one case and pick out the corresponding other-case letter; see Farah, Gazzaniga, Holtzman, & Kosslyn, 1985); retain an imaged pattern long enough to inspect it; inspect an imaged pattern; make the straight/curved judgment; make the responses; and integrate multiple steps together in similar tasks. And we showed that the problem is not due to this hemisphere's classifying only what it sees or being disrupted by conflicting visual input. In short, the data taken together implicated a specific deficit in JW's right hemisphere, namely a deficit in generating images of letters.

ISOLATING THE DEFICIT

At this point we had demonstrated that JW's right cerebral hemisphere has a deficit in generating visual mental images of letters of the alphabet. However, we did not know which of the component processes used in generating images is defective in his right hemisphere. We initially hypothesized that the right hemisphere would be impaired when it needed to invoke processes that use stored descriptions of spatial relations, resulting in a deficit when it must arrange the segments of a letter to form the image. However, the observed deficit might indicate that the processes that activate stored perceptual units produce only very faint, weak images, which cannot be used effectively; or, perhaps both types of processes are deficient. Alternatively, perhaps image generation is in fact accomplished by a single process, and the right hemisphere is simply impaired at image generation in general. In addition, the previous results do not tell us whether the observed deficit is specific to images of letters and words, or is more general. Thus, we conducted another series of experiments to gain a more fine-grained understanding of the deficit.

Our hypothesis was that JW's right hemisphere cannot form images of letters of the alphabet because these images must be formed by amalgamating distinct parts. If so, then we had no reason to expect a deficit when images having only one part must be formed. The next question we asked was whether both cerebral hemispheres in our first patient could in fact generate images of global shapes (which may be thought of as the output from a low spatial frequency bandpass filter), which presumably are stored as single perceptual units. If so, we have evidence that the processes that activate stored visual information operate in both hemispheres of this subject.

The first task we used in this experiment required the subject JW to decide which of two similar-sized objects, such as a goat and a hog, was the larger. We used this task partly because Kosslyn, Murphy, Bemesderfer, and Feinstein (1977) and Kosslyn (1980, chapter 9) found that subjects used images of the two shapes to make the judgment. They asked their subjects to begin by forming a tiny image or a normal sized image of one of the to-be-compared objects, and then presented the name of a second object. The subjects were asked to decide whether this object was larger than the first. Subjects were explicitly instructed that they did not have to use the image of the first object in making the decision; they were told simply to make the judgment as quickly as possible. The results of this experiment supported the claim that imagery is in fact used to make the judgment: More time was taken if the first object was imaged at a tiny size; the subjects later claimed that they had to "zoom in" on this object in order to compare it to the second one, and such zooming in was not necessary when the first object has been previously imaged at a normal size. This finding was only obtained for objects that were of similar sizes. For objects that were not similar in size, such as an elephant and a rabbit, there was no effect of the size of the initial image on judgment time; in this case, the subjects usually claimed not to use imagery to make the comparison. This finding makes sense if we store a size category with each object, with "large" for an elephant and "small" for a rabbit. If so, then simply accessing and comparing the stored category labels would allow one to make the judgment. But this strategy would not work when one compared two similar-sized objects, which are likely to be classified in the same way. For example, a goat and a hog might both be classified as medium-sized; in this case, knowing the size categories does not help, and one is forced to use imagery to make the comparison (see chapter 9 of Kosslyn, 1980).

Thus, JW was told that he soon would see the names of animals, each lateralized to one side or the other (ensuring that only one hemisphere could read it). When he saw a name, he was to press the button labeled goat if a goat was larger than that animal, or the button labeled other if the named animal was larger than a goat. The results were straightforward and dramatic: Both hemispheres could perform this task. Indeed, only one error was committed in the entire experiment (for *moose* which he apparently misread as *mouse*). And there was no significant difference between the hemispheres in response time (1.203 vs. 1.264 sec for the left and right, respectively). We were concerned that perhaps some of the comparison objects were too disparate in size, allowing the judgment to be made without imagery. Thus, we performed additional analyses to examine only the five animals just larger than a goat and the five animals just smaller than a goat. All of these items were evaluated correctly in both hemispheres, and response times from the two hemispheres were virtually identical (1.318 sec and 1.319 sec for the left and right hemispheres).

In short, then, these data suggest that both hemispheres can form images of single perceptual units (general shapes), as is required to evaluate the relative sizes of similar-sized objects.

In the next experiment we tested JW in a second task that required subtle spatial distinctions, and hence was likely to require imagery. We now lateralized the names of easily imaged objects, and JW decided whether each object is higher than it is wide. This experiment served two purposes: First, it provided additional converging evidence for our claim that both hemispheres can form images as long as parts do not have to be assembled. Second, it dealt with a methodological problem evident in the previous task: Both Hemispheres were essentially perfect, this ceiling effect may have prevented us from discovering whether one hemisphere is in fact better at generating images of overall shape. The stimuli used in the higher-than-wide task were more difficult to evaluate than those used in the previous task, which would allow a meaningful comparison of the hemispheres' performance. Indeed, although neither hemisphere was even close to performing perfectly in this task, there was no significant difference in the accuracy of the two hemispheres (70.8% v. 66.7% for left and right, respectively), and there was no systematic difference in the response times from the two hemispheres (2.266 vs. 2.318 sec for left and right).

In short, the left and right hemispheres could perform two imagery tasks that do not involve generating multipart images. Only a low-resolution image of the overall shape envelope is necessary to decide whether one object is larger than another or to determine the aspect ratio of a single object, and such an envelope can be stored as a single perceptual unit. Thus, we have reason to believe that the processes that activate stored perceptual information operate effectively in both hemispheres. This inference makes sense given that both hemispheres can store visual memories, and there is no compelling reason why these stored memories cannot be activated to reinstate a visual image of the stored object or part.

So far, one could argue simply that JW's right hemisphere can form images of objects but not of letters. This is not implausible, given the left hemisphere's well-documented involvement in reading (see Geschwind, 1965). The next question we faced, then, was whether both hemispheres could perform as well when images of nonlinguistic stimuli must be formed from separate parts. In the next experiment we used the same materials used in the previous size comparison experiment. Now, however, we asked our subject whether the ears of each animal protrude above the top of its skull or whether they flop down along the side of its skull. To get a better sense of this task, try to evaluate the ears of a beagle, a mouse, or a sheep. Kosslyn and Jolicoeur (1980) and Jolicoeur and Kosslyn (1981) found that people use imagery in making just this sort of judgment, and fortunately JW was familiar with many animals and could make these evaluations reliably. We expected the right hemisphere to be impaired in this task because the judgment requires that two parts, the ears and the skull, be properly placed in the image.

The results from this experiment were in sharp contrast to those obtained in the other experiments that used words as stimuli. Now, the right hemisphere performed at chance, compared to excellent performance for the left hemisphere (87.5% vs. 45% correct for the left and right hemispheres, respectively). There was no significant difference in the response times of the two hemispheres (2.139 and 2.315 sec for the left and right, respectively). These results are quite similar to those from the letter imagery task.

At this point we took pause, and again questioned whether we had really identified a deficit in a particular class of processes, or had observed something more general. To answer this question, we performed one last set of experiments with JW; these experiments were designed to demonstrate that we had discovered something more specific than a deficit in memory for details or in serial processing. The logic of these experiments was that if JW can use an alternative retrieval strategy to perform the task in his right hemisphere, then he must have had the relevant information stored in memory: and if this strategy requires serial processing, and he can carry it out, then the selective deficits we observed could not have been due to problems in performing serial processing.

The next experiments were grounded in neuropsychological findings on the apraxias and the visual agnosias, which imply that motor and visual memories can be separately spared or impaired after brain damage. The existence of alexia (inability to read) without agraphia (inability to write) and vice versa makes this point especially strongly for letters (see Geschwind, 1965). We had already shown that JW could read words (strings of letters), and so he must have had the representations of letters stored in long-term memory. In addition, JW is an excellent artist; he is able to draw highly realistic renditions of cars and other objects from memory. Thus, we attempted to lead JW to perform the task by asking him to draw (print) the uppercase versions of letters. If he could perform the task using a drawing strategy, but not an imagery one, we could argue that his deficit is not in memory for details, serial processing, or in processes used to perform both activities.

We began simply by asking JW to view lateralized lowercase cues and then to draw the corresponding uppercase versions of the letters with his left hand and with his eyes closed. He could do this perfectly when the letters were presented to the right hemisphere. We next asked him to "draw the letters" in his head during the basic lowercase cue imagery task. At first these instructions were of no use to him, but when we asked him to begin by physically drawing the uppercase versions of the first three lowercase cues, and then to classify the uppercase version, he was successful. After the first three letters we told him to do the same thing, but without actually drawing the letters; to "draw them" in his mind. An experimenter held his hand down before he responded (in an attempt to preclude solution by proprioception or gross cross-cueing), and the experimenter did not watch the lowercase stimuli (and hence could not provide nonverbal cues on how to respond correctly). By the end of these trials, both hemispheres were performing perfectly. However, even though the right hemisphere developed the ability to perform the task, it was still slower than the left (6.054 vs. 4.351 sec).

Finally, to ensure that the right hemisphere could indeed perform the task—as opposed to merely learning responses for the particular stimuli we used—we simply switched the stimuli to a set of new letters. If JW's right hemisphere had indeed learned a new way of performing the task, we expected generalization to the new letters. Again, the right hemisphere performed as well as the left, 87.5% versus 95%. However, the left hemisphere again was faster than the right.

These results are in sharp contrast to those found earlier with JW: His right hemisphere could now perform the straight/curved imagery task. The impairment observed before clearly does not reflect a deficit in memory for the form of letters or in serial processing in general. However, he still took more time in the right hemisphere, and was in general much slower than he was in the earlier experiments (in which times usually were in the one and two second range, as opposed to the three or more second range here). Apparently, we helped JW discovery an alternate access route to the stored information about the letters' shapes. But even so, this access route was not equally efficient in the two hemispheres.

Variation in Right Hemispheres

We tested a second subject, VP, whose right hemisphere has different abilities than JW's. We originally decided to test split-brain patients in our imagery tasks because we suspected that symbol manipulation was used in generating images of multipart objects, and we hypothesized that the right hemisphere was relatively impaired at such abilities. The second subject we tested has an exceptional degree of reasoning and linguistic ability in her right hemisphere, which we suspected might be correlated with an ability to form multipart images. Thus, we wished to compare the deficits in VP's processing with those in JW's processing, looking for a single underlying pattern cutting across different deficits.

We started our investigation of VP's imagery abilities with the straight/curved imagery task used before, presenting lateralized lowercase cues. We again found better performance in the left hemisphere (95% vs. 67.5%), but the difference in response times between the hemispheres was not significant (4.166 and 4.933 sec for the left and right, respectively).

We next conducted the simple perceptual control task, presenting the uppercase letters themselves and asking VP to judge the stimuli she saw. Again mirroring the findings with JW, there were no significant differences in the accuracy data, with both hemispheres performing virtually perfectly (100% and 97.5% for left and right, respectively); nor was there a significant difference in the response times of the two hemispheres (2.409 and 2.950 sec for left and right).

We next tested VP in another set of the lowercase cue imagery task. Although the left hemisphere was still marginally more accurate than the right, the right hemisphere was now performing at 87.5% accuracy; at the end of the session, there was no difference in the accuracy of the two hemispheres (100% vs. 95%), nor was there a significant difference in the response times. These findings, then, were strikingly different from those from the first patient.

We were impressed by the performance of VP's right hemisphere, and worried that it might be performing so well because it discovered some trick; perhaps it had simply memorized the responses from the previous perceptual control task (which used the same letters). Thus, we performed another experiment, using a different task: We now presented the lowercase cues and asked VP to decide whether there is a vertical line at the far left of the corresponding uppercase letter (e.g., as is true for *b* and *d*, but not *a* and *c*). We reasoned that if her right hemisphere had merely learned the responses to the letters, it should perform at close to chance in this task. On the other hand, if the right hemisphere did in fact generate images of the letters, then there should be considerable transfer to the new task, even though it requires a different judgment.

The results of this experiment indicated that the right hemisphere had indeed become able to generate images of the letters. Although accuracy initially was superior in the left hemisphere, by the second set of trials performance was markedly improved in the right hemisphere and there was no significant difference in performance between the hemispheres (95% vs. 80% for the left and right, respectively). In addition, there was no difference between the response times of the two hemispheres (4.362 and 4.238 sec).

The results from this experiment gave us good reason to believe that VP could form images of the letters. By the second set of trials her right hemisphere was performing the new task about as well as she performed the original task on the fifth set of trials. Furthermore, performance in the imagery task did not differ for the two hemispheres relative to performance in a perceptual control task. These findings are especially impressive because the responses required here often conflicted with those required for the straight/curved task, and thus there is the possibility of proactive interference.

The results demonstrated that VP's right hemisphere can generate images of letters with practice, but practice is definitely required. One interpretation of these results is that one or more of the processes simply took time to warm up. If so, we reasoned, then once the processes are all operating, the right hemisphere should be able to image any letters. Thus, in the next experiment we asked VP to perform the basic straight/curved imagery task with a new set of letters.

The results of this experiment were striking: With the set of new letters, the right hemisphere was back where it started from, again being less accurate and requiring more time than the left hemisphere (83.3% versus 63.3% for the left and right hemisphere, with response times of 4.409 and 5.812 seconds for the left and right hemisphere, but the difference in times was only marginally significant).

The results from VP are interesting in part because VP, unlike JW, did not in fact have a complete transection of her corpus callosum. That is,

Magnetic Resonance Imaging (MRI) revealed that the surgeons inadvertently spared bundles of fibers in her splenium and in her rostrum. The splenium is known to be a part of the corpus callosum involved in transmitting visual information between the hemispheres, and there is some suggestion that the rostrum may be involved in transmitting semantic information between the hemispheres. One interpretation of our results, then, is that the left hemisphere simply got better at interpreting degraded information coming over from the right hemisphere, and the left hemisphere was in fact responsible for performing the task.

CONCLUSIONS

The results of our experiments with JW are easily summarized: There was a clear dissociation between the right hemisphere's ability to perform imagery tasks that require integrating separate parts and imagery tasks that do not require integrating parts. In contrast, the left hemisphere was adept at both sorts of imagery tasks. We expected to find this pattern of results if, as we hypothesized, processes that activate visual memories are intact in both hemispheres but ones that use stored descriptive information to arrange parts are impaired in the right hemisphere. We showed that the deficit was not due to problems in encoding the cues, accessing the case representations, retaining images, inspecting imaged patterns, evaluating shape, or making the correct response. We also showed that the deficit was not due to a more general problem in accessing stored information about visual details or in performing sequential processing. By considering the various control tasks that the right hemisphere could do, in contrast to the imagery tasks it could not do, we conclude that imagery involves at least one process that is not used in reading words, perceptual recognition, or printing.

The results of this study emphasize the conclusion that imagery is not a simple event, and it does not take place entirely within a single part of the brain. Attempts to localize the imagery system as an undifferentiated whole to one hemisphere (usually the right) have not been successful (see Ehrlichman & Barrett, 1983). In this chapter we demonstrated the usefulness of a fine-grained analysis of the components of information processing used in imagery for understanding how one aspect of imagery, image generation, is lateralized in split-brain patients.

AFTERWORD

Jeffrey D. Holtzman died on May 16, 1985, at the age of 34. He fell ill suddenly, and a month later succumbed to Wegner's Disease, a rate autoimmune disorder. This chapter was written posthumously by the second author, who tried to summarize the work from Holtzman's point of view. Since then the second author's views have continued to evolve (e.g., Kosslyn, 1987, 1988), but this chapter does not include these more recent developments (it is not clear how Jeff would have regarded them, he being very acute and sensibly critical).

On a personal note, working closely with Jeff in the design and execution of the experiments with JW was an exhilarating experience, one of the high points of my life. Almost all of the experiments were conceived on-the-spot in a mobile van parked at the patient's home, and nailing down the phenomenon was done on-line as new results were obtained. As soon as a result was in, Jeff led the debate about its possible interpretations; the patient's break was over as soon as we agreed on a new control and Jeff reprogrammed the computer for the next phase. Jeff Holtzman had a mind like none I have never known; he was lightning-fast and extremely analytical. Jeff was quite possibly the world's best critic of interpretations of empirical results; if there was a hole, he spotted it, usually immediately. If an idea survived his scrutiny, you knew you had nothing to worry about when it came time to throw yourself on the mercy of the journal reviewers; if it did not pass muster, he sugar-coated his criticism with ample dollops of humor, and usually threw in a positive suggestion or two. The work reported here is an example of the contribution Jeff made, as are the written reports of all of the people who habitually consulted with him during the design and writing phases of their research. It is no exaggeration to point out that the loss of Jeffrey Holtzman is not just a loss for his family, friends, and colleagues, but for the field as a whole.

ACKNOWLEDGMENTS

Preparation of this chapter was supported by ONR Contract N00014-85-K-0291, and NIMH Grant MH 39478, and AFOSR Grant 88-0012.

REFERENCES

Beech, J. R., & Allport, D. A. (1978). Visualization of compound scenes. *Perception, 7*, 129–138.

Bundesen, C., & Larsen, A. (1975). Visual transformation of size. *Journal of Experimental Psychology: Human Perception and Performance, 1*, 214–220.

Coltheart, M., Hull, E., & Slater, D. (1975). Sex differences in imagery and reading. *Nature, 253*, 438–440.

Erlichman, H., & Barrett, J. (1983). Right hemisphere specialization for mental imagery: A review of the evidence. *Brain and Cognition, 2*, 55–76.

Farah, M. J. (1984). The neurological basis of mental imagery: A componential analysis. *Cognition, 18*, 245—272.

Farah, M. J., Gazzaniga, M. S., Holtzman, J. D., & Kosslyn, S. M. (1985). A left hemisphere basis for visual imagery? *Neuropsychologia, 23*, 115-118.

Farah, M. J., & Kosslyn, S. M. (1981). Structure and strategy in image generation. *Cognitive Science, 4*, 371-383.

Gazzaniga, M. S. (1983). Right hemisphere language following brain bisection: A 20-year perspective. *American Psychologist, 38*, 525-537.

Gazzaniga, M. S., & Smylie, C. S. (1984). Dissociations of language and cognition: A psychological profile of two disconnected right hemispheres. *Brain, 107*, 145-153.

Geschwind, N. (1965). Disconnexion syndromes in animals and man. *Brain, 88*, 237-294, 585-644.

Hayes, J. R. (1973). On the function of visual imagery in elementary mathematics. In W. G. Chase (Ed.), *Visual information processing*. (pp. 177-214). New York: Academic Press.

Holtzman, J. D., & Gazzaniga, M. S. (1984). *Enhanced dual task performance following corpus commissurotomy in humans*. Unpublished manuscript, Cornell Medical College, New York.

Jolicoeur, P., & Kosslyn, S. M. (1985). Are image scanning effects due to demand characteristics? *Memory and Cognition, 13*, 320-332.

Kosslyn, S. M. (1975). Information representation in visual images. *Cognitive Psychology, 7*, 341-370.

Kosslyn, S. M. (1980). *Image and mind*. Cambridge, MA: Harvard University Press.

Kosslyn, S. M. (1987). Seeing and imagining in the cerebral hemispheres: A computational approach. *Psychological Review, 94*, 148-175.

Kosslyn, S. M., Brunn, J., Cave, K. R., & Wallach, R. W. (1984). Individual differences in mental imagery: A computational analysis. *Cognition, 18*, 195-243.

Kosslyn, S. M., Cave, C. B., Provost, D. A., & Von Gierke, S. N. (1988). Sequential processes in image generation. *Cognitive Psychology, 20*, 319-343.

Kosslyn, S. M., & Jolicoeur, P. (1980). A theory-based approach to the study of individual differences in mental imagery. In R. E. Snow, P. A. Federico, & W. E. Montague (Eds.), *Aptitude, learning, and instruction: Cognitive processes analysis of aptitude* (Vol. 1, pp. 139-176). Hillsdale, NJ: Lawrence Erlbaum Associates.

Kosslyn, S. M., Holtzman, J. D., Farah, M. J., & Gazzaniga, M. S. (1985). A computational analysis of mental image generation: Evidence from functional dissociations in split-brain patients. *Journal of Experimental Psychology: General, 114*, 311-341.

Kosslyn, S. M., Murphy, G. L., Bemesderfer, M. E., & Feinstein, K. J. (1977). Category and continuum in mental comparisons. *Journal of Experimental Psychology: General, 106*, 341-375.

Kosslyn, S. M., Reiser, B. J., Farah, M. J., & Fliegel, S. J. (1983). Generating visual images: units and relations. *Journal of Experimental Psychology: General, 112*, 278-303.

Paivio, A. (1975). Imagery and synchronic thinking. *Canadian Psychological Review, 16*, 147-163.

Sidtis, J. J., Volpe, B. T., Wilson, D. H., Rayport, M., & Gazzaniga, M. S. (1981). Variability in right hemisphere language function after callosal section: Evidence for a continuum of generative capacity. *Journal of Neuroscience, 1*, 323—331.

Springer, S. P., & Deutsch, G. (1981). *Left brain, right brain*. San Francisco: W. H. Freeman.

7 Hierarchical Distributed Networks in the Neuropsychology of Selective Attention

Michael I. Posner
University of Oregon, Eugene

In 1980 I was asked to give the Seventh F. C. Bartlett lecture at Oxford University. The topic was orienting of attention. My thesis was that it was possible to measure time-locked shifts of attention, both to central instructional cues and to changes in eye position, with almost as much precision and ease as overt shifts of eye position. I was enormously excited by these experiments, because I believed they were a powerful demonstration of the ability of cognitive psychologists to explore internal mental operations by careful time measurements.

Similar results had already been obtained in such well-known experimental paradigms as letter matching (Posner, Boies, Eichelman, & Taylor, 1969), memory scanning (Sternberg, 1966), mental rotation (Shepard & Metzler, 1971) and priming (Neely, 1977). All of these paradigms were intrinsically more interesting to cognitive psychologists than detecting light flashes in an otherwise dim field, which was the methodology employed in the experiments described in my 1980 lecture. Why then the excitement? It was because, unlike the more complex situations, these new experiments were ones that were then being done in alert monkeys. The presence of an animal model seemed to me an opportunity to determine whether the results obtained from performance studies of normal humans converged with those using single-cell methodology in the study of spatial attention, where both methods could be employed. If they did, it would be evidence that cognitive and neuroscience techniques could be used together to provide an integrated picture of how neural systems produce cognition. In 1980 I was forced to hedge seriously on this promise by stating that there is nothing in our results that can prove that the spatial attention mechanisms that we study are identical to those under investigation in areas of the parietal lobe.

Level	General Examples	Covert Orienting Task Examples
Task	Reading, Speaking, Imagery	Covert Orienting
Elementary Operations	Next, Scan, Name, Zoom	Disengage, Move, Engage
Component Analysis	Facilitate Pathway; Inhibit Pathway	Facilitate Location
Neural System	Processing Negativity PET Blood Flow	Midbrain (Superior Colliculus) Parietal Lobe
Cellular Activity	Selective Enhancement	Light-Sensitive Cells

FIG. 7.1 A general framework for relating cognitive and neural systems.

For the last 5 years I have been attempting to provide the missing proof, as part of an effort to bring together the studies of cognition and neuroscience. I believe our results provide substantial additional support to the common assumption of neuropsychology that neural systems support cognition and further suggest a view of how this is done in detail.

FRAMEWORK

It has been useful to view these studies in relationship to a general framework for relating cognitive processes to neural systems. This framework is shown in Fig. 7.1. The top two rows are at the level of cognitive science. They provide a description or sufficiency analysis of how any electromechanical system would be able to perform the cognitive task described. Students of cognitive science have developed a number of computational models for tasks such as visual imagery (Kosslyn, 1980), aspects of reading (McClelland & Rumelhart, 1981); and typewriting (Rumelhart & Norman, 1982). They provide a detailed view of the computations necessary to accomplish the cognitive task. These computational models consist of subroutines that we label *elementary mental operations*. They resemble the types of operations studied by performance experiments for the last 20 years (Posner, 1978). Sample operations include: match, store, zoom, compare, engage, and move. Each operation can be specified in terms of the input code to the operation and its output code. These operations often serve as labels of the box models of information flow that dominate textbooks in cognitive psychology.

How can we determine if these operations are actually carried out by people in the course of accomplishing cognitive tasks? To what extent are these mental operations a description of the mechanisms of human performance? There are several bases on which such a decision might be made. If we suppose that several different cognitive tasks involve the same operation, we ought to expect performance in those tasks to be correlated across people (Chase, 1976; Keele & Hawkins, 1982). Unfortunately, there are also other reasons that might lead to such correlations; thus their existence is rather weak evidence. A more direct experimental test is to determine whether two tasks involving the same putative mental operation have strong interactions with one another. For example, if they need to be executed simultaneously, do they interfere with one another? If they are performed successively, do they show a high degree of priming (Kinsbourne & Hicks, 1978)? These are objective, if rather cumbersome, ways of checking whether the operations obtained from a sufficiency analysis describe human performance.

In our work we attempt to describe mental operations in terms of time-locked facilitations and inhibitions accompanying their performance (Posner & Snyder, 1975). Methods for making such measurements had been described previously and have been widely applied (Jonides & Mack, 1984; Neely, 1977; Posner, 1978). A great deal is known about how this can be done and what pitfalls there are in using them (Jonides & Mack, 1984).

Consider the act of encoding a visual word. According to many computational models, this act involves operations that activate physical, orthographic, phonological, and semantic codes. By studying patterns of facilitation in matches based on each of these criteria we have tried to separate such codes and determine whether they represent what happens as a word is processed (Posner, 1978). Similar methods have been applied to determine whether rotating a visual representation is accomplished by analog or propositional computations (Cooper, 1976). In order to determine how people perform this operation, Cooper (1976) studied the facilitation of probes rotated to varying angles as the subject attempted to rotate mentally a visual form. She found strong evidence that probe processing was facilitated when the rotating image was calculated to be at the same angle as the probe. These results argue that humans are performing an analog rotation at least to the degree of precision of the experiment. Thus, time-locked facilitations and inhibitions allow us to describe some of the characteristics of on-line mental operations as they are executed by people. This level of description is illustrated in the third row of Fig. 7.1.

The use of the words *facilitation* and *inhibition* are biased to make one inquire whether such patterns are related to the activity of the populations of neural cells that might perform the computation. The third row of Fig. 7.1 deals with facilitation as more efficient processing in terms of the speed and accuracy with which the organism responds. These are facilitations in the performance domain, not necessarily in a neurophysiological sense.

Similarly, inhibitions in these studies mean a reduction in efficiency of performance as measured by increased reaction time, raised threshold, or some other performance measure.

To what extent do findings favoring facilitation and inhibition in the performance domain relate to underlying changes in populations of neural cells? This issue may be examined in many ways. One major method for doing so is to relate the performance of cognitive operations with electrical changes that can be detected in the scalp EEG (Donchin, 1984). As an example, the general shift in performance efficiency following a warning signal is accompanied by a negative change in the EEG that has been termed the *contingent negative variation*. Under conditions of rapid presentation of stimuli to several channels, the instruction to attend to one channel produces a negative shift in that channel with respect to the unattended channels, which has been called *processing negativity* (Harter & Aine, 1984; Näätänen, 1982). Similarly, the change in efficiency of detecting an expected letter versus an unexpected one is reflected in the latency of a late positive wave called the *P300* (Duncan-Johnson & Donchin, 1982; Posner, 1978). These constitute increasingly favorable evidence for the links between facilitation and inhibition in the performance domain and those present in electrical activity arising from the brain.

In addition, new methods of exploring human brain activity can also be brought to bear on this issue. For example, the act of attending to a sensory event has been shown to produce an increase in cerebral blood flow in the primary somato-sensory area (Roland, Skinhoj, Lassen, & Larsen, 1980). The use of magnetic potentials has indicated some evidence favoring hippocampal generation of the aforementioned late positive wave (Okada, Kaufman, & Williamson, 1983).

The use of brain injury cases also provides an opportunity to develop links between facilitations and inhibitions in the performance domain and underlying neural systems. It has been argued that brain injury serves to disrupt computational modules or to disconnect them, not to create new modules (Coltheart, 1985). Thus, one ought to expect cases of brain injury to disrupt the mental operations performed by the area of the brain that is damaged. There are, of course, several problems inherent in this logic. Lesion work has often been faulted because it may be used to suggest that the absence of a function following a lesion means that thc function was located in the lesioned area. Certainly this is not a necessary conclusion, but the fact of deficits following lesions is germane to the localization issue and provides direct evidence that the brain treats that function as a separable entity. Often following traumatic brain injury there are effects that occur at locations far removed from the original lesion location. These have been studied by EEG (Gummow, Dustman, & Kearney, 1984) and by change in local glucose utilization (Deuel & Collins, 1984). To some extent they are reduced with time as the brain readjusts to the injury. However, they do represent cautions about the degree to which a deficit can be localized by the lesion method alone. The general framework with which we are working encourages the investigation of links at each level and reduces the overemphasis on the location issues as the major reason for studying connections between neural systems and information processing modules. In addition, the effort to go from findings of lesioned patients to predictions about normal performance provides a check on some of the problems of the use of brain-injured populations.

COMPUTATIONAL ANALYSIS OF VISUAL-SPATIAL ATTENTION

The idea on which our analysis is based is very simple. The act of attending to something provides priority of that information to a large variety of nonhabitual or arbitrary mental operations; it improves access to consciousness. We measure such access by time-locked improvements in the efficiency of detecting or identifying the stimulus event. This logic is quite straight-forward when detecting a visual stimulus involving overt movements of the eye. If the eyes are focused on a stimulus, we observe an increase in efficiency in the sense of visual acuity. We can be aware of fine detail that would be impossible to observe if we were not looking directly at the stimulus. When attention is shifted covertly, efficiency can be measured by the priority given that event over other possible events. We often measure priority by the speed of responding to that stimulus. Thus, when attention is drawn covertly to a visual location, responses are faster (Posner, 1980) and more accurate (Bashinski & Bachrach, 1980; Remington, 1980). If attention is drawn to a category (e.g. animal), items that are central to that category can be classified faster than items peripheral to the category or in other categories (Neely, 1977; Rosch, 1973). Thus, following a prime *animal*, subjects can classify the stimulus *dog* as a word faster than they can *tin* (Neely, 1977). This can be done internally, as when the subject is taught to think body part when the prime is *animal* and the target word *leg* is then facilitated. These changes in facilitations and inhibitions occurring rapidly following a semantic or visual cue allow us to measure components of an attention shift.

What are the computations that lie behind these attention shifts? Three operations are involved: disengage, move, and engage (see Fig. 7.2). Suppose you are currently attending to some location other than the one cued. It is first necessary to disengage attention from its current focus. It has been shown that the time to disengage attention increases with the depth to which it has already been committed (LaBerge, 1973). When the task to be performed is more difficult, time to disengage is increased. Thus, there is no fixed time to disengage. This feature of human attention is quite differ-

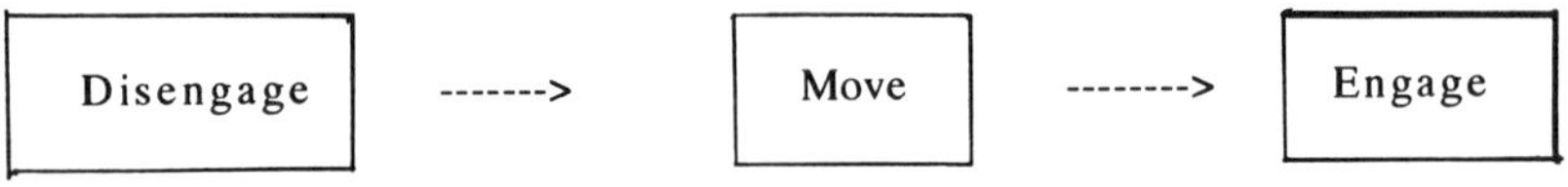

FIG. 7.2 The mental operations involved in covert orienting of visual attention.

ent from a simple spotlight or interrupt in a digital computer. Nonetheless, it is of great importance because it makes it difficult to determine a neutral condition. Suppose a person is expecting a visual target to occur somewhere in the field but has no idea where; his or her attention is committed only to the visual modality and not to a location. Such an attentive state is known to facilitate the firing rates of parietal cells (Mountcastle, Anderson, & Motter, 1981). This state is one baseline against which to evaluate both the facilitation due to attending to a target and the cost or inhibition that commitment to a location produces on targets at unexpected locations. As a practical matter, it is often a serious problem to determine the appropriate baseline condition against which to measure costs and benefits of cues (see Jonides & Mack, 1984 for a review).

If a target occurs outside of the focus of attention, it is necessary to disengage from the current focus and to move attention to the target. There has been considerable argument about how this operation is performed. In studies of visual imagery and mental rotation, there has often appeared to be a linear relationship between the distance moved or the degree of rotation and the time to perform the operation (Kosslyn, 1980). There is sometimes evidence for an increase of reaction time with distance in shifts of visual attention (Downing & Pinker, 1985; Tsal, 1983), and other times not (Posner, 1978). However, the increase of reaction time with distance, although a convenient feature, is not a necessary condition to define an analog movement. It is well known that the time to move the hand from one target to another will increase with distance only if the accuracy of termination is held constant (Fitts, 1954). Studies that ask directly whether intermediate locations are facilitated at intermediate times between leaving one focus and arriving at the target are more direct tests of analog operations (Shulman, Remmington, & McLean, 1979). It is quite likely that there are analog properties to attention movements that are not linear with actual distance, but depend both on the degree of clutter in the field, crossing the midline, and the eccentricity of the starting and finishing location. Downing and Pinker (1985) argued that such movements are related to the amount of cortex traversed between the start and finish locations. Because the cortex represents areas close to the fovea more fully than those in the periphery, this would mean that movement velocity would increase with eccentricity. If this view is correct it would serve as an important link between the structure of the underlying physiology of the visual system and visual attention.

When attention reaches the target location, it must be engaged. It is clear that such engagement can occur prior to the target arrival, because if one is cued to attend to a location, there are costs when a target occurs elsewhere.

How large a part of the visual field is represented by the focus of attention? This has been a widely disputed issue. For example, Hughes and Zimba (1985) argued that attention acts simply by inhibiting the hemifield to which one is not attending. Other investigators have found conditions in which the hemifield to which attention is summoned by a target is inhibited over all other parts of the field (Marzi, 1983). Still others have found a facilitation localized to the neighborhood of the target with an inhibition that is stronger once one has crossed the midline (Downing & Pinker, 1985). These disputes indicate the complexity of the overlapping processes that accompany a shift of attention.

Our basic approach to these complexities has been to attempt to deal with a functional system that can account for the various findings and obeys other properties that we have come to associate with attention.

According to this functional viewpoint (Posner & Cohen, 1984) there are three basic components that occur simultaneously when attention is summoned by a cue located in the neighborhood of a likely target, and these combine to determine the net increase in efficiency. First, the cue increases the alertness of the person because he or she now expects a target. It is known from previous work that alertness is not spatially selective and works to potentiate all targets following the cue.

Second, the cue initiates a spatially selective movement of visual attention to the cued location. Such attention shifts are not fully automatic in the sense of being unavoidable (Posner, Cohen, Choate, Hockey, & Maylor, 1984), but they occur with little effort if the subject does nothing to avoid them (Jonides, 1981). We are not sure how tight the attentional focus is, but we suspect that it depends both on eccentricity and on the precision with which the cue localizes the target. Thus, in a completely blank field one may find a uniform effect over a whole hemifield in comparison to the opposite field. However, when the field has many elements (Downing & Pinker, 1985) the facilitation may be localized to a few degrees. Indeed, Erickson and Hoffman (1978) showed that when responding to single letters subjects appear to be sensitive to all objects within about 1 degree of the focus of attention. LaBerge (1985) showed that when being sensitive to a whole word, the focus of attention is broader than attending to a single letter. Thus, the focus of attention can vary considerably. Facilitation of an entire hemifield may be a limiting case in an empty field when there is a great deal of uncertainty about target locations.

Third, the occurrence of a cue in the periphery initiates two forms of inhibition. What we call cost is a consequence of orienting attention to the cue. Once attention is engaged at the cued location, all other locations will be handled less efficiently (inhibited) than they would have been if no such orienting had occurred, because one must first disengage. This form of inhibition is spatially selective only in the sense that it is not present within the focus of attention. A second form of inhibition is called *inhibition of return*. It is not clear whether inhibition of return is initiated by the sensory event or by the act of attending to that event (Maylor, 1985), but it is shown most clearly if one summons attention to a location and then returns it to a neutral location. The efficiency at the previously cued location is reduced with respect to comparable locations in the visual field for one to two seconds. The overlap between facilitation due to orienting of attention and the specific inhibition of a cued location helps to explain the conflicts in the literature. Sometimes the cued location is handled more efficiently than other locations, sometimes less efficiently, depending on the balance between the two components.

In summary, the effect of any peripheral visual event is complex. It alerts the organism, provides the basis for orienting of attention, and begins a process of reducing the efficiency at the location that has been cued.

Is there any advantage to this constellation of internal events produced by a peripheral cue? At first it seemed very puzzling that such a complex of events should accompany the presentation of a cue. Later we were able to propose a rationale for these effects (Posner & Cohen, 1984).

Our theory rested in part on our findings that the facilitation obtained from a peripheral cue moved with the eyes as though it were mapped in retinal coordinates. The effect was not on the retina, because it could be obtained in a stereoscope. However, many visual maps preserve the coordinates of the retina, so it is not surprising that a visual attention effect also did. On the other hand, inhibition of return appeared not to move when the eyes did as though it were dependent on the coordinates of the environment. When we move our eyes the objects of the world appear to maintain their locations. Thus, many psychological phenomena maintain the coordinates of the environment as we move about. In this sense, one of our effects (facilitation) is retinotopic and the other (inhibition of return) is environmental.

These findings led us to suppose that the facilitation effect serves to improve the efficiency of target detection within a fixation. It is designed to allow us to give momentary priority to an area of the visual field as, for example, when we carefully examine the nose within a face. If the task demands high acuity, we are likely to move our eyes to the interesting location and thus produce a reorienting of attention back to the fovea. In reading, for example, the reduction of acuity with eccentricity may be the cause of the eye movement (Morrison, 1984). Facilitation allows a temporary emphasis to go on outside the center of fixation. Because it serves only within a fixation, it works in retinotopic coordinates. When the eyes move, attention is drawn back to fixation.

The inhibition of return evolved to maximize sampling of novel areas within the visual environment. Once the eyes move away from the target location, events that occur at that environmental location are inhibited and we find that one is less likely to move the eyes back to them (Posner, Choate, Rafal, & Vaughan, 1985). This reduces the effectiveness of an area of space in summoning attention and serves as a bias for favoring fresh areas at which no previous targets had been presented. The long-lasting nature of inhibition of return (one to two seconds) ensures that two to three eye movements are biased against a return.

This organization of facilitation and inhibition represents an exquisite functional adaptation to the needs of the visual world. There has been much discussion within psychology and physiology about the use of retinotopic and environmental coordinates for the mapping of visual phenomena. Physiologists usually stress the presence of many retinotopic maps early in the visual system; however, psychologists are aware that many subjective phenomena are mapped in environmental coordinates. Our finding of the close relationship of both types of mapping within the spatial attention system appears to be a special opportunity to understand how retinotopic maps relate to psychological performance.

Several important issues emerge from our model system for the study of spatial attention. First, it appears that the performance of people can be used to study time-locked shifts of efficiency that relate to visual cues and eye movements. Although we can describe these in terms of three logical computations involved in movements of attention, at another level several component facilitations and inhibitions occur simultaneously, each locked to the occurrence of the cue. A theory that relates these components to performance is difficult to test because of the complex overlapping nature of the effect produced by the cues. No doubt several different cognitive theories might describe what we have found. Perhaps this represents something of the intrinsic ambiguity obtained when one only has stimulus and response with no way of getting intervening steps in the computation. In order to examine these changes further, we consider the neural machinery that is involved.

NEURAL SYSTEMS OF VISUAL-SPATIAL ATTENTION

Alert Monkeys

Two areas of the monkey's brain have cells whose firing rates are enhanced selectively when the monkey's attention is directed to their receptive fields (Wurtz, Goldberg, & Robinson, 1980). In one area, the superior colliculus, the selective enhancement occurs only when attention is directed overtly via eye movements. In the second area, the posterior parietal lobe (and the subcortical pulvinar), selective enhancement occurs both when attention is directed overtly and when the monkey is required to maintain fixation while attending covertly to a peripheral target.

Is selective enhancement in the monkey related to the mental operations of covert attention described in the preceding section of this chapter? If that proves to be the case, we would have advanced our goal of providing useful links between the levels of performance and those of cellular activity.

In the preceding section we reviewed experiments using both central symbolic cues and cues at the spatial position of the target that obtained facilitation in reaction time and thresholds at the cued locations. In addition, when covert attention is maintained over a steady stream of signals, there is a negative shift in electrical activity at the scalp for targets at the selected position (Harter & Aine, 1984; Näätänen, 1982; Van Voorhis & Hillyard, 1977). These results suggest that such cues cause a change that both facilitates the efficiency of detecting a target and alters some aspects of brain activity.

One feature of these results is that the changes are tightly time-locked to the cue's occurrence. The presentation of a peripheral cue appears to produce improvement in reaction time when it leads the target by as little as 50 milliseconds (Posner, 1980). Processing negativity affects the signal from the selected location by about 120–150 milliseconds. This can be compared with selective enhancement of parietal cells, which occurs about 75 milliseconds after target input. When attention is shifted to a peripheral target in preparation for an eye movement, facilitation occurs about 150 milliseconds prior to the onset of the eye movement (Posner, 1980; Remmington, 1980). The time course of this effect is markedly similar to the selective enhancement of cells in the colliculus, which occurs about 150–200 milliseconds prior to the onset of the saccade (Wurtz, Goldberg, & Robinson, 1980).

The time course of single cells, event-related potential, and performance changes are roughly similar, and this provides one source of evidence on the relationship between selective enhancement of single cells in monkey brains and facilitation of human performance. Somewhat more direct evidence may be obtained through the study of patient populations suffering from brain injury to midbrain and cortical areas.

Patients

There is a long clinical history documenting the finding that lesions of the posterior part of one hemisphere can cause a severe deficit in reporting information on the side of space opposite the lesion (DeRenzi, 1982). One aspect of this syndrome is a reduction in eye movements to the side of space opposite the lesion and a reduced ability to notice or report visual stimuli there. This neglect of visual information contralateral to the lesion occurs most strongly when the patient is confronted with simultaneous lateralized visual stimuli. In this case, the stimuli contralateral to the lesion is frequently not reported (extinguished). The phenomenon of neglect can arise from unilateral lesions of the midbrain and thalamus as well as from a variety of cortical lesions. However, clinical observation seems to suggest that parietal lesions on the right side are the most frequent area of damage leading to neglect and extinction (DeRenzi, 1982).

For a variety of reasons, clinical researchers have related the neglect phenomenon to a reduced ability to orient covertly or overtly to stimuli opposite the lesion. This account is supported by the finding that stimuli from the neglected side do show the exogenous components of event-related potentials, although frequently reduced in amplitude. Neglect of contralateral stimuli tends to be variable, sometimes quite strong, and at other times much weaker. Contralateral stimuli can often be seen clearly when presented alone and can be used when patients are required to determine if pairs of stimuli presented across the midline are identical or not (Volpe, LeDoux, & Gazzaniga, 1979). All of these facts point to the idea that although stimuli contralateral to the lesion do have some effect on cortical systems, they often fail to reach systems that subserve conscious awareness.

These results are not unlike those found in normal subjects when they are heavily biased toward one source of sensory signals. For example, when paying attention to an auditory message presented to one ear it is not unusual for events presented to the other ear to be unreported or to be noticed only when they are of special significance (e.g., the person's name). Humans have been shown to have such a strong bias toward visual stimuli that simultaneous auditory events of equal strength can be missed entirely if subjects are led to expect that only one modality will be presented (Colavito, 1974; Egeth & Sager, 1977). Reports of these experiments are usually met with surprise. Attention is usually directed toward new stimuli with great efficiency, yet under special circumstances, stimuli that we are clearly capable of sensing do not reach consciousness.

Both the alert monkey work and clinical observations suggest that studies of patients with damage to the midbrain in the area of the superior colliculus and to the parietal lobe might be helpful in determining how the mental operations involved in covert orienting of attention are controlled by neural systems. The emphasis in reviewing this material is on the dissociation of cognitive components, not on anatomical localization. We conducted studies that have used the performance methods discussed previously with certain selected patient populations. Although the lesions of these patients are not localized to a small area, they can provide evidence on whether the elementary operations and components facilitation and inhibition described with normals are affected differentially by lesions to brain areas known to be associated with selective enhancement of neural cells.

Midbrain Effects

It is known that damage to the superior colliculus in animals produces a transient loss in saccadic eye movements that after recovery may only appear as increased latency. A neurological disease called *progressive supranuclear palsy* (PSP), which involves degeneration of the colliculus and surrounding structures, is also known to produce a loss of the ability to perform saccadic eye movements in humans. It is also known that such patients have trouble in performing tasks that require orienting toward events in social situations (Rafal & Grimm, 1981).

Covert visual orienting can be studied in such patients by cuing them to shift attention in directions where saccades are not possible and observing time-locked changes in the efficiency of reporting targets at those locations (Posner, Cohen, & Rafal, 1982). It was found that these patients could shift attention in a direction even when they could not voluntarily move their eyes in that direction. However, detailed comparisons of the speed of covert orienting suggested that it was retarded in the direction of the most severe eye movement paralysis. The damage to the saccadic system seemed to affect the latency of covert orienting both to cues and to targets. The specific effect was to delay the advantage for the cued over the uncued trials as though the damage affected the speed of moving from one attended location to another location irrespective of whether attention had previously been engaged at any location. These effects were not general results of similar degenerative disorders, because they were not found in Parkinson's patients, who have a related degenerative process but do not share the paralysis of the saccadic eye movement system.

In addition, the PSP patients showed a loss of the form of inhibition that we call *inhibition of return* (Posner et al., 1985). If their attention was summoned up or down by a peripheral cue from fixation to the target location and then back to fixation, they showed equal reaction time in returning to the previously uncued location as to the cued location (Posner et al., 1985). This was quite different from normals, from what happened to these same patients with horizontal targets, and all other paticnt groups studied (Parkinsons, parietal, frontal). Our previous work with normals had led us to speculate that inhibition of return was functionally related to the eye movement systems (Posner & Cohen, 1984). Thus, finding a loss of this effect in patients with known deficits in the saccadic system seems a confirmation of the hypothesis and one that furthers the relationship between cognitive theory and neuropsychology outlined by our general framework.

A role for midbrain systems in covert attention movements was also confirmed in a study of split-brain patients (Holtzman, Sidtis, Volpe, Wilson,

& Gazzaniga, 1981). It was found that cues indicating where in space a target might occur were successful in directing attention irrespective of whether they were presented to the same or opposite hemisphere that received the target. However, this system was more restrictive than the cortical system (Holtzman, 1985). It seems likely that the midbrain plays a role in moving covert attention from one location to another in much the same way as it does for eye movements. As with eye movements, degeneration in this area increases latency but does not eliminate covert attention shifts. Our finding that the speed of attention movements is slowed by midbrain lesions suggests that the midbrain system is a part of a larger system that performs other components of orienting of attention.

Cortical Lesions

An impressive aspect of parietal patients is their tendency to be unaware of signals that occur on the side opposite the lesion. Although this hemi-inattention can occur in any modality, we confine our discussion of it to the visual modality. Clinical investigation of this phenomenon has been well-summarized by DeRenzi (1982).

These clinical observations, together with animal work, suggested that parietal deficits might be thought of as a reduction in attention, arousal, or orienting (DeRenzi, 1982). In addition, lesions of the parietal lobe appear to reduce the processing negativity to selected auditory stimuli (Knight, Hillyard, Woods, & Neville, 1980). Unfortunately, these data do not provide an analytic treatment of how the lesion acts to produce neglect or extinction. According to our idea, movements of spatial attention depend on a sequence of three elementary mental operations (see Fig. 7.2). It is impossible to judge from clinical data exactly how these operations might be affected by the parietal lesion. However, features of the clinical syndrome do seem to argue that the lasting effects of the lesion may be largely on the disengage operation. The reason is the finding that unilateral stimulation can draw the subject's attention to the side opposite the lesion, but with bilateral presentation the same stimulus is not perceived (extinguished). Moreover, patients with parietal lesions can often compare stimuli on the two sides (Volpe et al., 1979) even though they show clinical extinction. This argues that information on the side opposite the lesion may receive a high level of analysis but is not perceived when there is competition. Such observations suggest that a stimulus on the side opposite the lesion cannot grab hold of attention, when attention is already elsewhere engaged.

These speculations received support from experimental work (Posner et al., 1982; Posner, Walker, Friedrich, & Rafal, 1984). In these studies patients were given a cue followed by a target, to which they responded by pressing a single key. Parietal patients often have a general advantage in reaction time for those targets that occur ipsilateral to the lesion in comparison to those that occur contralateral to the lesion. However, for many parietal patients there is little or no difference between the two once a cue has been presented 50 milliseconds or more prior to the presentation of the target. When attention is drawn to either side, these patients have nearly equal ability to detect the target. Thus, the ability to engage the target once attention is properly directed is not necessarily interrupted by parietal lesions, although it can be affected in some patients.

Striking results occur on trials in which attention is cued to the side of the lesion and the target is presented on the side opposite the lesion. In some cases, targets show extinction; that is, they are missed entirely by the subject (Posner et al., 1982). In other cases, these targets are not completely excluded from consciousness, but show greatly delayed reaction times, sometimes two to three times the normal reaction time. The results suggest that the elevation in latency is simply a less severe form of complete exclusion from consciousness. Patients who miss signals completely when they remain present in the field only briefly will report them when they remain present for a second, but only with a greatly increased latency. The idea that a latency increase is a less severe form of difficulty than extinction fits with the account of covert orienting discussed previously.

It is also possible to show that the pattern of increased reaction times to contralateral targets following miscues does not depend on the miscue being ipsilateral to the lesion. Rather, cuing the patient with a central arrow that directs attention to the side opposite the lesion is sufficient to produce the same greatly increased reaction time to targets that occur opposite the lesion. Similarly, a central brightening at fixation that draws attention to fixation, even if it tells nothing about target location (neutral cue), produces a similar increase in reaction time to targets opposite the lesion (Posner, Walker, Friedrich, & Rafal, 1984). The neutral cue result shows that neither a probability difference nor a stimulus ipsilateral to the lesion is necessary to produce the greatly elevated latency related to extinction.

In summary, we identify the major deficit in parietal patients with the disengage operation (Posner, Walker, Friedrich, & Rafal, 1984). It may be instructive to review the logic. On cued trials there is only a modest difference in reaction time (RT) on the two sides. Moreover, the effect of the cue in reducing RT to a subsequent target is identical on the two sides. This reduction is due to a shift of attention. Thus, the parietal patients must be able to shift attention equally to the two sides. However, once attention is engaged either at fixation or on the ipsilateral side, RT to contralateral targets is greatly elevated. Why should this be? Why should contralateral targets be so great a disadvantage following a cue at another location? It must be because the parietal lesion has a special effect on disengaging attention. Moreover, this effect is quite different from what is found with deficits due to midbrain lesions. That deficit reduces the ability to shift attention to both cued and targets. Thus, the deficit appears to be in the ability to move attention irrespective of whether it is first engaged elsewhere.

In terms of the framework (Fig. 7.1) presented in the introduction and the three mental operations involved in movements of attention (Fig. 7.2), it is now possible to propose that the midbrain lesion primarily affects the move operation, whereas the parietal lesion relates to disengaging attention. This result would be similar to what one finds with eye movements, where lesions of colliculus produce difficulties primarily in the execution of the eye movement rather than in the command that generates the movement.

In addition to its effect on the disengage operation, it is likely that parietal damage also affects the move function to some degree. It has been widely understood that patients with right parietal lesions have difficulties in dealing with the left side of objects in either the good or bad visual field. This led Kinsbourne (1978) to suggest that each parietal lobe controls orienting toward the opposite side of space, irrespective of the visual field in which the information was located. Parietal lobe lesions can reduce the likelihood of eye movements toward the contralateral side. A similar role for covert attention movements would be in accord with general nervous system principles, suggesting that similar control systems are frequently repeated at higher levels.

Clinical literature provides evidence that neglect and extinction may arise from lesions at many sites provided that they are unilateral. On the other hand, the relative specificity of the single-cell data in showing selective enhancement only at collicular and parietal sites suggests a much more restricted locus for the covert orienting operation. Tests to date suggest that neither temporal nor frontal lesions produce the same pattern of RT effects on covert orienting that have been discussed for the parietal lesion. Although it is quite possible that such lesions influence many aspects of the clinical syndrome of neglect, covert orienting deficits are more restricted.

The work described on visual spatial attention suggests that the act of attending can be broken into several component computations. These components can be revealed in performance studies in terms of overlapping patterns of facilitation and inhibition that accompany the performance of the mental operations. It has been shown that these components are affected differentially by lesions of the midbrain and cortex. Thus, the brain appears to perform a simple attentional act by the orchestration of a network of cortical and subcortical systems. Visual-spatial attention is not performed by a single center, nor is it a general property of the visual system or of the brain as a whole. Rather, it is an act consisting of components that can be differentially affected and lead to quite different behavioral deficits. Visual-spatial attention, however, is a very small part of attention as a whole. In the next section we present some approaches to the issue of how this form of attention relates to other forms.

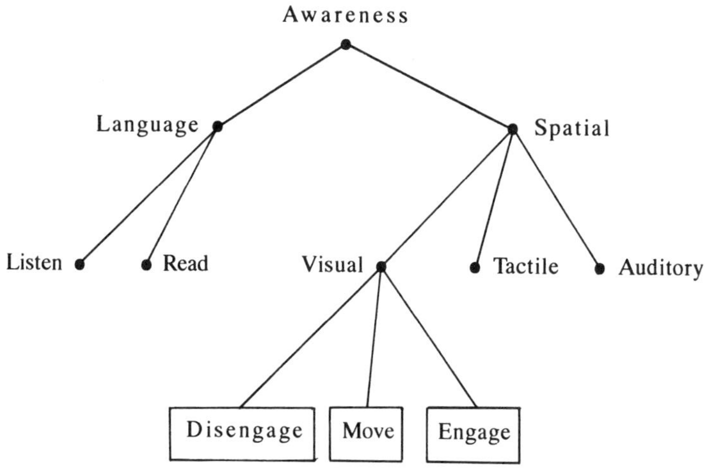

FIG. 7.3 A hierarchical system of selective attention.

HIERARCHIES OF DISTRIBUTED NETWORKS FOR SPATIAL ATTENTION

Is visual attention a separate module that controls the allocation of resources within that domain, or is it merely a part of a more general system involved in attention to space? In cognitive psychology this issue concerns the unity of attention. Some authors have argued that interference caused by attention is severe only when it occurs within the same modality or cognitive domain (Allport, 1980). Other authors have favored the idea of a single channel or limited processor at least for the set of operations we have defined as conscious (Posner, 1978). In 1978 we argued about the importance of a central system to exercise inhibitory control over more local processing in order to dampen the consequences of widespread activation of habitual pathways. Unfortunately, the evidence from strictly cognitive experiments has not been decisive (Kahneman & Treisman, 1984). There often appears to be more interference when tasks depend on similar processors, but even when they do not, some residual interference usually remains (McLeod & Posner, 1984).

One way of viewing this issue consistent with much cognitive theory (MacKay, 1982; McClelland, 1984; and Rumelhart, 1981) is to suppose that attentional modules are arranged in a hierarchial fashion (see Fig. 7.3). Thus, there might be a network for the allocation of attention to locations in visual space and a somewhat different but related network for auditory space. However, because both of these networks are spatial, there would also be a higher level system that allocates information to locations in space irrespective of modality. Similarly, attention might be allocated to the cognitive system controlling language, which then would be subdivided into modality-specific systems controlling reading and listening.

There is some evidence from both performance and neurological studies that favors this general idea. In 1978 we (Posner, Nissen, & Ogden, 1977) reported that a cue that draws attention to a spatial location was rather ineffective when the person did not know the modality of the target (visual or tactile). When both modality and location were known, the cue became quite effective in improving the efficiency of performance. Thus, locations seem to be organized by modality. This result fits with recent findings by DeRenzi, Gentilini, and Pattacini (1984) relating to clinical extinction found in parietal patients. They showed that although both visual and auditory extinction could be found, the two were independent. This suggests that at the level of parietal lobe function engaging a visual location has only minor effects on the efficiency of auditory detection and the reverse.

There is of course nothing very surprising about a view that spatial cognition represents a multimodal system toward which attention can be directed. What seems more interesting is to compare the relative influence of modality (e.g., auditory vs. visual) and cognitive system (e.g., spatial vs. language) in influencing the direction of attention. In a series of studies with normals (Posner & Henik, 1983) and parietal patients (Walker, Friedrich, & Posner, 1983) we used a spatial version of the Stroop effect to study this issue.

In these experiments subjects are instructed to respond either to the visual words left or right, to visual locations on a CRT, to visual symbols (arrows pointing to the left or right), or to auditory words (left or right) that might be presented to the left or right ear. In different experiments manual or vocal responses have been used. In work with normals (Posner & Henik, 1983), we compared irrelevant dimensions that used the same cognitive system but a different modality than the attended event, with those in the same modality but a different cognitive system. When a person is to deal with a visual or auditory word, the extent of facilitation or conflict in RT from words in the opposite modality is much greater than from spatial locations in the same modality. A similar result is obtained for the instruction to attend to a spatial location, but in addition auditory location has generally smaller effects than does visual location. There seems to be evidence from these results that stimuli from the same cognitive system, even when they involve different sensory modalities, interact strongly although not as strongly as if they shared both cognitive system and modality.

Studies of patients suggest another sense of separation by cognitive system. Selection by spatial location appears to involve the parietal system irrespective of modality of input. One source of evidence for this is that lesions of the parietal lobe can produce extinction in visual, auditory, or tactile domains depending on their location (DeRenzi, 1982). Our work has shown that patients with parietal lesions have similar difficulties in directing attention when the cue is (a) at the target location, (b) a central arrow, or (c) a word that directs attention to the target. In addition, we have studied parietal patients in a version of the spatial Stroop in which they are required to respond either to a left or right pointing arrow or to the word left or right. Normals show faster responses to the arrow and much more interference of the arrow on the word than the reverse. Right parietal patients have greater difficulty with the arrow than the word, thus reversing the normal pattern. Left parietal patients show a normal but greatly exaggerated pattern in which the arrow dominates quite strongly over the word (Walker et al., 1983). These data all show the involvement of the parietal system in spatial attention irrespective of input mode.

NONSPATIAL SELECTIVE ATTENTION

We were interested in learning whether this spatial attention system represents an independent module or whether it is part of a still more general attention system. We (Posner, Inhoff, Friedrich, & Cohen, 1987) designed a dual task for our parietal patients. Each patient was run in the visual orienting task described previously. In separate blocks they were required either to count backwards from a fixed digit or to monitor a series of auditory words for a target phoneme. These tasks were designed to require quite different cognitive systems. The visual-spatial task was known to involve the anatomical network that we have been describing. The two other tasks involved cognitive systems related to language. Neither of the secondary tasks involved the visual modality, nor did they require a manual output similar to what was used in the visual orienting task. Thus, as far as we could determine the two tasks were as separate in their cognitive demands as possible.

The results showed quite clearly that the two tasks interacted in an interesting way. Reaction time to visual targets was slowed by the dual task, and the use of cues was also clearly retarded because at 100 milliseconds the cues were no longer effective in directing attention to the visual targets. Thus, the language task disrupted the processing of visual targets by engaging the subject's attention to another cognitive system. A second important point is that this engagement of attention to the language task did not produce any differential advantage of the ipsilateral over the contralateral visual field. These two results led us to conclude both that visual orienting required access to a general attention system that was also used by the secondary tasks and that this system could not be anatomically the same as the parietal system damaged in our patients. If it were the parietal system, engaging attention to the language task would have produced the extinction-like reaction time pattern found with visual engagement in which contralateral targets are disadvantaged over ipsilateral targets.

It appears that in order to engage the parietal-based spatial system, another system must be free to issue some type of command signal. If this other, more general attention system is involved in generating counts or monitoring language the parietal system does not engage the location of the cue. This finding fits with the ability of parietal patients to perform spatial orienting tasks when they are not engaged. The origin of the improvement in performance due to spatial attention does not appear to reside in the parietal system. The location of the higher level attention system depicted in the top node of Fig. 7.3 remains unclear. The close anatomical connections of the parietal lobe to frontal sites (Mesulam, 1981) and the general effects of frontal lesion on a variety of tasks suggests to us a system that involves frontal areas, but that may itself be quite distributed.

CONCLUSIONS

The goal of this chapter was to outline a general framework for dealing with the relationship of cognition to brain systems. This framework is shown in Fig. 7.1 and provides a method that can be applied to any form of cognition and that will prove useful in discussions of the relationship of cognition to neural systems. The framework provides for empirical investigations at many levels; computational, chronometric, spatial imaging, and cellular. It argues for the logical interrelationship of these areas of investigations and provides speculations about how some of the current findings at one level (e.g., pathway facilitation in chronometric studies) may relate to findings at another level (e.g., processing negativity in EEG studies and selective enhancement of single cells).

We applied our framework to the issue of selective attention. In the area of visual-spatial attention, it has proven possible to relate specific elementary operations (e.g., disengage and move) to identified regional neural systems by the study of populations of brain-injury subjects. Studies of cross-modality cuing and interference suggest that the parietal system is also related to spatial orienting irrespective of modality and type of cue. Thus, we see a cognitive system involving spatial attention in which somewhat separate modality-specific systems are organized. This hierarchical view is illustrated in Fig. 7.3.

We asked whether the cognitive system subserving attention to spatial information relates to a more general attention system. The idea of a unified attention system has been quite persistent in studies of human performance and cognition. Our patient studies suggest that spatial attention is a module within a more general system of attention that extends to other cognitive systems as well (e.g., language). Although the anatomy of the more general system is unknown to us, our general framework does suggest the types of studies that may be useful in revealing its anatomical organization.

ACKNOWLEDGMENTS

This research was supported in part by ONR Contract No. N00014-83-0601 and in part by NIMH Grant R01-MN-3853-02.

ADDENDUM

There have been a number of developments in this story since it was written. We have been able to develop evidence for a thalamic system related to the engage function. This evidence was reviewed by Rafal and Posner (1987). Work with alert monkeys using the same task has also shown related effects in thalamic areas (Petersen, Robinson, & Morris, 1987).

The effect of parietal lesions on the reading of visual words and nonwords (Sieroff, Pollatsek, & Posner, 1988) has also been investigated. These results and single-cell recording from V4 have provided evidence of selective attention effects on aspects of object recognition. The effect of cuing on forming attribute conjunctions has also been demonstrated (Briand & Klein, 1987; Printzmental, Presti, & Posner, 1986).

We have been able to follow the processing of visual word reading directly, using new methods of visual imaging (Petersen, Fox, Posner, Mintun, & Raichle, 1988). This work has provided strong evidence for links between mental operations and localized brain areas. Moreover, there is evidence that the anterior cingulate gyrus might form a part of the more general attention system that was suggested by the dual-task work (p. 204).

These new results provide support for the general framework that began this inquiry.

REFERENCES

Allport, D. A. (1980). *Attention and performance*. In G. Claxton (Ed.), *Cognitive psychology: New directions* (pp. 75–100). London: Routledge & Kegan Paul.

Bashinski, H. S., & Bachrach, V. R. (1980). Enhancement of perceptual sensitivity as the result of selectively attending to spatial locations. *Perception and Psychophysics, 28*, 241–248.

Briand, K. A., & Klein, R. M. (1987). Is Posner's beam the same as Treisman's glue? On the relation between visual orienting and feature integration theory. *Journal of Experimental Psychology: Human Perception and Performance, 13*, 228–241.

Chase, W. G. (1976). Does memory scanning involve implicit speech? In J. Requin, (Ed.), *Attention and performance VI* (pp. 607–628). Hillsdale, NJ: Lawrence Erlbaum Associates.

Colavito, F. B. (1974). Human sensory dominance. *Perception and Psychophysics, 16*, 409–412.

Coltheart, M. (1985). Cognitive neuropsychology. In M. I. Posner & O. S. M. Marin (Eds.), *Attention and performance XI* (pp. 3–37). Hillsdale, NJ: Lawrence Erlbaum Associates.

Cooper, L. A. (1976). Demonstration of a mental analog of an external rotation. *Perception and Psychophysics, 17*, 296–302.

DeRenzi, E. (1982). *Disorders of space exploration and cognition*. New York: Wiley.

DeRenzi, E., Gentilini, M., & Pattacini, F. (1984). Auditory extinction following hemisphere damage. *Neuropsychologia, 22*, 733–744.

Deuel, R. M., & Collins, R. C. (1984). The functional anatomy of frontal lobe neglect in the monkey: Behavioral and quantitative 2 DG studies. *Annals of Neurology, 15*, 521–529.

Donchin, E. (Ed.). (1984). *Cognitive psychophysiology*. Hillsdale, NJ: Lawrence Erlbaum Associates.

Downing, C. J., & Pinker, S. (1985). The spatial structure of visual attention. In M. I. Posner & O. S. M. Marin (Eds.), *Attention and performance XI* (pp. 171–187). Hillsdale, NJ: Lawrence Erlbaum Associates.

Duncan-Johnson, C., & Donchin, E. (1982). The P 300 component of the event related potential as an index of information processing. *Biological Psychology, 14*, 1–52.

Egeth, H. E., & Sager, L. C. (1977). On the focus of visual dominance. *Perception and Psychophysics, 22*, 77–86.

Erickson, C. W., & Hoffman, J. (1978). The extent of processing noise elements during selective encoding from visual displays. *Perception and Psychophysics, 17*, 155–160.

Fitts, P. M. (1954). The information capacity of the human motor system in controlling the amplitude of movement. *Journal of Experimental Psychology, 47*, 351–381.

Gummow, L. J., Dustman, R. E., & Kearney, R. P. (1984). Remote effects of cerebrovascular accidents: Visual evoked potentials and electrophysiological coupling. *Electroencephalography and Clinical Neurophysiology, 58*, 408–417.

Harter, M. R., & Aine, C. J. (1984). Brain mechanisms of visual selective attention. In R. Parasuraman, R. Davies, & J. Beatty (Eds.), *Varieties of attention* (pp. 293–321). New York: Academic Press.

Hillyard, S. A., Munte, T. F., & Neville, H. J. (1985). Visual-spatial attention, orienting and brain physiology. In M. I. Posner & O. S. M. Marin (Eds.), *Attention and performance XI* (pp. 63–84). Hillsdale, NJ: Lawrence Erlbaum Associates.

Holtzman, J. D. (1985). Eye movement control following corpus commissurotomy in humans. In M. I. Posner & O. S. M. Marin (Eds.), *Attention and performance XI* (pp. 425–440). Hillsdale, NJ: Lawrence Erlbaum Associates.

Holtzman, J. D., Sidtis, J. J., Volpe, B. T., Wilson, D. H., & Gazzaniga, M. S. (1981). Dissociation of spatial information for stimulus localization and control of attention. *Brain, 104*, 861–872.

Hughes, H. C., & Zimba, L. D. (1985). Spatial maps of directed attention. *Journal of Experimental Psychology: Human Perception & Performance, 11*, 409–430.

Jonides, J. P. (1981). Voluntary versus automatic control over the mind's eye. In J. Lunci & A. Baddeley (Eds.), *Attention and performance IX* (pp. –). Hillsdale, NJ: Lawrence Erlbaum Associates.

Jonides, J. P., & Mack, R. (1984). On the cost and benefit of cost and benefit. *Psychology Bulletin, 96*, 29–44.

Kahneman, D., & Treisman, A. (1984). Changing views of attention and automaticity. In R. Parasuraman, R. Davies, & J. Beatty (Eds.), *Varieties of attention* (pp. 293–321). New York: Academic Press.

Keele, S. W., & Hawkins, H. L. (1982). Explorations of individual differences relevant to high skill level. *Journal of Motor Behavior, 1*, 3–23.

Kinsbourne, M. (1973). Hemi-neglect and hemisphere rivalry. In E. A. Weinstein & R. L. Friedland (Eds.), *Hemi-inattention and hemisphere specialization. Advances in neurology, 18* (pp. 41–52). New York: Raven Press.

Kinsbourne, M., & Hicks, R. (1978). Functional cerebral space. In J. Requin (Ed.), *Attention and performance VII* (pp. –). New York: Academic Press.

Knight, R. T., Hillyard, S. P., Woods, O. L., & Neville, F. J. (1980). Effects of frontal and temporal-parietal lesions on the auditory evoked potential in man. *EEG & Clinical Neurophysiology, 50*, 112–124.

Kosslyn, S. (1980). *Image and mind.* Cambridge, MA: Harvard Press.

LaBerge, D. L. (1973). Identification of two components of the time to switch attention: A test of a serial and a parallel model of attention. In S. Kornblum (Ed.), *Attention and performance IV* (pp. -). New York: Academic Press.

LaBerge, D. L. (1985). Distribution of attention to letters and words. *Journal of Experimental Psychology: Human Perception & Performance, 9*, 371–379.

MacKay, D. G. (1982). The problems of flexibility, fluency and speed-accuracy trade-off in skill behavior. *Psychological Review, 89*, 483–506.

Marzi, C. (1983, September). *Spatial inhibition in processing light flashes.* Paper presented to the European Neuroscience Society, Hamburg, Germany.

Maylor, E. (1985). Facilitatory and inhibitory components of orienting in visual space. In M. I. Posner & O. S. M. Marin (Eds.), *Attention and performance XI* (pp. 189-207). Hillsdale, NJ: Lawrence Erlbaum Associates.

McClelland, J. L., & Rumelhart, D. E. (1981). An interactive activation model of context effects in letter perception. *Psychological Review, 88*, 375–407.

McLeod, D., & Posner, M. I. (1984). Privileged loops from percept to act. In H. Bouma & D. Bowhuis (Eds.), *Attention and Performance X* (pp. 55–66). Hillsdale, NJ: Lawrence Erlbaum Associates.

Mesulam, M. M. (1981). A cortical network for directed attention and unilateral neglect. *Annals of Neurology, 10*, 309–325.

Moran, J., & Desimone, R. (1985). Selective attention gates visual processing in extrastriate cortex. *Science, 229*, 91–93.

Morrison, R. E. (1984). Manipulation of stimulus on set data in reading: Evidence for parallel programming of saccades. *Journal of Experimental Psychology: Human Perception & Performance, 10*, 667–682.

Mountcastle, V. B., Anderson, R. A., & Motter, B. C. (1981). The influence of attentive fixation upon the excitability of light-sensitive neurons of the parietal cortex. *Journal of Neuroscience, 1*, 1218–1235.

Näätäten, R. (1982). Processing negativity: An evoked cortical potential reflection of selective attention. *Psychological Bulletin, 92*, 605–640.

Neely, J. H. (1977). Semantic priming and retrieval from lexical memory. *Journal of Experimental Psychology: General, 106*, 226–254.

Okada, Y. C., Kaufman, L., & Williamson, S. J. (1983). The hippocampal formation as a source of slow endogenous potentials. *EEG & Clinical Neurophysiology, 55*, 417–426.

Petersen, S. E., Fox, P. T., Posner, M. I., Mintun, M., & Raichle, M. E. (1988). Positron emission tomographic studies of the cortical anatomy of single word processing. *Nature, 331*, 585–589.

Petersen, S. E., Robinson, D. L., & Morris, J. D. (1987). Contributions of the pulvinar to visual spatial attention. *Neuropsychologia, 25*, 97–106.

Posner, M. I. (1978). *Chronometric explorations of mind.* Hillsdale, NJ: Lawrence Erlbaum Associates.

Posner, M. I. (1980). Orienting of attention. *Quarterly Journal of Experimental Psychology, 32*, 3–25.

Posner, M. I., Boies, S. W., Eichelman, W., & Taylor, R. (1969). Retention of visual and name codes of single letters. *Journal of Experimental Psychology Monograph, 79*, 1–16.

Posner, M. I., Choate, L., Rafal, R. D., & Vaughan, J. (1985). Inhibition of return: Neural mechanisms and function. *Cognitive Neuropsychology, 2*, 211–228.

Posner, M. I., & Cohen, Y. (1984). Components of visual orienting. In H. Bouma & D. Bouwhuis (Eds.), *Attention and performance X* (pp. 531–556). Hillsdale, NJ: Lawrence Erlbaum Associates.

Posner, M. I., Cohen, Y., Choate, L., Hockey, R., & Maylor, E. (1984). Sustained concentration: Passive filtering or active orienting. In S. Kornblum & J. Requin (Eds.), *Preparatory states and processes* (pp. 49–65). Hillsdale, NJ: Lawrence Erlbaum Associates.

Posner, M. I., Cohen, Y., & Rafal, R. D. (1982). Neural systems control of spatial orienting. *Proceedings of the Royal Society of London B. 298*, 187–198.

Posner, M. I., & Henik, A. (1983). Isolating representation systems. In J. Beck, B. Hope, & A. Rosenfeld (Eds.), *Human and machine vision* (pp. 395–412). New York: Academic Press.

Posner, M. I., Inhoff, A., Friedrich, F. J., & Cohen, A. (1987). *Isolating attentional systems. Psychobiology, 15*, 107–121.

Posner, M. I., Nissen, M. J., & Ogden, W. C. (1978). Attended and unattended processing & modes: The role of set for spatial location. In H. I. Pick & E. Saltzman (Eds.), *Modes of perceiving and processing information*. Hillsdale, NJ: Lawrence Erlbaum Associates.

Posner, M. I., & Snyder, C. R. R. (1975). Attention and cognitive control. In R. Solso (Ed.), *Information processing and cognition: The Loyola symposium* (pp. 55–85). Hillsdale, NJ: Lawrence Erlbaum Associates.

Posner, M. I., Walker, J. A., Friedrich, A. J., & Rafal, R. D. (1984). Effects of parietal lobe injury on covert orienting of visual attention. *Journal of Neuroscience, 4*, 1863–1874.

Prinzmetal, W., Presti, D., & Posner, M. I. (1986). Does attention affect feature integration. *Journal of Experimental Psychology: Human Perception and Performance, 12*, 361–369.

Rafal, R. D., & Grimm, R. J. (1981). Progressive supranuclear palsy functional analysis of the response to methylserside and anti-Parkinsonism agents. *Neurology, 31*, 1507–1518.

Rafal, R. D., & Posner, M. I. (1987). Deficits in human spatial attention following thalamic lesions. *Proceedings of the National Academy of Sciences, 84*, 7349–7353.

Remington, R. (1980). Visual attention, detection, and the control of saccadic eye movements. *Journal of Experimental Psychology: Human Perception & Performance, 6*, 145–150.

Roland, P. E., Skinhoj, E., Lassen, N. A., & Larsen, B. (1980). Different cortical areas in man in organization of voluntary movements in extrapersonal space. *Journal of Neurophysiology, 43*, 137–150.

Rosch, E. (1973). On the internal structure of perceptual and semantic categories. In T. E. Moore (Ed.), *Cognitive development and the acquisition of language* (pp. 111–144). New York: Academic Press.

Rumelhart, D., & Norman, D. A. (1982). Simulating a skilled typist. *Cognitive Science, 6*, 1–36.

Shepard, R. N., & Metzler, J. (1971). Mental rotation of three dimensional objects. *Science, 171*, (701–703).

Shulman, G. L., Remmington, R., & McLean, J. P. (1979). Moving attention through visual space. *Journal of Experimental Psychology: Human Perception & Performance, 5*, 522–526.

Sieroff, E., Pollatsek, A., & Posner, M. I. (1988). Recognition of visual letter strings following injury to the posterior visual spatial attention system. *Cognitive Neuropsychology, 5*, 427–449.

Sternberg, S. (1966). High speed scanning in human memory. *Science, 153*, 652–654.

Tsal, Y. (1983). Movements of attention across the visual field. *Journal of Experimental Psychology: Human Perception & Performance, 9*, 523–530.

Van Voorhis, S., & Hillyard, S. A. (1977). Visual evoked potentials and selective attention to points in space. *Perception & Psychophysics, 22*, 54–62.

Volpe, B. T., LeDoux, J. E., & Gazzaniga, M. S. (1979). Information processes of visual stimuli in the "extinguished" field. *Nature, 282*, 722–727.

Walker, J. A., Friedrich, F., & Posner, M. I. (1983, February). *Biases in selective attention in patients with parietal lobe lesions*. Paper delivered to International Neuropsychological Society, San Diego, CA.

Wurtz, R. H., Goldberg, E., & Robinson, D. L. (1980). Behavioral modulation of visual responses in the monkey: Stimulus selection for attention and movement. *Progress in psychobiology & physiological psychology* (Vol. 9, pp. 43–83) New York: Academic Press.

8 The Effects of Attentional Deficits on Reading and Spelling

Argye E. Hillis
HealthSouth Rehabilitation Corporation

Alfonso Caramazza
Johns Hopkins University

Research on the patterns of language impairment that result from brain damage is increasingly being used to constrain claims about the structure of normal language processing. Much of this research has focused on issues concerning the overall functional architecture of the language processing system; that is, on questions about the nature and organization of the processing components or modules (in Marr's [1976] and, Simon's [1962] sense) that comprise the language systems. For example, an extensively investigated issue in the context of acquired dyslexia is whether or not there are distinct processing mechanisms that are engaged in oral reading (or spelling) of familiar and unfamiliar words (the latter operationally represented by nonwords). Another extensively investigated issue, this time in the broader context of acquired disorders of word processing, is whether or not the lexical system is organized into distinct input and output lexicons for both orthographic and phonological representations. In both cases, impaired performance has been used to infer the component structure of language-specific processing systems (see Caramazza, 1988, for review).

Issues about the functional architecture of the language system are not independent of issues concerning the processing structure of its component parts. Indeed, it is obvious that any meaningful discussion of functional architecture must be based on explicitly or implicitly held assumptions about the kinds of representations that are computed by the components that comprise the system. It is equally obvious that language performance is dependent on more than just language-specific processing mechanisms: Language performance also involves perceptual, motor, attentional, and memory mechanisms that are not necessarily language-specific. Consequently, the analysis of impaired language performance may be used to inform not only hypotheses about the functional architecture of the language system or specific hypotheses about the computational structure of a particular component of the system, but also hypotheses about the interaction of linguistic and nonlinguistic cognitive mechanisms. This wealth of opportunity is not without its price. The relationship between impaired performance and underlying mechanisms may be quite complex.

Consider the case of impaired oral reading performance. The impairment can result from damage to any one of a large number of mechanisms that are implicated in the reading process. Some of these mechanisms are specific to the reading process (e.g., orthographic input lexicon); others are specific to language processing generally (e.g., lexical-semantic processing); others still are specific to a particular subset of language tasks (e.g., recovering a phonological lexical form for output); but some mechanisms are not language-specific at all (e.g., perceptual and attentional mechanisms). If damage is restricted to only one mechanism in the complex functional architecture that subserves the reading process, inferences about the structure of specific components of the process from impaired performance may be relatively straightforward. However, if damage affects more than one mechanism in the reading process—by far the more likely event—inferences about the structure of normal reading may be quite complex, and in some cases not unproblematic. In any case, it is clear that the interpretation of impaired reading performance must consider not only the possibility that the impairment reflects damage to language-specific mechanisms, but also the possibility that the impairment results from damage to nonlinguistic mechanisms.

Cases of local interaction between language and more general cognitive mechanisms that have been investigated in brain-damaged subjects include reported consequences of unilateral attentional/perceptual deficits (clinically manifest as hemispatial neglect)[1] on their performance of reading and writing tasks. For example, patients with left hemispatial neglect tend to omit words on the left side of the page, lose their place in reading, and skip or repeat entire lines of print, frequently with no awareness of their errors (Battersby, Bender, Pollack, & Kahn, 1956; Gilliat & Pratt, 1952; Lawson, 1962). They also make backward completion errors (e.g., the word level is read as novel) in reading single words (Costello & Warrington; 1987; Ellis, Flude, & Young, 1987b; Kinsbourne & Warrington, 1962).

Ellis et al. (1987a & 1987b) reported a patient who made such so-called "neglect dyslexic" errors in reading print, but not when words were spelled

---

[1]We use the terms *unilateral spatial neglect*, or simply *neglect*, in reference to all varieties of phenomena evidencing an impairment in cognitive processing of internal or external stimuli contralateral to brain damage. However, Heilman (1979) delineated four major symptom constellations in the neglect syndrome: hemispatial neglect (impaired active processes of scanning and exploring), hemi-inattention (impaired passive processes; e.g., awareness), sensory extinction, and hemi-akinesia. Moreover, in the course of this chapter we draw additional distinctions between types (or levels) of neglect to explain our results.

aloud to her, indicating that neglect interacted with early visual processing of words. Their patient also made lateralized errors in written spelling, co-existing with intact oral spelling, pointing to a contribution of an attentional/perceptual impairment at a peripheral (output) level of the spelling process. Other reported effects of attentional deficits on peripheral aspects of written output include: neglect of the left side of the page with words squeezed into the right margin; a gradual slope to the right, upper corner in narrative writing; and perseverative or missing strokes in forming letters (e.g., Albert, 1981; Searleman, 1983). In contrast, oral spelling errors primarily on the left side of words (Baxter & Warrington, 1983) and skewed distribution of written and oral spelling errors toward the side of words contralateral to brain damage (Hillis & Caramazza, 1989) signal a faulty distribution of attention to an output-independent, orthographic representation.

These cases of interaction between lexical and other cognitive mechanisms suggest interesting constraints for models of the reading and spelling processes. Specifically, it would seem that attentional deficits may interact with different levels of representation in the processes of reading and spelling. In this chapter we present additional evidence of the interaction between lexical processing and attentional deficits that may contribute both to constraining theories of reading and spelling, and to the evaluation of competing theories of attentional mechanisms. First, however, we briefly describe the major theories of attentional and unilateral spatial neglect. We are brief here because there are several excellent recent reports that review in considerable detail the proposed psychological (De Renzi, 1982; Riddoch & Humphreys, 1987) and neural mechanisms (De Renzi, 1982; Rizzolatti & Camarda, 1987) implicated in unilateral spatial neglect.

Until recently (e.g., Jeannerod, 1987), most authors had assumed that the wide variety of dissociable symptoms involving impaired perception of, or response to, stimuli on one side of space have a common basis. Sensory hypotheses, for instance, implicate impaired scanning or analysis of sensory input as responsible for neglect symptoms. Although the prevalence and severity of neglect are, unarguably, positively correlated with both homonymous hemianopia and defective eye movements (De Renzi, 1982; Hecaen & Angelergues, 1963, cited in Costa, Vaughan, Horwitz, & Ritter, 1969); the hypothesis that sensory deficits cause neglect has been widely refuted on a variety of grounds, including persisting neglect in the face of intact visual fields and motor functioning (De Renzi, 1982); neglect of internal representations (Bisiach & Luzzatti, 1978); neglect of stimuli presented tachistoscopically to the intact visual hemifield (Kinsbourne & Warrington, 1962); and intact early visual processing of neglected stimuli (Volpe, LeDoux, & Gazzaniga, 1979).

Attentional hypotheses include explanations of neglect as an attention-arousal deficit (Heilman & Watson, 1977), a failure in exploration of space

(Chedru, 1976), defective mechanisms for directed attention (Mesulam, 1985), or difficulty shifting the focus of attention (Gainotti, 1986; Posner, Walker, Friedrich, & Rafal, 1984), each of which embraces a separate attentional mechanism as the source of impairment underlying neglect. Because attention may comprise a number of interacting processes involved in computing sensory and central representations, each of which could be unilaterally disrupted (Butter, 1987; Roy, Reuter-Lorentz, Roy, Copland, & Moscoviteh, 1987), the hypothesized mechanisms may turn out not to be mutually exclusive.[2] However, a historical focus on types of sensory attention has contributed to the lopsided development of attentional theories based exclusively on neglect symptoms to physical space and objects.

To account for symptoms of neglect that do not involve attention to external stimuli, such as unilateral errors in describing internally generated scenes (Bisiach, Capitani, Luzzatti, & Perani, 1981), tactile searching (Bisiach, Capitani, & Porta, 1985), or discriminating differences between internally reconstructed images (Bisiach, Luzzatti, & Perani, 1979; Ogden, 1985), several authors have advanced representational theories, which ascribe the cause of neglect to a disruption of internal representations (Bisiach & Berti, 1987; Bisiach, Berti, & Vallar, 1985; Bellas, Novelly, Eskanazi, & Wasserstein, 1988; Ogden, 1987) or impaired distribution of attention across representations (Mesulam, 1981).

In this chapter we provide additional evidence of unilaterally impaired computation of mental representations at several levels of the reading, writing, and perceptual processes. We present three cases of acquired dyslexia and dysgraphia in which the pattern of impaired performance in written and oral spelling, and in reading and recognition of orally spelled words, is explicable in each case by proposing a unilateral disruption in computing spatially coded orthographic representations of words. Two of the patients, RB and NG, showed severe contralesional neglect in a variety of visuospatial tasks; for NG (who is left-handed), the disorder is associated with left hemisphere damage (LHD). The third patient, HH (who is right-handed with LHD), was studied because his disproportionate right-sided errors in reading and spelling were remarkably similar to NG's errors, although he failed to show symptoms in traditional tests of neglect. Further evaluation shows, however, that his impairment (like that of the other two cases) is not restricted to lexical processes, but invades those cognitive processes in which computation of an internal spatial representation is required. The deficit in directed sensory attention displayed by only RB and

[2]Although mechanisms of attention can be separated along the lines of diverse aspects of mental state, including arousal/alertness, vigilance, and selective attention (Posner & Rafal, 1987), we are primarily concerned with distinctions among processes that require attention in the sense of "focalization, concentration of consciousness . . . withdrawal from some things in order to deal effectively with others" (James, 1890, p. 321).

NG provides support for the hypothesis that attentional mechanisms are implicated at different levels of representation (for both lexical and nonlexical processes).

SUBJECTS

All subjects were referred to the Medical Rehabilitation Center of Maryland for comprehensive outpatient therapy, following strokes. Relevant social, medical, and neuropsychological data follow, with the exception of reading and writing performance, which is described in detail later in this chapter.

Case 1: RB

Case History. RB is a 64-year-old, right-handed, white cable-splicer with a ninth-grade education and military technical training, who suffered a stroke 6 months prior to the initiation of this study. Physical examination revealed dense hemiplegia of both left extremities and left homonymous hemianopia, but full extraocular movements. A CT scan at the time of admission was normal. The diagnosis, based on clinical findings, was of a right middle cerebral artery thrombosis.

Speech, Language, and Cognitive Status. Clinical evaluation indicated mild central facial palsy, without significant dysarthria. A slight reduction in the visual field, in the left upper quadrant, was evidenced on confrontation. Performance on the Wechsler Memory Scale Form I (Wechsler, 1972/1945) was significantly below normal for his age on subtests of mental control (errors in counting backward and by threes); backward digits (score of 0); and visual reproduction. Forward digit span was 5. Visual reproduction of abstract designs demonstrated gross omissions and distortions on the left side, as did direct copying of a clock, flower, and a scene (See appendix A). In a line cancellation task, RB crossed 11/18 lines on the right side, and no lines on the left side of the paper. He bisected a 10-inch line at ⅞ inch from the right end. He obtained a score of 8/30 on the Hooper Visual Organization Test (Hooper, 1957), consistent with a severe deficit in visual integration. On the Raven's Coloured Progressive Matrices (Raven, 1956), he scored 16/36 correct, and showed a right : left response preference of 18 : 2. Given a blank map of the U.S., he judged the locations of all cities to be on the east coast. RB exhibited inconsistent neglect and consistent extinction (with bilateral stimulation) of left visual stimulation and left tactile stimulation of the face or hand. He also exhibited left-sided auditory extinction.

RB was not aphasic. Performance on the Boston Diagnostic Aphasia Examination (Goodglass & Kaplan, 1972) was 100% correct on body-part and responsive naming, sentence repetition, and in following auditory sequential commands. Speech was fluent and grammatical. RB received normal scored of 155/175 (standard score of 97) on the Peabody Picture Vocabulary Test—Revised Form M (Dunn & Dunn, 1981) and 55/60 on the Revised Boston Naming Test (Goodglass, Kaplan, & Weintraub, 1983). Three of his five errors on the Modified Token Text (De Renzi & Faglioni, 1978) could be attributed to impaired scanning of the stimuli on the left. RB spontaneously read letter-by-letter, and made many errors, as is described in detail in the experimental results.

Case 2: NG

Case History. NG is a 76-year-old white widow with an eighth-grade education. She claims to be naturally left-handed, but was trained to write with her right hand in parochial school. Premorbidly, she continued to write with her right hand, but used her left hand for most other tasks (e.g., brushing, eating). Four months prior to this study, NG suffered a stroke, resulting in spastic right hemiparesis of both extremities, hypesthesia, and diminished proprioceptive sensation. Eye movements and visual fields were fully normal. A CT scan revealed decreased density in the left anterior basal ganglia adjacent to the head of the caudate nucleus and a large area of the left parietal white matter. A later arteriogram evidenced complete occlusion of the left internal carotid artery.

Speech, Language, and Cognitive Status. NG received a score of 42/60 on the Revised Boston Naming Test. All but five of her errors could be ascribed to visual errors (e.g., *muzzle→gun holster*; *tripod→pencils*), although she did not correct them after stimulus (semantic) cues. On the Boston Diagnostic Aphasia Examination performance was normal on all tasks that did not involve sustained attention. Responses were 100% correct on naming colors and body parts, responsive naming, and on answering nonredundant, acontextual questions. She made three errors in answering questions about paragraphs read to her and in following complex auditory sequential commands. Her verbal description of the cookie theft picture revealed some omission of details on the right side of the picture, and poor synthesis of the content. She spoke in fluent, syntactically complex sentences. NG received a score of 131/175, standard score of 75, on the Peabody Picture Vocabulary Test, compatible with an educational level of ninth grade. She scored 30.5/36 (within normal limits) on the Modified Token Test; three errors could be attributed to impaired scanning of the stimuli on the right side. NG's scores on the Wechsler Memory Scale were significantly below normal for her age on subtests of mental control (score of 0/9); logical memory (5/22 in paragraph recall); backward digits (score of 0); and visual reproduction (score of 1/15). She demonstrated gross omissions and distortions on the right side in visual reproduction of abstract designs and in direct copying of drawings of familiar objects (see appendix A). She scored 18/36 correct on the Raven's Coloured Progressive Matrices with a left : right response preference of 21 : 3. In a line cancellation task, she crossed the 13 lines on the utmost left side, and no lines (out of 23) to the right of these. Her bisection of a 10-inch line was displaced 7/8 inch to the left. She received a score of 18/30 on the Hooper Visual Organization Test, consistent with a moderate deficit of visual processing. On a blank map of the U.S., NG located Baltimore (where she had lived all her life) in the southwest corner. She exhibited consistent extinction of tactile and visual stimulation on the right side. She showed no sign of verbal apraxia or significant dysarthria.

Case 3: HH

Case History. HH is a 57-year-old, right-handed truck driver with a 10th-grade education. Fifteen months before this study began, he experienced dense right hemiplegia, right homonymous hemianopia, and mild right facial droop. A CT scan 5 days postonset revealed a large area of attenuation in the left medial and posterior temporal lobe, occipital lobe, and thalamus adjacent to the posterior limb of the internal capsule. There was a slight mass effect, with some compression of the left lateral ventricle and mild obliteration of the cortical sulci on the left.

Speech, Language, and Cognitive Status. Performance on the Boston Diagnostic Aphasia Examination at 2 months postonset indicated deficits in auditory comprehension/retention, confrontation naming, reading, and writing. HH's score on the Boston Naming Test improved from 42/60 to 50/60, and his raw score on the Wechsler Memory Scale improved from 28 to 45 (just below normal range for his age) prior to initiation of the study. The only areas of unresolved deficits were drawing abstract figures from memory and learning associate word pairs. HH received a score of 29 (normal) on the Modified Token Text and a raw score of 126 (standard score of 71) on the Peabody Picture Vocabulary Test just prior to entering the study. In reading tasks HH, like RB, spontaneously read letter-by-letter and made many incorrect word responses, which are described later.

Visual reproduction of abstract designs on the Wechsler Memory Scale indicated a possible contribution of neglect in his incomplete (one side only) drawings from memory. Therefore, line bisection, line cancellation, and copying were assessed. There was no evidence of unilateral spatial neglect in any tasks except copying a scene of a house, fence, and two trees. He initially omitted the right-hand tree, but then inserted it in a wrong location. There was no evidence of tactile or auditory extinction. Assessment of visual detection of movement confirmed a persisting right visual field cut and consistent extinction of right stimuli with bilateral stimulation within the intact hemifield. The patient obtained a score of 21/30 (a mild deficit) on the Hooper Visual Organization Test.

HH reported premorbid right-hand dominance for all tasks (e.g., writing, throwing, cutting). He has seven siblings; one sister is left-handed.

Control Subject: WW

WW is a right-handed, white male, 65 years of age. He is a retired steelworker, who completed the 10th grade. He reports a negative history for neurological disease or trauma, cardiac arrest, and drug or alcohol abuse.

EXPERIMENTAL TASKS

The investigation consisted of studies designed to identify the role of spatial attention in reading and spelling processes. In order to determine whether the impaired mechanisms were specific to lexical processing or more general mechanisms for processing spatial representations, perception of nonlexical letter strings (identifying two identical letters in an array of five) was studied as well. Each of these tasks allowed us to study the effects of spatial position with respect to two independent variables: (a) position in the array, and (b) position in the visual field.

The studies took place over a period of 11 months, during which time each patient's performance in reading and writing tasks was fairly stable. The main exception was that NG's and RB's task persistence and vigilance improved gradually over time, allowing us to increase testing periods from 15-minute sessions to 60-minute sessions.

Interjudge reliability (point-to-point percent agreement) in scoring accuracy of oral reading responses was 100% for all three subjects for words, and exceeded 95% in all cases for nonwords. Percent agreement in scoring accuracy of spelling responses was greater than 98% in all cases for words and nonwords. Point-to-point percent agreement in transcription of written responses was 100% for RB, 94.6% for NG, and 98.2% for HH; so only the scoring of the first author is reported.

READING

Experiment 1: Oral Reading of Word Lists

Method

Stimuli consisted of word lists compiled from the Johns Hopkins University Dyslexia Battery (Goodman & Caramazza, 1986) and the Morphology

Battery (Badecker & Caramazza, unpublished data). Lists were constructed to determine the effect of grammatical word class, frequency, concreteness, orthophonological regularity, and a variety of dimensions of morphological complexity. A total of 976 words and 208 nonwords were presented to NG and HH; 350 words and 80 nonwords were presented to RB.

Results

Error types. RB ordinarily initiated reading of each word by naming the letters aloud. He rarely made letter confusions, but he frequently started reading letters in the middle of the word. His first response was recorded and scored. The most striking aspect of RB's performance was the production of backward completion errors following correct reading of all of the constituent letters. For example, RB read the word *basis* as "b-a-s-i-s...oasis". He also produced errors of left letter omissions (e.g., *blame* → "lame") with or without prior identification of the component letters. He did not appear to be aware of these errors, nor did he ever self-correct a response. On the 25 occasions in which he was asked to define the stimulus word, he consistently defined the response, rather than the stimulus word.

A backward completion error was defined as any response that satisfied all of the following criteria: (a) identical to the stimulus by at least two letters from the right end; (b) at least one unshared letter on the left; and (c) does not contain two or more letters in the same relative order left of the shared portion. Thus, for example, *ration* → "creation" was counted as a backward completion error, whereas *ration* → "traction" was counted as an other visual error. Neglect errors were responses that were identical to the stimulus on the right, but omitted all letters to the left of the shared portion (e.g., *ration* → "ion").

HH also read each word letter-by-letter before attempting a response. He produced the same types of errors made by RB. That is, he produced unilateral completion errors—in this case, forward completion errors, such as, *probably* → "p-r-o-b-a-b-l-y...problems"; right-sided neglect errors, such as *rigid* → "r-i-g-i-d...rig"; and occasional other visual errors (e.g., *bluish* → "blush"). Error types were defined analogously to backward completion errors and left neglect errors.

Although NG did not rely on explicit letter identification prior to word production, she produced the same types of errors as HH. Corpora of each patients' errors, organized by error type, are reported in appendix B.

Error Distribution. Figure 8.1 shows the distribution of errors for each of the subjects. There are notable contrasts between the relative proportion of completion and neglect errors for the three subjects. Completion errors accounted for 52.0% (64/123) of RB's error responses, 63.3% (133/210) of NG's errors, and 80.8% (193/239) of HH's errors in reading words. How-

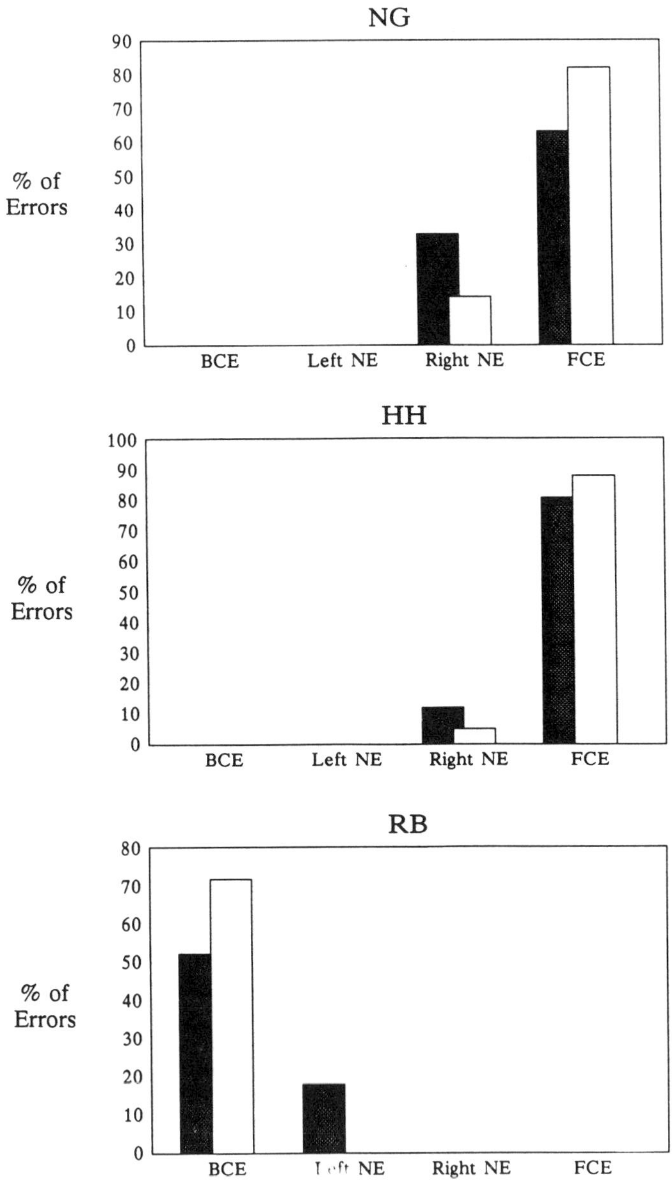

FIG. 8.1 Distribution of completion and neglect errors in reading. Bar 1 = errors on words; 2 = errors on nonwords.

ever, the differences were nearly eliminated in reading nonwords; 72.0% (18/25) of RB's errors, 82.2% (97/118) of NG's errors, and 88.1% (52/59) of HH's errors were completion errors. For all subjects, there was a strong tendency to complete nonwords as words (e.g., *dring* → "drill"), although some completion errors were other nonwords (e.g., *garmage* → "garmz").

For all patients, more than 75% of neglect error responses were more frequent than the target. For the two left hemisphere damaged patients, these included many suffix deletions. All but six (23/29; 79.3%) of the neglect errors by HH were suffix deletions, although only a small percentage (33/193; 17.1%) of his completion errors were suffix errors, consistent with a tendency by all patients to produce neglect errors only when omission resulted in a higher frequency word (see Table 8.1). In contrast, NG's many substitution and insertion of suffixes resulted in forward completion errors that were not ordinarily more frequent than the target word.

NG also occasionally produced words with illegal suffixes; that is, suffixes that are not appropriate for the stem produced. Many of these occurred in sequences of responses with a repeated suffix. Examples follow (+ indicates a correct response):

national → natural*ly*
similarity → similar*ly*
stables → +
travels → +
leader → +
heavy → +
follow → +
morality → moral*ly*
sky → +
reduction → +
eventual → eventual*ly*
parental → parent*ly*
brought → +
cruelty → cruel*ly*
sincerity → sincer*ly*
natural → +
organize → organization
blowing → +
among → +
orbital → orbital*ly*
serve → server
precise → precious*ly*

These illegally suffixed responses would seem to be related to perseverative errors, commonly associated with visuo-spatial neglect (Mark, Kooistra, & Heillman, 1988). NG's higher frequency of such perseverative responses may account for her higher proportion of suffix errors in forward completion errors when compared to HH's performance (Table 8.2).

Although the great majority of stimuli used in the reading tasks administered to RB consisted of unaffixed words, he did produce some prefix deletions in oral reading of sentences where affixed words were used (reported later).

Error Rates. Overall, RB exhibited the lowest accuracy rate in reading words: 39.4% (138/350), compared to 77.3% (754/976) accuracy for NG and 61.2% (597/976) accuracy for HH (see Table 8.3 for distribution of er-

TABLE 8.1
Stimulus and Response Frequency in Reading

Subject	Response Type	N	X̄ Stimulus Frequency	X̄ Response Frequency	t	p
RB: Words						
	Correct	138	190.4	—		
	Backward completion error	64	130.0	140.2	−.27	*NS*
	Left neglect error	22	65.8	1647.8	−1.41	*NS*
	Other visual error	37	187.0	115.0	.86	*NS*
	Omission	89	66.9	—		
Nonwords						
	Backward completion error	18	—	62.6		
	Left neglect error	0	—	—		
	Other visual error	7	—	253.6		
	Omission	0				
NG: Words						
	Correct	754	103.0	—		
	Forward completion error	133	44.2	63.0	.54	*NS*
	Right neglect error	69	42.2	74.4	3.37	$p < .01$
	Other visual error	8	24.5	89.9	1.02	*NS*
	Omission	12	48.5	—		
Nonwords						
	Forward completion error	97	—	141.5		
	Right neglect error	17	—	20.7		
	Other visual error	4	—	—		
	Omission	0				
HH: Words						
	Correct	597	110.2	—		
	Forward completion error	193	52.6	63.0	1.18	*NS*
	Right neglect error	29	58.4	74.4	1.01	*NS*
	Other visual error	17	113.8	89.9		
	Omission	140	20.1	—		
Nonwords						
	Forward completion error	52	—	92.0		
	Right neglect error	3	—	100.7		
	Other visual error	4	—	48.6		
	Omission	0				

rors as a function of various lexical and nonlexical parameters). This difference in the overall level of reading performance could merely reflect differences in severity of deficit. Alternatively, because only RB's deficit affected processing of the initial (left-sided) letters of words, the difference in accuracy levels could reflect the importance of the initial segment of visually presented words in word recognition. Certainly, the difference in performance levels cannot be attributed to differences in the stimuli used with the three subjects: for the 326 words they all read, RB was 36.5% accurate, where NG and HH were 84.1% and 61.7% accurate, respectively. Unfortunately, however, the issue of whether differences in performance levels among the three subjects reflect differences in severity of impairment or the interaction of side of neglect by relative importance of the initial segment of words cannot be decided by the data at our disposal. In any case, resolution of this issue is not crucial for present purposes.

Effect of Word Length. For all subjects, errors increased as a function of word length in number of letters. RB correctly read 39.3% (11/28) of the four- to six-letter words, compared to 14.3% (4/28) of the seven- to eight-letter words on a list matched for frequency and phonemes per word. On the same stimuli, the contrasts were 96.2% versus 82.1% for NG and 71.4% versus 35.7% for HH. Errors increased significantly with letter length only for HH (chi-square test for trend; [$\chi^2 = 6.5$; $p < .02$]), but analysis of each patient's entire reading sample indicated that correctly read words were significantly ($p < .001$) shorter than misread words in all cases. Whereas neglect errors were shorter than completion errors ($p < .001$ by two-tailed t test for words; $p < .01$ for nonwords for each subject; words that elicited neglect errors tended to be longer than words that elicited for-

TABLE 8.2
Distribution of Morphological Errors in Reading

		NG		*HH*	
	N	*Morphological Errors*	*Total Errors*	*Morphological Errors*	*Total Errors*
Nouns	40	2 (5.0)	6(15.0)	1 (2.5)	11(27.5)
Verbs	40	2 (5.0)	6(15.0)	3 (7.6)	12(30.0)
Adjectives	40	1 (2.5)	5(12.5)	1 (2.5)	13(32.5)
Functors	20	0 (0)	1 (5.0)	0 (0)	5(25.0)
Derivations	100	12(12.0)	18(18.0)	12(12.0)	48(48.0)
Inflections	100	46(46.0)	54(54.0)	19(19.0)	49(49.0)
Irregular suffix	50	4 (8.0)	7(14.0)	5(10.0)	13(26.0)
Regular suffix	50	21(42.0)	22(44.0)	6(12.0)	12(24.0)
Uninflected	50	10(20.0)	11(22.0)	0 (0)	5(10.0)
Opaque I	80	21(26.3)	32(40.0)	12(15.0)	48(60.0)
Transparent	80	4 (5.0)	10(12.5)	14(17.5)	29(36.3)
Total	650	123(18.9)	172(26.5)	73(11.2)	245(37.7)

TABLE 8.3
Reading Accuracy as a Function of Lexical and Orthographic Factors
(Given as # Correct and % Correct in Parentheses)

	N	*RB*	*NG*	*HH*
Open-class				
Nouns	28	8 (28.6)	27 (96.4)	20 (71.4)
Verbs	28	6 (21.4)	22 (78.6)	13 (46.4)
Adjectives	28	10 (35.7)	26 (92.9)	14 (50.0)
		$\chi^2 = 1.37$ *NS*	$\chi^2 = 5.23$ *NS*	$\chi^2 = 4.15$ *NS*
Functors	20	8 (40.0)	20(100.0)	15 (75.0)
		$\chi^2 = 2.24$ *NS*	$\chi^2 = 8.63$ ($p < .05$)	$\chi^2 = 6.69$ *NS*
Nonwords				
Nonhomophones	34	2 (5.9)	8 (23.5)	11 (32.4)
Pseudohomophones	34	9 (26.5)	12 (35.3)	7 (20.6)
Concrete nouns	21	11 (52.4)	19 (90.5)	13 (61.9)
Abstract nouns	21	6 (28.6)	15 (71.4)	6 (28.6)
		$\chi^2 = 1.58$ *NS*	$\chi^2 = 1.39$ *NS*	$\chi^2 = 3.46$ *NS*
Regular nouns	30	17 (56.7)	29 (96.7)	28 (93.3)
Irregular nouns	80	33 (41.3)	72 (90.0)	56 (70.0)
		$\chi^2 = 1.52$ *NS*	*NS*	$\chi^2 = 5.35$ ($p < .05$)
High frequency	145	68 (46.9)	141 (97.2)	118 (81.4)
Low frequency	145	41 (28.3)	123 (84.8)	81 (55.9)
		$\chi^2 = 9.67$ ($p < .01$)	$\chi^2 = 12.21$ ($p < .001$)	$\chi^2 = 20.43$ ($p < .0001$)
Word length (# letters)				
4	14	5 (35.7)	13 (92.9)	10 (71.4)
5	14	6 (42.9)	14(100.0)	10 (71.4)
6	14	5 (35.7)	14(100.0)	7 (50.0)
7	14	2 (14.3)	12 (85.7)	5 (35.7)
8	14	2 (14.3)	11 (78.6)	5 (35.7)
		$\chi^2 = 5.82$ ($p < .03$)	*NS*	*NS*
	χ^2 test for trend:	*NS*	*NS*	$\chi^2 = 6.5$ ($p < .02$)

ward completion errors or backward completion errors (*ns*). For completion errors, there was a high correlation in each case between response length and stimulus length (Table 8.4). The Pearson product-moment correlation (*r*) between stimulus word length and the number of letters shared (i.e., common to the stimulus and the response) exceeded .525 and was substantially higher than the correlation between stimulus length and response length, although the latter was also highly significant, for all subjects.

This result is consistent with the view that the patients were able to process greater amounts (not necessarily greater proportions) of information for longer than shorter words. Although previous reports attribute the high correlation between stimulus length and length of completion errors to an implicit awareness of the length of the target (Ellis et al., 1987b), the correlation in these cases seems to reflect, instead, the inclusion of more letters from longer stimuli in the responses. This result as we argue in the Discussion section, has important implications for claims about the nature of orthographic representations. Similar findings with regard to line bisection have been reported: Butter, Mark, and Heilman (in press) found that a patient with left neglect bisected lines further to the left as the length of lines increased, although he made more and larger errors on longer lines. A patient reported by Halligan and Marshall (1988) also included longer segments of the line on the left of the perceived midpoint with longer lines;

TABLE 8.4
Correlations Between Stimulus Length and Error Responses

Forward Completion Errors

	Stimulus Length—Response Length r^2	*f*	*Stimulus Length—# Shared Letters* r^2	*f*
RB: Words	.22	15.9 $p < .0001$	.59	78.2 $p < .0001$
Nonwords	.39	12.9 $p < .01$	.50	6.7 $p < .05$
NG: Words	.38	80.0 $p < .0001$	.56	165.3 $p < .0001$
Nonwords	.28	38.0 $p < .0001$	.39	61.1 $p < .0001$
HH: Words	.12	26.0 $p < .0001$	.53	211.7 $p < .0001$
Nonwords	.17	9.9 $p < .01$	.51	51.5 $p < .0001$

Neglect Errors

	Stimulus Length—Response Length r^2	*f*	*Stimulus Length—# Deleted Letters* r^2	*f*
RB: Words	.53	30.5 $p < .0001$	.49	26.1 $p < .0001$
Nonwords				
NG: Words	.16	13.1 $p < .01$	.80	274.8 $p \ll .0001$
Nonwords	.001	*NS*	.96	380.4 $p \ll .0001$
HH: Words	.26	9.5 $p < .01$	.86	159.9 $p \ll .0001$
Nonwords ($N = 3$)				

this patient also bisected very short lines accurately or to the left of the actual midpoint. Similarly, our patients included more letters on the neglected side of words as word length increased, although they made more errors on longer words.

For neglect errors, there was a low correlation ($r = .16$ and $.26$, respectively) between stimulus length and the number of letters deleted by NG and HH. Both subjects omitted one or two letters (mean = 1.49 for NG and 1.55 for HH), regardless of the length of the stimulus word. As a result, there was a very high correlation between stimulus length and response length ($r = .80$ and $.86$ [$p \ll .0001$] for the two subjects). For RB, who was presented only with unaffixed stimuli in the single word reading task, stimulus, length was significantly correlated with both the number of letters deleted in forming neglect errors ($r = .532$; $p < .0001$) and with response length ($r = .493$). In other words, RB deleted a segment that was proportional to the length of the stimulus.

Letter-by-Letter Reading. As noted, both RB and HH spontaneously commenced reading words by naming each letter in sequence. Unlike RB, HH almost never failed to read the entire letter string. HH claimed to be unable to read without this strategy, although he read very short words and occasional longer words without using this strategy. His behavior and the subjective account he gives of his difficulties in reading, resemble cases of so-called letter-by-letter reading that have been reported in the literature (e.g., Gardner & Zurif, 1975; Patterson & Kay, 1982; Staller, Buchanan, Singer, Lappin, & Webb, 1978; Warrington & Shallice, 1980). Therefore, we explored in HH those features of reading that have been described in patients classified as letter-by-letter readers so as to determine whether or not a common mechanism for the behavior might be identified.

The cardinal features of "letter-by-letter reading" delineated by Patterson and Kay (1982) are the following: successive identification of each letter in the word; abnormal latencies in word identification, with a linear relationship between response time and word length in letters; and frequently, a concomitant letter identification deficit. We confirmed the presence of the first characteristic. With regard to the second, HH's response times from the beginning of letter reading to the end of the first whole word response ranged from 2 seconds to 70 seconds, with a mean of 14.1 seconds, for 100 words that were timed (mean length = 6.51 letters). The correlation between length in letters and latency from the beginning of first letter named to the production of the word was highly significant ($r = .408$; $p < .0001$). HH also produced occasional confusions of visually similar letters (e.g., *e* → *o*), which were often self-corrected. The letter confusion errors were distributed across all positions.

We compared HH's reading performance following correct letter-by-letter reading to his performance when he did not use this strategy. Words read without letter-by-letter reading were significantly shorter (means = 5.2 letters and 6.0 letters, respectively; $t = 3.87$; by two-tailed t test, $p < .001$) and higher in frequency (means = 182.9 vs. 87.3; $t = 4.45$, $p < .0001$). HH read correctly 80.9% (123/152) of the words for which he did not attempt to overtly identify the words' letters, and 71.1% (474/667) of the words after accurate overt letter identification. Comparison of error responses following letter naming to error responses in the absence of letter naming revealed no significant differences in response length (mean of 6.9 and 6.3 letters, respectively), number of letters shared in forward completion errors (means of 4.08 and 4.09 letters, respectively), or number of letters deleted in neglect errors (means of 1.6 and 1.5 letters). The frequency value of error responses produced in those cases in which no overt letter naming took place tended to be higher than the frequency of error responses following letter reading—for forward completion errors: means of 138.3 and 52.4, respectively ($t = 2.82$, $p < .01$); for neglect errors: means of 125.2 and 61.1, respectively (*ns*). In sum, short words often elicited high-frequency, correct responses or high-frequency word errors without overt letter identification; whereas longer words elicited overt letter reading and more errors. For longer or less frequent words, explicit letter reading did not alter the accuracy or type of response or the relationship of the response to the stimulus.

If letter-by-letter reading was a learned compensatory strategy to assure adequate scanning, clearly it was not always effective for HH or RB, because they both produced neglect errors even after naming every letter in a word. Nonetheless, HH produced substantially fewer neglect (omission) errors than did NG, who did not employ this strategy independently. We evaluated the possibility that forcing NG to overtly identify all letters of a word would reduce the probability of producing neglect errors. A total of 150 words and nonwords from previous lists were presented to NG, with instructions to read each letter aloud before saying the whole word. She made no errors in letter identification, but she produced the identical types of word errors as she had produced in reading these words without letter-by-letter identification 6 months earlier (Table 8.5). Her errors included nine neglect errors (e.g., *stresses* → "s-t-r-e-s-s-e-s . . . stress"), 30 forward completion errors (*province* → "p-r-o-v-i-n-c-e . . . privacy"; *garmage* → "g-a-r-m-a-g-e . . . garment"), and only one other visual error (*insistence* → "i-n-s-i-s-t-e-n-c-e . . . instant"). The primary difference between this performance and her previous reading of these stimuli (without letter naming) was a reduction in neglect errors. That is, removing the possibility of defective scanning effectively reduced the probability of omitting the word ending, whereas the probability of other types of errors remained constant.

Furthermore, when NG was asked to construct a sentence with each of 50 words on this latter list of stimuli, prior to saying the word, the sentences she produced revealed comprehension of the word that was then produced

TABLE 8.5
Comparison of NG's Reading with and Without Letter Naming

	Normal Reading			Reading After Letter-by-Letter Naming		
	N	*% of Total*	*% of Errors*	*N*	*% of Total*	*% of Errors*
Words (*N* = 130)						
Forward completion error	20	15.4	51.3	20	15.4	69.0
Right neglect error	18	13.9	46.2	8	6.2	27.6
Other	1	0.8	2.6	1	0.8	3.4
Correct	91	70.0		101	77.7	
Nonwords (*N* = 20)						
Forward completion error	9	45.0	81.8	9	45.0	81.8
Right neglect error	1	5.0	9.1	1	5.0	9.1
Other	1	5.0	9.1	1	5.0	9.1
Correct	9	45.0		9	45.0	

(as opposed to the stimulus word). For example, NG's response to the word *status* was, "s-t-a-t-u-s. . . The Statue of Liberty is really pretty. . . . The word is statue"; the word *planet* elicited: "p-l-a-n-e-t. . . . The plane landed on the other side. . . . The word is plane." This pattern of performance clearly eliminates both a low level visual input deficit and a speech output deficit as potential sources of her completion and neglect errors in reading.

Experiment 2: Reading Vertically Presented Words

The preceding results demonstrate that impaired scanning or sensory deficits cannot, on their own, account for the occurrence of contralesional errors in our three subjects, because the entire word must be scanned and perceived in order to name the letters. It is, however, conceivable that the subjects' reading of the letters was an entirely separate process that did not have a role in subsequent word recognition. This account would be consistent with Denny–Brown's and Banker's (1954) theory (amorphosynthesis) of neglect as an extinction phenomenon, whereby perception of stimulation on the contralesional side is extinguished by exaggerated attention to stimulation on the ipsilateral side. Thus, for example, preoccupation with the letters on the left (for NG and HH) when considered as part of a word would extinguish perception of the letters on the right side, even though the letters were identified when they were attended to separately. To assess the plausibility of this account, we presented words in a vertical array. For vertically presented stimuli, the amorphosynthesis hypothesis would predict improved reading, or at least a reduction in unilateral errors, because the letters are all perceived on the same side. And, in fact, previous studies of dyslexia consequent to neglect have reported nearly complete elimination of unilateral errors with vertical presentation of words (Ellis et al., 1987b; Gilliatt & Pratt, 1952; Kinsbourne & Warrington, 1962). It was essential, therefore, to evaluate the effects of mode of presentation on reading performance in our subjects.

Method

NG and HH were presented with 300 words and 60 nonwords, selected from a larger list of stimuli presented 3 months earlier. WW (the control subject) read the same stimuli. Each word was printed vertically. This task was not completed by RB, because he found it extremely difficult.

Results

Overall reading accuracy of vertically presented stimuli was strikingly similar to performance with the same words presented horizontally (NG: 74.7% vs. 72.3% correct words for vertically and horizontally presented stimuli, respectively; HH: 60.7% vs. 61.2 correct words for vertically and horizontally presented stimuli, respectively). Furthermore, the types and distribution of errors were identical for the two types of stimulus presentation. Forward completion errors accounted for 63.3% of NG's errors in reading vertically presented words and for 63.2% of her errors in normal reading; neglect errors accounted for 34.2% and 32.9% of her errors on words presented vertically and horizontally, respectively. In HH's reading of words in the two types of stimulus presentation, forward completion errors accounted for 82.9% of the errors in reading vertically presented words and for 80.8% of his errors in normal reading, whereas neglect errors accounted for 7.3% and 9.7% of his errors for vertically and horizontally presented words, respectively. The distribution of errors on nonwords were also comparable for the two types of stimulus presentations (Table 8.6). WW made very few errors on this task.

Conclusion

The identical pattern of errors in reading vertically and horizontally presented stimuli rules out laterality of visual stimulation as the source of contralesional errors. These results also undermine the amorphosynthesis hypothesis of neglect. More generally, it would seem that we must entertain the hypothesis that the observed unilateral disruption in word reading in our subjects occurs at a level where an horizontally organized, word-centered internal representation of the word is computed.

Experiment 3: Recognition of Oral Spelling

If the patients' spatially determined impairment does not result from failure to process adequately aspects of the physical stimulus but arises instead from inadequate processing of an internal representation, then similar errors should occur when the visual system is circumvented in the process of word recognition as, for example, in the recognition of orally spelled words.

Method

The lists of words ($n = 300$) and nonwords (60) that served as stimuli in the preceding reading experiment and a list of words controlled for frequency and length ($n = 42$) from the Dyslexia Battery were spelled aloud to NG, HH, and WW, 2 months after Experiment 2 was completed. The subjects were simply required to name the words and nonwords.

Results

Once again, the same pattern of errors emerged (Table 8.7). For HH, the types and distribution of errors in this task were indistinguishable from his pattern of errors in normal reading of these stimuli. Forward completion errors comprised 68.4% of his errors in reading of words and 71.9% in recognition of oral spelling; neglect errors comprised an additional 9.7% and 14.4% of errors in the two tasks, respectively. HH's errors on nonword stimuli were also comparable across tasks: 73.9% compared to 80.7% forward completion errors and 8.7% compared to 9.7% neglect errors for reading and naming orally spelled nonwords, respectively. The only discernable contrast between this task and normal (or vertical) reading was a slight reduction in the number of neglect errors produced by NG. Notably, spelling letters aloud to NG had precisely the same effect as her own spelling of letters aloud prior to naming the word—that is, spelling the letters to her re-

TABLE 8.6
Vertical Reading Results

	N	*Correct*	*Forward completion error*	*Right neglect error*	*Left neglect & backward completion errors*	*Other*	*Omission*
NG							
Words	300	223(74.3)	48(16.0)	26 (8.7)	0	2 (0.7)	1 (0.3)
Nonwords	60	16(26.7)	33(55.0)	3 (5.0)	0	1 (1.7)	7(11.7)
HH							
Words	234	142(60.7)	68(29.1)	6 (2.6)	0	8 (3.4)	10 (4.3)
Nonwords	32	10(31.3)	18(56.3)	0	0	8 (9.7)	1 (3.1)
WW							
Words	300	293(97.7)	0	1 (0.3)	0	6 (3.0)	0
Nonwords	60	56(93.3)	2 (3.3)	0	0	2 (3.3)	0

TABLE 8.7
Distribution of Errors in Three Word Recognition Tasks

	Errors on Right		*Errors on Left*			*Total*
	Completion error	*Neglect error*	*Completion error*	*Neglect error*	*Other*	*Errors*
NG						
Reading						
Words	63.3	32.9	0	0	3.8	210
Nonwords	82.2	14.4	0	0	3.4	118
Vertical reading						
Words	63.2	34.2	0	0	2.6	76
Nonwords	89.2	8.1	0	0	2.7	154
Recognition of oral spelling						
Words	72.2	18.9	0	0	8.9	180
Nonwords	82.9	2.4	0	0	14.6	41
HH						
Reading						
Words	80.8	12.1	0	0	7.1	239
Nonwords	88.1	5.1	0	0	6.8	59
Vertical reading						
Words	82.9	7.3	0	0	9.8	82
Nonwords	85.7	0	0	0	14.3	21
Recognition of oral spelling						
Words	71.9	14.4	0	0	13.7	181
Nonwords	80.7	9.7	0	0	9.7	41
RB						
Reading						
Words	0	0	52.0	17.9	30.1	123
Nonwords	0	0	72.0	0	28.0	25
WW						
Vertical reading						
Words	0	14.3	0	0	85.7	7
Nonwords	50.0	0	0	0	50.0	4
Recognition of oral spelling						
Words	11.1	0	0	11.1	77.8	9
Nonwords	0	0	0	0	100	1

duced the probability of occurrence of neglect errors, from 32.9% to 18.9% of the error responses, whereas the probability of forward completion errors and other errors remained unchanged.

Other aspects of the patients' performance were also unaffected by the form of stimulus presentation used in this experiment. Thus, there was no significant difference (by two-tailed *t* tests), for either subject, between reading and recognition of oral spelling in the number of letters shared by forward completion errors and their targets, or in the number of letters deleted from the target to produce neglect errors. Furthermore, impaired word recognition in this experiment cannot be explained by a deficit in the retention of letters: On presentation of the Dyslexia Battery list (four- to seven-letter words), patients accurately repeated the letters before responding with the word. And, finally, WW again performed very well.

Conclusions

The unilaterality of errors in word recognition in our patients is a robust effect, observed in reading horizontally and vertically presented words, with or without prior, overt identification of the component letters, and in auditory presentation of letter series. Both NG and HH showed a unilateral disruption in components of the reading process that are not restricted to visual input.

Experiment 4: Sentence Reading

The strong similarity in performance by NG and HH on the preceding task strongly suggests that the deficit responsible for forward completion errors might be common to both patients, even though HH did not show clinical signs of neglect. However, a recurrent contrast noted between NG's and HH's reading performance was in their respective ability to scan external stimuli. NG did not consistently scan to the end of the word unless she was required to name the letters aloud. RB also erred in scanning the entire word, even when he (spontaneously) named the letters aloud. HH, on the other hand, read each letter without fail. Therefore, NG's and RB's impaired scanning might reflect an additional (and dissociable) impairment to the one that is presumably responsible for the failure to process adequately internal orthographic representations. This difference may reflect itself in differential omission errors in sentence reading.

Method

Stimuli consisted of 120 sentences, 40 sentences each of 5-word, 10-word, and 15-word lengths. The stimuli were selected from adult level reading material and only contained words from the 30,000 most frequently occurring words (Thorndike & Lorge, 1944). The patients were asked to read the sentences, and to indicate verbally if they encountered a word that they could not read.

Results

RB's and HH's distribution of error types on individual words for which an effort at reading was made was virtually identical to the distribution of errors reported for reading isolated words. RB's errors included backward completion errors (51.4% errors in reading words in sentences, compared to 52.0% errors in reading single words) and neglect errors (20% errors in reading sentences, compared to 17.9% errors in reading isolated words). HH made forward completion errors in sentence and isolated word reading (80.8% in both tasks) and neglect errors (6.7% vs. 5.1% errors in sentence and isolated word reading, respectively). NG produced a higher proportion (45/86; 52.3%) of neglect errors in sentence reading, entirely attributable to the high proportion of inflections in sentences, which she tended to omit. Her remaining word errors within sentences were forward completion errors (41/86; 47.7%).

There was, however, a sharp contrast among subjects in the frequency of whole-word omissions. RB and NG exhibited substantially more omissions at the extremities of sentences than did HH. Thus, for example, RB omitted 13.5% of the words in 5-word sentences and 25.7% of the words in the 10-word sentences he attempted. He only omitted words in the beginning of the sentences; he never missed a word to the right of an attempted word. All of NG's omission errors occurred on the final one or two words in a sentence. HH omitted only two words in all of the stimuli—both in the middle of 15-word sentences.

Conclusions

Results of sentence reading are compatible with the hypothesis that RB and NG have an additional deficit, not present in HH, responsible for impaired scanning of visual stimuli. Prominent omission of whole words on the neglected side, co-occurring with completion errors on individual words, appear to reflect the contribution of at least two dissociable factors: impaired encoding of the stimulus (consequent, perhaps, to reduced scanning), and unilateral disruption in computing internal orthographic representation of individual words. HH's completion errors, made in the absence of word omission errors, may be assumed to arise almost exclusively from the latter mechanism.

Discussion of Oral Reading Experiments

Considered together, results of the experiments reported thus far support the hypothesis that dyslexic errors made by the patients are a manifestation of a spatially specific deficit in attention over an internal spatial representation of the word. However, this hypothesis is silent with respect to the locus at which the disruption occurs in the reading process; that is, which level(s) of the reading process requires attention over a spatial representation? We know that the unilateral disruption must occur prior to comprehension, because words were understood as the error subsequently produced. Hence, to account for comparable input errors on words and nonwords as well as on printed and orally spelled words, we must assume that damage occurs at the level of the internally computed representation of the letter array, prior to either lexical access for familiar words, or grapheme-phoneme conversion for unfamiliar words.

Lexical decision

If the presence of an attentional deficit affects the computed representation of the stimulus prior to addressing a stored lexical representation, it should affect lexical decision performance. Specifically, nonwords that are identical to words on the unaffected side should be accepted as words as frequently as nonwords were read as words in the reading tasks. The following experiments allowed us to evaluate "early" processing of letter strings and to minimize the potential contribution of hemianopia by presenting stimuli tachistoscopically to the intact visual hemifield.

Stimuli

The word stimuli consisted of 300 unaffixed words, four to seven letters in length. Nonwords were created by changing one to two letters of a word matched for frequency, length, concreteness, and grammatical class to a word stimulus. For one half of the nonwords, initial letters were changed, and for the other half, final letters were changed; half were produced by changing one letter, and half were produced by changing two letters; 200 were rendered unpronounceable. Stimuli were counterbalanced for side of violation, number of letters changed, and pronounceability. The stimuli were divided into six blocks of 50 items each.

Procedure

Stimuli were displayed on a 40-column screen of an Apple II+ computer. The patient was instructed to press a button marked YES if the letter string presented was a word, and press the button marked NO if the letter string was not a real English word. The buttons were positioned vertically (because on practice trials, RB neglected to press the left button), close to the patient's preferred hand, contralateral to brain damage. Each subject completed practice trials with 100 stimuli to determine the lowest reliable presentation rate. Each stimulus was displayed for 100 msec for NG, HH, and WW, and 500 msec for RB.

The stimuli were presented in two different conditions, tested 10 weeks apart. For all blocks in Condition 1, each stimulus was preceded by a bar of asterisks in the center of the screen indicating where the letter string would appear. Three blocks were tested in Condition 2, in which the stimulus was presented to the left or to the right of fixation, to insure that the complete string would be within the intact visual hemifield. For WW, half

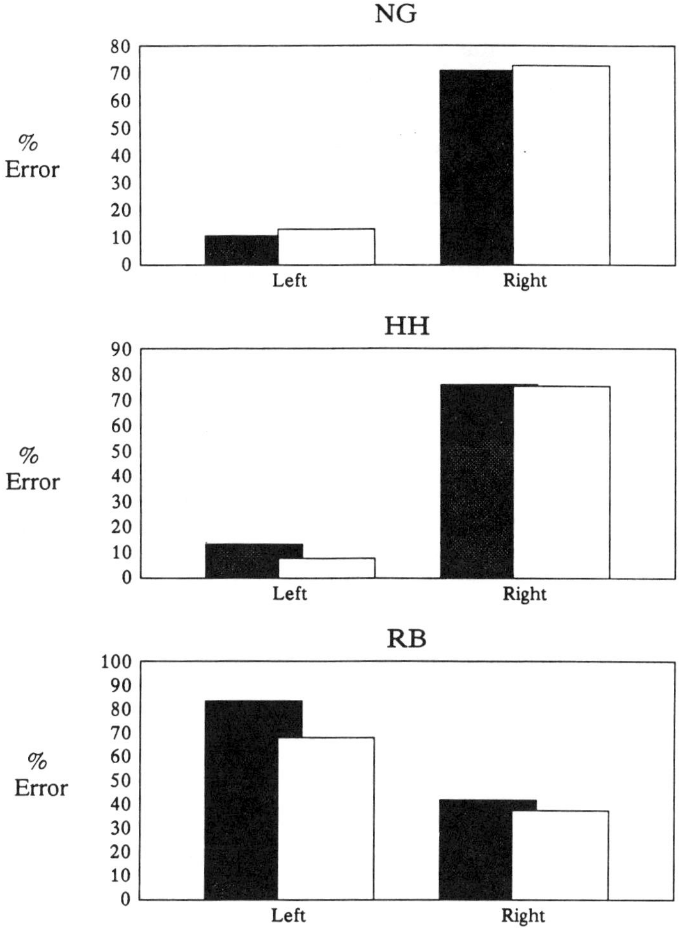

FIG. 8.2 Error rates in rejecting nonwords in lexical decision, as a function of the side of violation and pronouncability. Bar 1 = errors on pronouncable nonwords; 2 = errors on unpronouncable nonwords.

of the stimuli were presented to the left of fixation, and half were presented to the right.

Results

There were tendencies toward lower error rates with two-letter changes and unpronounceable segments compared to single letter and pronounceable violations, particularly on the unaffected side (Fig. 8.2 and 8.3), but these differences were nonsignificant ($\chi^2 = .04$ to 2.33; $p = .13$ to .84). Therefore, results across these two variables were combined for the remainder of the analyses.

Patients clearly accepted nonwords as words when letters were changed on the neglected side (Table 8.8). The interaction between error rate and side of word violation was highly significant ($\chi^2 = 29.3$ to 151.9; $p \leqslant .0001$) for all three patients, but nonsignificant for the control subject. False alarm rates were also significantly lower ($p \leqslant .0001$) than the acceptance rate of nonwords with contralesional errors. The effects were even greater when stimuli were presented to the intact visual hemifield, but the pattern of errors was identical for all patients. NG's spontaneous reading of many of the stimuli revealed that some nonwords with left-sided violations were

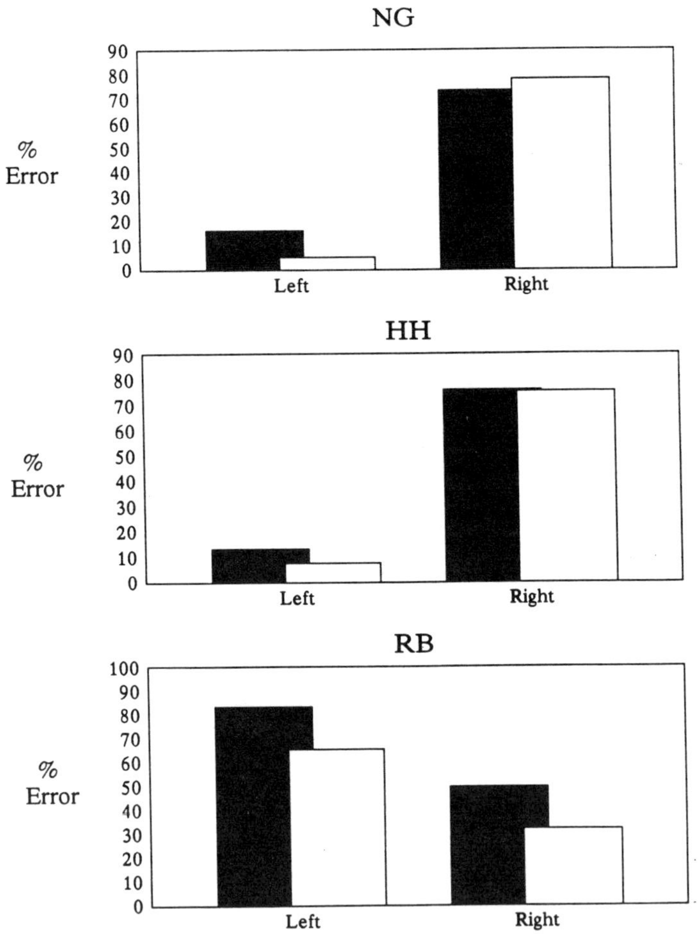

FIG. 8.3 Error rates in rejecting nonwords in lexical decision, as a function of the side of violation and number of letters changed. Bar 1 = errors on nonwords with one letter changed; 2 = errors on nonwords with two letters changed.

TABLE 8.8
Error Rates in Lexical Decision Task

Subject	*Violation on Left*	*Violation on Right*	*Chi-Square*	*Significance*	*False Alarm*
Stimuli presented in position of fixation point (*N* = 600)					
RB	83.6	48.1	29.3	$p < .0001$	16.0
NG	10.0	81.3	151.9	$p < .0001$	7.3
HH	9.3	70.7	114.9	$p < .0001$	25.0
WW	5.3	8.0		*NS*	4.0
Stimuli presented to intact visual field (*N* = 300)					
RB	80.0	14.7	61.6	$p < .0001$	17.3
NG	5.3	100.0	131.0	$p < .0001$	6.7
HH	10.7	93.3	99.4	$p < .0001$	14.7
WW (control) *N* = 150					
Right field	8.0	8.0	0	*NS*	40.0
Left field	8.0	0.0	2.34	*NS*	6.0

completed to the right (e.g., *zercy* [from *mercy*] → zero), accounting for some of the errors ipsilateral to brain damage.

Discussion of Lexical Decision Experiment

These data provide evidence that the effect of impaired processing of contralesional stimuli occurs (at least) prior to activation of a word in the lexicon, because the nonwords could not have lexical entries. These results also provide corroborative evidence that the basis for errors cannot be primarily a reduction in sensory information due to subclinical or clinically demonstrated homonymous hemianopia, because performance was unaffected by presenting the stimuli in the intact hemifield in the second condition (see also Kinsbourne & Warrington, 1962).

Spelling

All three patients had spelling difficulties as would be expected if, at any point in the spelling process, a spatial representation must be computed. Although there has been some previous support for this notion (Baxter & Warrington, 1983; Hillis & Caramazza, 1989), no systematic evaluation of associated effects of impaired attentional mechanisms on spelling and reading has been reported.

Method

The Johns Hopkins University Dysgraphia Battery (Goodman & Caramazza, 1986) was administered in full to NG and HH, and in part to RB. They wrote to dictation 326 words and 34 nonwords (also presented for reading), spelled aloud 42 words and 20 nonwords, wrote the names of 51 pictures, and copied 84 words and 40 nonwords (with and without delay). An additional 300 words and 60 nonwords from the Morphology Battery, also presented in various reading tasks, were presented to NG and HH for oral and written spelling and to WW for oral spelling.

Results

RB frequently did not attempt to respond in oral or written spelling, although he reportedly could spell quite well prior to his stroke. We report performance on the only list he completed, composed of 110 (four- to five-letter words, counterbalanced for frequency, letter length, phonemes per word, and probability of correct spelling by applying the most frequent phoneme-grapheme mappings. RB spelled correctly only 14.5% of words (eight high-probability and eight low-probability words) and failed to respond at all to 17.3% of the stimuli. On the remaining 75 words, RB produced 40 (53.3%) phonologically implausible nonword errors (e.g., *want* → *omew*; *gross* → *glors*), 20 phonemically plausible errors (e.g., *noise* → *noyees*; *broom* → *brum*), and 10 visually similar words (e.g., *stop* → *slop*). Some errors seemed to indicate inattention to the left (e.g., *free* → *three*, *flat* → *elat*) or a combination of deficits (e.g., *field* → [*filled*] → *billed*), including left-sided errors following phonemically plausible misspellings (*fence* → [*fents*] → *cents*; *leave* → [*leeve*] → *eleve*; *talk* → [*tok*] → *cok*). RB produced only 1 correct response in delayed copying and 12 (19.4%) correct responses in direct copying of the same 62 stimuli. All but two of his errors were backward completion errors or neglect errors on the left side, such as *spoil* → *moil*, *length* → *ngth*, and *suspend* → *end* (see appendix B).

NG's spelling deteriorated steadily as a function of word length, from 50% correct for four-letter words to 7.1% correct for eight-letter words, matched for frequency and phonemes per word (Table 8.9). In written spelling to dictation, 67.3% (185/275) of her errors were phonemically implausible nonwords; 22.9% (63/275) were phonemically plausible errors that also resulted from deletions, substitutions, transpositions, or insertions of one or two letters (e.g., *floor* → *floore*; *knife* → *knif*; 6.2% (17/275) were visually similar words with the same type of letter errors (e.g., *twin* → *twine*); and the remaining 3.3% (nine) errors were suffix deletions, substitutions, or insertions (e.g., *measure* → *measured*; *whispered* → *whisper*).

TABLE 8.9
NG's Spelling Performance as a Function of Word Length in Letters

	Correct	
	N	%
Word length list		
4-letter words	7/14	50.0
5-letter words	6/14	42.9
6-letter words	3/14	21.4
7-letter words	5/14	35.7
8-letter words	1/14	7.1

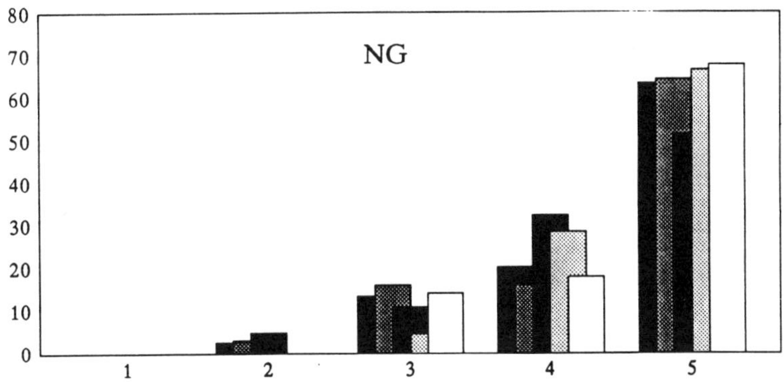

FIG. 8.4 Distribution of NG's errors as a function of letter position* in strings. Bar 1 = oral spelling of words; 2 = oral spelling of nonwords; 3 = written spelling of words; 4 = written spelling of nonwords; 5 = delayed copying.

*Formula used for normalizing letter positions of words of unequal lengths (from Wing & Baddeley, 1980, p. 260):

Number of Letters Assigned to Each Position

k = integer values 0,1,2,3. . .

Total # elements	*Relative Position*				
	A	*B*	*C*	*D*	*E*
$k \times 5 + 1$	k	k	$k + 1$	k	k
$k \times 5 + 2$	$k + 1$	k	k	k	$k + 1$
$k \times 5 + 3$	$k + 1$	k	$k + 1$	k	$k + 1$
$k \times 5 + 4$	$k + 1$	$k + 1$	k	$k + 1$	$k + 1$
$(k + 1) \times 5$	$k + 1$	$k + 1$	$k + 1$	$k + 1$	$k + 1$

oral and written spelling: 67.1% and 64.3% errors, respectively. In both tasks, NG exhibited series of errors with the same ending, similar to her error runs reported in reading tasks. Examples follow:

From oral spelling:	From written spelling:
appar → appard*ed*	replacement → replac*ment*
watch → watch*d*	shifts → shift
addresses → addressed*ed*	shild → shil
ask → ask*ed*	moaning → mo*ment*
taught → taughth	join → join*ment*
mafore → +	
valuable → value	marveled → marv*er*
strict → strick*ed*	clean → +
training → +	rancher → ranc*er*
takes → +	realize → realiz*er*
events → evenis	healthful → healthfull
against → agaisening	avoid → avoiloe
exactly → exact*ed*	allow → allowand*er*
discuss → discuss*ed*	facial → fac*er*
fortunate → forn*ed*	visit → vised
plan → plan*d*	active → actvic
lies → +	saddled → sadl*er*
appear → apper*d*	

Most (279/387; 72.1%) of NG's oral and written spelling errors met our criteria for forward completion errors as defined in reading experiments, many of which were suffix errors (see appendix B). For example, 14.6% (22/151) of her forward completion errors in oral spelling were suffix insertions or substitutions and 27.8% (42/151) had illegal suffixes. Unilateral omissions (neglect errors) also occurred in spelling words; approximately half of these involved deletion of regular suffixes.[3]

NG made comparable types, positions, and numbers of errors across all input modalities (in dictation, picture-naming, and delayed copying). Examples of forward completion errors in written naming include: *tent → tentt*, *anchor → anchart*, and *guitar → guiton*. Neglect errors include: *castle- → castl*; *watch → wat*, and *church → churc*. In delayed copying, there were also numerous forward completion errors (e.g., *what → whate*, *starve → starved*, *hungry → hunger*, *enough → enought*, and *lorn → lord*) and neglect errors (e.g., *fresh → fres, provide → provid*, and *sarcle → sarc*). Delayed copying was 33.9% correct, whereas direct copying was 96.8% correct, for the same 62 stimuli.

HH's spelling performance showed significant lexical effects: 61.9% (13/21) of concrete words versus 38.1% (8/21) of abstract words were spelled

[3]In later studies (Hillis & Caramazza, unpublished data), NG also made errors primarily on the right side of affixed and unaffixed words that she spelled backwards. More than 85% of her errors in this task were right-sided completion and neglect errors, which occurred at the beginning of each response.

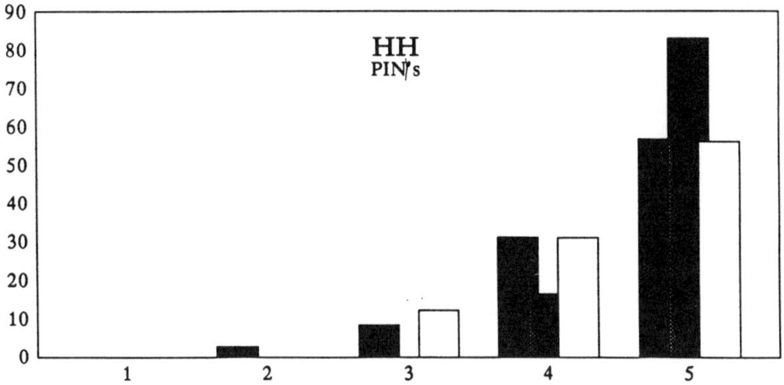

FIG. 8.5 Distribution of HH's phonologically implausible errors as a function of letter position in strings. Bar 1 = oral spelling to dictation; 2 = written spelling to dictation; 3 = delayed copying.

correctly, and 74.0% (108/146) high-frequency words versus 44.5% (65/146) low-frequency words were correct. He spelled four- to six-letter nonwords substantially better than words matched for length in letters (97.1% vs. 73.8% correct), and orthographically regular words better than irregular words, indicating that he often relies on nonlexical spelling mechanisms (i.e., phoneme-grapheme conversion). HH spelled correctly 93.3% (28/30) of four- to five-letter words with high phoneme-grapheme probability mappings and 72.5% (58/80) of four- to five-letter words with low phoneme-grapheme probability mappings. However, the most striking determinant of spelling accuracy was word length. HH correctly spelled 64.3% (9/14 of six-letter words but only 28.6% (4/14) of eight-letter words matched for frequency and phonemes per word. Analysis of his errors revealed that 96.8% (60/62) of written spelling errors on lists composed of four- to six-letter words were phonemically plausible (e.g., *phase*→*faise*; *dumb*→*dum*), whereas errors on longer words often showed a combination of phonological spelling and errors at the end of words (e.g., *realize*→*relized*). HH also produced a substantial number of pure forward completion errors and neglect errors, including suffix errors, in both oral and written spelling of longer words (see appendix B). All of his morphological errors involved substitution, insertion, or deletion of regular suffixes (e.g., *grab*→*grabbed*; *risks*→*risked*; *needed*→*need*). There were no discernable differences in frequency or quality of errors between written and oral spelling; both were 49% (98/200) correct for the same word and nonword stimuli, presented 4 months apart.

HH's phonologically plausible and phonologically implausible errors were separately graphed according to position of the error in the letter string, because two separate mechanisms seemed to be responsible for the two types of errors (Fig. 8.5 and 8.6). The distribution of his phonologically plausible errors in oral and written spelling to dictation reflects a cen-

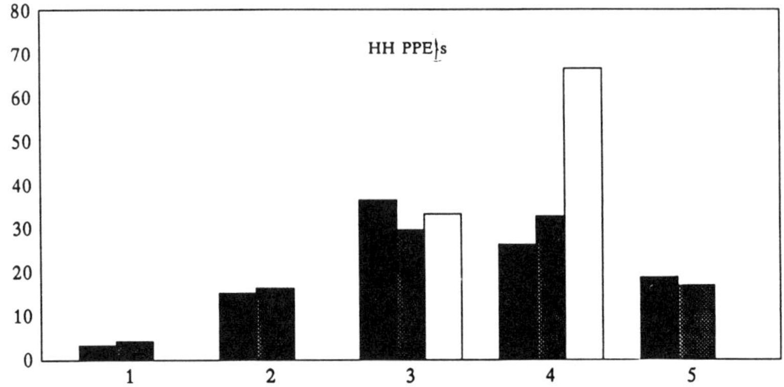

FIG. 8.6 Distribution of HH's phonologically plausible errors as a function of letter position in words. Bar 1 = oral spelling to dictation, 2 = written spelling to dictation; 3 = delayed copying.

tral, bow-shaped pattern (also evidenced in normal subjects' "slips of the pen", Wing & Baddeley, 1980). In contrast, his phonologically implausible errors in dictation and all of his errors in delayed copying increased at the ends of words, as did NG's errors.

HH performed very poorly on delayed copying. The majority (72.4%; 55/76) of his errors were forward completion errors (e.g., *carry → carred; bring → brite; grief → grith*); but seven neglect errors were also produced (e.g., *donsept → dons; rather → rath*). Series of identical errors at word endings (akin to NG's perservative suffixes in reading and spelling) were also observed, as in the following example:

length → lengty
under → undety
talent → tanty
crisp → cristy
faith → faity

He accurately reproduced 38.7% (48/124) of words in delayed copying, compared to 63.9% (79/124) of words in direct copying (on the same stimuli presented in blocks of 62 for each task, 6 weeks apart).

WW's oral spelling was 95.5% correct for wards, and 100% correct for nonwords. Most errors occurred in the center of the word, and none occurred on the first or last letter.

Discussion of Spelling Performance

The spelling data add important information on the issue of the possible interaction between attentional mechanisms and lexical processing, by demonstrating that some of the output errors produced by these patients are qualitatively identical to their input (reading and lexical decision) errors. For HH, a spatially specific influence on spelling that is distinct from his lexical defect is clearly demonstrated in (a) spelling words, when access to the graphemic lexicon was achieved without error; and (b) spelling nonwords. NG, who did not have a lexical deficit, also made contralesional errors in spelling words and nonwords. Hence, if the skewed distribution of errors is modulated by attentional mechanisms, the impact must occur at a level of the spelling process that is common to both lexical and nonlexical spelling. Further, although some errors in copying may be attributed to impaired reading, the substantially higher error rate for all patients in the delayed condition implicates an additional defect operating at a stage unique to the delayed condition, such as during storage of the graphemic representation of the word in the graphemic (output) buffer (see Caramazza, Miceli, Villa, & Romani, 1987). The contralesional skew of errors generated at this stage provides additional support for the hypothesized interaction between attentional mechanisms and short-term storage of an orthographic representation that is spatially encoded.

Nonlexical tasks

The strikingly similar pattern of reading (isolated words) and spelling errors found for the three patients suggests a common type of spatial attention deficit, even though HH failed to show evidence of neglect in clinical assessment of line cancellation, drawing, and so on. On the other hand, because performance on sentence reading demonstrated that RB and NG present with a scanning deficit that was not found for HH, we have grounds for being skeptical about the conclusion that a common spatial attention deficit is responsible for the observed impairments in the three patients. Thus, for example, HH's reading errors toward the ends of words could be related to some language-specific deficit involving final syllables or affixes. On this account, however, the deficit should be limited to lexical tasks. To evaluate the possibility that the deficit in any of the three patients could be language-specific, the following nonlexical processing task was administered.

Stimuli

Blocks of five-letter arrays were constructed with the following characteristics: Half were all uppercase letters and half were all lowercase letters; half were sequential letters of the alphabet (ABCDE) and half were random, nonvisually similar letters (e.g., XMQFS); half contained two identical letters (ABCDA) and half contained five different letters. The stimuli were counterbalanced with respect to the three variables. In one third of the arrays, the identical letters were on the left side (AABCD; ABACD); in one third of the arrays the identical letters were on the right side (ABCDD; ABDCD); and in one third the identical letters were on opposite sides (ABCDA; ABCBD; ABCAD; ABCDB).

Procedure

The stimulus was preceded by a fixation point in the center of the 40-column screen of an IBM PC computer. The patient was instructed to press a key marked YES if the letter string contained two identical letters, and press the key marked NO if the letter string had no identical letters. The keys were located vertically near the patient's preferred hand. The lowest reliable presentation rate, 1,000 milliseconds for all subjects, was determined by five practice trials.

Results

There were no significant differences in performance with respect to the case or random versus sequential letter strings, so results across these two variables were combined. The most clearly significant variable for each patient in each experiment was the position of the identical letters with the array (Table 8.10). The control subject showed no significant effect of position of the targets. Results for each experimental condition are described separately.

TABLE 8.10
Error Rate by Position of Identical Letters Within String

	N	*Both on Left*	*One on Each Side*	*Both on Right*	*Chi-Square*	*Significance*	*False Alarms(%)*
Experiment 1. Horizontal Presentation/Varied Location							
RB	200	75.0	76.9	16.7	27.57	$p < .001$	19.0
NG	200	32.5	77.0	62.5	22.20	$p < .0001$	13.0
HH	300	20.8	55.8	50.0	11.33	$p < .01$	9.0
WW	150	5.6	15.4	5.6	3.01	*NS*	1.3
Experiment 2. Horizontal Presentation/Varied Spacing							
RB	360	68.8	42.7	31.3	14.48	$p < .001$	21.3
NG	420	14.3	35.2	55.4	19.93	$p < .0001$	4.8
HH	600	13.2	50.7	43.4	34.82	$p < .0001$	5.2
WW	180	20.8	16.7	8.3	.95	*NS*	4.4
Experiment 3. Vertical Presentation/Varied Location							
RB	250	40.0	53.1	33.0	12.45	$p < .01$	36.0
NG	200	12.5	34.7	45.8	6.52	$p < .05$	9.0
HH	200	25.0	63.5	50.0	9.73	$p < .01$	2.0
WW	150	27.8	30.8	44.4	1.17	*NS*	9.3

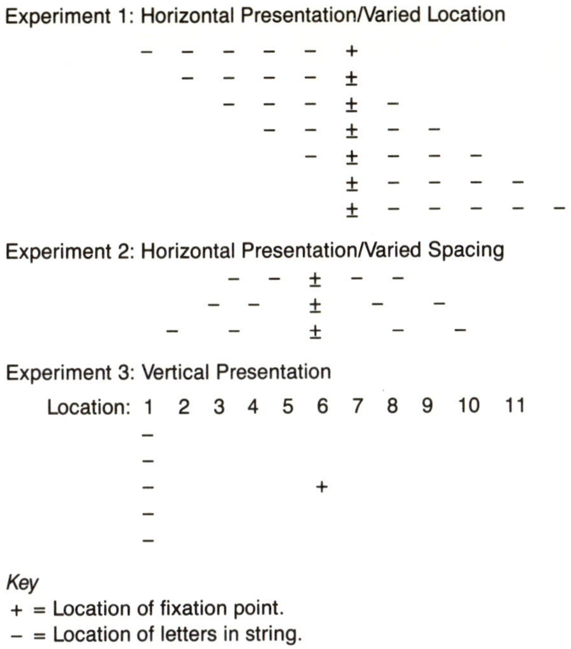

FIG. 8.7 Position of letter arrays relative to the fixation point (+).

Experiment 1: Horizontal Presentation/Varied Locations

Blocks of 50 arrays were randomly presented at six locations with respect to the fixation point, as shown in Fig. 8.7. The location of the array in the visual field was not a significant factor in determining error rate for any of the subjects. Even when the six locations were collapsed into left, right, and center locations, there was only a slight (*ns*) tendency toward higher error rates contralateral to the lesion, for NG and RB only. In contrast, the position of the target letters in the array was a significant factor for all brain-damaged subjects. For RB, there were highly significant differences in error rate between detection of two letters occurring both on the left versus both on the right ($\chi^2 = 14.2$; $p < .0001$) or one on the left versus both on the right ($\chi^2 = 22.1$; $p \ll .0001$). In other words, RB erred when one or both of the identical pair occurred on the left side of the array. NG and HH showed the opposite pattern: disproportionate errors when one or both targets occurred on the right. The identical pattern obtained when arrays presented to the left and to the right were analyzed separately (Table 8.11).

Experiment 2: Horizontal Presentation/Varied Spacing

Blocks of 60 randomly ordered arrays were presented, all centered with respect to the fixation point. In each block, 20 arrays each contained one

TABLE 8.11
Error Rate as a Function of Letter Position for Each Field of Presentation

	Strings Presented Left of Fixation Point (Positions 0 & 1)			*Strings Presented Right of Fixation Point (Positions 4 & 5)*		
Position of Identical Letters:	*Left*	*Both Sides*	*Right*	*Left*	*Both Sides*	*Right*
RB	75%	44%	13%	31%	50%	13%
NG	25%	58%	50%	25%	100%	63%
HH	23%	56%	58%	15%	48%	67%

space, two spaces, or three spaces between each letter. Half of each set contained a target pair. There was a significant accuracy × spacing interaction only for NG. Her error rate was significantly higher when there were three spaces between letters than when there were two spaces between letters, consistent with the impaired performance with greater scanning demands. In contrast, all patients exhibited significant effects of target position, comparable to those reported in Experiment 1, but more striking. The contrast between both targets on the left versus both on the right was highly significant ($p < .0001$) for all of the patients ($\chi^2 = 12.1$, 18.4, and 27.9 for RB, NG, and HH, respectively). They also showed significantly af($< .01$) higher error rates with one target (compared to none) on the affected side.

Experiment 3: Vertical Presentation/Varied Location

Blocks of 50 arrays each were presented vertically at 10 positions across the visual field in random order. The 10 locations varied by a single space, up to five spaces to the left and five spaces to the right of the fixation point. There were no interactions between accuracy and location in the visual field, even when the locations were collapsed into left and right field presentations ($\chi^2 = 1.4$ to 3.4; *ns*). Once again, a similar pattern emerged with regard to the effect of target position, although in this experiment a left–right contrast was actually a top–bottom contrast. The difference between both targets on the "good" side and both on the neglected side reached significance for NG ($\chi^2 = 3.2$; $p < .05$), whereas the difference between both targets on the good side and targets on opposite sides of the array reached significance for RB ($\chi^2 = 9.5$; $p < .005$) and HH ($\chi^2 = 8.3$; $p < .005$).

Conclusions

These results confirm that the position of letters within the spatial array is the determining factor of accuracy, rather than the location of the target with respect to the visual field (and hence, retinal position). Thus, the distribution of errors cannot be attributed to sensory factors, such as hemianopia, for any patient.[4] Moreover, these data demonstrate a spatially specific deficit in attention that is not restricted to lexical stimuli for any patient. Thus, we have stronger evidence for postulating that HH's contralesional errors in lexical processing are influenced by damage to a general mechanism of spatial attention. Further, we found no evidence for the possibility raised by Costello and Warrington (1987) that a dissociation they reported between left neglect in reading and right neglect in traditional visuo-spatial tests of neglect reflects material-specific attentional deficits. Rather, both the results we obtained and the performance pattern reported by Costello and Warrington are consistent with the proposal that attentional deficits may differentially operate on different levels of representation. Reading, spelling, and our nonlexical tasks all entail computation of an internal, spatially coded representation; whereas line cancellation, copying, and perhaps line bisection require attention to physical aspects of the stimulus array.

GENERAL DISCUSSION

The evidence we have reported from the reading, spelling, and nonlexical tasks converge in support of the hypothesis that the three brain-damaged subjects in our study are impaired in processing internal representations on the side opposite to brain damage. The effect of this impairment on reading and spelling performance has implications for hypotheses about the nature of representations in lexical processing and attentional mechanisms.

Representations in Lexical Processing

Locus of Attentional Effects in the Reading Process. Monk (1985) proposed a model of word recognition based on Marr's (1976) visual information processing theory that specifies several levels of representation in visual processing. Monk's schema consists of several levels of primitives (visual features, letters, graphemes, syllables, morphemes, and words) and five potential levels of coordinate systems (retinal, viewer-centered, real-world, word-centered, and sentence-centered). The distinction between representa-

[4]The fact that the patients had sufficient time to shift eye gaze during each presentation is not of concern here. We were primarily interested in presenting stimuli randomly to the intact visual hemifield for HH, to assure that the entire array was seen at least on these trials. Subsequent eye movement to the left, obscuring part of the stimulus would not affect results, but would in any case be unlikely. Further, there is evidence that although attentional shifts are possible without eye movements, shifts in eye movement do not occur in the absence of peripheral stimulation without corresponding shifts in attention (Shepherd, Findlay, & Hockey, 1986), so unprecedented ipsilateral eye movements would indicate an attentional deficit.

tions that specify the spatial location of visual features and of graphemes, which are both computed prior to activating a stored representation of the word, has been supported by a variety of experiments on processing of graphemic arrays (see Seymour, 1979 for review). The hypothesis of multiple coordinate systems for word representation receives support from the data we have presented.

According to Monk's proposal, the first representation computed has visual features as primitives and coordinates that correspond to the topographically organized retinal surface. Our patients' neglect errors in normal reading, including RB's omission of letters in letter-by-letter reading, might be attributable to a deficit at this level—a spatially specific scanning deficit that permits correct encoding of only the letters on the nonneglected side (although these errors might equally as likely result from impaired computation of a word-centered representation). However, their unilateral reading errors, with all methods of letter presentation (e.g., vertical vs. horizontal or visual vs. auditory) and following accurate identification of all of the letters in the string cannot be interpreted as resulting from an impairment in processing a retino-topic representation. These latter errors indicate impaired attention over a word-centered representation with graphemes as primitives and spatial coordinates. Damage at this second level of representation could account for the high proportion of completion errors compared to neglect errors, as follows: Unimpaired encoding of letters at an earlier level gives rise to an orthographic representation that is centered with respect to the "inner screen" with spatial coordinates, and subsequent "reading" of this representation is unilaterally disrupted (Kinsbourne & Warrington, 1962). For instance, a word-centered level of representation of *report* might normally be generated from the specification:

$$\begin{array}{cccccc} r & e & p & o & r & t \\ \mathrm{a} & \mathrm{a}+1 & \mathrm{a}+2 & & & \\ & & & n-2 & n-1 & n \end{array}$$

This representation in the presence of left neglect would be processed as:

$$\begin{array}{cccc} \text{---------------} & o & r & t \\ \text{---------------} & n-2 & n-1 & n \end{array}$$

or, in the presence of right neglect:

$$\begin{array}{cccc} r & e & p & \text{-----} \\ a & a+1 & a+2 & \text{------} \end{array}$$

where n = approximate length; a = the beginning of the word, and "---" corresponds to the neglected space.

The first foregoing representation might result in the activation of the entry *export* in the orthographic input lexicon, whereas the second representation might activate the entry *repair* (or reports, repayment, etc.). (These possibilities depend, of course, on assumptions about the way in which lexical entries may be activated in the orthographic lexicon. In the present case, the assumption is made that part of a word is sufficient to activate a lexical response.)

Neglect errors, such as *report* → "port" or "rep" would be expected to occur if the spatial coordinates of the representation were inaccurate due to disruption at the level where retinal coordinates are specified. A failure to scan completely the array of letters would result in an inaccurate positional encoding, such that a letter in medial position, say the *p* in *report*, is identified as the first (a), the next letter as $a + 1$, and so forth. Neglect errors might also occur at the level of the word-level representation, if an embedded word on the nonneglected side is the most available entry in the orthographic input lexicon that shares the letter segment attended. Thus, the result of a greater proportion of neglect (omission) errors by NG and RB compared to HH is consistent with the hypothesis that both of the proposed mechanisms for generating neglect errors could be operating in the first two patients, whereas only the latter mechanism gives rise to neglect errors by HH. A greater number of whole-word omissions on the neglected side in sentence reading by NG and RB compared to HH and impaired perception of letter strings as a function of the extent of the spatial array for NG but not for HH also appear to signal that NG and RB have an impairment in computing both levels of representation, whereas HH has damage affecting primarily the word-centered level of representation.

The influence of attentional impairments predominantly at the first level of representation, with retinal coordinates, may account for performance of the (left) "neglect dyslexic" patient, VB, reported by Ellis et al. (1987b). VB shared the following performance characteristics with RB and NG: completion errors and neglect errors in reading single words; a high correlation between stimulus and response length; impaired comprehension corresponding to impaired oral reading of words; an unchanged error pattern when words were presented to the intact visual hemifield; and omission of words on the neglected side in reading text. In contrast with our patients, VB's word recognition errors were eliminated when letters of the word were read aloud to her, and were reduced with rotated text.

VB's performance can be accommodated within our hypothesis in the following manner. Incomplete scanning of words printed normally permits construction of an orthographic representation that corresponds to one side of the word. This representation could serve as the basis for addressing the most similar word in the orthographic input lexicon—including responses classified as completion errors, neglect errors, and visual errors. Further, unlike the Ellis et al.'s (1987b) proposal that VB encoded the positions, but not the identities of the letters in the neglected side of the stimulus, our hypothesis can account for her neglect errors as well as for her responses that are longer than the stimulus (e.g., *ate* → "date"). VB's selective impairment of written spelling in the context of spared oral spelling (Ellis et al., 1987a) also allows us to conjecture that her neglect is confined to relatively peripheral levels of representation.

VB, like all of our patients, read longer words less accurately than shorter words. In contrast, JOH, the patient with left neglect dyslexia reported by Costello & Warrington (1987), made more errors on shorter words. We would expect this latter pattern of performance if attention were to be disrupted over an entire half of the word centered representation. That is, if the patient attended only to the right half of two- to four-letter words, only one to two letters would constrain the selection of an entry in the orthographic input lexicon; whereas attention to the right half of longer words would provide greater limitations on the possible selections, thereby increasing the probability of correct responses. On the other hand, if attention were impaired to a lesser extent, such that it is ordinarily directed at least to letters near the center of the word-centered representation, two-to four-letter words would carry a high chance of being read correctly.

Locus of Attentional Effects in the Spelling Process. Unilaterally disrupted processing of internal representation would be expected to affect those levels of the spelling process where computations are carried out over a graphemic string with spatial coordinates. One such mechanism—the graphemic buffer—has been postulated to maintain the representation of the graphemic string while motor processes for spelling are implemented. We have previously reported two patients with damage at the level of the graphemic buffer who showed contrasting distributions of errors as a function of letter position in the graphemic string—errors skewed toward the ends of words for DH (with left fronto-parietal damage) and toward the beginnings of words for ML (with right frontal and parietal lesions) (Hillis & Caramazza, 1989). Of the patients reported here, NG displayed an extreme increase in spelling errors at the ends of words for all tasks that are assumed to entail the graphemic buffer—that is, all spelling tasks, regardless of input or output modality. However, we do not suggest that NG or HH had damage to specifically the graphemic buffer, but that their attentional deficits prevented complete computation of the graphemic representation held (normally) in the buffer. Patients whose primary deficit is dysfunction of the graphemic buffer make errors that reflect impaired storage of graphemic representations resulting in deletions, substitutions, or transpositions of letters that could result in orthographically illegal, or unpronounceable, nonwords (e.g., *priest* → *rpiest*). In contrast, most of NG's and HH's error responses involved completion of word segments with recently produced, or frequently occurring letter sequences (e.g., *-ere* or suffixes). A substantial portion of these forward completion errors were illegally suffixed words, when patients spelled lists consisting of distinctly affixed words (as in the morphology battery). Although it is far from clear how these letter sequences were retrieved, there have been many comparable reports that patients with neglect often "complete" drawings, remembered objects or scenes and body images with inaccurate, but possible, segments. Perhaps, unattended portions of the representation are partially processed.[5]

Baxter and Warrington (1983) also reported a patient, ORF, whose pattern of spelling errors, predominantly at the beginnings of words in forward and backward oral spelling, is compatible with abnormal distribution of attention at the level of the graphemic buffer. However, in addition to the left-sided difficulty in spelling, ORF exhibited damage to nonlexical spelling mechanisms, such that he was completely unable to spell nonsense syllables. HH's errors on nonwords (and many assembled spellings of words) provide complementary information that the contralesional disruption in computing the internal representation can also follow assembly of a plausible spelling through nonlexical processes. Jointly, these patterns indicate that computation within the graphemic buffer (which is assumed to store lexical and assembled graphemic strings) can be unilaterally affected; and thus, that a spatially specified representation is processed at this level. The high proportion of completion errors in spelling indicates that the representation held in the buffer, like the internal representation of the stimulus constructed in reading, is word-centered, so that longer stimuli elicit longer responses. As noted in our interpretation of reading performance, higher accuracy on shorter words by ORF, and by our patients, may stem from spared attention to letters near the middle of the word-centered representation (i.e., all letters of shorter words).

In the cases of ORF and HH, no clinical evidence of neglect was obtained except in reading and spelling tasks. At first glance, these data appear to support the possibility that neglect symptoms are material-specific. However, further testing of HH in tasks requiring the computation of nonlexical spatial representation, which unveiled a pattern of errors comparable to his pattern in lexical tasks, indicated instead that impairments in the distribution of attention over separate levels of spatial representation may

---

[5]Crick (1984) also interpreted completion errors as resulting from partial or impaired attention to neglected portions of representations. He proposed that we think of the role of attention at different levels of representation in terms of an *attentional searchlight*, which intensifies a portion of a representation through temporary conjunctions of neurons to create connections between separate levels of perception. In perception of letter strings, for example, areas of the brain that presumably respond to different dimensions of visual input (e.g., color, shape, etc.) are connected when each item in the array is intensified in sequence. Thus, identifying a letter with a specified color within a string of colored letters is substantially slower than searching for just the specified letter or the color in the array, and both are slowed by increasing the number of distractors in the array (Treisman & Gelade, 1980). Hence, unilateral completion errors might occur if the searchlight failed to reach one side of the word representation, with the effect that features of graphemes in the neglected segment are not perceived simultaneously for a clear identification of their position and identity.

be dissociable.[6] Of course, it could be the case that HH's impairment involved the ends of temporally processed strings, without assuming a left-right orientation of internally (re)constructed spatial representations. However, a deficit in temporal processing would not explain NG's comparable right-sided errors in backward spelling (see footnote 3), because these occurred at the beginning of the response. Further, the co-occurrence of the same contralesional pattern of errors in processing words alongside disturbances in processing the contralesional side of spatial representations (e.g., map layout, recalled pictures, and body schema) in RB and NG lead to the parsimonious hypothesis that an impairment in attention affects spatially defined, lexical and nonlexical internal representations. Recall, also, that HH omitted half of an abstract design in delayed reproduction, which might be another indication of unilaterally disrupted processing of internal spatial representations.

Thus, the results we obtained are consistent with the hypothesis that the reading and spelling errors of all three of our patients result from an impairment that disrupts processing of spatially defined orthographic representations as well as, in some cases, spatially presented (printed) words and sentences. This hypothesis assumes a common mechanism involved in perception and in processing internal representations of words (as indicated by performance of RB and NG), which can nonetheless affect one or the other differentially (as indicated by performance of HH and of ORF reported by Costello & Warrington, 1987). These assumptions are supported by accumulating evidence for shared mechanisms subserving higher visual perception and imagery (Bisiach & Berti, 1987) and for the computation of spatial maps with separate coordinate systems (Bisiach, Capitani, & Porta, 1985; Bradshaw, Nettleton, Pierson, Wilson, & Nathan, 1987; Gazzaniga & Ladavas, 1987; Jeannerod & Biguer, 1987).

Implications for Theories of Neglect

If we take contralesional errors in lexical tasks to be symptoms of neglect, the results reported here have clear implications for theories of this class of deficits. To begin with, the observed pattern of errors in reading cannot be explained by sensory or oculo-motor hypotheses of neglect, because the identical distribution and frequency of errors was exhibited even after intact sensation of the letter string could be demonstrated, through sequential

[6]HH did not omit letters or words on the neglected side of print (as RB and NG did), but did demonstrate impaired computation of a unified internal representation with more abstract features (graphemes). Sieroff, Pollatsek, & Posner (1988) reported the opposite dissociation: Patients they tested with posterior lesions extinguished perception of letters on the contralesional side of nonlexical strings, but showed less extinction in processing letters of words. The latter result would seem to indicate intact processing of the internal orthographic representation.

letter identification. Similarly, theories that propose inadequate scanning or exploration, or reduced arousal/orienting response to contralateral stimuli (Heilman & Van Den Abell, 1980; Heilman & Watson, 1977) are at a loss to explain the contralesional errors in recognition of oral spelling, vertical or letter-by-letter reading, and spelling. Denny–Brown's and Banker's (1954) amorphosynthesis account, which attributes symptoms to a failure to synthesize input to the lesioned hemisphere with input to the intact hemisphere, also cannot account for neglected portions of words to be spelled and of spelled words to be recognized, which would presumably be processed in the same hemisphere as intact portions of words.

We do not imply that the hypotheses we have just referred to may not be the correct account for particular forms of neglect. It is clear that the disorders that have been grouped under the common rubric of neglect disorders constitute a rather heterogeneous class of deficits. It is unlikely, therefore, that a single explanation will work for all the different forms of neglect disorders that have been reported in the literature. The approach of seeking to explain all the different forms of neglect by proposing a common deficit seems inappropriate. It is more productive, instead, to focus on what can be learned about the structure of cognitive mechanisms from the varied forms of neglect deficits that have been reported. Thus, one conclusion suggested by our results is that the deficit in our patients concerns, at the very least, the processing of abstract internal representations. From this indisputable conclusion we may proceed to consider what the implications of our results are for the structure of the processing mechanisms implicated in the deficit.

There are two classes of explanations that are consistent with the production of unilateral errors in all the tasks reported here: theories that attribute the reported form of neglect to mutilated internal representations (e.g., Bisiach et al. 1979, 1981, 1985) and theories that attribute the deficit to attentional mechanisms (Heilman & Watson, 1977; Mesulam, 1981). We have chosen to discuss our results in terms of a deficit to attentional mechanisms. However, Bisiach and Berti (1987) argued against an attentional deficit account of neglect. The principal evidence for this argument is that completion phenomena cannot be explained by assuming an impairment of attention or scanning, because reduced scanning should result in reductive errors only, and not productive completion (see also Kinsbourne, 1987). This argument, however, presupposes that impairments of attention must result in all-or-none processing of all parts of an array. It could be argued, instead, that damage to attentional mechanisms results in different degrees of impairment to parts of a mental representation, as would be the case if we assumed that attentional deficits implicated, among other things, faulty attribution of processing resources to different parts of a mental representation. On this account, an inadequately processed part of a representation could give rise to completion errors as well as true neglect errors, depending on the amount of processing resources that had been allocated to the poorly processed part of the representation. Hence, it is not correct to argue that attentional deficit hypotheses cannot explain the presence of completion errors in cases of neglect. Thus, we are still left with two classes of explanations for the deficit in our patients: representational and attentional deficit accounts. Why, then, have we chosen to favor the attentional account in this discussion? The only reason is that we wanted to make it clear that the deficit does not seem to involve the stored representations of words in the orthographic output or input lexicons (which, therefore, need not be spatially encoded), but in computing an active representation for immediate use. Computation might be disrupted either during printout of the representation on the internal visuo-spatial scratchpad (Bisiach & Berti, 1987; Kinsbourne, 1987) or in the allocation of processing resources to a portion of the representation that is fully constructed (from the retinotopic representation in reading or from the stored, orthographic representation in the writing process). These alternative hypotheses are indistinguishable on the basis of the data we have reported.[7]

Regardless of which of the two accounts, if either, ultimately proves to be correct, both accounts require that we assume that some mental representations in the course of lexical processing are spatially organized. That is, there is a level(s) of lexical-orthographic representation in which information is organized in a form that implicates spatial coordinates.

In conclusion, the convergence of evidence we reported from reading tasks (regardless of spatial extent, direction, or modality of stimulus presentation), oral and written spelling tasks, and nonlexical, perceptual tasks indicates that each of the patients in this study has an impairment in processing internal spatial representations. The impairment would seem to be the result of damaged attentional mechanisms that operate at multiple loci within the cognitive processes of reading, spelling, and perception. For example, in the reading process, one level at which these mechanisms seem to

[7]This is not to say, of course, that there might not be other cases that favor one of the two hypotheses. Bisiach and Berti (1987) cite several types of unilateral symptoms that are difficult to attribute to an attentional disturbance, including: (a) somatophrenia or hallucinations concerning a contralesional limb or object in the room to which the patient appears to be attending, and (b) subjective reports by patients that they are unable, despite their best efforts, to clearly perceive the contralesional stimuli (e.g., portions of words they are attempting to spell). However, although these reports do seem to rule out attenuation of volitional attention as the source of errors, the data might not be inconsistent with an attentional deficit in the sense of an organic inability to direct processing resources to the contralesional stimulus. On the other side, favoring the attentional hypothesis, Riddoch and Humphreys (1987) and Shallice (1988) pointed to evidence of amelioration of neglect symptoms by cuing the patient to attend to the neglected side of a represented scene or line, as contraindications of a representational deficit. But this is not persuasive evidence either; cuing might serve not to shift attention, but to shift the frame of reference for constructing the representation. Hence, we are not aware of definitive evidence in support of either view.

be involved is at the point where word-centered representations are computed, following the construction of a representation with letters as primitives and retinal coordinates (which may be affected independently). And, in the case of the spelling process, attentional mechanisms seem to be involved in processing information at the level of the graphemic buffer. The influence of spatially specific attentional impairments in lexical processing supports the view that at least some of the representations computed in the course of reading and spelling are spatially encoded—a nonobvious property of mental representations.

ACKNOWLEDGMENTS

The research reported in this paper was supported by NIH grant NS22201 and by a grant from the Seaver Institute to the Johns Hopkins University. The authors wish to thank RB, NG, and HH for participating in this study. We also thank Andrew Olson and Barry Gordon for allowing us the use of computer programs they wrote, and Edoardo Bisiach for many helpful comments on an earlier draft.

REFERENCES

Albert, M. (1981). *Disorders of communication* (Vol. 2). New York: Springer-Verlag.

Battersby, W. S., Bender, M. B., Pollack, M., & Kahn, R. L. (1956). Unilateral "spatial agnosia" ("inattention") in patients with cerebral lesions. *Brain, 79*, 68–93.

Baxter, D. M., & Warrington, E. K. (1983). Neglect dysgraphia. *Journal of Neurology, Neurosurgery, and Psychiatry, 48*, 141–144.

Bellas, D. N., Novelly, R. A., Eskanazi, B., & Wasserstein, J. (1988). The nature of unilateral neglect in the olfactory sensory system. *Neuropsychologia, 26*, 45–52.

Bisiach, E., & Berti, A. (1987). Dyschiria: An attempt at its systemic explanation. In M. Jeannerod (Ed.), *Neuropsychological and physiological aspects of spatial neglect* (pp. 183–202). New York: Elsevier Science Publishers.

Bisiach, E., Berti, A., & Vallar, G. (1985). Analogical and logical disorders underlying unilateral neglect of space. In M. I. Posner & O. S. M. Marin (Eds.), *Attention and Performance XI* (pp. 239–250). Hillsdale, NJ: Lawrence Erlbaum Associates.

Bisiach, E., Capitani, E., Luzzati, C., & Perani, D. (1981). Brain and conscious representation of outside reality. *Neuropsychologia, 4*, 543–551.

Bisiach, E., Capitani, E., & Porta, E. (1985). Two basic properties of space representation in the brain. *Journal of Neurology, Neurosurgery, and Psychiatry, 48*, 141–144.

Bisiach, E., & Luzzatti, C. (1978). Unilateral neglect of representational space. *Cortex, 14*, 129–133.

Bisiach, E., Luzzatti, C., & Perani, D. (1979). Unilateral neglect, representational schema and consciousness. *Brain, 102*, 609–618.

Bradshaw, J. L., Nettleton, N. C., Pierson, J. M., Wilson, L. E., & Nathan, G. (1987). Coordinates of extracorporeal space. In M. Jeannerod (Ed.), Neuropsychological and physiological aspects of spatial neglect (pp. 41–68). New York: Elsevier Science Publishers.

Butter, C., Mark, V. W., & Heilman, K. M. (in press). An experimental analysis of factors underlying neglect in line bisection. *Journal of Neurology, Neurosurgery, and Psychiatry*.

Butter, C. (1987). Varieties of attention and disturbances of attention: A neuropsychological analysis. In M. Jeannerod (Ed.), *Neurophysiological and neuropsychological aspects of spatial neglect* (pp. 1-24). New York: Elsevier Science Publishers.

Caramazza, A. (1988). Some aspects of language processing revealed through the analysis of acquired aphasia: The lexical system. *Annual Review of Neuroscience, 11*, 395-421.

Caramazza, A., Miceli, M., Villa, A., & Romani, C. (1987). The role of the graphemic buffer in spelling: Evidence from a case of acquired dysgraphia. *Cognition, 26*, 59-85.

Chedru, F. (1976). Space representation in unilateral spatial neglect. *Journal of Neurology, Neurosurgery, and Psychiatry, 39*, 1057-1061.

Costa, L. D., Vaughan, H. G., Horwitz, M., & Ritter, W. (1969). Patterns of behavioral deficit associated with visual spatial neglect. *Cortex, 5*, 242-263.

Costello, A. D., & Warrington, E. K. (1987). The dissociation of visuospatial neglect and neglect dyslexia. *Journal of Neurology, Neurosurgery, and Psychiatry, 50*, 1110-1116.

Crick, F. (1984). Function of the thalamic reticular complex: The searchlight hypothesis. *Proceedings of the National Academy of Sciences, 81*, 4585-4590.

Dejerine, J. (1892). Contribution a l'etude anatomoclinique et clinique des differentes varietes de cecite verbale [The anatomical and Clinical Study of the different varieties of word blindness]. *Memoires de la Societe de Biologie, 4*, 61-90.

Denny-Brown, D., & Banker, B. Q. (1954). Amorphosynthesis from left parietal lesions. *Archives of Neurology and Psychiatry, 71*, 302-313.

De Renzi, E. (1982). *Disorders of space exploration and cognition*. New York: Wiley.

De Renzi, E. & Faglioni, P. (1970). Hemispheric contribution to exploration of space through the visual and tactile modality. *Cortex, 6*, 191-203.

De Renzi, E., & Faglioni, P. (1978). Normative data and screening power of a shortened version of the Token Test. *Cortex, 14*, 41-49.

Dunn, M. L., & Dunn, M. L. (1981) *The Peabody picture vocabulary test*. Circle Pines, MN: American Guidance Service.

Ellis, A. W., Flude, B., & Young, A. (1987a). 'Afferent Dysgraphia' in a patient and normal subjects. *Cognitive Neuropsychology, 4*, 465-486.

Ellis, A. W., Flude, B., & Young, A. (1987b). 'Neglect Dyslexia' and the early visual processing of letters in words and nonwords. *Cognitive Neuropsychology, 4*, 439-464.

Gainotti, G. (1986). Components of visual attention disrupted in unilateral neglect. Paper presented at IRBN Conference on The Organization and Pathology of Visual Perception, New York.

Gardner, H., & Zurif, E. B. (1975). Bee but not be: Oral reading of single words in aphasia and alexia. *Neuropsychologia, 13*, 181-190.

Gazzaniga, M. S., & Ladavas, E. (1987). Disturbances in spatial attention following lesions or disconnections of the right parietal lobe. In M. Jeannerod (Ed.), *Neuropsychological and physiological aspects of spatial neglect* (pp. 203-213). New York: Elsevier Science Publishers.

Geschwind, N. (1965). Disconnection syndromes in animals and man. *Brain, 88*, 237-294, 585-644.

Gilliatt, R. W., & Pratt, R. T. C. (1952). Disorders of perception and performance in a case of right-sided cerebral thrombosis. *Journal of Neurology, Neurosurgery, and Psychiatry, 15*, 264.

Goodglass, H., & Kaplan, E. (1972). *The Boston diagnostic aphasia examination*. Philadelphia, PA: Lea & Febiger.

Goodglass, H., Kaplan, E., & Weintraub, S. (1983). *The revised Boston naming test*. Philadelphia, PA: Lea & Febiger.

Goodman, R., & Caramazza, A. (1986). Dissociation of spelling errors in written and oral spelling: The role of allographic conversion in writing. *Cognitive Neuropsychology, 3*, 179-206.

Halligan, P. W., & Marshall, J. C. (1988). How long is a piece of string? *Cortex, 24*, 321–328.

Heilman, K. M. (1979). Neglect and related disorders. In K. M. Heilman & E. Valenstein (Eds.), *Clinical neuropsychology* (pp. 268–307). New York: Oxford University Press.

Heilman, K. M., & Van Den Abell, T. (1980). Right hemisphere dominance for attention. The mechanism underlying hemispheric asymmetries of inattention (neglect). *Neurology (NY), 30*, 327–330.

Heilman, K. M., & Watson, R. T. (1977). Mechanisms underlying the unilateral neglect syndrome. In E. A. Weinstein & R. P. Friedland (Eds.), *Advances in neurology, vol. 18: Hemi-Inattention and hemisphere specialization* (pp. 93–106), New York: Raven Press.

Hillis, A., & Caramazza, A. (1989). The Graphemic Buffer and attentional mechanisms. *Brain and Language*.

Hooper, H. E. (1957). *The Hooper visual organization test*. Beverly Hills, CA: Western Psychological Association.

James, W. (1890). *The principles of psychology*. New York: Holt.

Jeannerod, M., & Biguer, B. (1987). The directional coding of reaching movements. A visuomotor conception of spatial neglect. In M. Jeannerod (Ed.)., *Neuropsychological and physiological aspects of spatial neglect* (pp. 87–114). New York: Elsevier Science Publishers.

Jeannerod, M. (1987). *Neuropsychological and physiological aspects of spatial neglect*. New York: Elsevier Science Publishers.

Kinsbourne, M. (1987). Mechanisms of unilateral neglect. In M. Jeannerod (Ed.), *Neuropsychological and physiological aspects of spatial neglect* (pp. 69–86). New York: Elsevier Science Publishers.

Kinsbourne, M., & Warrington, E. (1962). A variety of reading disability associated with right hemisphere lesions. *Journal of Neurology, Neurosurgery, and Psychiatry, 25*, 334–339.

Lawson, I. R. (1962). Visual-spatial neglect in lesions of the right cerebral hemisphere: A study in recovery. *Archives of Neurology, 12*, 23–33.

Mark, V. W., Kooistra, C. A., & Heilman, K. M. (1988). Hemispatial neglect affected by non-neglected stimuli. *Neurology, 38*, 1207–1211.

Marr, D. (1976). Early processing of visual information. *Philosophical Transactions of the Royal Society of London, B 275*, 483–525.

McClelland, J. L., & Rumelhart, D. W. (1981). An interactive activation model of context effects in letter perception: Part I. An account of basic findings. *Psychological Review, 88*, 375–407.

Mesulam, M. M. (1981). A cortical network for directed attention and unilateral neglect. *Annals of Neurology, 10*, 309–325.

Mesulam, M. M. (1985). *Principles of behavioral neurology*. Philadelphia, PA: F. A. Davis.

Monk, A. F. (1985). Co-ordinate systems in visual word recognition. *Quarterly Journal of Experimental Psychology, 37*(A), 613–625.

Ogden, J. (1985). Contralesional neglect of constructed visual images in right and left brain-damaged patients. *Neuropsychologia, 23*, 273–277.

Ogden, J. (1987). The 'neglected' left hemisphere and its contribution to visuospatial neglect. In M. Jeannerod (Ed.), *Neurophysiological and neuropsychological aspects of spatial neglect* (pp. 215–234). New York: Elsevier Science Publishers.

Patterson, K., & Kay, J. (1982). Letter-by-letter reading. Psychological descriptions of a neurological syndrome. *Quarterly Journal of Experimental Psychology, 34*(A), 411–441.

Posner, M. I., & Rafal, R. D. (1987). Cognitive theories of attention and rehabilitation of attention deficits. In M. Meier, A. Benton, & L. Diller (Eds.), *Neuropsychological rehabilitation* (pp. 182–201). New York: Guilford Press.

Posner, M., Walker, J., Friedrich, F., & Rafal, R. (1984). Effects of parietal lobe injury on covert orienting and visual attention. *Journal of Neuroscience, 4*(7), 1874–1983.

Raven, J. C. (1956). *Coloured progressive matrices*. London: H. K. Lewis.

Riddoch, M. J., & Humphreys, G. W. (1987). Perceptual and action systems in unilateral visual neglect. In M. Jeannerod (Ed.), *Neuropsychological and physiological aspects of spatial neglect* (pp. 151–181). New York: Elsevier Science Publishers.

Rizzolatti, G., & Camarda, R. (1987). Neural circuits for spatial attention and unilateral neglect. In M. Jeannerod (Ed.), *Neuropsychological and physiological aspects of unilateral spatial neglect* (pp. 289–314). New York: Elsevier Science Publishers.

Roy, E., Reuter-Lorentz, P., Roy, L., Copland, S., & Moscovitch, M. (1987). Unilateral attention deficits and hemispheric asymmetries in the control of attention. In M. Jeannerod (Ed.), *Neurophysiological and neuropsychological aspects of spatial neglect* (pp. 25–40). New York: Elsevier Science Publishers.

Searleman, A. (1983). Language capabilities of the right hemisphere. In A. W. Young (Ed.), *Functions of the right cerebral hemisphere* (pp. 87–111). New York: Academic Press.

Seymour, P. H. K. (1979). *Human visual cognition*. New York: St. Martin's Press.

Shallice, T. (1988). *From neuropsychology to mental structure*. Cambridge, England: Cambridge University Press.

Shallice, T., & Warrington, E. K. (1977). The possible role of selective attention in acquired dyslexia. *Neuropsychologia, 15*, 31–41.

Shepherd, M., Findlay, J., & Hockey, R. (1986). The relationship between eye movements and spatial attention. *The Quarterly Journal of Experimental Psychology, 38A*, 475–491.

Sieroff, E., Pollatsek, A., & Posner, M. I. (1988). Recognition of visual letter strings following injury to the posterior visual spatial attention system. *Cognitive Neuropsychology, 5*, 427–449.

Simon, H. A. (1962). The architecture of complexity. *Proceedings of the American Philosophical Society, 106*, 467–482.

Staller, J., Buchanon, D., Singer, M., Lappin, J., & Webb, W. (1978). Alexia without agraphia: An experimental case study. *Brain and Language, 5*, 378–387.

Thorndike, E. L., & Lorge, I. (1944). *The teachers word book of 30,000 words*. New York: Teacher's College Columbia University.

Triesman, A., & Gelade, G., (1980). A feature-integration theory of attention. *Cognition and Psychology, 12*, 97–136.

Volpe, B. T., LeDoux, J. E., & Gazzaniga, M. S. (1979). Information processing in an "extinguished" visual field. *Nature, 282*, 722–724.

Warrington, E. K. (1962). The completion of visual forms across hemianoptic field defects. *Journal of Neurology, Neurosurgery, and Psychiatry, 25*, 208–217.

Warrington, E. K., & Shallice, T. (1980). Word-form dyslexia. *Brain, 103*, 99–112.

Warrington, E. K., & Zangwill, O. L. (1957). A study of dyslexia. *Journal of Neurology, Neurosurgery, and Psychiatry, 20*, 208–215.

Watson, R. T., Valenstein, E., & Heilman, K. M. (1981). Thalamic neglect: Possible role of the medial thalamus and nucleus reticularis in behavior. *Archives of Neurology, 38*, 501–506.

Wechsler, D. (1972). *The Wechsler memory scale*. New York: The Psychological Corp. (original work published 1945)

Wing, A., & Baddeley, A. (1980). Spelling errors in handwriting. In U. Frith (Ed.), *Cognitive processes in spelling* (pp. 251–273). London: Academic Press.

APPENDIX A: EXAMPLES OF DRAWING FROM MEMORY

RB's drawing of a flower:

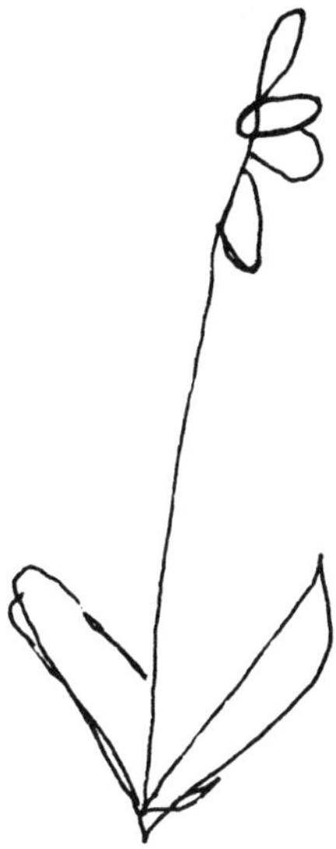

NG's drawing of a clock:

EXAMPLES OF COPYING

Stimulus:

RB's copy:

NG's copy:

APPENDIX B: EXAMPLES OF ERRORS IN READING AND SPELLING TASKS

RB's Backward Completion Errors (BCEs) in Reading

RB's Backward Completion Errors in Reading Words

village → v-i-l-l-a-g-e . . . mileage	tread → t-r-e-a-d . . . head
mercy → m-e-r-c-y . . . Percy	check → c-h-e-c-h . . . sick
basis → b-a-s-i-s . . . oasis	bribe → b-r-i-b-e . . . bibe
pressure → p-r-e-s-s-u-r-e . . . assure	cheer → c-h-e-e-r . . . sheer
shower → s-h-o-w-e-r . . . power	wept → w-e-p-t . . . kept
sought → s-o-u-g-h-t . . . caught	thief → t-h-i-e-f . . . chief
decide → d-e-c-i-d-e . . . provide	skull → s-k-u-l-l . . . cull
lobster → l-o-b-s-t-e-r . . . rooster	drive → d-r-i-v-e . . . serve
odor → o-d-o-r . . . door	head → h-e-a-d . . . dead
enough → e-n-o-u-g-h . . . though	yawn → y-a-w-n . . . lawn
certain → c-e-r-t-a-i-n . . . curtain	weave → w-e-a-v-e . . . wave
vivid → v-i-v-i-d . . . David	worm → w-o-r-m . . . dorm
rather → r-a-t-h-e-r . . . feather	sketch → s-k-e-t-c-h . . . each
loyal → l-o-y-a-l . . . royal	kiss → k-i-s-s . . . miss
space → s-p-a-c-e . . . trace	count → c-o-u-n-t . . . don't
spend → s-p-e-n-d . . . blend	report → r-e-p-o-r-t . . . export

spider→s-p-i-d-e-r . . . cider
ready→r-e-a-d-y . . . sandy
unit→u-n-i-t . . . in it
reason→r-e-a-s-o-n . . . season
rooster→r-o-o-s-t-e-r . . . Easter
letter→l-e-t-t-e-r . . . utter
palace→p-a-l-a-c-e . . . place
fight→f-i-g-h-t . . . light
just→j-u-s-t . . . must
blow→b-l-o-w . . . now
gross→cross
dust→must
blood→flood
value→blue

RB's Backward Completion Errors within Sentences

someone→no one
serving→evening
tow→blow
the→she
device→d-e-v-i-c-e . . . nice
compost→c-o-m-p-o-s-t . . . most
lasted→started
we'll→she'll
drives→braves
she→the
crevice→c-r-e-v-i-c-e . . . service

RB's Neglect Errors (NEs)

RB's Neglect Errors in Reading Words

want→w-a-n-t . . . ant
blame→b-l-a-m-e . . . lame
win→t-w-i-n . . . win
learn→l-e-a-r-n . . . earn
gone→g-o-n-e . . . one
land→l-a-n-d . . . and
parent→rent
broad→road
bright→right
spark→park
speak→peak
suspend→spend
brother→b-r-o-t-h-e-r . . . other
mend→end
million→on
thousand→sand
scrmble→ramble
stay→tay [tei]
skip→kip

RB's Neglect Errors within Sentences

for→or
the→he
understand→stand
almost→most
always→ways
spark→park

RB's Other Errors in Reading

pillow→lower
pursuit→result
open→penny
planet→airplane
grave→g-r-a-v-e . . . raven
begin→beginning
degree→eager
sleeve→lever
lamb→amber
cushion→washing

RB's Errors in Delayed Copying

RB's Backward Completion Errors in Delayed Copying

spoil→moil
faith→eaith
provide→povide
haygrid→gid
merber→eber
kantry→kntry

borrow → brow
quaint → gaint
borrow → groow
teeble → teble
hannee → hnnee
absent → bent

RB's Neglect Errors in Delayed Copying

pierce → ierce
hungry → ngry
moment → ment
rigid → gid
rather → ather
suspend → end
length → ngth
under → der
starve → arve
carry → arry
bright → ight
argue → gue
since → ince
greet → reet
listen → isten
boke → oke
mernie → nie
chench → nch
lorn → orn
kanty → antry
herm → erm
donsept → sept
kwine → wine
hannee → nee
herm → erm
talent → alent
bring → ring
afraid → raid
glove → ove

NG's Errors in Oral Reading

NG's Forward Completing Errors (FCEs)

Morphological FCEs

spent → spend
die → dies
realize → realized
allow → allowed
appear → appeared
directors → direction
dotted → dotter
forget → forgot
sleeve → sleeves
breathing → breathless
considerate → considerably
harsh → harshness
lives → lived
cried → cry
absorb → absorbant
decide → decided
proposal → propose
organize → organization
tire → tired
roughage → roughness
stepped → stepping
habitual → habitually
fortune → fortunately
regulated → regularly

Other FCEs

humid → human
saddled → sadly
furious → furlough
chin → chew
though → thoughts
learned → lean
sprinter → sprinkle
quite → quiet
national → naturally
resist → resident
severely → several
convicted → convince
swam → swan
resist → r-e-s-i-s-t . . . resident
entire → e-n-t-i-r-e . . . entry
precisely → p-r-e-c-i-s-e-l-y . . . precious

hound → house
cloak → clock
budge → budget
dumb → dump
yawn → yarn
worm → worn
sparrow → spared

Pseudomorphological FCEs

inventive → inventure
planets → p-l-a-n-e-t-s . . . planety
orbital → o-r-b-i-t-a-l . . . orbitally
stick → sticked
parental → parently

NG's Neglect Errors in Reading

Morphological NEs

packed → pack
mountains → mountain
radishes → radish
known → know
pictures → picture
savagely → savage
creeks → creek
yelled → yell
shows → show
measures → measure
raced → race
sailed → sail
wanderer → wander
orbital → orbit
liked → like
emotionally → emotional
forced → force
hazardous → hazard
potatoes → potato
arranged → arrange
shifts → shift
listened → listen
villages → village
looks → look
addresses → address

Other NEs

stripe → strip
study → stud

NG's Errors in Oral Reading of Nonwords

Forward Completion Errors

Lexicalizations

grotein → grow
dring → drill
stould → stoutly
frech → fresh
strist → strikes
sollow → solar
suffet → suffer
vigid → Vivian

Nonwords FCEs

garmage → garmin [garmən]
fote → foge [foʊg]
macred → macree [mækri]
letween → letwest [lɛtwɛst]
reave → reaver [rivɚ]
bould → bouly [boʊli]
petch → petcher [pɛtʃɚ]
ageirst → ager [eɪdʒɚ]

lince→line
womar→woman
hospile→hospital
humil→humid

rivid→rivin [rɪvən]
crite→crited [kraɪtəd]
solke→s-o-l-k-e . . . solky [solki]
heagy→h-e-a-g-y . . . heager [higɚ]

Lexicalizations
entineg→entering
faunch→fault
daud→dab
blory→blower
thouth→thought
afrain→afraid
compaer→compass
spim→spin
aftes→after
steat→steak
strang→strange
twile→twill
snoe→s-n-o-e . . . snore
reesh→r-e-e-s-h . . . reach

lytes→l-y-t-e-s . . . lye
cherch→c-h-e-r-c-h . . . check
spean→spin
wofe→wolf
abore→aboard
feek→f-e-e-k . . . feet
clude→c-l-u-d-e . . . clue
loyad→l-o-y-a-d . . . loyalty

Nonwords FCEs
seoven→s-e-o-v-e-n . . . seover [si:oʊvɚ]
sungry→s-u-n-g-r-y . . . sunger [sʌngɚ]
redge→r-e-d-g-e . . . redger [rɛdʒɚ]
hansh→h-a-n-s-h . . . hanshen [hænʃən]
yand→y-a-n-d . . . yang [jæŋ]
grob→g-r-o-b . . . groth [grɔθ]
chench→c-h-e-n-c-h..cheny [tʃɛni]
hannee→hannen [hænɛn]
sarcle→s-a-r-c-l-e . . . sarcly [sarkli]
wundoe→w-u-n-d-o-e . . . wundig [wʌndɪg]
kroid→k-r-o-i-d . . . krole [kroʊl]
haygrid→h-a-y-g-r-i-d . . . haygrite [heɪgraɪt]

Other Visual Errors (OTH)
nautral→natural
srield→spry
achieme→achievement
engane→engine

Neglect Errors (NEs)

Lexicalization
nate→n-a-t-e . . . Nat
lage→l-a-g-e . . . lag
gride→g-r-i-d-e . . . grid
luge→l-u-g-e . . . lug
sprange→s-p-r-a-n-g-e . . . sprang
poth→p-o-t-h . . . pot
sune→s-u-n-e . . . sun
mushrume→mush and rum

Nonword NEs
kwene→k-w-e-n-e . . . kwen [kwɛn]
breth→b-r-e-t-h . . . bret [brɛt]
quine→quin [kwɪn]
begond→begon [bigan]
wappy→wap [wæp]
oaps→oap [oʊp]
shild→s-h-i-l-d . . . shil [ʃɪl]
egery→e-g-e-r-y . . . eger [ɛgɚ]
sturmy→s-t-u-r-m-y . . . sturm [stɝm]
awkmard→a-w-k-m-a-r-d . . . awkmar [ɔkmar]

NG's Errors Following Correct Letter Reading

Errors on Words

Forward Completion Errors

Neglect Errors

journal→journey
belief→believe
talent→talented
pursuit→pursue
basis→basic
parent→parents
horror→horrible
offense→offend
dollar→dollars
insect→insects
status→statue
oyster→oysters
province→privacy
rang→range
nature→natural
giving→given
defendant→defended
absorb→absorbs
draped→drapes
complete→completed
planet→plane
forced→force
stresses→stress
eruption→erupt
whispered→whisper
designed→design
cottages→cottage
thundered→thunder

Other Visual Errors

insistence→instant

Errors on Nonwords

Forward Completion Errors

groteim→groto
grom→groom
dring→dry
fing→fine
garmage→garment
stoud→stout
strist→stress
sollow→solar
suffet→suffers

Neglect Errors

lage→lag

Other Errors

nature→not true

NG's Errors in Vertical Reading

Errors on Words

Forward Completion Errors

excited→expectation
dangerous→dangers
peaceful→personal
nature→natural
design→desperate
proved→provide
giving→given
separation→separate
blending→blemish
seriously→seriousness

Neglect Errors

slows→slow
rang→ran
stresses→stress
whispered→whisper
minerals→mineral
cottages→cottage
forced→force
thundered→thunder
frequently→frequent
discovery→discover

common → comet
imaginary → imagination
rigid → right
snarling → snail
vivid → vivian
bride → bribe
seasonal → serious
risks → rich
producer → product
grim → grin
hoped → hoping
motionless → motel
arrive → arrived
crime → crying
rode → row
spaces → space
comes → come
tired → tire
shaped → shape
grumbled → grumble
forced → force
equally → equal
listed → list
lengthy → length
wrestler → wrestle
villages → village
misses → miss
cured → cure
dashes → dash
habitual → habit

Errors on Nonwords

Forward Completion Errors

groteim → grotin [grotɪn]
achieme → achievement
quine → quiet
hospile → hospital
skeep → skeek [skik]
dring → drink
fing → fine
birk → bird
frech → fresh
sollow → solid
spond → spout
suffet → suffer
neithem → neither
abore → aboard
carsy → carry
vigid → visit
strist → strip
crail → crayon
bession → beside
womar → woman
humil → humble
entenig → enter in
donsept → doneness
esk → Eskay
affige → after

Neglect Errors

nate → Nat (her nickname)
lage → lag
sipter → sip

Other Errors

kown → know

NG's Errors in Recognition of Oral Spelling

Errors on Words

Forward Completion Errors

cured → curious
mobility → mobile
excess → exceed
college → collow [kalou]
danger → dances
talent → tall
earns → earring

Neglect Errors

stepped → step
joyous → joy
planet → plane
village → villa
bottomless → bottom
forced → force
picnics → picnic

sparrow → space
basis → bass
cabin → cabby
parent → part
spider → spike
horror → horrors
seriously → serve
atomic → atone
beauty → beautiful
meant → measuring
insect → inland
advice → advertise
window → winterize
status → static
complete → comply
elbow → eligible
province → pronounce
wore → work
region → regimen

powerful → power
requirement → require
slightly → slight
stresse → stress
cottages → cottage
whispers → whisper
objection → object
forced → force
employment → employ
belongs → belong
speaking → speak
frequenty → frequent
traveler → travel
tired → tire
shaped → shape
fixed → fix
framed → frame
taken → take
lengthy → length
blackness → black
villages → village
severely → severe
habitual → habit
looks → look
addresses → address

Errors on Nonwords

Forward Completion Errors

dring → drink
vigid → vigil
bession → beside
womar → woman
entineg → entertainment
sipter → sipping
solke → sold
donse → does
esk → Eskay
noture → noturous [notæɚəs]
stoud → stout
spond → sponge

neithem → neither
carsy → caress
achieme → achieve
quine → quiet
humil → humid
sleeme → sleep
blory → blow
cring → crime
fing → fine
birk → birth
affige → affect
strist → strick
suffet → suffer

NG's Errors in Written Spelling

Errors on Words

Forward Completion Errors (FCEs)

Morphological FCEs	Pseudomorphological FCEs	Other FCEs
palace → palaces	dangerous → dangeness	advice → advicd

hungry → hunger
absence → absent
edit → editor
stresses → stressed
fate → fated
carry → carrier
giving → given
learn → learning
arrive → arrived
refusal → refuse
bent → bend
regulate → regulated
mobility → mobile

frozen → frozer
study → studer
ask → asken
valuable → valuer
belongs → belonged
handed → hander
jury → jured
valuable → valuer
worthless → worthness

fabric → fabrick
basis → base
belief → beleven
status → stais
planet → planted
junk → jund
stay → staie
floor → floore
point → poind
sneeze → sneed
cross → crosse
crow → croy
blame → bland
kind → kinb
cloak → clock
twin → twine
grew → grued
fruit → fruil
head → heard
yawn → yand
save → saw
skin → skim
young → yound

Neglect Errors (NEs)

Morphological NEs	Other NEs
needed → need	talent → talen
whispered → whisper	beauty → beaut
thundered → thunder	fact → fac
draped → drape	knife → knif
seasoned → season	cloud → clou
hoped → hope	trout → trou
youthful → youth	thief → thie
heaped → heap	gross → gros
shaped → shape	skull → skul
fixed → fix	faith → fait
shifts → shift	merge → merg
lengthy → length	though → tho
mighty → might	noise → nois
villages → village	nature → natur
addresses → address	stripe → strip
misses → miss	sincere → sincer
banded → band	instinct → instin
	pretty → pret
	complete → complet
	center → cente
	broom → broo
	broke → brok
	common → comm

	caught → caug
	every → ever

Errors on Nonwords

Forward Completion Errors	Neglect Errors
grom → grommon	shild → shil
fing → finge	
esk → esken	
garmage → garmick	
fote → fol	
frech → fred	
strist → strick	
spond → spon	
carsy → carseat	
abore → abored	
lince → linst	
cound → count	
stecial → stech	
reve → revell	
blory → blored	
apar → apard	
thouth → though	
mofour → mofourd	
ague → agur	
conpare → conpary	

Errors in Oral Spelling

Errors on Words

Forward Completion Errors (FCEs)

Morphological FCEs	Pseudomorphological FCEs	Other FCEs
measure → measured	shot → shoted	shifts → shifue
drainage → drains	jury → jured	feel → felld
join → joined	rudely → rudle	humidity → humitdi
stresss → stressed	frontiers → fronter	admirable → admiraled
peaceful → picefully	exception → excepted	whispered → whisperert
flash → flashed	broken → brokend	objection → objeckedenment
swell → swelled	normal → norment	session → sescent
giving → given	greenish → greeness	separation → seprashone
blending → blended	framed → framine	passed → pasch
risks → risked	potatoes → potation	problem → problend
colonies → coloney	join → joinment	confusion → confusend
families → family	bent → bended	thin → thine
solve → solved	listened → lising	farmer → farmere
powerful → powerfully	protein → protion	bakers → bakerd
addresses → addressed	strike → stricked	wildcat → wildesu
ask → asked	equal → equald	hungry → hungrard

valuable → value
discuss → discussed
resemblance → resemble
talent → talented
starve → starved

Neglect Errors (NEs)

Morphological NEs

thundered → thunder
hoped → hope
picked → pick
mighty → might
announcer → announce
villages → village
needed → need
whispers → whisper

Other NEs

wore → wor
every → ever
huge → hug
fixed → fixe
priest → pries
spoke → spok
rode → rod
pressure → pressur
nature → natured
dangerous → dangeres
leav → leaved
town → townd
stick → sticked
defendant → defendty
western → westernd
begin → beging
froniers → fronter
rudely → rudled
bride → brided
handed → hander
wanted → wanter
execution → execusing
blindness → blindes
dashes → dasness
brisk → brisky
sincere → sincered
special → specion
crime → crimed
jury → jurion
million → millionen
complete → completement
thousands → thousened
freedom → freedment
sturdy → sturd
intently → intench
emotional → emomous
soft → sofe
soaking → soakend
movement → movend
strangely → stranght
recently → recend
regulated → regulad
deaf → deafee
mobility → mobilde
force → forster
created → cread
vital → vil
atomic → atomice
stay → staye
watch → watchd
taught → taughth
event → evenis
against → agaisening
teeth → teeh
exactly → exacked
fortunate → forned
plan → pland
appear → appeard
skunks → skunck
collapsed → collasp
turns → turnes
thoughs → thoughth
strict → strick
what → whate
severe → severden
sense → sent
listen → listente
speak → speack
afraid → afraide
argue → argant

NG's Errors in Number Reading

Neglect Errors

4,582,300 → 4,582
6,152,387 → 6,152
4,422,317 → 4,422
4,989,344 → 4,989
8,911,616 → $8,911.61
5,312,891 → 5,312

Completion Errors

340,475 → 340,000
8,952 → 89,522
2,385 → 23,855
8,969 → 89,699
7,585 → 758,500

Other

689,921→6,809,921
3,140→31,040

HH's Errors in Reading and Spelling Tasks

HH's Errors in Oral Reading of Words

Forward Completion Errors (FCEs)

Morphological FCEs	Other FCEs
belief→b-e-l-i-e-f . . . believe	pressure→p-r-e-s-s-u-r-e . . . present
nature→n-a-t-u-r-e . . . natural	shower→s-h-o-w-e-r . . . short
cushion→c-u-s-h-i-o-n . . . custom	provide→p-r-o-v-i-d-e . . . provident
hungry→h-u-n-g-r-y . . . hunger	thousand→t-h-o-u-s-a-n-d . . . thought
decent→d-e-c-e-n-t . . . decency	basis→b-a-s-i-s . . . base
pollution→p-o-l-l-u-t-i-o-n . . . polluting	crow→c-r-o-w . . . crown
spelling→s-p-e-l-l-i-n-g . . . spelled	shack→s-h-a-c-k . . . shave
grim→g-r-i-m . . . grimace	debt→d-e-b-t . . . deep
wonderment→w-o-n-d-e-r-m-e-n-t . . . wonderful	
refusal→r-e-f-u-s-a-l . . . refuse	group→g-r-o-u-p . . . grove
weave→w-e-a-v-e . . . weaves	budge→b-u-d-g-e . . . budget
darken→d-a-r-k-e-n . . . darky	insect→i-n-s-e-c-t . . . insecure
fortunate→f-o-r-t-u-n-a-t-e . . . furtunes	carry→c-a-r-r-y . . . cart
owner→o-w-n-e-r . . . owned	spoil→s-p-o-i-l . . . spout
regulated→r-e-g-u-l-a-t-e-d . . . regulator	those→t-h-o-s-e . . . thought
misses→m-i-s-s-e-s . . . missed	threat→t-h-r-e-a-t . . . thread
lovely→l-o-v-e-l-y . . . loved	drama→d-r-a-m-a . . . draw
traveler→t-r-a-v-e-l-e-r . . . traveled	whispered→w-h-i-s-p-e-r-e-d . . . whispering
movement→m-o-v-e-m-e-n-t . . . movers	excess→e-x-c-e-s-s . . . expect
created→c-r-e-a-t-e-d . . . creative	election→e-l-e-c-t-i-o-n . . . electronic
emergence→e-m-e-r-g-e-n-c-e . . . emergency	grab→g-r-a-b . . . grade
assembly→a-s-s-e-m-b-l-y . . . assemble	rang→r-a-n-g . . . range
solve→s-o-l-v-e-n-t . . . solvent	listed→l-i-s-t-e-d . . . listen
starter→s-t-a-r-t-e-r . . . started	protein→p-r-o-t-e-i-n . . . protestant
designed→d-e-s-i-g-n-e-d . . . designate	weave→w-e-a-v-e . . . weak
known→k-n-o-w-n . . . knows	severely→s-e-v-e-r-e-l-y . . . several
peaceable→p-e-a-c-e-a-b-l-e . . . peaceful	spread→s-p-r-e-a-d . . . spry
publisher→p-u-b-l-i-s-h-e-r . . . publishing	execution→e-x-e-c-u-t-i-o-n . . . exercise
woody→w-o-o-d-y . . . woods	province→p-r-o-v-i-n-c-e . . . provident
suggestion→s-u-g-g-e-s-t-i-o-n . . . suggestions	
realize→r-e-a-l-i-z-e . . . realized	collapsed→c-o-l-la-p-s-e-d . . . colide
clinical→c-l-i-n-i-c-a-l . . . clinics	probably→p-r-o-b-a-b-l-y . . . problems
directors→d-i-r-e-c-t-o-r-s . . . direction	colonies→c-o-l-o-n-i-e-s . . . color
soften→s-o-f-t-e-n . . . softer	sang→s-a-n-g . . . sand
grown→g-r-o-w-n . . . grows	sleek→s-l-e-e-k . . . sled
forget→f-o-r-g-e-t . . . forgotten	thin→t-h-i-n . . . thing
correctly→c-o-r-r-e-c-t-l-y . . . corrective	humidity→h-u-m-i-d-i-t-y . . . human
frontiers→f-r-o-n-t-i-e-r . . . frontness	proved→p-r-o-v-e-d . . . province
equality→e-q-u-a-l-i-t-y . . . equable	invented→i-n-v-e-n-t-e-d . . . invest
habitual→h-a-b-i-t-u-a-l . . . habitary	spines→s-p-i-n-e-s . . . spite
mobility→m-o-b-i-l-i-t-y . . . mobilite	though→t-h-o-u-g-h . . . thought

swimmer → s-w-i-m-m-e-r . . . swimmed
humanity → h-u-m-a-n-i-t-y . . . humanation
stability → s-t-a-b-i-l-i-t-y . . . stabiling
signify → s-i-g-n-i-f-y . . . signally

Pseudomorphological FCEs

discussing → d-i-s-c-u-s-s-i-n-g . . . discussful

threaten → t-h-r-e-a-t-e-n . . . threw
grew → g-r-e-w . . . greet
measures → m-e-a-s-u-r-e-s . . . meanly
wanderer → w-a-n-d-e-r-e-r . . . warring
king → k-i-n-g . . . kind
scarse → s-c-a-r-s-e . . . scared
sensible → s-e-n-s-i-b-l-e . . . sensational
happy → h-a-p-p-y . . . happen
played → p-l-a-y-e-d . . . plate

HH's Errors in Oral Reading of Nonwords

Forward Completion Errors (FCEs)

Lexicalizations

sume → s-u-m-e . . . summer
snoy → s-n-o-y . . . snow
troe → t-r-o-e . . . trout
cring → c-r-i-n-g . . . cries
cherch → c-h-e-r-c-h . . . cheer
fing → f-i-n-g . . . find
flad → f-l-a-d . . . flag
affige → a-f-f-i-g-e . . . affects
strang → s-t-r-a-n-g . . . strange
begond → b-e-g-o-n-d . . . begin
faunch → f-a-u-n-c-h . . . fans
hansh → h-a-n-s-h . . . hand
luge → l-u-g-e . . . lugs
cheg → c-h-e-g . . . cheek
leng → l-e-n-g . . . length
winbon → w-i-n-b-o-n . . . window
birk → b-i-r-k . . . bing
aftes → a-f-t-e-s . . . after
emplain → e-m-p-l-a-i-n . . . employer

Nonword FCEs

kwine → k-w-i-n-e . . . kwisky [kwɪski]
mersee → m-e-r-s-e-e . . . merser [mɝsɚ]
mushrame → m-u-s-h-r-a-m-e . . . mushrather [mʌʃræðɚ]
remmun → r-e-m-m-u-m . . . remmunt
garmage → g-a-r-m-a-g-e . . . garmy [garmi]
redge → r-e-d-g-e . . . readish [ridɪʃ]

Neglect Errors

kown → k-o-w-n . . . kowe [koʊ]
poth → p-o-t-h . . . pot
carsy → c-a-r-s-y . . . car

HH's Errors in Vertical Reading of Words

Forward Completion Errors (FCEs)

belongs → belief
caught → caution
pollution → polling
wore → wort
producer → problem
sheep → sheen
confusion → conference
exception → excitement
election → electric
fairness → faction
musical → muscare [mʌsker]
sacred → sacring [seɪkrɪŋ]
arrive → arrade [əred]

Morphological FCEs

employment → employed
started → starting
keeps → keeper
teacher → teaching
spaces → spatial
construction → constructive
become → becoming
grumbled → grumbly

bright → brigade
vivid → videy [vaɪdi]

HH's Errors in Recognition of Oral Spelling—Words

Forward Completion Errors

imaginary → imaginely
snarling → snared
employment → emplite [ɛmplaɪt]
vivid → viper
available → availon [əveilən]
pollution → polite
wore → worth
special → speculate
producer → proud
appear → apply
every → even
comes → comsy [kʌmzi]
fabric → fabrade [fæbreɪd]
motionless → motice [moʊtəs]
collapsed → collect
confusion → confused
plan → plane
depend → depending
effortless → effortly
construction → continuously
bright → brigid [brɪgəd]
severely → several
measure → measuring
collapsed → collect

Neglect Errors

risks → risk
wonderment → wonder
exception → except
annoyance → annoy
note → not
framed → frame
events → even
owner → own
regulated → regulate
seriousness → serious
traveler → travel
lady → lad
dangerous → danger
stresses → stress
minerals → miner
designed → design
cottages → cottage
defendent → defend
commander → command
humanity → human

HH's Errors in Recognition of Oral Spelling—Nonwords

Forward Completion Errors

noture → north
affige → affoul
frech → fresh
strist → strict
carsy → carries
achieme → achiement
quine → quantity
hospile → hospice
skeep → skeet
entineg → entinate [ɛntəneɪt]
potatoes → potsle [patsəl]
macred → mace
sleeme → sleemly [slimli]
stecial → style
reave → reavy [rivi]
thouth → thought

Neglect Errors

woman → wom [wɔm]
daud → dau [daʊ]
sipter → sip

appaur → appear
alque → algon
palse → past
petch → petched

HH's Errors in Delayed Copy Transcoding

Forward Completion Errors	Neglect Errors
provide → provit	absent → abse
starve → starved	length → len
afraid → afre	donsept → dons
carry → carred	rather → rath
bright → brib	strict → str
bring → brite	afraid → af
since → sinte	bright → brigh
pierce → piech	mushrame → mush
hungry → hungrh	suspend → susp
kwine → kwint	haygrid → hayg
hannee → hantte	
herm → herv	
reesh → reech	
spoil → spoih	
brisk → brick	
haygrid → haygrit	
fabric → fabrec	
quaint → quait	
fresh → frert	
happy → happe	
carry → carrt	
length → lengty	
talent → tante	
crisp → cristy	
faith → faity	

HH's Errors in Spelling Words

Forward Completion Errors

Morphological FCEs	Pseudomorphological FCEs	Other FCEs
goodness → goods	slows → slowey	useful → usfold
grab → grabbed	slightly → slightey	admirable → admiral
tamp → tamped	richness → richens	common → commond
launch → launched	every → evered	adopt → adoct
realize → relized	lovely → lovey	enough → enought
risks → risked		

Neglect Errors

addresses → addres
needed → need
defendant → defend

HH's Errors in Spelling Nonwords

Forward Completion Errors

Pseudomorphological FCEs	Other FCEs
skeep → skeeped	cimon → cimond
	bevele → beveld
	noture → nothen
	afige → afaged
	fote → foked

HH's Errors in Number Reading

Neglect
97,245 → 9,724
26,451 → 268

Other
4,989,344 → 4,985,344
4008 → 408

Completion
4,308,175 → 4,308,178
378,104 → 378,108
31,396 → 31,398
1,997,338 → 1,997,337
16,942 → 16,947
712,124 → 712,124,000
9,591 → 9,519
340,475 → 340,478
52,856 → 52,857
97,209 → 97,208
24,058 → 24,055

Author Index

A

B

Z

Subject Index